Authors
& Artists
for Young
Adults

ISSN 1040-5682

Authors & Artists for Young Adults

VOLUME 47

GALE®

THOMSON

GALE

Detroit • New York • San Diego • San Francisco • Cleveland • New Haven, Conn. • Waterville, Maine • London • Munich

THOMSON

GALE

Authors and Artists for Young Adults, Volume 47

Project Editor
Scot Peacock

Editorial
Katy Balcer, Sara Constantakis, Anna Marie Dahn, Alana Joli Foster, Arlene M. Johnson, Michelle Kazensky, Julie Keppen, Joshua Kondek, Lisa Kumar, Thomas McMahon, Jenai Mynatt, Judith L. Pyko, Mary Ruby, Anita Sundaresan, Maikue Vang, Denay L. Wilding, Thomas Wiloch

Research
Michelle Campbell, Nicodemus Ford, Sarah Genik, Barbara McNeil, Tamara C. Nott, Gary J. Oudersluys, Tracie A. Richardson, Cheryl L. Warnock

Permissions
Debra Freitas, Shalice Shah-Caldwell

Imaging and Multimedia
Dean Dauphinais, Robert Duncan, Leitha Etheridge-Sims, Mary K. Grimes, Lezlie Light, Michael Logusz, Dan Newell, David G. Oblender, Christine O'Bryan, Kelly A. Quin, Luke Rademacher

Composition and Electronic Capture
Carolyn A. Roney

Manufacturing
Stacy L. Melson

LIBRARY OF CONGRESS CATALOG CARD NUMBER 89-641100

ISBN 0-7876-5176-1
ISSN 1040-5682

Printed in the United States of America
10 9 8 7 6 5 4 3 2 1

Contents

Introduction

Authors and Artists for Young Adults is a reference series designed to serve the needs of middle school, junior high, and high school students interested in creative artists. Originally inspired by the need to bridge the gap between Gale's *Something about the Author,* created for children, and *Contemporary Authors,* intended for older students and adults, *Authors and Artists for Young Adults* has been expanded to cover not only an international scope of authors, but also a wide variety of other artists.

Although the emphasis of the series remains on the writer for young adults, we recognize that these readers have diverse interests covering a wide range of reading levels. The series therefore contains not only those creative artists who are of high interest to young adults, including cartoonists, photographers, music composers, bestselling authors of adult novels, media directors, producers, and performers, but also literary and artistic figures studied in academic curricula, such as influential novelists, playwrights, poets, and painters. The goal of *Authors and Artists for Young Adults* is to present this great diversity of creative artists in a format that is entertaining, informative, and understandable to the young adult reader.

Entry Format

Each volume of *Authors and Artists for Young Adults* will furnish in-depth coverage of twenty to twenty-five authors and artists. The typical entry consists of:

—A detailed biographical section that includes date of birth, marriage, children, education, and addresses.

—A comprehensive bibliography or filmography including publishers, producers, and years.

—Adaptations into other media forms.

—Works in progress.

—A distinctive essay featuring comments on an artist's life, career, artistic intentions, world views, and controversies.

—References for further reading.

—Extensive illustrations, photographs, movie stills, cartoons, book covers, and other relevant visual material.

A cumulative index to featured authors and artists appears in each volume.

Compilation Methods

The editors of *Authors and Artists for Young Adults* make every effort to secure information directly from the authors and artists through personal correspondence and interviews. Sketches on living authors and artists are sent to the biographee for review prior to publication. Any sketches not personally reviewed by biographees or their representatives are marked with an asterisk (*).

Highlights of Forthcoming Volumes

Among the authors and artists planned for future volumes are:

Piers Anthony	Dennis Brindell Fradin	Alan Moore
Judd Apatow	George McDonald Fraser	Mette Newth
Toni Cade Bambara	Frank Gehry	Frank E. Peretti
Sue Ellen Bridgers	Adele Geras	Janet Quin-Harkin
Mel Brooks	Sue Grafton	Auguste Rodin
Octavia E. Butler	Lynn Hall	Darren Shan
Rachel Carson	Patricia Highsmith	Sonya Sones
Eoin Colfer	John Hockenberry	Theodore Sturgeon
Michael Crichton	Ron Howard	Amy Tan
Peter Dickinson	Chuck Jones	Cate Tiernan
Frederick Douglass	Sonia Levitin	Eudora Welty
Deborah Ellis	Carolyn Meyer	Walter Jon Williams

Contact the Editor

We encourage our readers to examine the entire *AAYA* series. Please write and tell us if we can make *AAYA* even more helpful to you. Give your comments and suggestions to the editor:

BY MAIL: The Editor, *Authors and Artists for Young Adults,* 27500 Drake Rd., Farmington Hills, MI 48331-3535.

BY TELEPHONE: (800) 347-GALE

Authors and Artists for Young Adults
Product Advisory Board

The editors of *Authors and Artists for Young Adults* are dedicated to maintaining a high standard of excellence by publishing comprehensive, accurate, and highly readable entries on writers, artists, and filmmakers of interest to middle and high school students. In addition to the quality of the entries, the editors take pride in the graphic design of the series, which is intended to be orderly yet appealing, allowing readers to utilize the pages of *AAYA* easily, enjoyably, and with efficiency. Despite the success of the *AAYA* print series, we are mindful that the vitality of a literary reference product is dependent on its ability to serve its readers over time. As critical attitudes about literature, art, and media constantly evolve, so do the reference needs of students and teachers. To be certain that we continue to keep pace with the expectations of our readers, the editors of *AAYA* listen carefully to their comments regarding the value, utility, and quality of the series. Librarians, who have firsthand knowledge of the needs of library users, are a valuable resource for us. The *Authors and Artists for Young Adults* Product Advisory Board, made up of school, public, and academic librarians, is a forum to promote focused feedback about *AAYA* on a regular basis, as well as to help steer our coverage of new authors and artists. The advisory board includes the following individuals, whom the editors wish to thank for sharing their expertise:

- **Eva M. Davis,** Teen Services Librarian, Plymouth District Library, Plymouth, Michigan

- **Joan B. Eisenberg,** Lower School Librarian, Milton Academy, Milton, Massachusetts

- **Francisca Goldsmith,** Teen Services Librarian, Berkeley Public Library, Berkeley, California

- **Harriet Hagenbruch,** Curriculum Materials Center/Education Librarian, Axinn Library, Hofstra University, Hempstead, New York

- **Monica F. Irlbacher,** Young Adult Librarian, Middletown Thrall Library, Middletown, New York

- **Robyn Lupa,** Head of Children's Services, Jefferson County Public Library, Lakewood, Colorado

- **Eric Norton,** Head of Children's Services, McMillan Memorial Library, Wisconsin Rapids, Wisconsin

- **Victor L. Schill,** Assistant Branch Librarian/Children's Librarian, Harris County Public Library/Fairbanks Branch, Houston, Texas

- **Caryn Sipos,** Community Librarian, Three Creeks Community Library, Vancouver, Washington

Acknowledgments

Grateful acknowledgment is made to the following publishers, authors, and artists for their kind permission to reproduce copyrighted material.

CATHERINE ASARO. Cover of *Ascendant Sun*, by Catherine Asaro. Tor, 2000. Reproduced by permission./ Bollinger, Peter, illustrator. From a cover of *Catch the Lightning*, by Catherine Asaro. Tor, 1996. Reproduced by permission./ Ayers, Alan, illustrator. From a cover of *The Phoenix Code* by Catherine Asaro. Bantam Books, 2000. Reproduced by permission./ Bell, Julie, illustrator. From a cover of *The Quantum Rose*, by Catherine Asaro. Tor, 2000. Reproduced by permission./ Asaro, Catherine, photograph by John Cannizzo. Reproduced by permission.

MARGARET ATWOOD. Rossetti, Dante Gabriel, illustrator. From a cover of *Alias Grace* by Margaret Atwood. Anchor Books, 1996. Reproduced by permission./ Cover of *The Blind Assassin* by Margaret Atwood. Random House, 2000. © The Curtis Publishing Co. Reproduced by permission./ Marcellino, Fred, illustrator. From a cover of *Cat's Eye*, by Margaret Atwood. Anchor Books, 1998. Cover copyright © 1998 by Fred Marcellino. Reproduced by permission./ Marcellino, Fred, illustrator. From a jacket of *The Handmaid's Tale*, written by Margaret Atwood. Anchor Books, 1998. Copyright © 1998 by Anchor Books. Reproduced by permission of the illustrator./ Atwood, Mary, photograph by Jerry Bauer. © Jerry Bauer. Reproduced by permission.

PETER S. BEAGLE. Beagle, Peter S., photograph by G. Richard Yamagata. Reproduced by permission.

WILLIAM BLAKE. Blake, William, painting by John Linnell. Public Domain./ Blake, William, illustrator. From an illustration in *English Romantic Writers*, edited by David Perkins. Harcourt Brace, 1967. © 1967 by Harcourt Brace Jovanovich, Inc./ Blake, William, illustrator. From an illustration in *The Marriage of Heaven and Hell*, by William Blake./ Blake, William, illustrator. From an illustration in *William Blake at the Huntington*, by Robert N. Essick. Harry N. Abrams Inc., Publishers, and The Henry E. Huntington Library and Art Gallery, 1994. Copyright © 1994 The Henry E. Huntington Library and Art Gallery.

T. CORAGHESSAN BOYLE. Neville, John, as Endymion Hart-Jones, and Matthew Broderick as William Lightbody. From a scene in *The Road to Wellville*, by T. Coraghessan Boyle. The Kobal Collection/Beacon/Dirty Hands. Reproduced by permission./ Boyle, T. Coraghessan, photograph by Jim Cooper. AP/Wide World Photos. Reproduced by permission.

BERNARD CORNWELL. Gregory, Bill, illustrator. From a cover of *The Winter King*, by Bernard Cornwell. St. Martin's Griffin, 1997. Reproduced by permission.

KATE DICAMILLO. Sheban, Chris, illustrator. From a jacket of *The Tiger Rising* by Kate DiCamillo. Candlewick Press, 2001. Jacket illustration © 2001 by Chris Sheban. Reproduced by permission./ DiCamillo, Kate, photograph. Reproduced by permission.

MARCEL DUCHAMP. *Apropos of Little Sister*, painting by Marcel Duchamp. © Burstein Collection/Corbis. © 2002 Artists Rights Society (ARS), New York/ADAGP, Paris/Estate of Marcel Duchamp. Reproduced by permission of Corbis and Artist Rights Society./ *Bicycle Wheel*, sculpture by Marcel Duchamp. © Philadelphia Museum of Art/Corbis. © 2002 Artist Rights Society (ARS) New York/ADAGP, Paris/Estate of Marcel Duchamp. Reproduced by Corbis and Artist Rights Society, Inc./ *Door 11, Rue Larrey*, photographer Marcel Duchamp. © Burstein Collection/Corbis and © 2002 Artists Rights Society(ARS), New York/ADAGP, Paris/Estate of Marcel Duchamp. Reproduced by permission of Corbis and Artists Rights Society, Inc./ Duchamp, Marcel, artist. Oil painting of *Nude Descending a Staircase, No. 2*. © Philadelphia Museum of Art/Corbis. Reproduced by Corbis Corporation./ Duchamp, Marcel, photograph. Corbis-Bettmann. Reproduced by permission.

LOUISE ERDRICH. Minor, Wendel, illustrator. From a cover of *The Beet Queen*, by Louise Erdrich. Bantam Books, 1989. Cover art © 1989 by Wendel Minor. Reproduced by permission of Bantam Books, a division of Bantam Doubleday Dell Publishing Group, Inc./ Erdrich, Louise, photograph. © Jerry Bauer. Reproduced by permission.

LINDA GREENLAW. Greenlaw, Linda, photograph by Robert F. Bukaty. AP/Wide World Photos. Reproduced by permission.

JOHN GRISHAM. Sheldon, Joshua, photographer. From a cover of *The Brethren,* by John Grisham. Island Books, 2001. Cover photo © Joshua Sheldon 2000. Reproduced by permission of Dell Publishing, a division of Random House, Inc./ O'Donnell, Chris, as Adam Hall, with Gene Hackman as Sam Cayhall. Scene from the film *The Chamber* by John Grisham. The Kobal Collection. Reproduced by permission./ Bailey, Brian, illustrator. From a cover of *The Firm*, by John Grisham. Island Books, 1992. Reproduced by permission of Dell Publishing, a division of Random House, Inc./ Danes, Claire and Matt Damon, photograph. Scene from the film *The Rainmaker.* The Kobal Collection. Reproduced by permission./ Grisham, John, photograph. Archive/Capri/Saga. Reproduced by permission.

DAN GUTMAN. Gonzales, Dan, illustrator. From a jacket of *The Kid Who Ran for President,* by Dan Gutman. Scholastic, 1996. Jacket illustration © 1996 by Dan Gonzales. Reproduced by permission.

LILLIAN HELLMAN. Gordon, Dorothy, in a scene from the play *The Children's Hour,* by Lillian Hellman. © Hulton-Deutsch Collection/Corbis. Reproduced by Corbis Corporation./ Redgrave, Vanessa, as Julia with Jane Fonda as Lillian Hellman. From a scene in the film *Julia.* The Kobal Collection/20th Century Fox. Reproduced by permission./ Hellman, Lillian, photograph. © Bettmann/Corbis. Reproduced by Corbis Corporation.

SPIKE JONZE. Scene from the 1999 film *Being John Malkovich,* directed by Spike Jonze. The Kobal Collection. Reproduced by permission./ Jonze, Spike. From a scene in *Three Kings,* directed by David O. Russell. The Kobal Collection. Reproduced by permission./ Jonze, Spike, photograph by Melissa Moseley. The Kobal Collection. Reproduced by permission.

FRIDA KAHLO. *Diego and I,* photograph of the painting by Frida Kahlo. AP/Wide World Photos. Reproduced by permission./ Kahlo, Frida, holdng an artist's brush to a painting. Bettmann/Corbis. Reproduced by permission./ Kahlo, Frida, standing near her painting *Las Dos Fridas,* photograph. Bettmann/Corbis. Reproduced by permission./ Kahlo, Frida, photograph. Bettmann/Corbis. Reproduced by permission.

JOY KOGAWA. Roth, Hal, photographer. From a cover of *Itsuka* by Joy Kogawa. Doubleday, 1994. Reproduced by permission./ Roth, Hal, photographer. From a cover of *Obasan,* by Joy Kogawa. Doubleday, 1994. Copyright © 1981 by Joy Kogawa. Reproduced by permission of Doubleday, a division of Bantam Doubleday Dell Publishing Group, Inc./ Broca, Lilian, illustrator. From a cover of *A Song of Lilith* by Joy Kogawa. Polestar, 2000. Art © 2000 by Lilian Broca. Reproduced by permission./ Kogawa, Joy, photograph. AP/Wide World Photos. Reproduced by permission.

JOYCE MCDONALD. Morgenstern, Michael, illustrator. From a cover of *Shades of Simon Gray* by Joyce McDonald. Delacorte Press, 2001. Reproduced by permission./ White, Craig, illustrator. From a cover of *Shadow People* by Joyce McDonald. Laurel-Leaf Books, 2002. Reproduced by permission./ Stabin, Victor, illustrator. From a jacket of *Swallowing Stones,* by Joyce McDonald. Delacorte Press, 1997. Jacket illustration © 1997 by Victor Stabin. Reproduced by permission of Delacorte Press, a division of Bantam Doubleday Dell Publishing Group, Inc./ McDonald, Joyce, photograph. Reproduced by permission of Joyce McDonald.

WILLIAM NICHOLSON. Marceau, Sophie. From a scene of *Firelight,* written and directed by William Nicholson. The Kobal Collection. Reproduced by permission./ Scene from the 1995 film *First Knight,* directed by Jerry Zucker. The Kobal Collection. Reproduced by permission./ Crowe, Russell as Maximus Decimus Meridius in a scene from the film *Gladiator,* directed by Ridley Scott, photograph. The Kobal Collection. Reproduced by permission./ Foster, Jodie. From a scene in *Nell,* screenplay by William Nicholson, directed by Michael Apted. The Kobal Collection. Reproduced by permission./ Hopkins, Anthony. From a scene in the film *Shadowlands,* screenplay by William Nicholson, directed by Richard Attenborough. The Kobal Collection. Reproduced by permission.

JILL PATON WALSH. Zelvin, Diane, illustrator. From a cover of *A Chance Child,* by Jill Paton Walsh. Sunburst, 1991. Cover illustration © 1991 by Diana Zelvin. Reproduced by permission./ Paton Walsh, Jill. From a jacket of *A Desert in Bohemia,* by Jill Paton Walsh. St. Martin's Press, 2000. Reproduced by permission./ Huber, Gretchen, illustrator. From a cover of *Fireweed,* by Jill Paton Walsh. Sunburst Books,

1988. Cover art © 1988 by Gretchen Huber. Reproduced by permission of Sunburst Books, a division of Farrar, Straus and Giroux, LLC./ Maggio, Vigui, illustrator. From a cover of *Grace* by Jill Paton Walsh. A Sunburst Book, Farrar, Straus & Giroux, 1994. Cover art © 1994 by Vigui Maggio. Reproduced by permission of Sunburst Books, a division of Farrar, Straus and Giroux, LLC./ Catalanotto, Peter, illustrator. From a cover of *The Green Book,* by Jill Paton Walsh. Sunburst Books, 1986. Cover art © 1986 by Peter Catalanotto. Reproduced by permission of Sunburst Books, a division of Farrar, Straus and Giroux, LLC.

EZRA POUND. Pound, Ezra. Cover of *Collected Early Poems of Ezra Pound,* edited by Michael John King. New Directions Books, 1982. Reproduced by permission./ Pound, Ezra, 1945, photograph. AP/Wide World Photos. Reproduced by permission.

PAM MUÑOZ RYAN. Selznick, Brian, illustrator. From an illustration in *Amelia and Eleanor Go for a Ride,* by Pam Muñoz Ryan. Scholastic Press, a division of Scholastic Inc., 1999. Text © 1999 by Pam Muñoz Ryan. Illustrations © 1999 by Brian Selznick. Reproduced by permission./ Cepeda, Joe, illustrator. From a jacket of *Esperanza Rising* by Pam Muñoz Ryan. Scholastic Press, 2000. Reproduced by permission.

DAVID SEDARIS. Cover of *Barrel Fever: Stories and Essays,* by David Sedaris. Back Bay Books, 1994. Reproduced by permission./ Cover of *Me Talk Pretty One Day,* by David Sedaris. Back Bay Books, 2001. Reproduced by permission./ Zeray, Peter, photographer. From a cover of *Naked,* by David Sedaris. Back Bay Books, 1997. Reproduced by permission.

MILDRED D. TAYLOR. Baracca, Sal, illustrator. From a cover of *Roll of Thunder, Hear My Cry* by Mildred D. Taylor. Bantam Books, 1984. Cover art © 1984 by Sal Baracca. Reproduced by permission of Bantam Books, a division of Random House, Inc./ Taylor, Mildred D., photograph. The Toledo Blade. Reproduced by permission.

CHRIS WARE. Ware, Chris. From an illustration in *The ACME Novelty Library #15: The Big Book of Jokes II.* Fantagrahics Books, 2001. Reproduced by permission./ Ware, Chris, illustrator. From an illustration in *Jimmy Corrigan: The Smartest Kid on Earth* by Chris Ware. Pantheon Books, 2000. Reproduced by permission of Random House, Inc./ Ware, Chris. Cartoon self-portrait of Chris Ware. Fantagraphics Books. Reproduced by permission.

Catherine Asaro

■ **Personal**

Born November 6, 1955, in Oakland, CA; daughter of Frank and Lucille Marie (Lavezo) Asaro; married John Kendall Cannizzo (an astrophysicist), August 9, 1986; children: Catherine Kendall. *Education:* University of California—Los Angeles, B.S. (highest honors; chemistry), 1978; Harvard University, M.A. (physics), 1983, Ph.D. (chemical physics), 1985; postdoctoral study at University of Toronto, 1985-87. *Hobbies and other interests:* Classical piano, ballet dancing, choir.

■ **Addresses**

Office—c/o Molecudyne Research, P.O. Box 1302, Laurel, MD 20725. *E-mail*—asaro@sff.net.

■ **Career**

Kenyon College, Gambier, OH, assistant professor of physics, 1987-90, affiliated scholar, 1990-91; Molecudyne Research, Laurel, MD, president, 1990—.

Consultant to Lawrence Livermore Laboratory, 1978-83, Biodesign, 1987, and Harvard-Smithsonian Center for Astrophysics, 1991. Visiting scientist at Max Planck Institute for Astrophysics, 1991-92. Dance teacher at Caryl Maxwell Classical Ballet Maryland.

■ **Member**

Science Fiction and Fantasy Writers of America, American Association of Physics Teachers, American Physicists Society, Tau Beta Pi, Sigma Xi.

■ **Awards, Honors**

Finalist, Nebula Award, 1997, for *The Last Hawk*; National Readers Choice Award, Prism Award, and HOMer Award for best novel, all 1999, all for *The Veiled Web*; National Readers Choice Award shortlist, and Prism Award for Futuristic/Fantasy writing, both 2000, both for *The Quantum Rose*.

■ **Writings**

The Veiled Web, Bantam Books (New York, NY), 1999. *The Phoenix Code*, Bantam Books (New York, NY), 2000.

"SAGA OF THE SKOLIAN EMPIRE" SERIES

Primary Inversion, Tor (New York, NY), 1995.
Catch the Lightning, Tor (New York, NY), 1996.
The Last Hawk, Tor (New York, NY), 1997.
The Radiant Seas, Tor (New York, NY), 1998.
Ascendant Sun, Tor (New York, NY), 2000.
The Quantum Rose, Tor (New York, NY), 2000.
Spherical Harmonic, Tor (New York, NY), 2001.

OTHER

Work represented in anthologies, including *Christmas Forever,* edited by David G. Hartwell, Tor (New York, NY), 1993, and *Analog.* Contributor to periodicals and scholarly journals, including *Analog, Journal of Chemical Physics, New York Review of Science Fiction, American Journal of Physics, International Journal of Quantitative Chemistry, Science Fiction Writers of America Bulletin, Science Fiction Age, Pirate Writings,* and *Physical Review Letters.* Columnist, *Tangent.* Editor and publisher, *Mindsparks: The Magazine of Science and Science Fiction,* 1993—.

■ **Sidelights**

Both a distinguished astrophysicist and a science-fiction writer, Catherine Asaro brings to her work more than a notional conception of the laws of physics and quantum mechanics. As Carl Hays noted in a *Booklist* review of Asaro's debut novel, *Primary Inversion,* the author "combines hard speculative science and first-rate storytelling to look at the galaxy's distant future." In the books in Asaro's "Skolian Empire" series, she combines science fiction and romance, each volume in the series a stand-alone title set in the same universe and dealing with the royal Skolia family. Asaro has also written more conventional sf artificial intelligence novels, as well as a plethora of professional articles on theoretical chemical physics—specifically using quantum theory to describe the behavior of atoms and molecules. And as if to push the envelope with activities, the novelist-physicist is a mother, wife, and a ballet dancer who teaches dance and has many dance performances to her credit. "Few writers in the world of science fiction successfully fuse love, romance and excitement with hard science," wrote a contributor for *Crescent Blues* online. "Yet Catherine Asaro pirouettes between the worlds of theoretical physics and action-oriented romance with the grace of a ballerina."

Asaro's love of physics did not happen just by chance; she was bound to become involved in science, one way or another. Her father, Frank Asaro, a

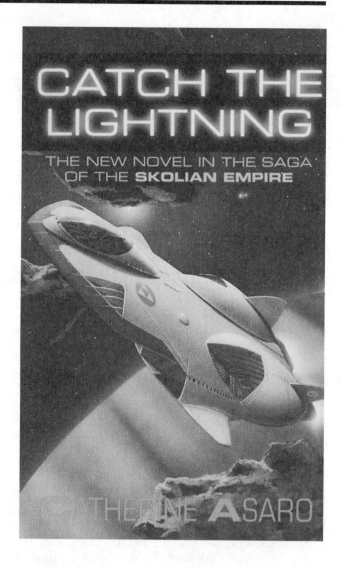

In Catherine Asaro's 1996 novel, the heroic Jagernaut Althor lands his injured starship on a future Earth where he meets a psychic teen who helps him return to his own world of Skolia.

nuclear chemist, was part of the scientific team that proposed the theory that an asteroid or comet struck the Earth sixty-five million years ago, causing mass extinctions, and possibly even wiping out the dinosaurs. Asaro's father "discovered the iridium anomalies that led to the theory," Asaro explained to the interviewer for *Crescent Blues.* "I've always liked solving scientific problems," the novelist added. "Gathering data, analyzing it, solving equations, finding answers—it fascinates me."

In addition to her love of the scientific process, Asaro was also interested in writing and dance. She studied and performed classical ballet; she also began writing. As an eight year old, she wrote half of a science-fiction novel "about a girl who helps the cat-like aliens on a distant planet fight their conquerors," as the author explained in an interview with *Amazon.com.* Asaro was forced to give up the saga, however, when her young heroine hides in a military installation . . . and the young would-be novelist realized she had no idea what a military installation looked like.

Graduating from the University of California—Los Angeles with highest honors in chemistry, Asaro went on to graduate school at Harvard University, earning her M.A. in physics and then changing her area of concentration to earn her doctorate in theoretical chemical physics in 1985. Asaro was not a single-minded science student throughout these years, however. She founded the Mainly Jazz Dance program at Harvard, and also went back to her early love—writing. "When I was working on my doctorate in chemical physics at Harvard, I decided to give writing a go again," she told *Amazon.com,* "as a way to unwind from my thesis. As soon as I started, it took over!" The universe she had been mulling over since she began her first novel years before suddenly began to take shape as a mature and detailed other world. Characters and plot took on real form, and this time around she had the background knowledge to accurately describe her separate universe. By the mid-1980s Asaro had written "Lucifer's Legacy," the short story that would ultimately become her first novel, *Primary Inversion.*

Meanwhile, Asaro married an astrophysicist and completed her postdoctoral study at the University of Toronto, at the Max Planck Institute in Germany, and at the Harvard-Smithsonian Center for Astrophysics. She worked as a professor of physics from 1987 to 1990, and then became president of her own research company, Molecudyne Research, in Laurel, Maryland. She also kept her hand in the academic world, publishing articles in prestigious journals such as *Physical Review Letters, Journal of Chemical Physics,* and *Chemical Physics Letters.*

Asaro explained in *Crescent Blues* that it was during her sojourn in Germany that she began to tinker with "Lucifer's Legacy," with the idea of expanding it into a novel. Serendipity also played a part in the process: A paper she published in the *American Journal of Physics* gave her the key to the physics she needed for an important part of the plot. In 1995 the story had found new life as *Primary Inversions,* and Asaro could add "published author" to her lengthy list of accomplishments.

Meet the Skolians

Primary Inversion is a futuristic tale in which three empires vie for domination of the galaxy. Inhabitants of Earth have ties to both the other empires:

the Skolians and the Traders, the latter a genetic experiment gone wrong who have evolved into a race who feel little pain and have no empathy. In fact, the Traders actually derive pleasure from the pain of others, especially Jagernauts. Although Skolians and Traders are enemies, Skolian princess Sauscony Valdoria becomes drawn to Jaibriol Qox, son of the Trader emperor, when her sensory capabilities reveal that Jaibriol, despite his ancestry, is her soul mate. However, Valdoria also learns that Jaibriol has been genetically contrived to overpower Skolians.

Primary Inversion met with praise from critics, including Hays, who praised it in *Booklist* as "an un-

Combining romance with science fiction, Asaro spins a tale of thwarted romance as Kamoj Argali must wed a wealthy landowner in order to keep her people from starvation.

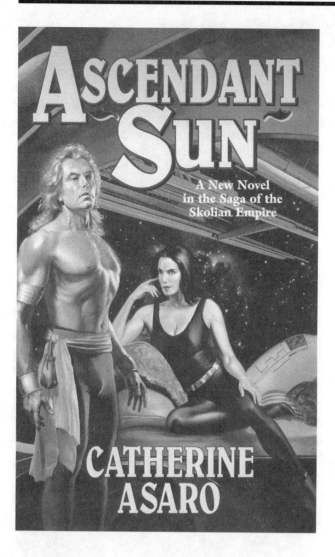

ASCENDANT SUN

A New Novel in the Saga of the Skolian Empire

CATHERINE ASARO

When adventurer Kelric returns to his home planet, he finds a changed world in which he must keep his identity secret in order to save what is left of his imprisoned family.

usually masterful first novel." A reviewer for *Publishers Weekly* also called attention to the wealth of hard science in the book—from "faster-than-light inversion drives" to computer networks—and maintained that Asaro "manages to anchor her story with thoughtful, engaging characters and an intriguing vision of the future."

Asaro followed *Primary Inversion* with *Catch the Lightning,* which relates continued conflicts between the Skolians and the Traders. In *Catch the Lightning,* Skolian Jagernaut Althor, destined to rule Skolia, lands his sabotaged space vehicle on an alternative Earth and befriends Tina Pulivok, a psychic teenager from 1980s Los Angeles. Inquisitive scientists, meanwhile, are conducting investigations into the

capabilities of Althor's craft. Althor, with the help of Tina and her friends, determines to recover his ship and return to his own world to undermine the Trader antagonists. Several critics were disappointed with *Catch the Lightning* due to the expectations set by Asaro's first foray into fiction. A *Kirkus Reviews* critic called it "an unexciting but solidly crafted, and at times absorbing narrative," but added that too many technical details and a slow plot weaken the book. While a *Publishers Weekly* reviewer wrote that the novel "fails to cohere and to deliver the vibrant reading experience" contained in *Primary Inversion,* the critic added that *Catch the Lightning* contains good characterization and "many fine passages."

With her third "Skolian Empire" novel, *The Last Hawk,* "Asaro continues to flesh out the old-fashioned concept of an interstellar empire with well-chosen detail," according to *Booklist* contributor Roland Green. Kelric, a fighter pilot and heir to the Skolian throne, crashes on the female-dominated planet Coba. While the women of this matriarchal society abhor killing, their fear that their world will no longer remain hidden and free from Skolian domination prompts them to keep Kelric captive. For twenty years, as both a concubine and prisoner, he remains on Coba and is traded or sold to various estates.

Realistic Language Paired with Science

With *The Last Hawk* Asaro began to fully develop the linguistic possibilities of her invented universe. As she explained to Terry Hickman in an interview for *Market List,* the language of the Skolian books is an amalgam of Mesoamerican, North African, and Indian. These peoples were abducted from Earth millennia ago by aliens and resettled in time and space; descendants of these earthlings populate the worlds of Skolia. "Coba is one the lost colonies," Asaro explained to Hickman. "The name is Mayan (Mesoamerican). Other names have North African or Indian roots. Languages evolve, of course, so the words in the book shouldn't be exactly like those derived from on Earth, at least not most of them."

Another intriguing aspect of *The Last Hawk* is the introduction of the game of Quis, a mathematical model for human relationships that is played with dice of rainbow hues. Asaro began to develop this game also while still in graduate school.

Critical reception of *The Last Hawk* was largely positive. A reviewer for *Library Journal* noted that this "intriguing novel combines hard speculative science . . . with romantic adventure." Asaro manages to avoid the usual "pitfalls" of the genre, maintained Greene in *Booklist,* "giving us an intelligent action story, with strong overtones of the better sort of romance." A contributor for *Publishers Weekly* added to the praise, noting that Asaro "has settled into a smoothly absorbing space-opera formula that mixes high-tech gimmickry with galactic politics and plenty of romance."

The Radiant Seas, volume four in the "Skolian Empire" series, is set in the twenty-third century, as the rivalry between the Skolians and the Eubians has now reached fever pitch. The book reprises the two protagonists of *Primary Inversion,* Valdoria and Jaibriol, who are heirs to their respective dynasties. The star-crossed lovers have faked their deaths so that they can raise a family together on an unknown planet. However, soldiers from the competing empire of Eube find the couple's son and kidnap him due to his value as heir to both empires. It is left to Valdoria to lead her warriors in a mission to free him. "Fierce battle scenes play off against intense family drama as the two powers use techniques of mind and machinery in their final effort," wrote Roberta Johnson in a *Booklist* review. A contributor for *Publishers Weekly* was less enthusiastic, however, maintaining that *The Radiant Seas* contains a surplus of "gratuitous" sex and torture and that the book "falls short of the state of the art even in space opera." Still, *Library Journal* reviewer Jackie Cassada predicted that Asaro's "mix of romantic intrigue and large-scale dynastic sf should have a broad appeal."

Series Takes a Daring Twist

With 2000's *Ascendant Sun,* "Skolian Empire" fans were reunited with the cybernetically enhanced Jagernaut Kelric, who is now on his way home after nearly two decades on Coba. However, once back in the Skolian Empire, he is dismayed to learn that Earth's Allied Forces have been deployed as a peace-keeping force in the wake of the destruction of the Radiance War and the elimination of the telepathic web that once connected the empires of Skolia, Eube, and Aristo. Kelric discovers that most of his family are dead and that he is heir to an empire that may no longer exist. Falling into the hands of the Aristos—who derive pleasure from the pain of their sex slaves—the unlucky Kelric discovers that this empire plans to assume absolute power by opening a space-time portal. Due to the dangers involved, he must do all in his power to stop them.

Praise greeted this fourth installment in the "Skolian Empire" series, a reviewer for *Publishers Weekly* commenting that "every element in the novel fits

HUMANITY'S GREATEST ACHIEVEMENT MAY PROVE TO BE ITS DEADLIEST....

THE PHOENIX CODE

CATHERINE ASARO

AUTHOR OF *THE VEILED WEB*

Megan O'Flannery is the only one with the expertise to fix an unstable defense-system android that has become self-aware and now runs amok in an underground research lab.

together" and dubbing *Ascendant Sun* "yet another fast-paced and pleasing entry" in the series. *Booklist* contributor Green found *Ascendant Sun* to be "the best of [Asaro's] Skolian Empire series." Noting the increasing blend of romance, sex, and violence in the Asaro's novels, Green remarked that the series "is beginning to be a Star Wars gone slightly kinky," but added that Asaro "continues to oblige seekers of fast-paced entertainment with literate page-turners."

A contributor to *Publishers Weekly* called the sixth "Skolian" novel, *The Quantum Rose,* a "freestanding page-turner as a romance, with a hard science framework." In this installment, beautiful Kamoj

Quanta Argali, governor of an impoverished province, has long been betrothed to Jax Ironbridge, governor of a wealthier neighboring province. But when the mysterious Havryl Lionstar arrives from a distant planet, things heat up. Havryl, an exiled prince of the Skolian line, comes into competition with Jax for Kamoj's hand, and meanwhile entangles local governors in the affairs of a much wider universe. Green wrote in *Booklist* that *The Quantum Rose* "bolsters [Asaro's] reputation for skillfully putting classic romance elements in an sf setting." Green also praised Asaro's "sound characterization, straightforward plotting, abundant world building detail, and . . . humor." Writing in *Library Journal*, Cassada noted that Asaro "details the lives of a trio of powerful individuals whose lives mirror the complexities of the worlds in which they move."

Going back in time for the seventh novel in the series, Asaro places the protagonist of *Spherical Harmonic* at the end of the Radiance War between Skolians and Traders, with both sides now claiming victory. The empire's psiberweb is not functioning, disrupting instantaneous communication and interstellar travel, and rival powers jockey for control. Into the interplanetary chaos comes Dyhianna Selei, heir to the Ruby Dynasty and believed to be dead, who appears on a moon of Opalite. Recovering her memory, Dyhianna must strive to keep the sadistic Traders from assuming power while also going in search of her husband and son.

"Fans of Asaro's 'Saga of the Skolian Empire' will not want to miss this installment," stated Diana Tixier Herald in *Booklist*, while also noting of *Spherical Harmonic* that the novel might be "bewildering" as a stand-alone read. A reviewer for *Publishers Weekly* agreed, writing that the "fast-paced" novel provides a "backstory with plenty of battles and political machinations that will no doubt delight fans of the series but may leave others scratching their heads." However, in *Library Journal* Jackie Cassada noted that Asaro's blend of "dynastic intrigue with theoretical physics . . . will appeal to fans of hard sf as well as grand-scale storytelling."

Strays Far from Skolia

With *The Veiled Web* and *The Phoenix Code*, Asaro left her fictional Skolian Empire. Published in 1999, *The Veiled Web* is, according to a reviewer for *Publishers Weekly*, "an uneasy blend of cyber-intrigue, exotic love and romantic cliché." The novel takes place in the near future, as Lucia del Mar, a ballerina and inveterate web-surfer, meets and falls in love with Rashid al-Jazari, the inventor of an artificial intelli-

gence system. Kidnaped by terrorists, the duo manage to outwit their abductors, who want Rashid's invention. Married in Morocco, the couple sets up house. Cloistered in her new Islamic home, Lucia befriends the human-like computer Zaki, which Rashid has invented. When the terrorists strike a second time, they destroy Rashid's invention but Lucia and her husband manage to weather their resulting marital problems. A *Publishers Weekly* reviewer found that while plotting and suspense elements of the novel did not work well, "the sensuous and respectful evocation of Islamic culture" is praiseworthy, and Zaki "comes to life as the tale's most quirky and moving character."

In *The Phoenix Code*, Asaro's second non-"Skolian Empire" novel, Megan O'Flannery is an artificial intelligence expert who has the opportunity to help develop a self-aware android. She becomes the human interface with the latest model, RS-4, who desperately wants to escape. Megan seeks the help of Raj Sundarum, a robotics expert, but the duo are soon taken captive by the android in its bid for freedom. Their only hope is to socialize RS-4 before it kills them both. Calling *The Phoenix Code* a "well-executed reworking of a classic sf tale," *Booklist* reviewer Green added that the tale is "lighthearted without being silly, and irresistible for at least one thorough reading." Cassada called *The Phoenix Code* a "fast-moving tale of sf intrigue," in a *Library Journal* review.

If you enjoy the works of Catherine Asaro, you might want to check out the following books:

Andre Norton, *Witch World*, 1963.
Marion Zimmer Bradley, *The Forbidden Tower*, 1977.
Dan Simmons, *Hyperion*, 1989.
Walter Jon Williams, *Metropolitan*, 1995.

Asaro, who writes on a laptop whenever she can squeeze the time into her busy schedule of revising manuscripts and attending conventions, now views herself as a full-time writer. She noted in her *Crescent Blues* interview: "Now that I'm writing so much, I don't do much science, because I don't have the time. It reached the point where I had to make a decision, full time writer or full time scientist. I had no doubts on that score." She also remarked in the same interview that devising the plots for her stories is great fun. "It's like a game. I can't believe I actually get paid to do this."

■ **Biographical and Critical Sources**

PERIODICALS

Analog Science Fiction/Science Fact, July-August, 1999, pp. 224-225; April, 2000, pp. 136-137.

Booklist, February 15, 1995, Carl Hays, review of *Primary Inversion,* p. 1064; November 1, 1997, Roland Green, review of *The Last Hawk,* p. 456; December 1, 1998, Roberta Johnson, review of *The Radiant Seas,* p. 655; February 1, 2000, Roland Green, review of *Ascendant Sun,* p. 1010; December 1, 2000, Roland Green, review of *The Phoenix Code* and *The Quantum Rose,* p. 698; November 1, 2001, Diana Tixier Herald, review of *Spherical Harmonic,* p, 463.

Kirkus Reviews, October 15, 1996, review of *Catch the Lightning,* p. 1500; September 15, 2001, p. 1329.

Library Journal, February 15, 1995, p. 186; November 15, 1996, p. 92; November 15, 1997, review of *The Last Hawk,* p. 79; December, 1998, Jackie Cassada, review of *The Radiant Seas,* p. 162; November 15, 2000, Jackie Cassada, review of *The Quantum Rose,* p. 101; December, 2000, Jackie Cassada, review of *The Phoenix Code,* p. 197; November 15, 2001, Jackie Cassada, review of *Spherical Harmonic,* pp. 100-101.

Magazine of Fantasy and Science Fiction, April, 2000, p. 34.

Publishers Weekly, January 16, 1995, review of *Primary Inversion,* p. 442; November 18, 1996, review of *Catch the Lightning,* p. 66; October 27, 1997, review of *The Last Hawk,* p. 57; November 23, 1998, review of *The Radiant Seas,* p. 63; November 8, 1999, review of *The Veiled Web,* p. 65; January 17, 2000, review of *Ascendant Sun,* p. 48; November 27, 2000, review of *The Quantum Rose,* p. 60; November 12, 2001, review of *Spherical Harmonic,* p. 41.

Wilson Library Bulletin, June, 1995, p. 96.

OTHER

Amazon.com, http://www.amazon.com/ (February 25, 2002), "Amazon.com Talks to Catherine Asaro."

Catherine Asaro Web site, http://www.sff.net/people/Asaro (February 26, 2002).

Crescent Blues, http://www.crescentblues.com/ (February 25, 2002), "Catherine Asaro: Fictional Fusion."

Market List, http://www.marketlist.com/ (February 25, 2002), Terry Hickman, "Catherine Asaro Interview."*

—Sketch by J. Sydney Jones

Margaret Atwood

■ Personal

Born November 18, 1939, in Ottawa, Ontario, Canada; daughter of Carl Edmund (an entomologist) and Margaret Dorothy (Killam) Atwood; married Jim Polk, 1967 (divorced 1977); married Graeme Gibson (a writer); children: (second marriage) Jess (daughter). *Education:* University of Toronto, B.A., 1961; Radcliffe College, A.M., 1962; Harvard University, graduate study, 1962-63, 1965-67. *Politics:* "William Morrisite." *Religion:* "Immanent Transcendentalist."

■ Addresses

Home—Toronto, Ontario, Canada. *Agent*—c/o Random House, 201 East 50th St., New York, NY, 10022.

■ Career

Novelist, poet, and educator. University of British Columbia, Vancouver, British Columbia, Canada, lecturer in English literature, 1964-65; Sir George Williams University, Montreal, Quebec, Canada, lecturer in English literature, 1967-68; York University, Toronto, Ontario, Canada, assistant professor of English literature, 1971-72; House of Anansi Press, Toronto, editor and member of board of directors, 1971-73; University of Toronto, writer-in-residence, 1972-73; University of Alabama—Tuscaloosa, writer-in-residence, 1985; New York University, New York, NY, Berg Visiting Professor of English, 1986; Macquarie University, North Ryde, Australia, writer-in-residence, 1987. Worked variously as a camp counselor and waitress.

■ Member

PEN International, Amnesty International, Writers' Union of Canada (vice-chairperson, 1980-81), Royal Society of Canada (fellow), Canadian Centre, American Academy of Arts and Sciences (honorary member), Anglophone (president, 1984-85), Canadian Civil Liberties Association (member of board, 1973-75).

■ Awards, Honors

E. J. Pratt Medal, 1961, for *Double Persephone*; President's Medal, University of Western Ontario, 1965; YWCA Women of Distinction Award, 1966, 1988; Governor General's Award, 1966, for *The Circle*

Game, and 1986, for *The Handmaid's Tale*; first prize in Canadian Centennial Commission Poetry Competition, 1967; Union Prize for poetry, 1969; Bess Hoskins Prize for poetry, 1969, 1974; City of Toronto Book Award, Canadian Booksellers' Association Award, and Periodical Distributors of Canada Short Fiction Award, all 1977, all for *Dancing Girls and Other Stories*; St. Lawrence Award for fiction, 1978; Radcliffe Medal, 1980; *Life before Man* selected a notable book of 1980, American Library Association; Molson Award, 1981; Guggenheim fellowship, 1981; named Companion of the Order of Canada, 1981; International Writer's Prize, Welsh Arts Council, 1982; Book of the Year Award, Periodical Distributors of Canada and Foundation for the Advancement of Canadian Letters, 1983, for *Bluebeard's Egg and Other Stories*; named Woman of the Year, *Ms.* magazine, 1986; Ida Nudel Humanitarian Award, Toronto Arts Award for writing and editing, and *Los Angeles Times* Book Award, all 1986, and Arthur C. Clarke Award for Best Science Fiction, and Commonwealth Literature Prize, both 1987, all for *The Handmaid's Tale*; Council for the Advancement and Support of Education silver medal, 1987; Humanist of the Year award, 1987; Booker Prize shortlist, City of Toronto Book Award, Coles Book of the Year Award, Canadian Booksellers' Association Author of the Year Award, Foundation for Advancement of Canadian Letters citation, Periodical Marketers of Canada Award, and Torgi Talking Book Award, all 1989, all for *Cat's Eye*; Harvard University Centennial Medal, 1990; Order of Ontario, 1990; Trillium Award for Excellence in Ontario Writing, and Book of the Year Award, Periodical Marketers of Canada, both 1992, both for *Wilderness Tips and Other Stories*; Commemorative Medal, 125th Anniversary of Canadian Confederation; Booker Prize shortlist, Trillium Award, Canadian Authors' Association Novel of the Year Award, Commonwealth Writers' Prize for Canadian and Caribbean Region, and *Sunday Times* Award for Literary Excellence, all 1994, and Swedish Humour Association's International Humourous Writer Award, 1995, all for *The Robber Bride*; Government of France's Chevalier dans l'Ordre des Arts et des Lettres, 1994, for *The Robber Bride*; Trillium Award, 1995, for *Morning in the Burned House*; Norwegian Order of Literary Merit, 1996; Booker Prize shortlist, and Giller Prize, both 1996, both for *Alias Grace*; International IMPAC Dublin Literary Award shortlist, Dublin City Library, 1998; Booker Prize, 2000, and Dashiell Hammett Award, International Association of Crime Writers, 2001, both for *The Blind Assassin*. Recipient of honorary degrees from Trent University, 1973, Concordia University, 1980, Smith College, 1982, University of Toronto, 1983, Mount Holyoke College, 1985, University of Waterloo, 1985, University of Guelph, 1985, Victoria College, 1987, University of Montreal, 1991, University of Leeds, 1994, Queen's University, 1994, and Oxford University, 1998, Cambridge University, 2001, and others.

■ Writings

NOVELS

The Edible Woman, McClelland Stewart (Toronto, Ontario, Canada), 1969, Little, Brown (Boston, MA), 1970.

Surfacing, McClelland Stewart (Toronto, Ontario, Canada), 1972, Simon & Schuster (New York, NY), 1973.

Lady Oracle, Simon & Schuster (New York, NY), 1976.

Life before Man, Simon & Schuster (New York, NY), 1979.

Bodily Harm, McClelland Stewart (Toronto, Ontario, Canada), 1981, Simon & Schuster (New York, NY), 1982.

Encounters with the Element Man, Ewert (Concord, NH), 1982.

Unearthing Suite, Grand Union Press, 1983.

The Handmaid's Tale, McClelland Stewart (Toronto, Ontario, Canada), 1985, Houghton (Boston, MA), 1986.

Cat's Eye, McClelland Stewart (Toronto, Ontario, Canada), 1988, Doubleday (Garden City, NY), 1989.

The Robber Bride, Doubleday (New York, NY), 1993.

Alias Grace, Doubleday (New York, NY), 1996.

The Blind Assassin, Random House (New York, NY), 2000.

POETRY

Double Persephone, Hawkshead Press, 1961.

The Circle Game, Cranbrook Academy of Art (Bloomfield Hills, MI), 1964, revised edition, Contact Press, 1966.

Kaleidoscopes Baroque: A Poem, Cranbrook Academy of Art (Bloomfield Hills, MI), 1965.

Talismans for Children, Cranbrook Academy of Art (Bloomfield Hills, MI), 1965.

Speeches for Doctor Frankenstein, Cranbrook Academy of Art (Bloomfield Hills, MI), 1966.

Expeditions, 1966.

The Animals in That Country, Little, Brown (Boston, MA), 1968.

What Was in the Garden, 1969.

The Journals of Susanna Moodie, Oxford University Press (Toronto, Ontario, Canada), 1970.

Procedures for Underground, Little, Brown (Boston, MA), 1970.

Power Politics, House of Anansi Press (Toronto, Ontario, Canada), 1971, Harper (New York, NY), 1973.

You Are Happy, Harper (New York, NY), 1974.

Selected Poems, 1965-1975, Oxford University Press (Toronto, Ontario, Canada), 1976, Simon & Schuster (New York, NY), 1978.

Marsh Hawk, Dreadnaught, 1977.

Two-headed Poems, Oxford University Press (Toronto, Ontario, Canada), 1978, Simon & Schuster (New York, NY), 1981.

Notes toward a Poem That Can Never Be Written, Salamander Press (Toronto, Ontario, Canada), 1981.

True Stories, Oxford University Press (Toronto, Ontario, Canada), 1981, Simon & Schuster (New York, NY), 1982.

Snake Poems, Salamander Press (Toronto, Ontario, Canada), 1983.

Interlunar, Oxford University Press (Toronto, Ontario, Canada), 1984.

Selected Poems II: Poems Selected and New, 1976-1986, Oxford University Press (Toronto, Ontario, Canada), 1986.

Morning in the Burned House, Houghton (Boston, MA), 1995.

Eating Fire: Selected Poetry, 1965-1995, Virago (London, England), 1998.

STORY COLLECTIONS

Dancing Girls and Other Stories, McClelland Stewart (Toronto, Ontario, Canada), 1977, Simon & Schuster (New York, NY), 1982.

Bluebeard's Egg and Other Stories, McClelland Stewart (Toronto, Ontario, Canada), 1983, Fawcett (New York, NY), 1987.

Murder in the Dark: Short Fictions and Prose Poems, Coach House Press (Toronto, Ontario, Canada), 1983.

Wilderness Tips and Other Stories, Doubleday (New York, NY), 1991.

Good Bones, Coach House Press (Toronto, Ontario, Canada), 1992, published as *Good Bones and Simple Murders,* Doubleday (New York, NY), 1994.

A Quiet Game: And Other Early Works, edited and annotated by Kathy Chung and Sherrill Grace, Juvenilia Press (Edmonton, Alberta, Canada), 1997.

OTHER

The Trumpets of Summer (radio play), Canadian Broadcasting Corporation (CBC-Radio), 1964.

Survival: A Thematic Guide to Canadian Literature, House of Anansi Press (Toronto, Ontario, Canada), 1972.

The Servant Girl (teleplay), CBC-TV, 1974.

Days of the Rebels, 1815-1840, Natural Science Library, 1976.

The Poetry and Voice of Margaret Atwood (recording), Caedmon, 1977.

Up in the Tree (juvenile), McClelland Stewart (Toronto, Ontario, Canada), 1978.

(Author of introduction) Catherine M. Young, *To See Our World,* GLC Publishers, 1979, Morrow (New York, NY), 1980.

(With Joyce Barkhouse) *Anna's Pet* (juvenile), James Lorimer, 1980.

Snowbird (teleplay), CBC-TV, 1981.

Second Words: Selected Critical Prose, House of Anansi Press (Toronto, Ontario, Canada), 1982.

(Editor) *The New Oxford Book of Canadian Verse in English,* Oxford University Press (Toronto, Ontario, Canada), 1982.

(Editor with Robert Weaver) *The Oxford Book of Canadian Short Stories in English,* Oxford University Press (Toronto, Ontario, Canada), 1986.

(With Peter Pearson) *Heaven on Earth* (teleplay), CBC-TV, 1986.

(Editor) *The Canlit Foodbook,* Totem, 1987.

(Editor with Shannon Ravenal) *The Best American Short Stories, 1989,* Houghton (Boston, MA), 1989.

For the Birds, illustrated by John Bianchi, Firefly Books (Toronto, Ontario, Canada), 1991.

(Editor with Barry Callaghan and author of introduction) *The Poetry of Gwendolyn MacEwen,* Exile Editions (Toronto, Ontario, Canada), Volume 1: *The Early Years,* 1993, Volume 2: *The Later Years,* 1994.

Princess Prunella and the Purple Peanut (juvenile), illustrated by Maryann Kovalski, Workman (New York, NY), 1995.

Strange Things: The Malevolent North in Canadian Literature (lectures), Clarendon/Oxford University Press (Toronto, Ontario, Canada), 1996.

Some Things about Flying, Women's Press (London, England), 1997.

(With Victor-Levy Beaulieu) *Two Solicitudes: Conversations* (interviews), translated by Phyllis Aronoff and Howard Scott, M & S (Toronto, Ontario, Canada), 1998.

(Author of introduction) *Women Writers at Work: The 'Paris Review' Interviews,* edited by George Plimpton, Random House (New York, NY), 1998.

Negotiating with the Dead: A Writer on Writing, Cambridge University Press (New York, NY), 2002.

Contributor to anthologies, including *Five Modern Canadian Poets,* 1970, *The Canadian Imagination: Dimensions of a Literary Culture,* Harvard University

Press, 1977, and *Women on Women*, 1978. Contributor to periodicals, including *Atlantic*, *Poetry*, *New Yorker*, *Harper's*, *New York Times Book Review*, *Saturday Night*, *Tamarack Review*, and *Canadian Forum*.

■ Adaptations

The Edible Woman was adapted for a stage play; *The Handmaid's Tale* was filmed by Cinecom Entertainment Group, 1990, and was adapted for an opera, with music by Poul Ruder, premiering at the Royal Danish Opera, 2000; *The Robber Bride* was optioned for a film by Irish Screen; *The Blind Assassin* was adapted for a four-part television mini-series by BBC's Channel Four, 2001.

■ Sidelights

The author of over sixty books, Margaret Atwood holds a unique position in contemporary Canadian literature. "Atwood is arguably the most recognizable writer in the country," noted John Bemrose in *Maclean's*. Likewise, Ann Marie Lipinski, writing in the *Chicago Tribune*, described Atwood as "one of the leading literary luminaries, a national heroine of the arts, the *rara avis* of Canadian letters." To limit Atwood geographically as a "Canadian" author, would be a gross injustice, however, for her books have received critical acclaim in the United States and Europe as well in as her native Canada, and she has won numerous literary awards. Her receipt of Great Britain's Booker Prize in 2000, proof of Atwood's international repute, is of particular significance to an author who was placed on the prestigious award's short list three times in the past.

Atwood's popularity with both critics and the reading public has surprised her. "It's an accident that I'm a successful writer," she told Roy MacGregor in *Maclean's*. "I think I'm kind of an odd phenomenon in that I'm a serious writer and I never expected to become a popular one, and I never did anything in order to become a popular one." In addition to being the darling of critics, she is a frequent guest on Canadian television and radio, her books are best sellers, and "people follow her on the streets and in stores," as Judy Klemesrud reported in the *New York Times*. According to MacGregor in *Maclean's*, Atwood "is to Canadian literature as Gordon Lightfoot is to Canadian music, more institution than individual."

Best known for novels such as *The Handmaid's Tale*, *The Robber Bride*, and *The Blind Assassin*, Atwood is also a poet of note, as well as a short-story writer,

essayist, children's author, and playwright with several radio scripts to her credit. She explores many of the same themes within these various genres, examining the relationship between humanity and nature or the disquieting aspects of human behavior, and looking at power as it pertains to gender and politics. Employing symbolism, irony, and self-conscious narrators, Atwood takes literary chances by employing techniques from science fiction and the detective novel in her detail-filled novels, poems, and short stories. Often dubbed a feminist author, Atwood is in fact a humanist, examining the human condition, both male and female, through the eye both of a poet and scientist.

Canadian Origins

Atwood's keen scientific eye may have come from her entomologist father, or perhaps her dietician mother. Born in 1939, in Ottawa, Ontario, Canada, she was raised in a tight-knit family that also included a brother and a sister. From infancy into her late adolescence, Atwood spent at least half the year living in the wilderness of northern Ontario and Quebec, where her father conducted research on forest insects for the government. While she was a busy child on such expeditions, hauling water and chopping wood, this wilderness experience also informed Atwood's perception. As Jerome H. Rosenberg noted in his *Margaret Atwood*, "The bush provided [Atwood] not only with knowledge but also a kind of wisdom, a way of seeing." Educated at home, Atwood relied on books of all sorts during these long sojourns away from civilization. As a six year old, she had already started dabbling with poetry, writing a series she called "Rhyming Cats."

In 1946 the family moved to Toronto, where Atwood's father held a university position; still, half the year was spent in Canada's north woods. By the time she reached high school Atwood had decided to become a professional writer. As she told Kim Hubbard in *People Weekly*, she was somewhat frightened by her decision, for she had few female role models in her chosen profession. "Emily Dickinson lived in a cupboard, Charlotte Brontë died in childbirth. They were weird like Christina Rossetti, or they drank or committed suicide like Sylvia Plath. Writing seemed like a call to doom. I thought I would probably get [tuberculosis] and live in a garret and have a terrible life."

Graduating from Toronto's Leaside High School in 1957, Atwood attended the University of Toronto's Victoria College and entered the English honors program. Studying under well-known critic

Northrop Frye, she became versed in the use of mythical and biblical imagery. As an undergraduate she wrote for the college literary magazine and had her first poem published at age nineteen.

In 1961, the year she graduated from college, Atwood published her first volume of poetry, *Double Persephone,* which won the E. J. Pratt Medal. She went on to earn her M.A. at Radcliffe College, studying Victorian literature, and also studied at Harvard University. Her second volume of poetry, 1964's *The Circle Game,* won a Governor General's Award. Atwood was by this time busy teaching at colleges in Canada. Though she began her literary career as a poet, it is for her novels that Atwood has become most widely known; she published her first novel, *The Edible Woman,* in 1969.

Early Novels

Atwood's concern for strong female characters emerges clearly in her novels, particularly in *The Edible Woman, Surfacing, Life before Man, Bodily Harm,* and *The Handmaid's Tale.* These novels feature female characters who are, Klemesrud reported, "intelligent, self-absorbed modern women searching for identity. . . . [They] hunt, split logs, make campfires and become successful in their careers, while men often cook and take care of their households." Like her poems, Atwood's novels "are populated by pained and confused people whose lives hold a mirror to both the front page fears—cancer, divorce, violence—and those that persist quietly, naggingly—solitude, loneliness, desperation," according to Lipinski.

The Edible Woman tells the story of Marian McAlpin, a young woman engaged to be married, who rebels against her upcoming marriage. Her fiancee seems too stable, too ordinary, and the role of wife too fixed and limiting. Marian's rejection of marriage is accompanied by her body's rejection of food; she cannot tolerate even a spare vegetarian diet. Eventually she bakes a sponge cake in the shape of a woman and feeds it to her fiancee because, she explains, "You've been trying to assimilate me." After the engagement is broken off, she is able to eat some of the cake herself.

Reaction to *The Edible Woman* was divided, some reviewers pointing to flaws commonly found in first novels. John Stedmond of *Canadian Forum* maintained that "the characters, though cleverly sketched, do not quite jell, and the narrative techniques creak a little." Linda Rogers of *Canadian Literature* found that "one of the reasons *The Edible Woman* fails as a novel is the awkwardness of the dialogue." Still, critics found the novel at least partially successful. Tom Marshall, writing in his *Harsh and Lovely Land: The Major Canadian Poets and the Making of a Canadian Tradition,* praised *The Edible Woman* as an effective comic novel, "even if the mechanics are sometimes a little clumsy, the satirical accounts of consumerism a little drawn out." *New York Times Book Review* contributor Millicent Bell termed it "a work of feminist black humor" and claimed that Atwood's "comic distortion veers at times into surreal meaningfulness." And Linda Hutcheon, writing in the *Dictionary of Literary Biography,* described *The Edible Woman* as "very much a social novel about the possibilities for personal female identity in a capitalistic consumer society."

MARGARET ATWOOD

THE HANDMAID'S TALE

In Margaret Atwood's 1985 novel, readers are presented with a dismal future Earth in which women are either selected by male overlords to serve as mothers to the next generation of humans or else relegated to a life of slavery.

Surfacing, Atwood's second novel, is "a psychological ghost story," as Marshall described it, in which a young woman confronts and accepts her past during a visit to her rural home. She comes to realize that she has repressed disturbing events from her memory, including an abortion and her father's death. While swimming in a local lake, she has a vision of her drowned father, which "drives her to a healing madness," Marshall stated. Hutcheon explained that "*Surfacing* tells of the coming to terms with the haunting, separated parts of the narrator's being . . . after surfacing from a dive, a symbolic as well as a real descent under water, where she has experienced a revealing and personally apocalyptic vision."

Many of the concerns voiced in Atwood's poetry also appear in *Surfacing.* The novel, Roberta Rubenstein wrote in *Modern Fiction Studies,* "synthesizes a number of motifs that have dominated [Atwood's] consciousness since her earliest poems: the elusiveness and variety of 'language' in its several senses; the continuum between human and animal, human being and nature; the significance of one's heritage . . . ; the search for a location (in both time and place); the brutalizations and victimizations of love; drowning and surviving." Margaret Wimsatt agreed with this assessment in *Commonweal.* "The novel," Wimsatt wrote, "picks up themes brooded over in the poetry, and knits them together coherently." Marshall asserted that both *The Edible Woman* and *Surfacing* "are enlargements upon the themes of [Atwood's] poems. In each of them a young woman is driven to rebellion against what seems to be her fate in the modern technological 'Americanized' world and to psychic breakdown and breakthrough."

In *Life before Man* Atwood dissects the relationships between three characters: Elizabeth, a married woman mourning the recent suicide of her lover; Elizabeth's husband, Nate, who is unable to choose between his wife and his lover; and Lesje, Nate's lover, who works with Elizabeth at a museum of natural history. All three characters are isolated from one another and unable to experience their own emotions, the fossils and dinosaur bones on display at the museum reflecting the sterility of their separate lives. As Laurie Stone noted in the *Village Voice, Life before Man* "is full of variations on the theme of extinction." Similarly, Rubenstein wrote in the *Chicago Tribune* that the novel is a "superb living exhibit in which the artifacts are unique (but representative) lives in progress."

Although *Life before Man* is what Rosellen Brown of *Saturday Review* called an "anatomy of melancholy," MacGregor pointed out a tempering humor in the

novel as well. *Life before Man,* MacGregor wrote, "is not so much a story as it is the discarded negatives of a family album, the thoughts so dark they defy any flash short of Atwood's remarkable, and often very funny, insight." Comparing the novel's characters to museum pieces and commenting on the analytical examination to which Atwood subjects them, Peter S. Prescott wrote in *Newsweek* that "with chilly compassion and an even colder wit, Atwood exposes the interior lives of her specimens." Writing in the *New York Times Book Review,* Marilyn French made clear that in *Life before Man,* Atwood "combines several talents—powerful introspection, honesty, satire and a taut, limpid style—to create a splendid, fully integrated work."

The title of *Life before Man,* French believed, relates to the characters' isolation from themselves, their history, and from one another. "This novel suggests that we are still living life before man, before the human—as we like to define it—has evolved." Prescott addressed the same point, noting that the novel's characters "do not communicate; each, in the presence of another, is locked into his own thoughts and feelings." This concern is also found in Atwood's three earlier novels, French argued, all of which depict "the search for identity . . . a search for a better way to be—for a way of life that both satisfies the passionate, needy self and yet is decent, humane and natural."

Atwood further explores this idea in *Bodily Harm.* In this novel Rennie Wilford is a Toronto journalist who specializes in light, trivial pieces for magazines. She is, Anne Tyler explained in the *Detroit News,* "a cataloguer of current fads and fancies." Isabel Raphael of the London *Times* called Rennie someone who "deals only in surfaces; her journalism is of the most trivial and transitory kind, her relationship with a live-in lover limited to sex, and most of her friends 'really just contacts.'" Following a partial mastectomy, which causes her lover to abandon her, Rennie begins to feel dissatisfied with her life. She takes on an assignment to the Caribbean island of St. Antoine in an effort to get away from things for a while. Her planned magazine story focusing on the island's beaches, tennis courts, and restaurants is distinctly facile in comparison to the political violence she finds on St. Antoine. When Rennie is arrested and jailed she gains a self-realization about her life. "Death," Nancy Ramsey remarked in the *San Francisco Review of Books,* "rather than the modern sense of ennui, threatens Rennie and the people around her, and ultimately gives her life a meaning she hadn't known before."

Bodily Harm, Frank Davey of the *Canadian Forum* asserted, follows a characteristic Atwood pattern: "Alienation from natural order . . . followed by descent into a more primitive but healing reality . . . and finally some reestablishment of order." Although Davey was "troubled" by the similarities between the novels and stated that "Atwood doesn't risk much," he concluded that *Bodily Harm is still a pleasure to read."* Other critics had few reservations about the novel. Anatole Broyard claimed in the *New York Times* that "the only way to describe my response to [*Bodily Harm*] is to say that it knocked me out. Atwood seems to be able to do just about everything: people, places, problems, a perfect ear, an exactly-right voice and she tosses off terrific scenes with a casualness that leaves you utterly unprepared for the way these scenes seize you." Tyler called Atwood "an uncommonly skillful and perceptive writer," and went on to state that, because of its subject matter, *Bodily Harm* "is not always easy to read. There are times when it's downright unpleasant, but it's also intelligent, provocative, and in the end—against all expectations—uplifting."

The Handmaid's Tale

In *The Handmaid's Tale*, Atwood turns to speculative fiction, creating the dystopia of Gilead, a future America in which Fundamentalist Christians have killed the president and members of Congress and imposed their own dictatorial rule. In this future world, polluted by toxic chemicals and nuclear radiation, few women can bear children; the birthrate has dropped alarmingly. Those women who can bear children are forced to become Handmaids, the official breeders for society. All other women have been reduced to chattel under a repressive religious hierarchy run by men.

The Handmaid's Tale is a radical departure from Atwood's previous novels. Her strong feminism, evident in earlier books, is dominant in *The Handmaid's Tale*. As Barbara Holliday wrote in the *Detroit Free Press*, Atwood "has been concerned in her fiction with the painful psychic warfare between men and women. In 'The Handmaid's Tale,' a futuristic satire, she casts subtlety aside, exposing woman's primal fear of being used and helpless." Atwood's creation of an imaginary world is also new. As Mary Battiata noted in the *Washington Post, The Handmaid's Tale* is the first of Atwood's novels "not set in a worried corner of contemporary Canada."

Atwood was moved to write her story only after images and scenes from the book had been appearing to her for three years. She admitted to Mervyn Rothstein of the *New York Times,* "I delayed writing it . . . because I felt it was too crazy." However, she eventually became convinced that her vision of

Avant-garde painter Elaine Risley returns to her Canadian hometown and is immediately overcome by memories of a painful coming of age that she now must confront.

Gilead was not far from reality; some of the anti-female measures she had imagined for the novel now actually existed. "There is a sect now, a Catholic charismatic spinoff sect, which calls the women handmaids," Atwood told Rothstein. "A law in Canada," Battiata reported, "[requires] a woman to have her husband's permission before obtaining an abortion." Atwood also pointed to repressive laws in the totalitarian state of Romania as well: "No abortion, no birth control, and compulsory pregnancy testing, once a month." *The Handmaid's Tale,* Elaine Kendall explained in the *Los Angeles Times Book Review,* depicts "a future firmly based upon actuality, beginning with events that have already taken place and extending them a bit beyond the inevitable conclusions. *The Handmaid's Tale* does not depend upon hypothetical scenarios, omens, or straws in the wind, but upon documented occurrences and public pronouncements; all matters of record." Stephen McCabe of *Humanist* called the novel "a chilling vision of the future extrapolated from the present."

Several critics voiced a disbelief in the basic assumptions of *The Handmaid's Tale*. Mary McCarthy complained in the *New York Times Book Review:* "I just can't see the intolerance of the far right . . . as leading to a super-biblical puritanism." Although agreeing that "the author has carefully drawn her projections from current trends," McCarthy asserted that "perhaps that is the trouble: the projections are too neatly penciled in. The details . . . all raise their hands announcing themselves present. At the same time, the Republic of Gilead itself, whatever in it that is not a projection, is insufficiently imagined." Richard Grenier of *Insight* objected that the Fundamentalist-run Gilead does not seem Christian: "There seems to be no Father, no Son, no Holy Ghost, no apparent belief in redemption, resurrection, eternal life. No one in this excruciatingly hierarchized new clerical state . . . appears to believe in God." Grenier also found it improbable that "while the United States has hurtled off into this morbid, feminist nightmare, the rest of the democratic world has been blissfully unaffected." Writing in the Toronto *Globe and Mail,* William French stated that Atwood's "reach exceeds her grasp" in *The Handmaid's Tale,* "and in the end we're not clear what we're being warned against." Atwood seems to warn of the dangers of religious fanaticism, of the effects of pollution on the birthrate, and of a possible backlash to militant feminist demands. The novel, French stated, "is in fact a cautionary tale about *all* these things . . . but in her scenario, they interact in an implausible way."

Despite this flaw, French saw *The Handmaid's Tale* as being "in the honorable tradition of *Brave New World* and other warnings of dystopia. It's imaginative, even audacious, and conveys a chilling sense of fear and menace." Prescott, writing in *Newsweek,* also compared *The Handmaid's Tale* to other dystopian novels. It belongs, he wrote, "to that breed of visionary fiction in which a metaphor is extended to elaborate a warning. . . . Wells, Huxley and Orwell popularized the tradition with books like 'The Time Machine,' 'Brave New World' and '1984'—yet Atwood is a better novelist than they." Christopher Lehmann-Haupt identified *The Handmaid's Tale* as a book that goes far beyond its feminist concerns. Writing in the *New York Times,* Lehmann-Haupt explained that the novel "is a political tract deploring nuclear energy, environmental waste, and anti-feminist attitudes. But it [is] so much more than that—a taut thriller, a psychological study, a play on words." Lindsy Van Gelder of *Ms.* agreed. The

novel, she wrote, "ultimately succeeds on multiple levels: as a page-turning thriller, as a powerful political statement, and as an exquisite piece of writing." Lehmann-Haupt concluded that *The Handmaid's Tale* "is easily Margaret Atwood's best novel to date."

Just as Atwood became a noticeably more political writer with *The Handmaid's Tale,* she became a more personal one with *Cat's Eye.* "Much of its detail is autobiographical," stated Hubbard in *People Weekly.* "Atwood's father, like her heroine's, was a forest entomologist who spent years traipsing with his wife and children through the backwoods of northern Ontario and Quebec collecting specimens." Elaine's mother, like Atwood's, was also an unconventional woman who refused to conform to the mold of 1940s housewife. Like *Cat's Eye* protagonist Elaine Risley, Atwood herself went to school only sporadically until she was twelve. The tragedy at the heart of *Cat's Eye,* however, is very different from anything in the novelist's life.

Cat's Eye is a retrospective told through the eyes of Elaine, a successful painter. Returning to her childhood home in Toronto to appear at an exhibition of her artwork, Elaine dwells on the unhappy memories the city evokes in her. After spending the first years of her childhood with her family in the woods, Elaine had found it difficult to be accepted by other girls after her family settled in Toronto.

Having set up this situation, Atwood explores the ways children can be just as cruel and deceiving as adults. Elaine's main tormentor is her "best friend" Cordelia. Cordelia makes Elaine the object of numerous pranks, one of which almost ends up killing Elaine. Meanwhile, Elaine feels helpless to defend herself and is unable to confide in her parents. As Cordelia enters her teen years, however, she becomes overweight and unhappy, and she eventually goes insane. By the book's conclusion, Elaine discovers how these events have influenced her art and her life.

One point Atwood wished to make with *Cat's Eye* is that women are no more noble or moral than men. Although other of her novels have also made this point, none makes it plainer than *Cat's Eye.* As Hermione Lee noted in the *New Republic,* "Under Atwood's sharp satire on girls' codes is a nightmare of persecution, which is the ugly heart of the novel. . . . Atwood's account of this torture is horrifyingly brilliant, and will strike home to anyone who was ever involved in childhood gang warfare, whether as bullier or bullied."

A bestseller, *Cat's Eye* has been praised by critics, several of whom point out the author's frank portrayal of often-unpleasant aspects of childhood. As

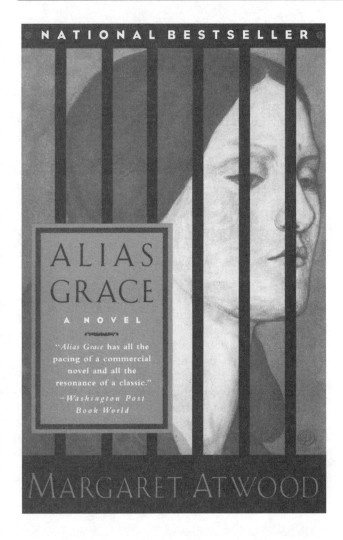

NATIONAL BESTSELLER

ALIAS GRACE

A NOVEL

"*Alias Grace* has all the pacing of a commercial novel and all the resonance of a classic."
—*Washington Post Book World*

MARGARET ATWOOD

Although Grace Marks was convicted of the brutal murder of her employer and his mistress, her lack of memory of the murders causes a curious physician to attempt to tap her unconscious and perhaps prove her innocence in this 1996 novel.

Philip Howard attested in the London *Times*, the "book is not just about growing up female in Toronto in the Forties: it is about life for all of us." *New York Times Book Review* critic Alice McDermott called *Cat's Eye* "emotionally engaging fiction" while in *People Weekly* Susan Toepfer remarked: "There is hardly a sentence in Atwood's book that will not cause a reader to linger in sometimes amused, sometimes horrified, always startling recognition. Perhaps Atwood's most striking achievement, *Cat's Eye* is a courageous, awesome undertaking whose crystal-sharp vision shines too eerily but unerringly true."

In 1993's *The Robber Bride* Atwood explores women's issues and feminist concerns, this time concentrating on women's relationships with each other—both positive and negative. Inspired by the Brothers Grimm's fairy tale "The Robber Bridegroom," the novel chronicles the relationships of college friends Tony, Charis, and Roz with their backstabbing classmate Zenia. Now middle-aged women, their paths and life choices have diverged, yet Tony, Charis, and Roz have remained friends. Throughout their adulthood, however, Zenia's manipulations have nearly destroyed their lives and cost them husbands and careers. Lorrie Moore, writing in the *New York Times Book Review*, called *The Robber Bride* "Atwood's funniest and most companionable book in years," adding that its author "retains her gift for observing, in poetry, the minutiae specific to the physical and emotional lives of her characters." Calling Zenia "charming and gorgeous," Moore further described her as "a misogynist's grotesque: relentlessly seductive, brutal, pathologically dishonest. . . . Perhaps Ms. Atwood intended Zenia . . . to be a symbol of all that is inexplicably evil: war, disease, global catastrophe." Judith Timson commented in *Maclean's* that *The Robber Bride* "has as its central theme an idea that feminism was supposed to have shoved under the rug: there are female predators out there, and they will get your man if you are not careful." Viewing the novel as "a sort of grown-up sequel to . . . *Cat's Eye*," Timson wrote that "the book seems to be saying that if you think little girls can be mean to each other, you should see what big ones can accomplish."

Atwood maintains that she had a feminist motivation in creating Zenia. The femme fatale all but disappeared from fiction in the 1950s, due to that decade's sanitized ideal of domesticity; and in the late 1960s came the women's movement, which in its early years encouraged the creation of only positive female characters. "I think we're now through with all that, and we can put the full cast of characters back on the stage," Atwood told Lauri Miller in an interview in the *San Francisco Review of Books*. "Because to say that women can't be malicious and intentionally bad is to say that they're congenitally incapable of that, which is really very limiting." Francine Prose, reviewing *The Robber Bride* for the *Washington Post Book World*, made a similar point, recommending the book "to those well-intentioned misguided feminists or benighted sexists who would have us believe that the female of the species is 'naturally' nicer or more nurturing than the male."

Alias Grace, while Atwood's first venture into historical fiction, has much common with her contemporary novels in its contemplation of "the shifting notions of women's moral nature" and "the exercise of power between men and women," *Maclean's* contributor Diane Turbide noted. Based on a true story

Atwood had previously explored in a television script titled *The Servant Girl, Alias Grace* centers on Grace Marks, a servant found guilty of murdering her employer and his mistress in northern Canada in 1843. Some doubt Grace's guilt, however, and as she serves out her sentence of life in prison with no memory of the murders, reformers agitate for clemency. In a quest for evidence to support their position, they assign a young doctor, Simon Jordan, who is versed in the new science of psychiatry, to evaluate her soundness of mind. Over many meetings, Grace tells the doctor the harrowing story of her life, which has been marked by extreme hardship. Much about Grace, though, remains puzzling: she is haunted by flashbacks of the supposedly forgotten murders and by a woman who died from a mishandled abortion. Jordan does not know what to make of Grace's tales.

Several reviewers found Grace a complicated and compelling character. "Sometimes she is prim, naive, sometimes sardonic; sometimes sardonic because observant; sometimes observant because naive," commented Hilary Mantel in the *New York Review of Books. Los Angeles Times Book Review* critic Richard Eder lauded Atwood for making Grace "utterly present and unfathomable" and her story "pure enchantment." Eder continued, "We are as anxious as Jordan to know what [Grace] is, yet bit by bit it seems to matter less. What matters is that she becomes more and more distinct and unforgettable." Turbide added that Grace is more than an intriguing character: she is also "the lens through which Victorian hypocrisies are mercilessly exposed."

Mantel also remarked upon the novel's portrait of Victorian life. "We learn as much about Grace's daily routine . . . as if Atwood had written a manual of antique housewifery, and yet the information neither intrudes nor slows the action," she observed. Atwood's use of period detail goes beyond mere background, Mantel asserted: "Other authors describe clothes; Atwood feels the clothes on her characters' backs." Prose, writing in the *New York Times Book Review,* was one critic who found the historical trivia excessive: "The book provides, in snippets, a crash course in Victorian culture. . . . Rather than enhancing the novel's verisimilitude, these mini-lessons underline the distance between reader and subject." Prose added that while "Some readers may feel that the novel only intermittently succeeds in transcending the burden of history, research and abstraction. . . . Others will admire the liveliness with which Ms. Atwood toys with both our expectations and the conventions of the Victorian thriller."

Historical research also plays a part in Atwood's Booker Prize-winning novel *The Blind Assassin.* "Dying octogenarian Iris Chasen's narration of the past carefully unravels a haunting story of tragedy, corruption, and cruel manipulation," summarized Beth E. Anderson in a *Library Journal* review of the novel, which involves multiple story lines. At the heart of the book is Iris's memoir retracing her marriage to wealthy and conniving industrialist Richard Griffen and the death of her sister Laura, her husband, and her daughter. Interspersed with these narrative threads are sections devoted to Laura's posthumous novel, titled *The Blind Assassin.* Iris "reveals at long last the wrenching truth about herself and Laura amid hilariously acerbic commentary on the inanities of contemporary life," wrote Donna Seaman in *Booklist,* dubbing the work a "spellbinding novel of avarice, love, and revenge."

Andersen noted that while some readers may guess how the story will pan out before the conclusion, "nothing will dampen the pleasure of getting there." Reviewing the novel in the *New York Times,* Michiko Kakutani called the book "absorbing," and further noted the intricate Russian-doll, story within a story framework: "To build suspense and create a narrative hall of mirrors, Ms. Atwood deftly cuts back and forth among three plot lines." Kakutani also commented that Atwood, writing with "uncommon authority and ease . . . conjures up the lives of the Canadian gentry in a small town," and concluded with high praise for Atwood's "virtuosic storytelling."

Michael Dirda, writing in the *Washington Post Book World,* also noted Atwood's leisurely prose style in the book, which he called "slightly reserved—formal and almost portentous, rhetorically balanced, aphoristic, emotionally muted." Remarking that though the prose was "wistful much of the time, *The Blind Assassin* nonetheless doesn't lack for the Atwood wit," said Dirda. He concluded that the book is "beautifully composed" and that "its smoothness, wit and mournful wisdom are deeply ingratiating." Writing in *Nation,* Brenda Wineapple felt that *The Blind Assassin* "presents a typical Atwood predicament: Women taught self-effacement, obedience, modesty and quiescence resolve to tell their stories, trusting that someone, somewhere will listen." And a contributor for *Time International* concluded, "A virtuoso feat of construction and psychological examination, *The Blind Assassin* suggests not only the tortuous paths that lead to understanding but also the subterfuges by which humans prevent themselves from confronting unpalatable truths about their own actions. Written with wit and compassion, this justly rewarded novel is a disturbing and moving entertainment."

Atwood as Poet

Atwood began her literary career quite momentously, winning awards for both her first two publications, *Double Persephone* and *The Circle Game*. These two books marked out the terrain all of Atwood's more recent poetry and much of her fiction has explored. *Double Persephone* concerns "the contrast between the flux of life or nature and the fixity of man's artificial creations," as Hutcheon explained in the *Dictionary of Literary Biography*. *The Circle Game* takes this opposition further, setting such human constructs as games, literature, and love against the instability of nature. Human constructs are presented as both traps and shelters, the fluidity of nature as both dangerous and liberating. Sherrill Grace, writing in her *Violent Duality: A Study of Margaret Atwood*, identified the central tension in all of Atwood's work as "the pull towards art on one hand and towards life on the other." This tension is expressed in a series of "violent dualities," as Grace termed it. Atwood "is constantly aware of opposites—self/other, subject/object, male/female, nature/man—and of the need to accept and work within them," Grace explained. "To create, Atwood chooses violent dualities, and her art re-works, probes, and dramatizes the ability to see double."

Linda W. Wagner, writing in *The Art of Margaret Atwood: Essays in Criticism*, asserted that in Atwood's poetry "duality [is] presented as separation." This separation leads her characters to be isolated from one another and from the natural world, resulting in their inability to communicate, to break free of exploitative social relationships, or to understand their place in the natural order. "In her early poetry," Gloria Onley wrote in the *West Coast Review*, "[Atwood] is acutely aware of the problem of alienation, the need for real human communication and the establishment of genuine human community—real as opposed to mechanical or manipulative; genuine as opposed to the counterfeit community of the body politic." Speaking of *The Circle Game*, Wagner wrote that "the personae of those poems never did make contact, never did anything but lament the human condition. . . . Relationships in these poems are sterile if not destructive."

Atwood's sense of desolation, especially evident in her early poems, and her use of frequently violent images moved Helen Vendler to claim in the *New York Times Book Review* that Atwood has a "sense of life as mostly wounds given and received." About *The Circle Game* and *Procedures for Underground*, Peter Stevens noted in *Canadian Literature* that both collections contain "images of drowning, buried life, still life, dreams, journeys and returns." In a review of *True Stories* for *Canadian Forum*, Chaviva Hosek

stated that the poems "range over such topics as murder, genocide, rape, dismemberment, instruments of torture, forms of torture, genital mutilation, abortion, and forcible hysterectomy," although Robert Sward of *Quill and Quire* explained that many reviewers of the book have exaggerated the violence and given "the false impression that all thirty-eight poems . . . are about torture." Yet, Scott Lauder of *Canadian Forum* spoke of "the painful world we have come to expect from Atwood."

Becomes Feminist Icon

Suffering is common for the female characters in Atwood's poems, although they are never passive victims. In more recent works they take active mea-

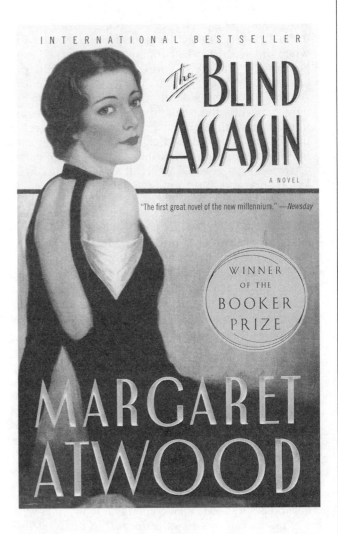

A brilliant novelist dies an untimely death—or so it seems—in Atwood's 2000 work that garnered a top British literary award.

sures to improve their situations. *West Coast Review* contributor Gloria Onley cited the poet's focus as "modern woman's anguish at finding herself isolated and exploited (although also exploiting) by the imposition of a sex role power structure." Atwood explained to Klemesrud in the *New York Times* that her suffering characters come from real life: "My women suffer because most of the women I talk to seem to have suffered."

By the early 1970s, the perception of Atwood as strident feminist made her into "a cult author to faithful feminist readers," noted *Chicago Tribune* reviewer Lipinski. This popularity within the feminist community was unsought. "I began as a profoundly apolitical writer," Atwood explained to Lindsy Van Gelder in *Ms.*, "but then I began to do what all novelists and some poets do: I began to describe the world around me."

Atwood's 1995 poetry collection, *Morning in the Burned House*, "reflects a period in Atwood's life when time seems to be running out," observed John Bemrose in *Maclean's*. Noting that many of the poems address grief and loss, particularly in relationship to her father's death and a realization of her own mortality, the book "moves even more deeply into survival territory." Bemrose further suggested that in this book Atwood allows the readers greater latitude for interpretation than in her earlier verse: "Atwood uses grief . . . to break away from that airless poetry and into a new freedom."

Advocate of Unique Canadian Voice

Atwood has achieved additional success with her short fiction and has also published essays. *Wilderness Tips and Other Stories*, published in 1991, is a collection of "ten neatly constructed, present-tense narratives," reported Merle Rubin in the *Christian Science Monitor*. While finding Atwood's writing style drab and unappealing, Rubin nevertheless praised the author for her "ability to evoke the passing of entire decades . . . all within the brief compass of a short story." The tales in Atwood's 1992 collection *Good Bones*, published in 1994 as *Good Bones and Simple Murders*, "occupy that vague, peculiar country between poetry and prose," according to Bemrose. Describing Atwood as "storyteller, poet, fabulist and social commentator rolled into one," Bemrose claimed in *MacLean's* that "the strongest pieces in *Good Bones* combine a light touch with a hypnotic seriousness of purpose." In the *New York Times Book Review*, Jennifer Howard labeled *Good Bones and Simple Murders* a "sprightly, whimsically feminist collection of miniatures and musings, as-

sembled from two volumes published in Canada in 1983 and 1992." A *Publishers Weekly* reviewer, who characterized the entries as "postmodern fairy tales, caustic fables, inspired parodies, witty monologues," declared each piece to be "clever and sharply honed."

In *Survival: A Thematic Guide to Canadian Literature* Atwood expresses her strong belief in Canadian nationalism. She discerns a uniquely Canadian literature, distinct from its American and British counterparts, and discusses the dominant themes to be found in it. Canadian literature, she argues, is primarily concerned with victims and with the victim's ability to survive. Atwood, Onley explained, "perceives a strong sado-masochistic patterning in Canadian literature as a whole. She believes that there is a national fictional tendency to participate, usually at some level as Victim, in a Victor/Victim basic pattern." But "despite its stress on victimization," Hutcheon wrote, "this study is not a revelation of, or a reveling in, [masochism]." What Atwood argues, Onley asserted, is that "every country or culture has a single unifying and informing symbol at its core: for America, the Frontier; for England, the Island; for Canada, Survival."

Several critics find Atwood's own work exemplifying this primary theme of Canadian literature. Her examination of destructive sex roles and her nationalistic concern over the subordinate position Canada plays with relation to the United States are variations on the victor/victim theme. As Marge Piercy explained in *American Poetry Review*, Atwood believes a writer must consciously work within his or her nation's literary tradition. She argues in *Survival*, according to Piercy, "that discovery of a writer's tradition may be of use, in that it makes available a conscious choice of how to deal with that body of themes. She suggested that exploring a given tradition consciously can lead to writing in new and more interesting ways." Because Atwood's own work closely parallels the themes she sees as common to the Canadian literary tradition, *Survival* "has served as the context in which critics have subsequently discussed [Atwood's] works," Hutcheon stated.

Atwood's prominent stature in Canadian letters rests as much on her published works as on her efforts to define and give value to her nation's literature. "Atwood," Susan Wood wrote in the *Washington Post Book World*, "has emerged as a champion of Canadian literature and of the peculiarly Canadian experience of isolation and survival." Hutcheon noted the writer's "important impact on Canadian culture" and believed that her oeuvre, "internationally known through transla-

If you enjoy the works of Margaret Atwood, you might want to check out the following books:

Anita Brookner, *The Misalliance*, 1986.
Connie Willis, *Impossible Things*, 1994.
Alice Adams, *Medicine Men*, 1997.

tions, stand as testimony to Atwood's significant position in a contemporary literature which must deal with defining its own identity and defending its value."

Although she has been labeled a Canadian nationalist, a feminist, and even a gothic writer, Atwood incorporates and transcends these categories. Writing in *Saturday Night,* Linda Sandler concluded that "Atwood is all things to all people . . . a nationalist . . . a feminist or a psychologist or a comedian . . . a maker and breaker of myths . . . a gothic writer. She's all these things, but finally she's unaccountably Other. Her writing has the discipline of a social purpose but it remains elusive, complex, passionate. It has all the intensity of an act of exorcism." Atwood's work succeeds because it speaks of universal concerns. "Atwood is a large and remarkable writer," Piercy maintained. "Her concerns are nowhere petty. Her novels and poems move and engage me deeply, can matter to people who read them." Wineapple perhaps sums up Atwood's major theme most succinctly: "At her best . . . Atwood's suppressed women of precocious sensibility tell their stories with prickly precision, sparing neither themselves nor anyone else. They hold on; they let go."

■ Biographical and Critical Sources

BOOKS

Beacham's Encyclopedia of Popular Fiction, Beacham Publishing (Osprey, FL), Volumes 1, 2, 4, 6, 1996, Volumes 9, 11, 1998.

Beran, Carol L., *Living over the Abyss: Margaret Atwood's "Life before Man,"* ECW Press (Toronto, Ontario, Canada), 1993.

Bloom, Harold, editor, *Margaret Atwood,* Chelsea House (Philadelphia, PA), 2000.

Bouson, J. Brooks, *Brutal Choreographies: Oppositional Strategies and Narrative Design in the Novels of Margaret Atwood,* University of Massachusetts Press (Amherst, MA), 1993.

Contemporary Literary Criticism, Gale (Detroit, MI), Volume 2, 1974, Volume 3, 1975, Volume 4, 1975, Volume 8, 1978, Volume 13, 1980, Volume 15, 1980, Volume 25, 1983, Volume 44, 1987.

Cooke, John, *The Influence of Painting on Five Canadian Writers: Alice Munro, Hugh Hood, Timothy Findley, Margaret Atwood, and Michael Ondaatje,* Edwin Mellen Press (Lewiston, NY), 1996.

Cooke, Nathalie, *Margaret Atwood: A Biography,* ECW Press (Toronto, Ontario, Canada), 1998.

Davidson, Arnold E., and Cathy N. Davidson, editors, *The Art of Margaret Atwood: Essays in Criticism,* House of Anansi Press (Toronto, Ontario, Canada), 1981.

Davidson, Arnold E., *Seeing in the Dark: Margaret Atwood's "Cat's Eye,"* ECW Press (Toronto, Ontario, Canada), 1997.

Dictionary of Literary Biography, Volume 53: *Canadian Writers since 1960,* Gale (Detroit, MI)), 1986.

Gibson, Graeme, *Eleven Canadian Novelists,* House of Anansi Press (Toronto, Ontario, Canada), 1973.

Grace, Sherrill, *Violent Duality: A Study of Margaret Atwood,* Vehicúle Press (Montreal, Ontario, Canada), 1980.

Grace, Sherrill, and Lorraine Weir, editors, *Margaret Atwood: Language, Text, and System,* University of British Columbia Press (Vancouver, British Columbia, Canada), 1983.

Hengen, Shannon, *Margaret Atwood's Power: Mirrors, Reflections, and Images in Select Fiction and Poetry,* Second Story Press (Toronto, Ontario, Canada), 1993.

Howells, Coral Ann, *Margaret Atwood,* St. Martin's Press (New York, NY), 1996.

Irvine, Lorna, *Collecting Clues: Margaret Atwood's Bodily Harm,* ECW Press (Toronto, Ontario, Canada), 1993.

Lecker, Robert, and Jack David, editors, *The Annotated Bibliography of Canada's Major Authors,* ECW Press (Toronto, Ontario, Canada), 1980.

Marshall, Tom, *Harsh and Lovely Land: The Major Canadian Poets and the Making of a Canadian Tradition,* University of British Columbia Press (Vancouver, BC, Canada), 1978.

McCombs, Judith, and Carole L. Palmer, *Margaret Atwood: A Reference Guide,* G. K. Hall (Boston, MA), 1991.

Michael, Magali Cornier, *Feminism and the Postmodern Impulse: Post-World War II Fiction,* State University of New York Press (Albany, NY), 1996.

Nicholson, Colin, editor, *Margaret Atwood: Writing and Subjectivity: New Critical Essays,* St. Martin's Press (New York, NY), 1994.

Nischik, Reingard M., editor, *Margaret Atwood: Works and Impact,* Camden House (Rochester, NY), 2000.

Rao, Eleanora, *Strategies for Identity: The Fiction of Margaret Atwood,* P. Lang (New York, NY), 1993.

Rosenberg, Jerome H., *Margaret Atwood*, Twayne (New York, NY), 1981.

St. James Guide to Young Adult Writers, 2nd edition, St. James Press (Detroit, MI), 1999.

Sandler, Linda, editor, *Margaret Atwood: A Symposium*, University of British Columbia (Vancouver, Ontario, Canada), 1977.

Stein, Karen F., *Margaret Atwood Revisited*, Twayne (New York, NY), 1999.

Sullivan, Rosemary, *The Red Shoes: Margaret Atwood Starting Out*, Harper Flamingo Canada, 1998.

Thompson, Lee Briscoe, *Scarlet Letters: Margaret Atwood's "The Handmaid's Tale,"* ECW Press (Toronto, Ontario, Canada), 1997.

Twigg, Alan, *For Openers: Conversations with Twenty-four Canadian Writers*, Harbour, 1981.

Woodcock, George, *The Canadian Novel in the Twentieth Century*, McClelland & Stewart (Toronto, Ontario, Canada), 1975.

PERIODICALS

American Poetry Review, November-December, 1973; March-April, 1977; September-October, 1979.

Atlantic, April, 1973.

Book Forum, Volume 4, number 1, 1978.

Booklist, June 1, 2000, Donna Seaman, review of *The Blind Assassin*, p. 1796.

Books in Canada, January, 1979; June-July, 1980: March, 1981.

Canadian Forum, February, 1970, John Stedmond, review of *The Edible Woman*, p. 267; January, 1973; November-December, 1974; December-January, 1977-78; June-July, 1981, Chaviva Hosek and Scott Lauder, review of *True Stories*; December-January, 1981-82, Frank Davey, "Life after Man," pp. 29-30.

Canadian Literature, autumn, 1971; spring, 1972; winter, 1973; spring, 1974; spring, 1977.

Chicago Tribune, January 27, 1980, Roberta Rubenstein, review of *Life before Man*; February 3, 1980; May 16, 1982; March 19, 1989.

Chicago Tribune Book World, January 26, 1986.

Christian Science Monitor, June 12, 1977; December 27, 1991, Merle Rubin, review of *Wilderness Tips and Other Stories*, p. 14; November 19, 1993, p. 19.

Commonweal, July 9, 1973, Margaret Wimsatt, review of *Surfacing*.

Communique, May, 1975.

Detroit Free Press, January 26, 1986, Barbara Holliday, review of *The Handmaid's Tale*.

Detroit News, April 4, 1982, Anne Tyler, review of *Bodily Harm*.

Essays on Canadian Writing, spring, 1977.

Globe and Mail (Toronto), July 7, 1984; October 5, 1985; October 19, 1985; February 15, 1986; November 15, 1986; November 29, 1986; November 14, 1987.

Hudson Review, autumn, 1973; spring, 1975.

Humanist, September-October, 1986, Stephen McCabe, review of *The Handmaid's Tale*.

Insight, March 24, 1986, Richard Grenier, review of *The Handmaid's Tale*.

Journal of Canadian Fiction, Volume 1, number 4, 1972.

Library Journal, August 9, 2000, Beth E. Andersen, review of *The Blind Assassin*.

Los Angeles Times, March 2, 1982; April 22, 1982; May 9, 1986; January 12, 1987; September 26, 2000, p. E1.

Los Angeles Times Book Review, October 17, 1982; February 9, 1986, Elaine Kendall, review of *The Handmaid's Tale*; December 23, 1987; November 14, 1993, pp. 3, 11; December 15, 1996, Richard Eder, review of *Alias Grace*, p. 2.

Maclean's, January 15, 1979; October 15, 1979, Roy MacGregor, review of *Life before Man*; March 30, 1981; October 5, 1992, John Bemrose, review of *Good Bones*; October 3, 1993, Judith Timson, "Atwood's Triumph," pp. 56-61; February 6, 1995, John Bemrose, review of *Morning in the Burned House*; September 23, 1996, Diane Turbide, "Amazing Atwood," pp. 42-45; October 14, 1996, p. 11; July 1, 1999, Atwood, "Survival, Then and Now," p. 54; September 11, 2000, John Bemrose, "Margaret's Museum," p. 54.

Malahat Review, January, 1977.

Manna, Number 2, 1972.

Meanjin, Volume 37, number 2, 1978.

Modern Fiction Studies, autumn, 1976, Roberta Rubenstein, review of *Surfacing*.

Ms., January, 1987, Lindsy Van Gelder, review of *The Handmaid's Tale*.

Nation, December 11, 2000, Brenda Wineapple, "The Killer Elite," p. 58.

New Leader, September 3, 1973.

New Orleans Review, Volume 5, number 3, 1977.

New Republic, April 10, 1989, Hermione Lee, review of *Cat's Eye*, pp. 38-40.

Newsweek, February 18, 1980, Peter S. Prescott, review of *Life before Man*; February 18, 1986, Peter S. Prescott, "No Balm in This Gilead," p. 70.

New York Review of Books, December 16, 1993, Gabrielle Annan, review of *The Robber Bride*, pp. 14-15; December 19, 1996, Hilary Mantel, review of *Alias Grace*, pp. 4-6.

New York Times, December 23, 1976; January 10, 1980; February 8, 1980; March 6, 1982, Anatole Broyard, review of *Bodily Harm*, p. 13; March 28, 1982, Judy Klemesrud, "Canada's High Priestess of Angst," p. 21; September 15, 1982; January 27,

1986, Christopher Lehmann-Haupt, review of *The Handmaid's Tale*, p. C24; February 17, 1986, Mervyn Rothstein, "Atwood Finds No Balm in Gilead," p. C11; November 5, 1986; October 26, 1993, Michiko Kakutani, review of *The Robber Bride*, p. C20; November 23, 1993, Sarah Lyall, "An Author Who Lets Women Be Bad Guys," pp. C13, C16; September 8, 2000, Michiko Kakutani, review of *The Blind Assassin*, p. E43.

New York Times Book Review, October 18, 1970, Millicent Bell, review of *The Edible Woman;* March 4, 1973; April 6, 1975; September 26, 1976; May 21, 1978; February 3, 1980, Marilyn French, review of *Life before Man,* pp. 1, 26; October 11, 1981; February 9, 1986, Mary McCarthy, "Breeders, Wives, and Unwomen," pp. 1, 35; February 5, 1989, Alice McDermott, "What Little Girls Are Really Made Of," pp. 1, 35; October 31, 1993, Lorrie Moore, review of *The Robber Bride,* pp. 1, 22; December 11, 1994, Jennifer Howard, review of *Good Bones and Simple Murders;* April 28, 1996, p. 22; December 29, 1996, Francine Prose, review of *Alias Grace,* p. 6; September 3, 2000, p. 7.

Observer (London, England), June 13, 1982.

Ontario Review, spring-summer, 1975.

Open Letter, summer, 1973.

Parnassus, spring-summer, 1974.

People Weekly, May 19, 1980; February 27, 1989, Susan Toepfer, review of *Cat's Eye,* pp. 22-23; March 6, 1989, Kim Hubbard, "Reflected in Margaret Atwood's *Cat's Eye,* Girlhood Looms as a Time of Cruelty and Terror," pp. 205-206.

Poetry, March, 1970; July, 1972; May, 1982.

Publishers Weekly, August 23, 1976; October 3, 1994, review of *Good Bones and Simple Murders;* August 28, 1995, pp. 107-108; October 7, 1996, p. 58; April 13, 1998, p. 65; July 24, 2000, review of *The Blind Assassin,* p. 67; July 24, 2000, "PW Talks to Margaret Atwood," p. 68.

Quill and Quire, April, 1981, Robert Sward, review of *True Stories;* September, 1984.

Room of One's Own, summer, 1975.

San Francisco Review of Books, January, 1982; summer, 1982; February-March, 1994, Lauri Miller, interview with Margaret Atwood, pp. 30-34.

Saturday Night, May, 1971; July-August, 1976; September, 1976; May, 1981; July-August, 1998, Rosemary Sullivan, "The Writer-Bride," p. 56.

Saturday Review, September 18, 1976; February 2, 1980, Rosellen Brown, review of *Life before Man.*

Saturday Review of the Arts, April, 1973.

Shenandoah, Volume 37, number 2, 1987.

Studies in Canadian Literature, summer, 1977.

Time, October 11, 1976.

Time International, November 27, 2000, "Wayward Sisters: This Year's Booker Prize Winner Is an Intricate Mystery That Elucidates a Nation's Recent History," p. 91.

Times (London, England), March 13, 1986; June 4, 1987; June 10, 1987; January 26, 1989, Philip Howard, review of *Cat's Eye;* November 8, 2000, p. 3.

Times Literary Supplement, March 21, 1986; June 12, 1987; September 29, 2000, p. 24.

Tribune Books (Chicago, IL), November 21, 1993, p. 1.

University of Toronto Quarterly, summer, 1978.

Village Voice, January 7, 1980, Laurie Stone, review of *Life before Man.*

Vogue, January, 1986.

Washington Post, April 6, 1986, Mary Battiata, review of *The Handmaid's Tale;* November 8, 2000, p. C10.

Washington Post Book World, September 26, 1976; December 3, 1978; January 27, 1980; March 14, 1982; February 2, 1986; November 7, 1993, Francine Prose, review of *The Robber Bride,* p. 1; September 3, 2000, Michael Dirda, review of *The Blind Assassin,* pp. 15-16.

Waves, autumn, 1975.

West Coast Review, January, 1973, Gloria Onley, review of *Surfacing.*

Writer's Digest, October, 2000, p. 34.

OTHER

Margaret Atwood Information Site, http://www.web.net/owtoad/ (February 27, 2002).*

Peter S. Beagle

■ Personal

Born April 20, 1939, in New York, NY; son of Simon and Rebecca (Soyer) Beagle; married Enid Elaine Nordeen, May 8, 1964 (divorced July, 1980); married Padma Hejmadi, September 21, 1988; children: (first marriage) Vicki, Kalisa, Daniel, Nordeen. *Education:* University of Pittsburgh, B.A., 1959; Stanford University, graduate study, 1960-61.

■ Addresses

Home—2135 Humboldt Ave., Davis, CA 95616. *Agent*—McIntosh & Otis, Inc., 310 Madison Ave., New York, NY 10017.

■ Career

Writer.

■ Member

American Civil Liberties Union (vice chair, Santa Cruz, CA, chapter, 1968-69).

■ Awards, Honors

Scholastic Writing Scholarship, 1955; Wallace Stegner writing fellow, 1960-61; Guggenheim Foundation award, 1972-73; guest of honor, Seventh World Fantasy Convention, 1981; Mythopoeic Fantasy Award for best novel, and Locus Award, both 1987, both for *The Folk of the Air*; *Locus* Award for Best Novel, 1994, for *The Innkeeper's Song*; *Locus* Award for Best Anthology, 1996, for *Peter S. Beagle's Immortal Unicorn*; *Locus* Award for Best Novella, 1997, for *The Unicorn Sonata*, and 1998; World Fantasy Award, 1998, for *Giant Bones*.

■ Writings

FICTION

A Fine and Private Place (also see below), Viking (New York, NY), 1960.

The Last Unicorn (also see below), Viking (New York, NY), 1968, published as *The Last Unicorn: A Fantastic Tale*, Bodley Head (London, England), 1968.

Lila the Werewolf (chapbook; also see below), Capra Press (Santa Barbara, CA), 1974, revised edition, 1976.

The Fantasy Worlds of Peter S. Beagle (contains *A Fine and Private Place, The Last Unicorn, Lila the Werewolf,* and "Come, Lady Death"), Viking (New York, NY), 1978.

The Folk of the Air, Del Rey (New York, NY), 1987.

The Innkeeper's Song, Penguin (New York, NY), 1993.

The Unicorn Sonata, illustrations by Robert Rodriguez, Turner Publications (Atlanta, GA), 1996.

The Magician of Karakosk, and Others (short fiction), Penguin (New York, NY), 1997.

Giant Bones, Roc (New York, NY), 1997.

Tamsin, Roc (New York, NY), 1999.

A Dance for Emilia, Roc (New York, NY), 2000.

SCREENPLAYS

The Zoo (television script), Columbia Broadcasting System, 1973.

The Dove, E.M.I., 1974.

The Greatest Thing That Almost Happened (television script), 1977.

The Lord of the Rings, Part One, United Artists, 1978.

The Last Unicorn, Marble Arch/Rankin-Bass, 1982.

Also author of the story and teleplay, "Sarek," an episode for *Star Trek: The Next Generation.*

OTHER

I See by My Outfit, Viking (New York, NY), 1965.

The California Feeling, photographs by Michael Bry and Ansel Adams, Doubleday (New York, NY), 1969.

(With Harry N. Abrams) *American Denim: A New Folk Art,* Warner (New York, NY), 1975.

(With Pat Derby) *The Lady and Her Tiger,* Dutton (New York, NY), 1976.

The Garden of Earthly Delights, Viking (New York, NY), 1981.

(Editor with Janet Berliner) *Peter S. Beagle's Immortal Unicorn,* HarperCollins (New York, NY), 1995.

(With Pat Derby) *In the Presence of Elephants,* Capra Press (Santa Barbara, CA), 1995.

Also author of opera libretto *The Midnight Angel,* 1993. Work has appeared in anthologies, including *New Worlds of Fantasy,* edited by Terry Carr, Ace Books (New York, NY), 1967; *New Worlds of Fantasy #3,* edited by Terry Carr, Ace Books, 1971; *Phantasmagoria,* edited by Jane Mobley, Anchor Books (New York, NY), 1977; *The Fantastic Imagination: An Anthology of High Fantasy,* edited by Robert H. Boyer and Kenneth J. Zahorski, Avon (New York, NY), 1977; *Dark Imaginings: A Collection of Gothic Fantasy,* edited by Boyer and Zahorski, Dell (New York, NY), 1978. Work also appears in a volume of *Prize Stories: The O. Henry Awards.* Author of introduction to *The Tolkien Reader,* Houghton Mifflin (Boston, MA), 1966; *Adventures of Yemima, and Other Stories,* by Abraham Soyer, translated by Rebecca Beagle and Rebecca Soyer, Viking (New York, NY), 1979; *The Best of Avram Davidson,* by Avram Davidson, Doubleday (New York, NY), 1979; and *Adventure in Unhistory,* by Davidson, Owlswick Press, 1993.

Contributor of articles and fiction to periodicals, including *Holiday, Seventeen, Today's Health, Saturday Evening Post, Venture, West, Atlantic,* and *Ladies' Home Journal.*

■ Adaptations

The Last Unicorn was adapted for an animated film, 1983; Erik Haagensen and Richard Isen created a musical comedy based on Beagle's novel titled *A Fine and Private Place,* Samuel French (New York, NY), 1992.

■ Sidelights

Peter S. Beagle is "the class act of fantasy writing," according to *Booklist* contributor John Mort. A writer whose highly regarded fantasy fiction has wrought comparisons to J. R. R. Tolkien, C. S. Lewis, Thomas Malory, and Lewis Carroll, Beagle hit the ground running as a young writer. His *A Fine and Private Place,* published by a mainstream rather than genre publisher in 1960, won praise from equally mainstream critics. His popular 1968 title, *The Last Unicorn,* "is a benchmark of contemporary mythic fantasy," according to a *Publishers Weekly* critic.

Beagle's enduring popularity began before the floodgates of literary fantasy opened in the 1970s and 1980s. He is, as William H. Archer of *Best Sellers* noted, "a writer whose work speaks so eloquently [that he] needs no comparison." Similar accolades have been garnered on the basis of Beagle's relatively small body of work: several novels and novellas, as well as short stories. In addition to this body of fiction works, the versatile Beagle, who has only earned his living by his pen, has also compiled anthologies, written nonfiction works, and worked in television and film.

Born April 20, 1939, in New York City, Beagle grew up in a family that valued literature and books. Both his parents were public school teachers, and his father's experiences as a high school and junior high history instructor taught him the only way to hold a student's interest was to bring out the story behind the dry facts. A further literary legacy came from a grandfather who penned fantasy stories in

Hebrew. Raised in the Bronx, Beagle became a dedicated reader at an early age, and by the time he reached sixth grade he had already declared his intent to be a writer. Attending the prestigious Bronx High School of Science, he contributed to the school literary magazine where his work attracted the attention of the fiction editor for *Seventeen* magazine.

"Fantasy, for me, is a way of seeing, rather than a definite state or style."

—*Peter S. Beagle*

With graduation approaching, Beagle submitted a poem and short story to the Scholastic Writing Awards contest. When his poem took first place, he won a scholarship to the University of Pittsburgh, where he studied creative writing, graduating in 1959. Early literary mentors of Beagle included the author Robert Nathan and poet Louis Untermeyer, the latter introducing him to literary agent Elizabeth Otis. While its author was still in college, Beagle's short story "Telephone Call" won first place in *Seventeen*'s short story contest. While at the University of Pittsburgh, Beagle also began what would be his first novel, *A Fine and Private Place*.

A Published Novelist

After graduation, Beagle spent time traveling in Europe; meanwhile *A Fine and Private Place* was sold to Viking in 1960. Set in a Bronx cemetery, the novel tells the story of Jonathan Rebeck, a bankrupt druggist who has given up on the world and gone to live in an isolated mausoleum. Rebeck lives on food stolen by a talking raven and spends his days playing chess and taking walks. He also talks to the ghosts of the recently deceased, but only for a short while; the ghosts soon forget their lives and, by forgetting, drift into their final sleep. Two such ghosts are Michael Morgan and Laura Durand, who meet in the cemetery, fall in love, and seek to avoid the oblivion that is their fate. Michael and Laura's relationship is echoed in the friendship between Rebeck and Mrs. Gertrude Klapper, a widow who visits her husband's grave in the cemetery. When it becomes necessary for Rebeck to leave the cemetery to resolve the dilemma of the two ghostly lovers, Mrs. Klapper provides the support he needs to do so.

A Fine and Private Place was received enthusiastically by critics who cited its vivid characters, both living and dead. Granville Hicks claimed in the *Saturday Review* that "Rebeck lives so close to death that it was quite a trick to give him substance, as Beagle succeeds in doing. . . . And there is the raven, one of the most entertaining characters in recent fiction and by no means one of the least credible." Harold Jaffe of *Commonweal* thought that "the allegorical truth of the characters [and] their situations developed leisurely, emanated naturally without violating the integrity of the fiction." Reviewing the novel in the *New York Times Book Review*, Edmund Fuller maintained that Beagle made "a striking debut on several counts." Among the most prominent of the book's attributes, according to Fuller, are "wit, charm and individuality—with a sense of style and structure notable in a first novel."

A Fine and Private Place won Beagle a Wallace Stegner writing fellowship to Stanford University's creative writing program, where he worked alongside other young authors such as Robert Stone, Ken Kesey, and Larry McMurtry. During his sojourn in California, Beagle also met Enid Nordeen, who would later become his first wife. Returning to New York, he attempted to reconnect with his former life, but decided he wanted to settle in California. Beagle's subsequent cross-country scooter adventure was immortalized in his first work of nonfiction, *I See by My Outfit*. In 1964 he married Enid, adopted her children, and settled into the life of a writer, attempting to support an instant family as a freelancer for magazines such as the *Saturday Evening Post*.

Beagle did not publish his second novel, *The Last Unicorn*, until 1968. It too received scholarly attention as well as considerable critical praise. Raymond M. Olderman, writing in his *Beyond the Waste Land*, called the book "a magnificent romance with a sweetly sorrowful happy ending." The novel tells the story of the world's last unicorn and her quest to discover the fate of the rest of her species. She is aided in her quest by Schmendrick the Magician, a bumbling wizard who performs simple tricks ineffectively but who can, on rare occasions, perform feats of true magic, and by Molly Grue, a peasant woman who has been searching for true wonder and finds it in the unicorn. The three companions discover that King Haggard, ruler of a waste land, has imprisoned the unicorns with the help of the Red Bull, a creature who inspires fear and forgetfulness. King Haggard has captured the unicorns because he enjoys their beauty and wishes to possess all of it. At the novel's end, the unicorns are set free and the waste land becomes fertile once more.

As with *A Fine and Private Place*, *The Last Unicorn* is concerned with a kind of death in life. Olderman believed that Beagle's unicorn "is the dream we have forgotten how to see, the thing whose absence makes our world a waste land; she is renewal and rebirth, the lost fertility and potency of life." Comparing *The Last Unicorn* to other novels dealing with a waste land theme, Olderman found the book concerned with moving "out of the waste land and into the magic of life, as in [*A Fine and Private Place*] where the main character literally moves out of a cemetery to rejoin the living."

Other critics have espoused varied interpretations of the novel. In *Critique* Don Parry Norford maintained that the book presents pairs of opposites: "the immortal and mortal, joy and sorrow, [and] life and death [which are] equally real halves of the same whole: you cannot have one without the other." What happened in King Haggard's realm, according to Norford, is the separation of these halves by the removal of the unicorns from the world. The result of this separation is the creation of a waste land. At the novel's end, with the freeing of the unicorns to live in the world of man, this separation is overcome and the waste land becomes fertile again.

"Beagle's language is rich, his deployment of it deft and fluid, and his eye for detail wonderfully keen."

—*Suzy McKee Charnas*

"A novel like this comes alive and stays alive on bright intensity of imagination, with style as a useful auxiliary," wrote Benedict Riely in the *New York Times Book Review*. "If the imagination is opulent enough the author can even exist without style, and a new myth may be created." Riely declared that Beagle "has both the opulence of imagination and the mastery of style. And a critic for *St. James Guide to Fantasy Writers* noted that *The Last Unicorn* is much more than a fairy tale for adults. Instead it is "a meditation on maturity, responsibility, and the assumption of expected roles." The same critic found the novel to be "far more than the sum of its disparate elements. . . . It is one of the enduring classics of American fantasy" and "the book for which Beagle will always be known and to which all his later work will be compared."

A Hiatus from Novels

During the 1970s and the 1980s Beagle published no full-length fiction. Instead he turned his hand to screenplays, adapting *The Last Unicorn* for an ani-

mated movie, among other projects, and even wrote a teleplay for an episode of *Star Trek: The Next Generation*. He also published nonfiction articles and books, reviews, and a novella, and enjoyed himself as a folk singer of local renown. In 1980 he divorced his first wife and eight years later married the author Padma Hejmadi.

Beagle's short fiction includes the novella *Lila the Werewolf* and the story "Come, Lady Death." *Lila the Werewolf*, originally published as *Farrell and Lila the Werewolf*, is the story of a young man who discovers that his lover becomes a werewolf at every full moon. George Cohen of the *Chicago Tribune* called it a "crazy, wonderful short story," although he conceded that the relationship between Farrell and Lila is "a bizarre affair to say the least." Darrell Schweitzer of the *Science Fiction Review* noted that the story's "linkage between lycanthropy and sex is one of the more interesting variants on the subject I've seen." "As far as I know," Beagle noted in his introduction to *The Fantasy Worlds of Peter S. Beagle*, "I was just spinning a tale, as always, and the equating of womanhood with lycanthropy, or sexual needs with blood and death, was entirely dictated by the story and the characters."

"Come, Lady Death" is set in eighteenth-century London, where a bored society matron invites Death to her party to liven things up. "Again Beagle manages to create genuinely living characters," Schweitzer observed, "and avoid all the clichés that usually turn up in such stories." Beagle claims he wrote the story in college "to see whether I could sneak it past Frank O'Connor [his English professor], who hated all fantasy."

Returns to the Novel

After a long stint as a screenwriter, Beagle returned to fantasy in 1987 with *The Folk of the Air*, which is set in southern California in modern times. Joe Farrell is reprised from *Lila the Werewolf* and is again the main character, a musician who arrives in California and moves in with Ben, an old friend from college. Joe soon takes up with a former girlfriend, Julie, who is a member of the League for Archaic Pleasures—a version of the real-life Society for Creative Anachronism—and Ben and Joe become involved with the many strange League members. Conflict ensues when a teenage witch named Aiffe succeeds in summoning a young man named Bonner who involves the characters in a duel of magic.

Once again, reviewers celebrated Beagle's style. Beagle, stated Gerald Jonas in the *New York Times Book Review*, "knows how to use language to keep the reader from peering too closely at the machinery of a tale. . . . The plot unfolds at a languorous but inexorable pace that seems entirely appropriate to the matters at hand." "Among other things," wrote Suzy McKee Charnas in the *Los Angeles Times Book Review,* "the book is a sympathetic study of characters who suffer from various sorts and degrees of discomfort in our time, and who long for real or imagined ages past." "Beagle's language is rich, his deployment of it deft and fluid, and his eye for detail wonderfully keen," added Charnas. "Scenes set at the doings of the League sparkle with wry, affectionate humor, and the magic . . . is wild and disorienting, as magic should be."

In 1993 Beagle again fulfilled reader's expectations with *The Innkeeper's Song.* Unlike *The Folk of the Air, The Innkeeper's Song* is set in a pre-industrial society in which power is manipulated by wizards and magicians. The story's viewpoint alternates between the various characters: three different women, "a young man consumed by love, the innkeeper, his servants, and a 'fox' who is sometimes a 'man' but who turns out to be neither," explained Jonas in the *New York Times Book Review.* Three strange women converge on the inn known as The Gaff and Slasher: Lal and her companion Nyateneri, and the maid Lukassa, whom Lal brought back to life after the young girl drowned. Lukassa, in turn, has been pursued by her childhood sweetheart, Tikat. Lal and Nyateneri have come to the inn at the request of their magician mentor to help him in combat with another wizard. When all these characters converge at the inn, magic awaits.

According to Jonas, Beagle sums up the moral of his story in a "characteristically complex" statement: "'Love each other from the day we are born to the day we die, we are still strangers every minute, and nobody should forget that, even though we have to.'" A critic for *Publishers Weekly* called *The Innkeeper's Song* a "multifaceted fantasy told from various points of view [which] plumbs the nature of life, death and love," and added "In elegant yet simple prose Beagle illuminates the shifting relationships among the various major and minor players . . . who people this affecting tale." *Booklist* contributor John Mort dubbed the work a "beautiful fantasy" and a "gentle, romantic, lyrical tale." "This is the kind of novel that absorbs you," added Tom Easton in *Analog,* while in *Locus* Gary K. Wolfe allowed that "*The Last Unicorn* may always be Beagle's best fantasy, but *The Innkeeper's Song* . . . is his best *novel.*"

Of Unicorns and Ghosts

Beagle returned to the land of mythical beasts in *The Unicorn Sonata,* set in contemporary Los Angeles. In the story, thirteen-year-old Joey Rivera hears magical music played by a mysterious boy named Indigo who comes into the music store where Joey works. Joey is captivated by the music that comes from Indigo's horn, and she begins to hear it everywhere. One day she follows the music into the magical realm of Shei'rah, where she discovers that Indigo is one of the Eldest, a race of unicorns threatened by a form of blindness. While Indigo would rather remain in the "real" world in human form, ultimately he helps Joey and her grandmother cure the plague of blindness. Despite the "slight" plot, a reviewer for *Publishers Weekly* found *The Unicorn Sonata* to be a "charming fantasy," the entire enterprise "enhanced by graceful prose laced with exquisite detail." *Booklist* contributor Ray Olson commented that "America's finest gentle fantasist manages to point up the best qualities of both real life and fantasy, of both Earth and Shei'rah."

Within the six novellas included in 1997's *Giant Bones,* Beagle introduces readers to traveling bards who work magic with songs and a hayseed wizard who manages to get the best of an evil queen. "Gentle yet biting, far-fetched and altogether common, Beagle's fairy tales invoke comparison with those associated with yet another great name, the Brothers Grimm," Mort maintained in *Booklist.* John Clute, writing in *Washington Post Book World,* called *Giant Bones* "clever, deeply self-conscious about the devices of fantasy, wholehearted to the point of sentimentality, and deft." *Locus* reviewer Faren Miller added to the praise, noting that the collection is a "work of mastery, with much to tell us of the truths within a fabulist's 'lies.'" "The whole range of human emotions is expressed in these wonderful tales," wrote Diane Yates in *Voice of Youth Advocates.* "Beagle is a writer who has continued to grow and mature . . . reading him is pure pleasure."

Beagle's novel *Tamsin* deals with the connection between an affluent, spoiled New York teen named Jenny Gluckstein and her kindred spirit, a three-hundred-year-old ghost. Jenny is initially miserable at being transplanted from her American home to the ramshackle old farm in Dorset, England that her new stepfather is restoring. Despite her city ways, however, Jenny is slowly drawn to the old house, as well as to the woods and fields surrounding it. She begins hearing voices, and one day she discovers a ghost—actually, two ghosts: one a cat and the other the animal's owner, Tamsin Willoughby. Tamsin is mourning her lost love, Edric; her soul is not at peace and thus she is trapped in a hidden chamber in the house. She and Jenny become unlikely allies in an effort to end this eternal torment. "Slipping effortlessly between Jenny's brash 1999 lingo, the raw primeval dialect of ancient Dorset and Tamsin's exquisite Jacobean English, Beagle has created a stunning tale of good battling evil, of wonder and heartbreak and of a love," wrote a reviewer for *Publishers*

Weekly. Jackie Cassada, reviewing *Tamsin* in *Library Journal,* called it a "gracefully written story," while *Booklist* reviewer Mort concluded that "although nowhere labeled as such, *Tamsin* is a fine young adult novel. Despite its meandering beginning, it may be the best of its kind this year."

Beagle returned to a U.S. setting for his 2000 novella *A Dance for Emilia,* "a charming reflection on dreams and the afterlife," according to a contributor for *Publishers Weekly.* In the story, actor Jack Holtz suddenly gets a call from Emily, the girlfriend of his deceased best friend, Sam Kagan. Sam left his cat, Millamant, to be cared for by Emily; now she reports to Jack that the cat is dancing crazily. One look at the cat and Jack knows that Sam has merged with the Abyssinian cat. Beagle takes his story back and forth from the present to the past, describing Jack and Sam's youth in Brooklyn in "concise yet lyric prose," according to a critic for *Publishers Weekly. Booklist* contributor Olson also lauded the novella, noting that there is a "bittersweet resolution to Beagle's characteristically warm take on a theme, spirit possession, that other fantasists exploit for chills only. Those who like their fantasy only a wee bit eerie shouldn't miss this little tale."

If you enjoy the works of Peter S. Beagle, you might want to check out the following books:

Patricia A. McKillip, *The Riddle-Master of Hed,* 1976.
David Brin, *The River of Time,* 1986.
Jane Yolen, *Here There Be Unicorns,* 1994.

Beagle once explained that he writes fantasy because "the fantastic turn of vision suits both my sense of the world as a profoundly strange and deceptive place, and my deepest sense of poetry, which is singing." His many fans around the world can only hope that such inspiration continues to fuel Beagle's imagination, and that his song goes on.

■ Biographical and Critical Sources

BOOKS

Carter, Lin, *Imaginary Worlds: The Art of Fantasy,* Ballantine (New York, NY), 1973.

Contemporary Literary Criticism, Volume 7, Gale (Detroit, MI), 1977.
Dictionary of Literary Biography Yearbook: 1980, Volume 80, Gale (Detroit, MI), 1981.
Olderman, Raymond M., *Beyond the Waste Land: A Study of the American Novel in the 1960s,* Yale University Press (New Haven, CT), 1972.
St. James Guide to Fantasy Writers, St. James Press (Detroit, MI), 1996.
St. James Guide to Young Adult Writers, 2nd edition, St. James Press (Detroit, MI), 1999.

PERIODICALS

Analog Science Fiction/Science Fact, October, 1987, pp. 180-181; April, 1994, Tom Easton, review of *The Innkeeper's Song,* pp. 166-68; December, 1997, pp. 151-152; February, 2000, pp. 132-133.
Best Sellers, April 1, 1968; September, 1976, William H. Archer.
Booklist, October 15, 1993, John Mort, review of *The Innkeeper's Song,* p. 394; October 15, 1995, p. 389; August, 1996, Ray Olson, review of *The Unicorn Sonata,* p. 1853; July, 1997, John Mort, review of *Giant Bones,* p. 1806; August, 1999, John Mort, review of *Tamsin,* p. 1984; August, 2000, Ray Olson, review of *A Dance for Emilia,* p. 2124.
Books and Bookmen, October, 1968.
Book World, April 7, 1968.
Chicago Tribune, June 5, 1960; November 26, 1978, George Cohen, review of *Lila and the Werewolf.*
Christian Century, August 31, 1960.
Christian Science Monitor, May 9, 1968.
Commonweal, June 28, 1968, Harold Jaffe, review of *The Last Unicorn.*
Critique, Volume 19, number 2, 1977.
Extrapolation, fall, 1979, pp. 230-237; spring, 1980.
Fantasiae, November-December, 1979.
Fantasy Review, April, 1987, Charles de Lint, "Well Worth the Wait," p. 33.
Galaxy, April, 1961; June, 1977.
Hollins Critic, April, 1968.
Kirkus Reviews, March 15, 1960; July 1, 1997.
Library Journal, May 1, 1960; June 1, 1960; February 15, 1968; October 15, 1993, p. 93; June 15, 1996; October 15, 1999, Jackie Cassada, review of *Tamsin,* p. 110.
Locus, June 30, 1976; September, 1993, Gary K. Wolfe, review of *The Innkeeper's Song,* pp. 23-24; October, 1993, p. 59; February, 1994, p. 36-37, 38; July, 1997, Faren Miller, review of *Giant Bones.*
Los Angeles Times, November 20, 1982, p. 1.
Los Angeles Times Book Review, February 1, 1987, Suzy McKee Charnas, review of *The Folk of the Air,* pp. 1, 9; January 13, 1991, p. 10.

Magazine of Fantasy and Science Fiction, January, 1988, pp. 31-32.

New Statesman, November 20, 1987, p. 31.

New Worlds, December, 1968.

New York Herald Tribune Book Review, May 29, 1960.

New York Times, November 19, 1982, p. N19.

New York Times Book Review, June 5, 1962, Edmund Fuller, "Unique Recluse"; March 24, 1968, Benedict Riely, "The Dragon Has Gout," pp. 4, 8; January 18, 1976, p. 6; September 23, 1979; June 20, 1982, p. 31; January 18, 1987, Gerald Jonas, review of *The Folk of the Air,* p. 33; November 14, 1993, Gerald Jonas, review of *The Innkeeper's Song,* p. 74.

People, January 10, 1983, p. 16.

Publishers Weekly, June 4, 1982, p. 64; December 12, 1986, p. 44; October 18, 1993, review of *The Innkeeper's Song,* p. 67; September 25, 1995, review of *Peter S. Beagle's Immortal Unicorn,* pp. 45-46; August 5, 1996, review of *The Unicorn Sonata,* p. 430; August 9, 1999, review of *Tamsin,* p. 348; October 2, 2000, review of *A Dance for Emilia,* p. 63.

San Francisco Chronicle, June 2, 1960.

Saturday Review, May 28, 1960, Granville Hicks, "Visit to a Happy Haunting Ground," p. 18; March 30, 1968.

Science Fiction Review, February, 1978, Darrell Schweitzer, review of *Lila and the Werewolf;* March-April, 1979.

Time, May 23, 1960.

Voice of Youth Advocates, Diane Yates, review of *Giant Bones.*

Washington Post Book World, October 26, 1997, John Clute, review of *Giant Bones.*

OTHER

Unofficially Peter S. Beagle, http://www.white-mountain.org/ (March 18, 2002).*

William Blake

Erdman, David V., editor, *The Complete Poetry and Prose of William Blake,* with commentary by Harold Bloom, Anchor, 1982.

SELF-ILLUSTRATED; PRIVATELY PRINTED BY BLAKE

Poetical Sketches, 1783.

There Is No Natural Religion, 1788.

All Religions Are One, 1788.

Songs of Innocence, 1789, expanded edition printed as *Songs of Innocence and of Experience,* 1794, edited by Geoffrey Keynes, 1967.

The Book of Thel, 1789, edited by Nancy Bogen, 1971.

The Marriage of Heaven and Hell, 1793, edited by Geoffrey Keynes, 1967.

Visions of the Daughters of Albion, 1793.

For Children: The Gates of Paradise, 1793, revised as *For the Sexes: The Gates of Paradise,* 1818.

America: A Prophecy, 1793.

Europe: A Prophecy, 1794.

The First Book of Urizen, 1794, published as *The Book of Urizen,* edited by Kay P. and Roger R. Easson, 1978.

The Song of Los, 1795.

The Book of Ahania, 1795.

Milton: A Poem in Two Books, 1804, edited by Kay P. and Roger R. Easson, 1979.

Jerusalem: The Emanation of the Giant Albion, 1804.

Laocoon, 1820.

The Ghost of Abel: A Revelation in the Visions of Jehovah, 1822.

■ Personal

Born November 28, 1757, in London, England; died August 12, 1827, in London, England; son of James (a hosier) and Catherine (Harmitage) Blake; married Catherine Boucher, August 18, 1782. *Education:* Studied at Henry Pars's drawing school, 1767-72, and Royal Academy, 1779. *Politics:* Radical. *Religion:* Mystical Christian.

■ Career

Author, poet, painter, illustrator, and engraver. Apprenticed to engraver James Basire, 1772-79; printseller in partnership with James Parker, 1784.

■ Writings

STANDARD EDITIONS

Keene, Geoffrey, editor, *The Complete Writings of William Blake,* Random House (New York, NY), 1957, revised edition, 1966.

POSTHUMOUS PUBLICATIONS

The Poetical Works of William Blake, edited by Michael Rossetti, Roberts Brothers (Boston, MA), 1875.

The Works of William Blake: Poetic, Symbolic, and Critical, memoir and interpretation by Edwin Ellis and William Butler Yeats, B. Quaritch (London, England), 1893.

The Letters of William Blake, edited by Archibald G. B. Russell, Scribner (New York), 1906.

The Letters of William Blake Together with His Life, edited with biography by Frederick Tatham, Methuen, 1906.

Auguries of Innocence, Guthrie & Housley, 1914.

The Land of Dreams: Twenty Poems by William Blake, edited and illustrated by Pamela Bianco, Macmillan, 1928.

The Portable Blake, edited by Alfred Kazin, Viking Press (New York), 1946.

Selections from Songs of Innocence and Experience, Archway Press, 1946.

Genesis, Cummington Press, 1951.

Selected Poetry and Prose, edited by Northrop Frye, Modern Library (New York), 1953.

The Letters of William Blake, edited by Geoffrey Keynes, Macmillan, 1956, 3rd edition, 1980.

Vala, edited by H. M. Margoliouth, Clarendon Press (Oxford, England), 1956, published as *The Four Zoas*, edited by G. E. Bentley, Jr. (London, England), 1963, edited by Bettina Tramontano Magono and David Erdman (Lewisburg, Pennsylvania), 1988.

(With William Hogarth) *The Beggar's Opera*, edited by Wilmarth S. Lewis and Philip Hofer, Harvard University Press (Cambridge, MA), 1965.

Tiriel, Oxford University Press, 1967.

(And illustrator) *A Grain of Sand: Poems for Young Readers*, edited by Rosemary Manning, Bodley Head (London, England), 1967.

England Awake! Awake! Awake!, Carr, 1968.

The Fly, illustrated by Paul P. Peich, Taurus Press, 1968.

The Tyger, Merrill, 1969.

The Chimney Sweeper, Taurus Press, 1969.

London, illustrated by Paul P. Peich, Taurus Press, 1969.

The Mental Traveller, illustrated by Emil Antonucci, Journeyman Press, 1970.

Infant Sorrow, illustrated by Duine Campbell, Black Knight Press, 1970.

The Divine Image, illustrated by Paul P. Peich, Taurus Press, 1970.

Jerusalem: Selected Poems and Prose, edited by Hazard Adams, Holt (New York), 1970.

Holy Thursday, illustrated by Paul P. Peich, Taurus Press, 1971.

Proverbs of Hell, illustrated by Duine Campbell, Black Knight Press, 1972.

The Pickering Manuscript, Pierpont Morgan Library, 1972.

The Clouded Hills: Selections from William Blake, edited by Catherine Hughes, Sheed & Ward, 1973.

The Notebooks of William Blake, edited by David Erdman and Donald Moore, Oxford University Press, 1973.

(And illustrator) *The Poems of William Blake*, edited by Aileen Ward, Cambridge University Press, 1973.

The Illuminated Blake: All of William Blake's Illustrated Works, Doubleday (New York, NY), 1974.

The Apocalyptic Vision, Manhattanville College Press, 1974.

Writings, edited by G. E. Bentley, Jr., Oxford University Press, 1978.

The Letters of William Blake, edited by Geoffrey Keynes, Clarendon Press (Oxford, England), 1980.

An Island in the Moon, Cambridge University Press, 1987.

The Lambeth Prophecies, edited by David Worrall, Princeton University Press (Princeton, NJ), 1994.

ILLUSTRATOR

The Protestant's Family Bible, Harrison, 1780.

Mary Wollstonecraft, *Original Stories from Real Life*, Johnson, 1791.

Gottfried A. Buerger, *Leonora*, Miller, 1796.

Edward Young, *The Complaint and the Consolation; or, Night Thoughts* (London, England), 1797.

William Hayley, *Ballads*, Chichester, 1805.

Robert Blair, *The Grave*, Gromek, 1808.

Geoffrey Chaucer, *The Prologue and Characters of Chaucer's Pilgrims, Selected from His Canterbury Tales*, Harris, 1812.

Virgilius Maro, *The Pastorals of Virgil*, Rivington, 1821.

Illustrations of the Book of Job, in Twenty-one Plates, Invented and Engraved by William Blake, privately printed, 1826.

Illustrations to the Divine Comedy (London, England), 1827.

Blake's Illustrations of Dante: Seven Plates, Designed and Engraved by William Blake (London, England), 1838.

John Milton, *Paradise Lost*, Lyceum Press, 1906.

John Milton, *On the Morning of Christ's Nativity*, Cambridge University Press, 1923.

John Milton, *Comus: A Mask*, Benn, 1926.

Blake's self-illustrated *Songs of Innocence and of Experience* has as its purpose to show "the Two Contrary States of the Human Soul."

John Milton, *Poems in English,* Nonesuch Press, 1926.

Pencil Drawings by William Blake, edited by Geoffrey Keynes, Nonesuch Press, 1927.

William Blake, 1757-1827: A Descriptive Catalogue of an Exhibition of the Works of William Blake, Philadelphia Museum of Art (Philadelphia, PA), 1939.

Engravings, edited by Geoffrey Keynes, Faber (London, England), 1950.

An Exhibition of the Illuminated Books of William Blake, Trianon Press (London, England), 1964.

Drawings of William Blake: Ninety-two Pencil Studies, edited by Geoffrey Keynes, Dover, 1970.

William Blake's Illustrations for John Milton's Paradise Regained, Press of Case Western Reserve University, 1971.

Watercolour Designs for the Poems of Thomas Gray, Trianon Press (London, England), 1971.

William Blake: Selected Engravings, St. Martin's Press (New York, NY), 1975.

The Complete Graphic Works of William Blake, edited by David Bindman, Putnam's (New York), 1978.

Adaptations

William Blake, a recording of poems read by Alan Bates and others, was produced by Argo, 1964; the film *Tyger, Tyger* was produced by Time-Life Films, 1969; the film *Holy Thursday* was produced by American Educational Films, 1970.

Sidelights

William Blake was an English writer, poet, and illustrator of the Romantic period. Romantic authors and artists emphasized the content of their works over the form, valued imagination and emotion, and celebrated nature and freedom. Kenneth Muir, writing in the *Reference Guide to English Literature,* called Blake "one of the best lyrical poets of the last 500 years." His first biographer, Alexander Gilchrist, said in his *Life of William Blake: Pictor Ignotus* that Blake "neither wrote nor drew for the many, hardly for the work'y-day men at all, rather for children and angels"; he called Blake "'a divine child,' whose playthings were sun, moon, and stars, the heavens and the earth." Prone to mystical visions throughout his life, Blake often incorporated these powerful images into his poems and engravings. His abiding concern with religious matters, and his strong opinions about the corruption of the modern world, are also frequent themes in his work. Writing in *Famous British Poets,* Sybil Norton and John Cournos explained that "to William Blake, God and the imagination were the same thing; that is, he conceived God as the spiritual power in man; apart from mankind he could find no meaning in God. He took pains to show that when he speaks of God's love and care he means these qualities as displayed by men and contained in men themselves."

Born in London on November 28, 1757, Blake was one of seven children, two of whom did not survive infancy. Young William was an unusual child, having visions of spirits when he was eight or ten years old, according to Gilchrist. The first of these occurred one day when William was walking in the countryside near London and saw "a tree filled with angels, bright angelic wings bespangling every bough like stars." In some of his visions, which continued throughout his life, he was visited by poets, including John Milton, and biblical prophets, such as Ezra, and he would have vague memories later in his life of having been visited by Jesus and Socrates.

Blake had no formal schooling and learned to read and write at home. Charles Reinhart in the *Dictionary of Literary Biography* recounted: "By all accounts Blake had a pleasant and peaceful childhood, made even more pleasant by his skipping any formal schooling. As a young boy he wandered the streets of London and could easily escape to the surrounding countryside." At the age of ten, he was sent to Henry Pars's drawing school. The family could not afford further instruction in art, so at fourteen Blake was apprenticed to an engraver, James Basire. "Basire seems to have been a good master," Reinhart noted, "and Blake was a good student of the craft. Blake was later to be especially grateful to Basire for sending the young student to Westminster Abbey to make drawings of monuments Basire was commissioned to engrave. The vast Gothic dimensions of Westminster and the haunting presence of the tombs of kings affected Blake's romantic sensibilities and were to provide fertile ground for his active imagination." It was at this time that Blake began writing poetry. In 1779 Blake left his apprenticeship and enrolled briefly at the Royal Academy before setting out to make his living as an engraver.

Marries Catherine Boucher

On August 18, 1782, after a one-year courtship, Blake married. "After one ill-fated romance, Blake met Catherine Boucher, an attractive and compassionate woman who took pity on Blake's tales of being spurned," Reinhart explained. "After a year's

One of Blake's best-known poems, "The Lamb," appears in *Songs of Innocence and of Experience.*

Blake published some of his poetry in 1783, under the title *Poetical Sketches.* The poems contain protests against war, tyranny, and King George III's treatment of the American colonies. Only about fifty copies were printed.

Blake's father died on July 4, 1784, and Blake used part of his inheritance to move to a new home where he opened a print shop with a friend and former fellow apprentice, James Parker. The business was unsuccessful, however, and soon closed, compelling Blake and his wife to move yet again. In 1787 Blake's favorite brother, Robert, died. Blake nursed Robert in his final illness and was with him when he died. According to Gilchrist, Blake believed he saw Robert's spirit ascending through the ceiling, "clapping its hands for joy." Later Blake had a vision in which, he claimed, Robert visited him and showed him the technique of "illuminated writing," or relief-etching: after producing a text and a drawing on a copper plate with an acid-resistant liquid, Blake would dip the plate in acid, which ate away the untreated surfaces and left the text and drawing in relief; he would then print the design on paper and color it with watercolors. He used the method for all of his books, beginning in 1788 with *There Is No Natural Religion,* a collection of aphorisms. The next year he wrote, illustrated, and printed *The Book of Thel,* a work of fantasy that, although not written specifically as a children's book, is considered his first book that is appropriate for children.

Publishes "Songs of Innocence"

Also in 1789 Blake produced *Songs of Innocence,* in which a young shepherd is inspired to write a series of poems by an angel child who appears to him as he wanders through the countryside playing his pipe. The shepherd says that he is writing his songs "In a book that all may read," and that they are "happy songs / Every child may joy to hear." Among the songs that reflect the happy world of childhood are "Laughing Song," "Spring," and "The Echoing Green." According to Muir, "*Songs of Innocence,* Blake's first illustrated poems, are simple without being naive, childlike without being childish, innocent without being insipid. Their subject is childhood as a symbolic representation of the Kingdom of Heaven" Alan Richardson in the *Dictionary of Literary Biography* described the book in these terms: "The title page of *Songs of Innocence* features a mother or nurse holding an open book, which two children, a boy and a girl, are eagerly reading. The group is sheltered by an apple tree (the branches of which frame the word *Innocence* in the title) with a vine growing around its trunk, suggesting the children's dependence on the adult and perhaps

courtship the couple were married on 18 August 1782. The parish registry shows that Catherine, like many women of her class, could not sign her own name. Blake soon taught her to read and to write, and under Blake's tutoring she also became an accomplished draftsman, helping him in the execution of his designs. By all accounts the marriage was a successful one, but no children were born to the Blakes. Catherine also managed the household affairs and was undoubtedly of great help in making ends meet on Blake's always limited income."

Another important woman in Blake's life was Harriet Mathew, who was introduced to the young artist by his friend John Flaxman, a well-known artist and engraver. Mathew was a society woman whose home was a meeting place for artists and musicians. With encouragement from Flaxman and Mathew,

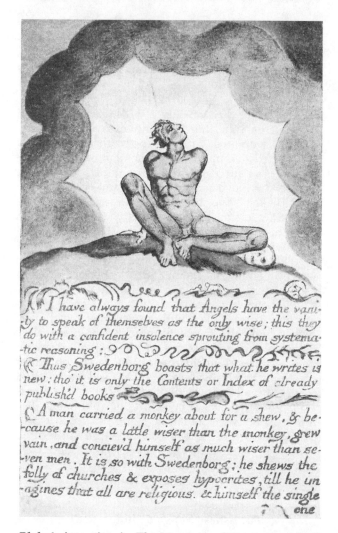

Blake's intention in *The Marriage of Heaven and Hell* **was to show that, through a union of opposites, a more complete humanity might be created.**

also the folds of a serpent and the inevitable loss of innocence." Roderick Mcgillis wrote in *Writers for Children* that *Songs of Innocence* was Blake's "great and lastingly influential work for children.... Blake is responsible for all aspects of the production of this remarkable work: he wrote the text, designed the pages, engraved both text and illustrations on copperplate, printed the plates, and bound and hand-colored them. Twenty-one original copies of *Songs of Innocence* are extant. Blake produced each one by hand, and each time he made the book he tried a new arrangement of the twenty-three poems."

Blake enlarged his *Songs of Innocence* in 1794 by adding more poems to it, calling the new book *Songs of Innocence and of Experience*. The title page of the book states that its purpose is to show "the Two Contrary States of the Human Soul." The "Songs of Innocence" deal with the state of soul that is possessed by children; they are optimistic and happy and affirm God's love. The "Songs of Experience" are gloomy and deal with evil. "The two states of innocence and experience," Reinhart explained, "are not always clearly separate in the poems, and one can see signs of both states in many poems." Reinhart argued that, within these poems, "the poet is both a pleasant piper playing at the request of his audience and a stern Bard lecturing an entire nation. In part this is Blake's interpretation of the ancient dictum that poetry should both delight and instruct. More important, for Blake the poet is a man who speaks both from the personal experience of his own vision and from the 'inherited' tradition of ancient Bards and prophets who carried the Holy Word to the nations."

Two of Blake's best-known poems appear in *Songs of Innocence and of Experience*: "The Lamb" in "Songs of Innocence" and "The Tyger" in "Songs of Experience." Children are the main characters in three pairs of companion poems, both poems in each pair having the same title and one of each pair appearing in "Songs of Innocence" and the other in "Songs of Experience": these poems are "The Chimney Sweeper," "A Little Boy Lost," and "Holy Thursday."

Speaking of the poems in this collection, Mcgillis found: "Blake is no sentimentalist. Innocence is not all laughter and merriment. It recognizes and sympathizes with grief and care ('On Another's Sorrow'), it is ignorant and gullible, easily manipulated ('The Little Black Boy,' 'The Chimney Sweeper'), fragile and vulnerable ('The Little Boy Lost'), and easily controlled and oppressed ('The School Boy,' 'Holy Thursday'). Blake's songs are 'happy' because they are prophetic, visions of human possibility that make us 'joy to hear' because we can only rejoice to be reminded of the power for change that we have within us. In short, Blake's *Songs of Innocence and of Experience* express human and poetic liberty. They break free of eighteenth-century conventions of children's literature and they speak of the means we have of unbinding ourselves from institutional convention and authority." Richardson concluded that, "as a creator of poems in children's forms virtually unrivaled for their high aesthetic standards, compelling rhythms and imagery, and subtle complexities, Blake provided an important example and challenge to late-nineteenth- and twentieth-century children's writers. There is little doubt that Blake will continue to inspire the children's writers—and the children—of future ages."

Produces "The Marriage of Heaven and Hell"

Between 1790 and 1793 Blake wrote and etched the long prophetic poem *The Marriage of Heaven and Hell,* which "brutally satirizes oppressive authority in church and state," according to Reinhart. Algernon Charles Swinburne, writing in his *William Blake: A Critical Essay,* described Blake's poem as "the greatest of all his books.... None of his lyrical writings show the same sustained strength and radiance of mind; none of his other works in verse or prose give more than a hint here and a trace there of the same harmonious and humorous power, of the same choice of eloquent words, the same noble command and liberal music of thought; small things he could often do perfectly, and great things often imperfectly; here for once he has written a book as perfect as his most faultless song, as great as his most imperfect rhapsody."

Blake's intention in *The Marriage of Heaven and Hell* was to show that, through a union of opposites, a more complete humanity might be created. Blake writes in the poem: "Without Contraries is no progression. Attraction and Repulsion, Reason and Energy, Love and Hate, are necessary to Human Existence." As P. H. Butter argued in the *Reference Guide to English Literature,* Blake believed that "full humanity is not to be attained by suppression, but by bringing all man's potentialities to fruition. Good and Evil, Heaven and Hell, Reason and Energy, Angel and Devil—the words being used in deliberately perverse ways—are to be 'married.' One can recognize profound truth here, and enjoy the exuberance of the writing, and still doubt whether Blake shows what he purports to do." Dan Miller, writing in *Studies in Romanticism,* found that *"The Marriage of Heaven and Hell* holds a special place in the Blake canon. It marks the transition from the early works, in which Blake's poetic vision is articulated primarily in single lyrics or groups of lyrics, to the prophecies, where that vision assumes narrative and systematic form."

Publishes "Milton" and "Jerusalem"

In 1800 Blake accepted an invitation from the poet William Hayley to move to the seaside village of Felpham, in Sussex, where Hayley lived. The Blakes rented a cottage there, and Hayley found engraving jobs for Blake. After 1800 Blake wrote no more works for children. He taught himself Greek, Latin, Hebrew, and Italian so that he could read classical works in their original language. He also composed his epic poem *Milton,* about the seventeenth-century poet John Milton. Although Blake and his wife were

happy in Felpham at first, Blake became dissatisfied with the restrictions Hayley put on his original work. In 1803 the Blakes moved back to London, where Blake engraved and printed *Milton* as well as *Jerusalem: The Emanation of the Giant Albion.*

Writing in the *Reference Guide to English Literature,* Butter found the poem to be "not mainly a narrative—rather a series of related visions." Butter also believed *Milton* to be "the most attractive, partly because the shortest, of William Blake's long prophetic poems. There are two main strands of narrative—the Bard's Song and the story of Milton's journey to self-renewal. The former is difficult, contains little of Blake's best writing, and may well be passed over at a first reading. All one needs to grasp is that it is the Bard's story of Satan's usurpation of the prophetic role that leads to Milton's recognition of his own errors. Milton descends to earth, enters into Blake, his successor, into whom Los, the eternal Prophet, also enters. He unites with his female counterpart Ololon. The scattered elements of full humanity come together, leading to the appearance of Jesus, the divine humanity, and bringing us to the brink of Apocalypse."

"Milton is primarily about inspiration," F. B. Beer explained in *British Writers,* "a manifesto for the role of the poetic genius in his time. The Milton who is Blake's model is a Milton appropriate to the new age, subduing the spectrous Puritan morals and rational devotion to law that rendered poems such as [Milton's] *Paradise Lost* inadequate for the future, and so releasing himself into the full vigor and self-giving illumination that Blake regards as his underlying qualities. The eighteenth-century world is seen as dominated by thinkers who wish to reduce it finally to quantitative measurement and the rule of law; it is the work of the poetic genius, by contrast, to explore the moment of illumination that can never be organized into any time scheme, to enter into the timelessness of certain sensuous experiences (the lark pouring out its song as it ascends the sky, the flower with its power to overwhelm the senses with its scent) and find in them the true significance of the world."

In *Jerusalem,* Blake "is mainly concerned with the necessity of mutual forgiveness and of self-annihilation, which to him were the essentials of Christ's teaching, and the conditions for the establishment of the Kingdom of Heaven on earth, and specifically in England," according to Muir. Butter, comparing *Jerusalem* to *Milton,* found that the latter poem "is a more patient work, devoted to Blake's belief that the long-term work of the artist is to continue making, giving forms to things, since this is the only true work of redemption that is possible in the world."

Later Years

Blake received little engraving work after his return to London, and he and his wife were forced to live frugally. He tried to stir up interest in his work by exhibiting some of his watercolors at the Royal Academy in 1808 and at his brother James's house in 1809. The critics were unimpressed for the most part, and some even suggested that the paintings indicated that the artist was insane. Blake became a recluse until 1818, when he met John Linnell, a young artist who helped him financially and also helped to create new interest in his work. In 1820 Blake was commissioned by another patron, Thomas Butts, to paint a series of watercolors illustrating the *Book of Job.* The paintings were engraved and printed in 1825 and are among his most highly regarded works. During the early 1820s Blake also began to gather a group of disciples, young artists who called themselves "the Ancients."

In 1825 Linnell commissioned Blake to design illustrations for Dante's *Divine Comedy.* Before he completed the series, Blake died on August 12, 1827. Gilchrist quotes a letter from "a now distinguished painter," George Richmond, who was present at Blake's death: "Just before he died his countenance became fair, his eyes brightened, and he burst out into singing of the things he saw in heaven."

If you enjoy the works of William Blake, you might want to check out the following:

The works of British Romantic poets John Keats, Lord Byron, Percy Bysshe Shelley, and William Wordsworth.
The works of British author John Milton, who wrote *Paradise Lost.*
The works of Irish poet and dramatist Willam Butler Yeats, who was greatly influenced by Blake.

In his own time Blake was known mainly as an artist and an engraver; his original literary works were hand-printed in small editions and not widely circulated. After his death, and especially after the publication of Gilchrist's biography, Blake began to be considered an important writer and influenced many later poets, including William Butler Yeats. His reputation ranges from being a successful writer of poems for children—his poems "Infant Joy," "Night," "Spring," "Play Time," "The Lamb," "The Tyger," and "Three Things to Remember" have appeared in many anthologies of children's poetry and are still used to introduce young people to literature—to a prophetic writer of almost Biblical power. Beer described Blake as possessing "a vehement energy that refuses to be bound by the demands of convention." Reinhart concluded that "from the relative obscurity of his reputation in his own time, Blake is now recognized as one of the major poets of the Romantic period and one of the most original and challenging figures in the history of English literature."

■ Biographical and Critical Sources

BOOKS

Adams, Hazard, *Blake and Yeats: The Contrary Vision,* Cornell University Press (Ithaca, NY), 1955.

Altizier, *The New Apocalypse: The Radical Christian Vision of William Blake,* Michigan State University Press, 1974.

Baker, C. H. Collins, *Catalogue of Blake's Drawings and Paintings in the Huntington Library* (San Marino, CA), 1938, revised edition, with Robert P. Wark, 1957.

Barnes, Walter, *The Children's Poets,* World Book Co., 1924.

Beer, John, *Blake's Humanism,* Manchester University Press (Manchester, England), 1968.

Bentley, G. E., Jr., and Martin K. Nurmi, *A Blake Bibliography,* 1964, published as *Blake Books,* by G. E. Bentley, Jr., Oxford University Press, 1977.

Bentley, G. E., Jr., *Blake Records,* Oxford, 1969, supplement, 1988.

Bentley, G. E., Jr., editor, *William Blake: The Critical Heritage,* Routledge & Kegan Paul, 1975.

Bentley, G. E., Jr., *The Blake Collection of Mrs. Landon K. Thorne* (New York, NY), 1971.

Bentley, G. E., Jr., *The Stranger from Paradise,* Yale University Press (New Haven, CT), 2001.

Bindman, David, *Blake* (catalogue) (Hamburg, Germany), 1975.

Bindman, David, *Blake as an Artist* (Oxford, England, and New York, NY), 1977.

Bindman, David, *Blake: Catalogue of the Collection in the Fitzwilliam Museum,* Cambridge, 1970.

Bindman, David, *Blake: His Art and Times* (catalogue) (New Haven, CT), 1982.

Bindman, David, *The Complete Graphic Works of Blake* (London, England), 1978.

Blake's poem "Infant Joy" has appeared in many anthologies of children's poetry and is still used to introduce young people to literature.

Blackstone, Bernard, *English Blake*, Archon Books, 1966.

Bloom, Harold, *Blake's Apocalypse*, Doubleday (New York, NY), 1963.

Bloom, Harold, editor, *Modern Critical Views: William Blake*, Chelsea House, 1985.

Bloom, Harold, editor, *William Blake's Songs of Innocence and of Experience*, Chelsea House, 1987.

Blunt, Anthony, *The Art of Blake* (London, England, and New York, NY), 1959.

British Writers, Scribner (New York, NY), 1980.

Bronowski, Jacob, *William Blake and the Age of Revolution*, Routledge & Kegan Paul, 1972.

Butlin, Martin, *A Catalogue of the Works of Blake in the Tate Gallery* (London, England), 1957.

Butlin, Martin, *Blake* (catalogue) (London, England), 1978.

Butlin, Martin, *The Paintings and Drawings of Blake* (New Haven, CT), 1981.

Chesterton, Gilbert K., *William Blake*, Dutton (New York, NY), 1910.

Cournos, Helen, and John Cournos, *Famous British Poets*, Dodd, 1952.

Damon, Samuel Foster, *William Blake: His Philosophy and Symbols*, 1924.

Damon, Samuel Foster, *A Blake Dictionary: The Ideas and Symbols of William Blake*, Brown University Press (Providence, RI), 1965, revised edition, University Press of New England, 1988.

Davis, Michael, *William Blake: A New Kind of Man*, University of California Press (Berkeley, CA), 1977.

Dictionary of Literary Biography, Gale (Detroit, MI), Volume 93: *British Romantic Poets, 1789-1832*, 1990, Volume 163: *British Children's Writers, 1800-1880*, 1996.

Digby, George, *Symbol and Image in William Blake*, Oxford University Press, 1957.

Dorfman, Deborah, *Blake in the Nineteenth Century: His Reputation as a Poet from Gilchrist to Yeats*, Yale University Press (New Haven, CT), 1969.

Dunbar, Pamela, *Blake's Illustrations to the Poetry of Milton*, 1980.

Easson, Roger R., and Robert N. Essick, *Blake, Book Illustrator*, 1972-79.

Erdman, David V., *Blake's Designs for Edward Young's Night Thoughts*, Oxford, 1980.

Erdman, David V., editor, *The Illuminated Blake* (New York, NY), 1974, (London, England), 1975.

Erdman, David V., editor, *The Poetry and Prose of William Blake*, 1965.

Essick, Robert N., and Morton D. Paley, *Robert Blair's "The Grave," Illustrated by Blake* (London, England), 1982.

Essick, Robert N., *Blake, Printmaker*, Princeton University Press (Princeton, NJ), 1980.

Essick, Robert N., *The Separate Plates of Blake: A Catalogue*, Princeton University Press (Princeton, NJ), 1983.

Essick, Robert N., *The Works of William Blake in the Huntington Collection*, (catalogue) (San Marino, CA), 1985.

Fox, Susan, *Poetic Form in Blake's Milton*, Princeton University Press (Princeton, NJ), 1976.

Frye, Northrop, editor, *Blake: A Collection of Critical Essays*, Prentice-Hall (Englewood Cliffs, NJ), 1966.

Frye, Northrop, *Fearful Symmetry: A Study of William Blake*, Princeton University Press (Princeton, NJ), 1947.

Gilchrist, Alexander, *Life of William Blake: Pictor Ignotus*, Macmillan, 1863, enlarged edition, 1880, edited by Ruthven Todd (London, England), 1942.

Gillam, D. G., *William Blake*, Cambridge University Press, 1973.

Hagstrum, Jean, *William Blake: Poet and Painter*, University of Chicago Press (Chicago, IL), 1964.

Harper, George Mills, *The Neoplatonism of William Blake*, University of North Carolina Press (Chapel Hill, NC), 1961.

Johnson, Mary L., and John E. Grant, *Blake's Poetry and Designs* (New York, NY and London, England), 1979.

Keynes, Geoffrey, and Edwin Wolf II, *Blake's Illuminated Books* (New York, NY), 1953.

Keynes, Geoffrey, *Blake Studies: Essays on His Life and Work*, 2nd edition, Clarendon Press (Oxford, England), 1971.

Keynes, Geoffrey, *Blake, Poet, Printer, Prophet* (London, England), 1964.

Keynes, Geoffrey, *Blake's Illustrations to the Bible* (London, England), 1957.

Keynes, Geoffrey, editor, *Blake: Complete Writings*, Oxford University Press, 1974.

Keynes, Geoffrey, *Engravings by Blake: The Separate Plates: A Catalogue Raisonné* (Dublin, Ireland), 1956.

King, James, *William Blake: His Life*, Weidenfeld and Nicolson (London, England), 1991.

Lindberg, Bo, *Blake's Illustrations of the Book of Job*, Abo, 1973.

Lister, Raymond, *Blake* (New York, NY), 1968.

Lister, Raymond, *Infernal Methods: A Study of Blake's Art Techniques* (London, England), 1975.

Lister, Raymond, *The Paintings of Blake*, Cambridge University Press, 1986.

Lister, Raymond, *William Blake: An Introduction to the Man and His Work*, Bell, 1968.

Margoliouth, Herschel M., *William Blake*, 1951.

McGillis, Roderick, *Writers for Children: Critical Studies of Major Authors since the Seventeenth Century*, edited by Jane M. Bingham, Scribner (New York, NY), 1988.

Mitchell, W. J. T., *Blake's Composite Art: A Study of the Illuminated Poetry,* Princeton University Press (Princeton, NJ), 1978.

Nesfeld-Cookson, Bernard, *William Blake: Prophet of Universal Brotherhood,* Crucible, 1987.

Paley, Morton D., editor, *Twentieth-Century Interpretations on "Songs of Innocence of Experience,"* Prentice-Hall (Englewood Cliffs, NJ), 1969.

Paley, Morton D., *Energy and Imagination: A Study of the Development of Blake's Thought,* Clarendon Press (Oxford, England), 1970.

Percival, Milton O., *William Blake's Circle of Destiny,* Octagon Books, 1977.

Pinta, Vivian De Sola, editor, *The Divine Vision: Studies in the Poetry and Art of William Blake,* Gollancz (London, England), 1957.

Raine, Kathleen, *Blake and Tradition,* [London, England], 1969.

Raine, Kathleen, *From Blake to "A Vision,"* Dolman Press, 1979.

Raine, Kathleen, *The Human Face of God: Blake and the Book of Job,* [London, England], 1982.

Roe, Albert S., *Blake's Illustrations to the Divine Comedy,* Princeton University Press (Princeton, NJ), 1953.

Schorer, Mark, *William Blake: The Politics of Vision,* Vintage Books, 1959.

Shaw, John Mackay, *Childhood in Poetry,* 3rd supplement, Gale (Detroit, MI), 1980.

Swinburne, Algernon Charles, *William Blake,* Hotten, 1868.

Taylor, Irene, *Blake's Illustrations to the Poems of Gray,* Princeton University Press (Princeton, NJ), 1971.

Todd, Ruthven, *Blake the Artist,* [London, England], 1971.

Tucker, Martin, editor, *The Critical Temper,* Volume IV (supplement), Frederick Ungar, 1979.

Wilke, Joanne, *William Blake's Epic: Imagination Unbound,* Croom Helm, 1986.

Willard, Helen D., *Blake: Water-Color Drawings* (catalogue), [Boston, MA], 1957.

Wilson, Mona, *The Life of William Blake,* Nonesuch Press, 1927, Oxford University Press, 1971.

Wolf-Gumpold, Kaethe, *William Blake: Painter, Poet, Visionary: An Attempt at an Introduction to His Life and Work,* Rudolf Steiner Press, 1969.

Writers for Children, Scribner (New York, NY), 1988.

PERIODICALS

Financial Times, June 23, 2001, Andrew Motion, "Spirit-Sightings and Glimpses of Heaven: The Hardworking Poet Is an Awkward Subject," p. 5.

Humanist, September-October, 1993, p. 36.

New York Times Book Review, March 15, 1992, p. 18.

Studies in Romanticism, winter, 1985, Dan Miller, "The Marriage of Heaven and Hell," pp. 491-509.

Time, June 18, 2001, Robert Hughes, "Chatting with the Devil, Dining with Prophets: Seer, Bard, and Oddball, Artist-Poet William Blake Poured His Passions into Uniquely Visionary Images," p. 79.*

T. Coraghessan Boyle

■ Personal

Middle name pronounced "kuh-*RAGG*-issun"; born Thomas John Boyle, December 2, 1948, in Peekskill, NY; changed middle name to Coraghessan c. 1965; son of Thomas John and Rosemary Post (McDonald) Boyle; married Karen Kvashay, 1974; children: Kerrie, Milo, Spencer. *Education:* State University of New York at Potsdam, B.A., 1968; University of Iowa Writers' Workshop, M.F.A., 1974, Ph.D., 1977.

■ Addresses

Home—Santa Barbara, CA. *Office*—Department of English, University of Southern California—University Park, Los Angeles, CA 90089. *Agent*—Georges Borchardt, 136 East 57th St., New York, NY 10022.

■ Career

Writer. University of Southern California—University Park, Los Angeles, professor of English, 1977—.

■ Awards, Honors

Coordinating Council of Literary Magazines Award for fiction, 1977; National Endowment for the Arts fellowship, 1977; St. Lawrence Prize, 1980; Aga Khan Prize, *Paris Review,* 1981, for excerpts from *Water Music;* PEN/Faulkner Award, 1988, for *World's End;* PEN Award for short story, PEN American Center, 1990, for *If the River Was Whiskey;* Prix Medicis *Étranger* for best foreign novel published in France, 1997, for *The Tortilla Curtain;* PEN/Malamud Award in the short story, 1999, for *T. C. Boyle Stories;* O. Henry Award, 1999, for "The Underground Gardens," and 2001, for "The Love of My Life."

■ Writings

NOVELS

Water Music, Little, Brown (Boston, MA), 1981.
Budding Prospects: A Pastoral, Viking (New York, NY), 1984.
World's End, Viking (New York, NY), 1987.
East Is East, Viking (New York, NY), 1991.
The Road to Wellville, Viking (New York, NY), 1993.
The Tortilla Curtain, Viking (New York, NY), 1995.
Riven Rock, Viking (New York, NY), 1998.
A Friend of the Earth, Viking (New York, NY), 2000.
Drop City, Viking (New York, NY), in press.

SHORT STORIES

The Descent of Man, Little, Brown (Boston, MA), 1979.

Greasy Lake and Other Stories, Viking (New York, NY), 1985.

If the River Was Whiskey, Viking (New York, NY), 1990.

Without a Hero, Viking (New York, NY), 1994.

T. C. Boyle Stories, Viking (New York, NY), 1998.

After the Plague, Viking (New York, NY), 2001.

Books published in Great Britain under name T. C. Boyle. Contributor of short stories to periodicals, including *Esquire, Paris Review, Atlantic Monthly,* and *Harper's.* Fiction editor, *Iowa Review,* c. early 1970s.

■ Adaptations

A film adaptation of *The Road to Wellville* starring Anthony Hopkins, Matthew Broderick, and Brigit Fonda was directed by Alan Parker and released by Columbia Pictures, 1994.

■ Sidelights

Known for his blend of black humor and slightly off-kilter characters, T. Coraghessan Boyle has garnered a reputation for inserting verbal pyrotechnics and a bizarre mix of subjects in his novels and story collections. Boyle finds humor and pathos in subjects ranging from African exploration to corn flake barons and even environmental degradation, and his stories are filled with quirky characters, lush descriptions, and cynical humor. Over the course of the 1980s and 1990s he went from relatively unknown short-story writer to bestselling novelist, his wildly imaginative stories eliciting comparisons to the works of John Barth, Thomas Pynchon, and Evelyn Waugh. *Los Angeles Times Book Review* writer Charles Champlin termed Boyle's prose "a presence, a litany, a symphony of words, a chorale of idioms ancient and modern, a treasury of strange and wondrous place names, a glossary of things, good food and horrendous ills," while *Times Literary Supplement* critic Thomas Sutcliffe described the author's style as "punctuated with fire-cracker metaphors, a showy extravagance with obscurities of language and an easy mediation between hard fact and invention." Michael Adams, writing in the *Dictionary of Literary Biography Yearbook, 1986,* acknowledged Boyle's debt to such masters of absurdist and experimental fiction as Barth, Pynchon, Franz Kafka, and James Joyce. He also observed: "For all Boyle's similarities to other artists, no Americans . . . write about the diverse subjects he does in the way he does."

A self-described "pampered punk" of the 1960s, Boyle did not set out to become a writer. Born in Peekskill, New York to Irish immigrant parents, Boyle led a life, as he saw it, full of rebellion and rock and roll. Both his parents were alcoholics who died before Boyle was thirty. Named Thomas John after his father, Boyle changed his name at seventeen to distance himself from his roots, taking a new middle name from his mother's side of the family. Boyle has reported that he did not read a book until he was eighteen, and then attended college as a music student at the State University of New York at Potsdam, where he began to compose plays and short stories after enrolling in a creative writing course on a whim. He continued to write short fiction after graduation, between his daytime job as a high school teacher—a position he admits he took to avoid serving in Vietnam—and his nightly drug and alcohol binges. One of his stories, "The OD and Hepatitis Railroad or Bust," was published in the *North American Review,* giving Boyle the confidence to apply to the respected University of Iowa Writers' Workshop. "The only one I'd ever heard of was Iowa," he explained to Anthony De-Curtis in *Rolling Stone,* "so I wrote to them, and they accepted me, because they accept you just on the basis of the work. I could never have gotten in on my record."

Writer in the Making

At Iowa Boyle studied under authors such as Vance Bourjaily, John Cheever, and the young John Irving, and also began to read widely. Some of his major literary influences during these years came from Barth, Pynchon, Gabriel García Márquez, Evelyn Waugh, Flannery O'Connor, and Jean Genet. In 1977 Boyle earned his Ph.D. at Iowa and took a position as professor of English and creative writing at the University of Southern California.

His Ph.D. dissertation, a collection of stories which were later published as *Descent of Man,* earned the young writer an instant reputation for strange characters and offbeat plots and comedy. The collection won the St. Lawrence Award for Short Fiction in 1980 and, according to Denis Hennessy in *Dictionary of Literary Biography,* "displays Boyle's overriding theme: the unavoidable reversion of humankind to a prelapsarian animality, a state of being characterized by physical coarseness and the absence of conscience." Hennessy further observed that a reader "rarely hears Boyle's voice of judgment in these stories; rather he seems to be snickering behind a first-person narrator or alongside an ostensibly omniscient teller, not with Joycean indifference of a creator paring his nails but with something approaching blissful complicity." Evident already in this first collection is Boyle's love of playing with language.

"Good literature is a living, brilliant, great thing that speaks to you on an individual and personal level. . . . I think the essence of it is telling a story. It's entertaining. It's not something to be taught in a classroom, necessarily. To be alive and be good, it has to be a good story that grabs you by the nose and doesn't let you go till The End."

—*T. Coraghessan Boyle*

In 1981 Boyle published his first novel, *Water Music*. The book tells of two men: Mungo Park, a Scottish explorer who actually existed and led expeditions to Africa in 1795 and 1805, and the fictional Ned Rise, a drunken con-man from the London slums. Much of *Water Music* is concerned with Park's African excursions, and it offers particularly vivid accounts of his adventures with curious natives; Rise, meanwhile, has been involved in such dubious activities as running a sex show, robbing graves, and peddling fake caviar. Together the two protagonists travel down the Niger on the 1805 expedition from which the real Park never returned. With *Water Music* Boyle developed his reputation as a prominent American humorist. Champlin characterized the novel as "dark and sprawling, ribald, hilarious, cruel, language-intoxicated, exotic, and original," and hailed Boyle as "an important new writer." Other critics offered similar praise: Sutcliffe deemed *Water Music* "compendious, funny and compelling" and cited Boyle's "tropically fecund imagination," while Jay Tolson wrote in the *Washington Post Book World* of Boyle's ability to present "his most implausible inventions with wit, a perfect sense of timing, and . . . considerable linguistic gifts." Although most reviewers responded enthusiastically to the humor in *Water Music*, some tempered their praise by questioning the work's flamboyant style.

Writing in the *New York Times Book Review*, Alan Friedman decried the novel's prose as "a freewheeling mixture of elegant polysyllabic rhetoric . . . with current colloquialisms" and claimed that it results in merely "an extended occasion for comic-strip pathos."

Like *Water Music, Budding Prospects* received both praise as an invigoratingly funny novel and criticism as a superficial work. *Prospects* tells the story of a depressed teacher who takes up growing marijuana in hopes of getting rich quick. Ironically, the protagonist learns the merits of hard work and responsibility in this illegal activity, which comes to nothing when one of the partners runs off with the profits. Michael Gorra of the *New York Times Book Review* called *Budding Prospects* an "energetically written and very funny" novel and declared that Boyle's "raw ability to make one laugh" is reminiscent of Kingsley Amis and Thomas Berger. But Gorra also contended that Boyle "stops at the surface too often, settling for one-liners . . . rather than working toward a more sustained comic display." Similarly, Eva Hoffman wrote in the *New York Times* that *Budding Prospects* is "often quite hilarious" but argued that it lacks depth; she accused Boyle of failing to sufficiently differentiate and develop his characters and claimed that he writes as if he were "dancing on the edges of language, afraid that if he slowed down for a minute, he might fall into a vacuum." Despite these objections, even Hoffman concluded that "Boyle possesses a rare and redeeming virtue—he can be consistently, effortlessly, intelligently funny."

Growing Popularity

Boyle continued to gain high praise as a humorist with his 1985 collection, *Greasy Lake and Other Stories*. Hennessy noted that this collection, published when Boyle was thirty-seven, "seems to be his commentary on life from the late 1960s, when he was one of the rebellious baby boomers, until the mid 1980s." As with the earlier *Descent of Man, Greasy Lake* offers bizarre action within seemingly normal settings. Among the many odd tales in the collection are "Ike and Nina," which relates a love affair between President Dwight Eisenhower and the wife of Soviet leader Nikita Khrushchev; "The Hector Quesadilla Story," which depicts an aging baseball player in a never-ending game; and "On for the Long Haul," which concerns a survivalist who moves his family to Montana only to discover that his new neighbor is an even more paranoid survivalist who loathes the newcomer's children and pets. In a *New York Times* review of *Greasy Lake*, Michiko Kakutani commended Boyle's "vigorous and alluring . . . use of language" as well as his ability to move from "the literary to the mundane without the slightest strain."

Boyle first began to achieve the widespread fame he so coveted with the 1988 publication of *World's End*. Set in the Hudson River Valley area of New York where Boyle himself grew up, *World's End* describes the intertwining of three families over ten generations. In 1663 the rich, tyrannical Van Warts own the land tended by the oppressed Van Brunts—land once belonging to the Mohonk family of Indians, until they gave it up to the Van Warts. In 1968 Walter Van Brunt crashes his motorcycle into an historical marker honoring the spot where a group of rebels were hanged, betrayed to the authorities by yet another Van Brunt. Walter's collision is just one instance in which the past and the present meet: as the novel progresses, jumping between the past and present, we see dozens of Van Brunts indentured to Van Warts, and we witness the same mistakes made time and time again. Even Walter, in the end, must come to terms with destiny.

Critics hailed *World's End* as a work finally worthy of Boyle's unique prose and fecund imagination. Despite the novel's prodigious length, John Calvin Batchelor wrote in the *Washington Post Book World*, the author "displays a talent so effortlessly satirical and fluid that it suggests an image of the author at a crowded inn of wicked wits in a tale-telling fight for best space at the hearth." *New Statesman* reviewer Geoff Dyer concurred: "Word for word Boyle has never been a cost-effective writer. Like a fast car he gets through a lot of fuel, guzzling up words in an amphetamine rush of similes. *World's End* is uneconomic in a very different way. Here he has embarked on such a long haul with such a freight of material that there is no point in hurrying."

World's End is shaped, primarily, by a sense of overwhelming, inescapable predestiny. The history of the Van Warts and Van Brunts was described by John Clute in the *Times Literary Supplement* as "a crushing machine, which limns a world without exit; nowhere in [the novel] does any moment of hilarity or joy or love do more than strengthen the grip of the past." Several critics found Boyle's inescapable destiny to be problematic. The characters "are not only invaded by the past but flattened by it," wrote Richard Eder in the *Los Angeles Times Book Review*. "Or rather, they are flattened by the awkwardness of having three centuries of fatality come to a point in them." "Even Walter's tale begins to sound increasingly contrived," noted Kakutani in the *New York Times*. "Instead of feeling that he's living out some inexorable family destiny, we end up suspecting that he is just another pawn in the author's elaborate chess game."

After the ambitious reach displayed in *World's End*, a few critics were dissatisfied with *If the River Was Whiskey*, Boyle's 1990 collection of short stories. Though as quirky and entertaining as his past story collections, some viewed this new book as the author's way of playing it safe, producing stories filled with his characteristic wit but lacking any real substance. "The writing is evocative, the craft stunning," explained *Village Voice* critic Sally S. Eckhoff. "But it's all wrapped up too tight to explode into the imagination. . . . At every story's end, we don't have much to savor but how good Boyle is." Nicholas Delbanco of Chicago's *Tribune Books* called the stories at times "simply silly—a five-finger exercise," while Kakutani lamented in the *New York Times* that Boyle's talents "are used, singly, for showy but shallow effects."

Still, as Delbanco pointed out, "there are worse problems than a prodigality of talent." "What keeps us reading," observed Francine Prose in the *Washington Post*, "are Boyle's humor, his imagination, his narrative gifts: the pleasure of watching a writer make each story more inventive than the last one." Eckhoff, too, happily conceded that in these stories Boyle "is completely in command. . . . On all counts, *If the River Was Whiskey* is impressive."

The critical response to Boyle's 1991 novel, *East Is East*, was similar to that of *If the River Was Whiskey*; Charles Dickinson of Chicago's *Tribune Books*, for example, called the novel "Boyle Lite. It is better than most fiction being written today, but because of the standard he has set for himself, a disappointment nonetheless." *East Is East* describes the attempts of Japanese-born Hiro Tanaka to find his long-vanished American father. Envisioning the thriving cities of New York, Philadelphia, and Boston, Hiro takes a job on a Japanese freighter, jumping from its bow as it sails near the eastern coast of the United States. He swims to the closest shore, that of Georgia's Tupelo Island—a soggy, insect-and-reptile-infested morass with little to offer in the way of food or shelter. At the far end of the island is a writers' colony full of eccentric and neurotic artists, and it is into their midst that Hiro, attempting to evade agents of the Immigration and Naturalization Service, finally lands.

Dickinson called *East Is East* "the kind of knowing, cynical farce that Boyle can toss off in his sleep. . . . The writing is seamless and slick, and in a few instances the equal of anything Boyle has yet produced, but without the power that informs his other novels." Julian Loose, writing in *New Statesman*, observed that the book "is at its funniest when portraying the colony's literati doing battle with writ-

John Neville and Matthew Broderick star in the film adaptation of Boyle's *The Road to Wellville*, a comedy focusing on the late nineteenth-century health cure fad.

er's block and one another," but that the novel as a whole "singularly fails as an allegory of cultural misunderstanding."

A Writer in His Prime

With 1993's *The Road to Wellville* and its movie adaptation the following year, Boyle's name came to be recognized by an ever-wider audience. The very title of the book went into the language, incorporated in headlines and in advertising slogans. A send-up of current and historical food fads, the novel is set in Battle Creek, Michigan in 1907, and deals with Dr. John Harvey Kellogg, the inventor of the corn flake, peanut butter, and many other foods intended to promote healthy eating. *The Road to Wellville*, punned Jim Neilson in the *Review of Contemporary Fiction*, "is paved with food inventions." To Kellogg's Battle Creek spa came the health-conscious people of the day, and in this fictional-

ized account Will and Eleanor Lightbody are among the guests in the winter of 1907, the husband there for his delicate stomach. On the train to the spa they meet entrepreneur Charlie Ossining who intends to make his fortune in the breakfast cereal business. A power struggle ensues with rival brands battling it out for market share, and spa guests undergoing every form of torture for their supposed good health. Louisa Ermelino, writing in *People Weekly* called the novel "wildly funny," a book that "blurs the line between fact and fiction, comic and tragic, to create a magnificent satire of 20th-century America's obsession with health." *Time*'s John Skow, however, felt that *Wellville* was simply "one of [Boyle's] better efforts, though effort is the key word here, and the result is, at best, a story that is amusing and interestingly odd but baffling in its intent." A contributor to *Publishers Weekly*, on the other hand, felt that Boyle hit the "bull's-eye" with this "rich plum of a book, full of ripely conceived characters, satire both broad and bitter, beautifully integrated period atmosphere, and writing that is colorful but considered." The same reviewer concluded, "Boyle has woven all this into a tale told with the broad humanism and compassionate eye of a great 19th-century novelist."

Boyle's 1994 short-story collection, *Without a Hero*, received high marks from readers and reviewers alike, though Hennessy, for one, felt the collection "failed to show much broadening of themes." Critic Ian Sansom, who in his *New Statesman* review of the collection frequently compared and contrasted Boyle with John Updike, wrote: "While Updike's stories descend with heavenly choirs from the *New Yorker*, Boyle's crawl up out of *Rolling Stone* and *Wig Wag*, yelling prophecies and denunciations. . . . For all [Boyle's] warnings about the road to excess, he is—like Updike—at his best when writing about life's unexpected failures and inevitable defeats." *Knight-Ridder/Tribune News Service* contributor Sandy Bauers similarly offered glowing words: "Boyle is superbly demented. He's the court jester of modern society, tweaking our icons. These are the sort of stories that the kid who flicked spitballs at the blackboard in grade school would write. Only now the kid has grown up; he has more finesse. Boyle's stories are more than funny, better than wicked. They make you cringe with their clarity. . . . [Boyle is] the absolute genius of description." If Hennessy had reservations about the sameness of themes, he also found that the final two stories in *Without a Hero*, "The Fog Man" and "Sitting on Top of the World," "combine wit and brilliantly deft word play in a haunting call to recognize the diminished glory of American civilization."

Boyle's most read and perhaps most controversial work, *The Tortilla Curtain*, was described by its publisher as a "*Grapes of Wrath* for the 1990s." Set in Southern California and involving the intersection of white, upper-middle-class Americans with poor, homeless Mexican illegals, the novel examines more than border relations and the corresponding struggle between the "haves" and the "have-nots" of the region. Barbara Kingsolver, writing in *Nation*, explained how the novel "addresses what has probably always been the great American political dilemma: In a country that proudly defines itself as a nation of immigrants, who gets to slam the door on whom?" While acknowledging that "Boyle has his finger firmly on the pulse of an American middle class whose fear of the iron curtain has been replaced by an obsession with one made of tortillas," *New Statesman* reviewer Julie Wheelwright also claimed that "Boyle explores powerful issues through his parallel characters, but they operate just shy of caricature. They are more symbolic figures than real inhabitants of a state wallowing in economic downturn. The Mexicans are naive, but es-

sentially good, while their Anglo counterparts grow increasingly ugly with rage." Despite similar complaints about the novel's characters, Kingsolver concluded: "What Boyle does, and does well, is lay on the line our national cult of hypocrisy. Comically and painfully he details the smug wastefulness of the haves and the vile misery of the have-nots." *The Tortilla Curtain* received the 1997 Prix Medicis Étranger as the best foreign novel published that year in France.

Set in the early part of the twentieth century in Santa Barbara, California, on an estate called Riven Rock, Boyle's 1998 novel *Riven Rock* tells the story of millionaire Stanley McCormick, who suffers from madness and sexual dysfunction. Katherine, his wife, who has not seen him in more than twenty years, remains ever hopeful that he will recover. Novelist D. M. Thomas, writing in the *New York Times Book Review*, noted the novel's theme of the dichotomous nature of men's love for women as both Madonna and whore, who are conflicted by thoughts of both desire and worship for them. But Thomas concluded that the novel's "promise of intellectual and emotional exploration . . . is not fulfilled."

Boyle's *T. C. Boyle Stories*, an impressive release containing all the stories from his four earlier collections, along with seven new stories, enjoyed considerable admiration upon its 1998 publication. Contending that Boyle's stories "concentrate his talents more powerfully than his seven novels," critic John C. Hawley explained in *America* that Boyle "plays with famous stories by Gogol, Kafka, Chekhov and Joyce, and imitates some of the best of his contemporaries—Barthelme, Coover, Lorrie Moore. He is very funny and Dickensian in his clearly drawn characters and in the cornucopia of plots that tumble out into page after fascinating page." Offering similar praise, a *Publishers Weekly* contributor called Boyle "a premier practitioner of short fiction" and praised the collection for its "narrative outtakes that are invariably amusing and, like Boyle's more serious work, mordant, worldly, and irreverent." Reviewing the collection in the *New York Times Book Review*, Jim Shepard wondered "who else of his generation could have assembled, by this point, a 'Collected Stories' the size of the Phoenix [Arizona] white pages?" Shepard noted a "staggering" sixty-eight stories in all, in almost seven hundred pages, in this collection which is marked with "overall inventiveness, flash and just plain entertainment value." Praise also came form Herbert Gold in the *Los Angeles Times Book Review*, who found Boyle's stories not only laugh-out-loud funny, but also often profound. "Not every yarn-spinner needs to be the philosopher king of an epoch," Gold wrote. "But when the spinner of yarns is as adept at composing his tapestry as T. Coraghessan Boyle is, he is a source of philosophy in others and, yes, he can call himself Maestro."

Boyle returned to the novel form with *A Friend of the Earth*, a critical look at environmentalism. Set in 2025 with most mammalian species extinct because of global warming, the novel focuses on Tyrone Tierwater, who thinks back to the late 1980s when he in fact predicted that such a disaster would happen. Tyrone was an early eco-terrorist, graduating beyond mere monkey wrenching. He spent years in prison for his environmental activism. Meanwhile his wife, Andrea, moving into the bureaucracy of the environmental movement Earth Forever!, felt threatened by her husband's role, and divorced him, but his daughter Sierra went on to be famed for her tree-sitting protests. In a sense, Boyle is after a rethinking of such classics as Edward Abbey's *The Monkey Wrench Gang*, questioning the ethos not only of developers, but also of environmental activists. "As disaster tales," wrote Lisa Zeidner in the *Washington Post*, "this is a sly, hip one," as well as "surprisingly solemn." Zeidner went on to note that in *A Friend of the Earth*, Boyle "sets himself the challenge of using his impressive arsenal of literary tricks and tropes in the service of a more earnest exploration." A contributor for *Publishers Weekly* also pointed out the seriousness of purpose in this "mordantly funny and inventive" novel which is "as unflinching as it is satirical." Kakutani, writing in the *New York Times*, also had praise for this new voice. "Up till now T. Coraghessan Boyle has been the Jim Carrey of fiction: all broad gestures and mimicry, nervous hyperbole and dazzling razzmatazz," Kakutani noted. "He's used his satiric gifts and bravura showmanship to give us a gallery of weirdos and bug-eyed misfits . . . and in doing so, he's energetically limned the lunatic fringe of America's Zeitgeist." With *A Friend of the Earth*, Kakutani noted, Boyle's humor is "as black as ever, [but] he demonstrates . . . that satire can coexist with psychological realism, comedy with compassion." In this novel, according to Kakutani, Boyle demonstrates that "he's not just a manic and maniacally talented performer, but that he's got the novelistic equivalent of solid acting chops as well." And Eric Zency, reviewing the same title in the *Los Angeles Times Book Review*, felt that Boyle's "work is the richer and more affecting" for setting himself new challenges. "It not only marks Boyle's progress as a literary talent but demonstrates his consistent ability to entertain."

In 2001 Boyle brought out his sixth collection of short stories, *After the Plague*, a series of "wickedly ironic, sometimes poignant, sometimes darkly humorous tales that speak directly to the human condition," according to David W. Henderson in *Library Journal*. Gathered here are stories dealing with topics from abortion to air rage to Internet voyeur cameras. Jonathan Levi, writing in the *Los Angeles Times Book Review*, detected a new voice within these stories. "Boyle's has always been a peculiar voice," Levi noted, "particularly in the short story form, which he has worked like a master trickster, the jester of the butt end of the 20th century." This "jewel-earringed jester rock 'n' roller who once sang in a coat he borrowed from James Dean, has grown a beard of a Jeremiah. Terrible things happen in these stories. Boyfriends sabotage their lovers, brothers their brothers, fathers their sons." Levi concluded that in an "age of war where the foe is indistinct and difficult to identify, Boyle has become the poet and the prophet of our time."

If you enjoy the works of T. Coraghessan Boyle, you might want to check out the following books:

Bill Crider, *Medicine Show*, 1990.
Frederick Barthelme, *The Law of Averages*, 2000.
Michael Chabon, *Werewolves in Their Youth*, 2000.

Speaking with Lewis Burke Frumkes in *Writer*, Boyle acknowledged his commitment to literature. "I think a lot of novelists, particularly academic novelists, lose track of the fact that literature is not something that is on the shelf in the academy, with the public out here being ignorant, and the writer is over here being equally ignorant, and you need some genius to mediate. Good literature is a living, brilliant, great thing that speaks to you on an individual and personal level. You're the reader. I think the essence of it is telling a story. It's entertaining. It's not something to be taught in a classroom, necessarily. To be alive and be good, it has to be a good story that grabs you by the nose and doesn't let you go till The End."

■ Biographical and Critical Sources

BOOKS

Contemporary Literary Criticism, Gale (Detroit, MI), Volume 36, 1986; Volume 55, 1989.

Dictionary of Literary Biography, Volume 218: *American Short-Story Writers since World War II,* Gale (Detroit, MI), 1999, pp. 70-77.

Dictionary of Literary Biography Yearbook, 1986, Gale (Detroit, MI), 1987.

Short Story Criticism, Volume 10, Gale (New York, NY), 1992.

PERIODICALS

America, April 23, 1994, p. 20; May 22, 1999, John C. Hawley, "An American Delight," p. 31.

Atlantic Monthly, November 1987, p. 122; October, 1990, p. 135.

Carolina Quarterly, fall, 1979, p. 103.

Entertainment Weekly, May 27, 1994, p. 79; April 28, 1995, p. 73.

Interview, January, 1988, p. 91.

Kirkus Reviews, June 1, 1995, p. 725.

Knight-Ridder/Tribune News Service, May 25, 1994, Sandy Bauers, review of *Without a Hero;* November 15, 2001.

Library Journal, August, 1996, p. 136; September 15, 1998, p. 115; August, 2000, p. 152; August, 2001, David W. Henderson, review of *After the Plague,* p. 168.

Los Angeles Times, June 17, 1982; October 7, 1987; April 21, 1988; April 6, 1990; October 3, 1990, p. E1; September 24, 1995, p. 4; September 15, 1996, p. 44; February 26, 1998, p. 5; April 28, 2001, p. A1.

Los Angeles Times Book Review, January 3, 1982, Charles Champlin, review of *Water Music;* May 6, 1984, p. 3; June 30, 1985; October 11, 1987, Richard Eder, review of *World's End,* p. 3; July 24, 1988, p. 10; May 21, 1989, p. 3; May 30, 1993, p. 2; November 22, 1998, Herbert Gold, "Of Frogs and Swains"; September 10, 2000, Eric Zency, "Future Shock"; September 30, 2001, Jonathan Levi, "Fifty Going Down."

Nation, April 7, 1979, p. 377; September 1, 1984, pp. 151-153; September 25, 1995, Barbara Kingsolver, review of *The Tortilla Curtain,* p. 326.

New Republic, February 10, 1979; June 12, 1989, p. 40; October 4, 1993, p. 43.

New Statesman, October 22, 1993, p. 38; February 10, 1995, Ian Samson, review of *Without a Hero,* p. 44; November 10, 1995, Julie Wheelwright, review of *The Tortilla Curtain,* p. 39.

New Statesman and Society, August 26, 1988, Geoff Dyer, review of *World's End,* p. 36; March 29, 1991, Julian Loose, review of *East Is East,* p. 31.

Newsweek, April 19, 1993, p. 62.

New Yorker, January 19, 1998, p. 68.

New York Review of Books, January 17, 1991, p. 31.

New York Times, May 19, 1979; May 19, 1984, Eva Hoffman, review of *Budding Prospects,* p. N15; May 22, 1985, Michiko Kakutani, review of *Greasy Lake and Other Stories,* p. C24; September 23, 1987, Michiko Kakutani, review of *World's End,* p. C27; May 2, 1989, Michiko Kakutani, review of *If the River Was Whiskey,* p. C18; September 7, 1990, p. C25; June 2, 1993, p. B1; April 25, 1994, p. B2; January 20, 1998, Michiko Kakutani, review of *Riven Rock,* p. E10; October 3, 2000, Michiko Kakutani, "In Dark Days, the Human Hyena Has the Last Laugh," p. B8; September 23, 2001, Janet Maslin, "Grand Delusion."

New York Times Book Review, April 1, 1979, p. 14; December 27, 1981, Alan Friedman, review of *Water Music,* p. 9; June 6, 1982; July 1, 1984, Michael Gorra, review of *Budding Prospects,* p. 18; June 9, 1985, p. 15; July 21, 1985; September 27, 1987, p. 1; December 6, 1987, p. 85; May 14, 1989, p. 1; May 6, 1990, p. 38; September 9, 1990, p. 13; April 25, 1993, p. 1; May 8, 1994, p. 9; December 3, 1995, p. 78; September 15, 1996, p. 44; February 8, 1998, D. M. Thomas, review of *Riven Rock,* p. 8; November 8, 1998, Jim Shepard, "The Damned Outnumber the Rest"; October 8, 2000, p. 24; September 2, 2001, p. 5.

New York Times Magazine, March 19, 1989, p. 57; December 9, 1990, p. 50.

People Weekly, May 24, 1993, Louisa Ermelino, review of *The Road to Wellville,* pp. 33-34; November 14, 1994, pp. 17-18.

Publishers Weekly, October 9, 1987, pp. 71-72; February 22, 1993, review of *The Road to Wellville,* p. 79; July 3, 1995, p. 47; July 22, 1996, p. 234; September 21, 1998, review of *T. C. Boyle Stories,* p. 71; June 19, 2000, review of *A Friend of the Earth;* October 1, 2001, p. 43.

Review of Contemporary Fiction, summer, 1994, Jim Neilson, review of *The Road to Wellville,* pp. 211-212.

Rolling Stone, January 14, 1988, Anthony DeCurtis, "A Punk's Past Recaptured," pp. 54-57.

Saturday Review, March 31, 1979.

Time, May 10, 1993, John Skow, review of *The Road to Wellville,* pp. 71-72.

Times (London, England) March 21, 1991.

Times Literary Supplement, June 20, 1980; February 26, 1982, Thomas Sutcliffe, review of *Water Music;* September 14, 1985; January 31, 1986; August 26, 1988, John Clute, review of *World's End,* p. 927; March 22, 1991, p. 19; October 27, 1995, p. 25; May 22, 1998, p. 9.

Tribune Books (Chicago, IL), October 11, 1987, p. 3; May 21, 1989, p. 7; July 15, 1990, Nicholas Delbanco, review of *If the River Was Whiskey,* p. 4; September 9, 1990, Charles Dickinson, review of *East Is East,* p. 5.

Village Voice, January 6, 1982, p 39; September 6, 1989, Sally S. Eckhoff, review of *If the River Was Whiskey.*

Voice Literary Supplement, November, 1987.

Wall Street Journal, September 7, 1990, p. A13.

Washington Post, May 23, 1989, Francine Prose, review of *If the River Was Whiskey;* September 3, 2000, Lisa Zeidner, "Apocalypso."

Washington Post Book World, February 7, 1982, Jay Tolson, review of *Water Music,* p. 10; June 23, 1985; November 1, 1987, John Calvin Batchelor, review of *World's End,* p. 4; March 9, 1988; April 20, 1988; September 2, 1990, p. 1; May 9, 1993, p. 5.

World Literature Today, summer, 2000, p. 591.

Writer, October, 1999, Lewis Burke Frumkes, "A Conversation with T. Coraghessan Boyle," p. 26.

OTHER

T. Coraghessan Boyle Web site, http://www.tcboyle. com (March 19, 2002).*

Bernard Cornwell

■ Personal

Born February 23, 1944, in London, England; came to the United States, 1980; married Judy Acker (a travel agent), October 20, 1980. *Education:* University of London, B.A., 1967.

■ Addresses

Home—Cape Cod, MA. *Agent*—Toby Eady Associates, Inc., 7 Gledhow Gardens, London SW5 0BL, England.

■ Career

British Broadcasting Corp. (BBC-TV), London, England, producer, 1969-76, Belfast, Northern Ireland, head of current affairs, 1976-79; Thames Television, London, editor of television news, 1979-80; freelance writer, 1980—.

■ Writings

NOVELS; "RICHARD SHARPE" SERIES

Sharpe's Eagle: Richard Sharpe and the Talavera Campaign, July 1809, Viking (New York, NY), 1981.

Sharpe's Gold: Richard Sharpe and the Destruction of Almeida, August 1810, Viking (New York, NY), 1982.

Sharpe's Company: Richard Sharpe and the Siege of Badajoz, January to April 1812, Viking (New York, NY), 1982.

Sharpe's Sword: Richard Sharpe and the Salamanca Campaign, June and July 1812, Viking (New York, NY), 1983.

Sharpe's Enemy: Richard Sharpe and the Defense of Portugal, Christmas 1812, Viking (New York, NY), 1984.

Sharpe's Honour: Richard Sharpe and the Vitoria Campaign, February to June 1813, Viking (New York, NY), 1985.

Sharpe's Regiment: Richard Sharpe and the Invasion of France, June to November 1813, Viking (New York, NY), 1986.

Sharp's Siege: Richard Sharpe and the Winter Campaign, 1814, Viking (New York, NY), 1987.

Sharpe's Rifles: Richard Sharpe and the French Invasion of Galicia, January 1809, Viking (New York, NY), 1988.

Sharpe's Revenge: Richard Sharpe and the Peace of 1814, Viking (New York, NY), 1989.

Waterloo, Viking (New York, NY), 1990, published as *Sharpe's Waterloo: Richard Sharpe and the Waterloo Campaign, 15 June to 18 June 1815*, Collins (London, England), 1990.

Sharpe's Devil: Richard Sharpe and the Emperor, 1820-1821, HarperCollins (New York, NY), 1992.

Sharpe's Battle: Richard Sharpe and the Battle of Fuentes de Onoro, May 1811, HarperCollins (New York, NY), 1995.

Sharpe's Tiger, HarperCollins (New York, NY), 1997.

Sharpe's Triumph: Richard Sharpe and the Battle of Assaye, September 1803, HarperCollins (New York, NY), 1999.

Sharpe's Fortress: Richard Sharpe and the Siege of Gawilghur, December 1803, HarperCollins (New York, NY), 2000.

Sharpe's Trafalgar: Richard Sharpe and the Battle of Trafalgar, 21 October 1805, HarperCollins (New York, NY), 2001.

Sharpe's Prey, HarperCollins (New York, NY), 2002.

NOVELS; "NATHANIEL STARBUCK CHRONICLES"

Rebel, HarperCollins (New York, NY), 1993.
Copperhead, HarperCollins (New York, NY), 1994.
Battle Flag, HarperCollins (New York, NY), 1995.
The Bloody Ground, HarperCollins (New York, NY), 1996.

NOVELS; "GRAILQUEST" SERIES

Harlequin, HarperCollins (London, England), 2000, published as *The Archer's Tale,* HarperCollins (New York, NY), 2000.
Gallows Thief, HarperCollins (New York, NY), 2002.
Vagabond, HarperCollins (New York, NY), 2002.

NOVELS; "WARLORD CHRONICLES"

The Winter King: A Novel of Arthur, St. Martin's Press (New York, NY), 1996.
Enemy of God: A Novel of Arthur, St. Martin's Press (New York, NY), 1997.
Excalibur: A Novel of Arthur, St. Martin's Press (New York, NY), 1998.

NOVELS; AS SUSANNAH KELLS

A Crowning Mercy, Collins (London, England), 1983.
The Fallen Angels, Collins (London, England), 1984.
Coat of Arms, Collins (London, England), 1986.

OTHER

Redcoat, Viking (New York, NY), 1988.
Wildtrack, Putnam (New York, NY), 1988.
Killer's Wake, Putnam (New York, NY), 1989.
Sea Lord, M. Joseph (London, England), 1989.
Crackdown, HarperCollins (New York, NY), 1990.
Stormchild, HarperCollins (New York, NY), 1991.
(Illustrator) Charles O'Neil, *The Military Adventures of Charles O'Neil,* Midpoint Trade Books, 1998.

Stonehenge: 2000 B.C., HarperCollins (New York, NY), 2000.
A Flight of Arrows (poems), HarperCollins (New York, NY), 2000.

■ Sidelights

The author of over three dozen historical novels, Bernard Cornwell is best known for his many novels detailing the life and adventures of Richard Sharpe during the Napoleonic age, which were adapted for a popular television series. Other well-known series from Cornwell include the "Warlord Chronicles," a trio of books about British King Arthur, the "Nathaniel Starbuck Chronicles," set during the American Civil War, the "Grail Quest," set during the Hundred Years' War, and a novel of Neolithic and Bronze Age Britain titled *Stonehenge.* Scrupulously researched and graphic in descriptions of violence and squalor, Cornwell's books aim to capture the spirit of the era in which they are set, whether it be the France of Napoleon's time or the Celtic Britain of the legendary King Arthur. In *Twentieth-Century Romance and Historical Writers,* Geoffrey Sadler acknowledged Cornwell as "a leading figure . . . in the field of the historical novel," adding that the author holds "a secure place among contemporary adventure writers." Modest about his achievements, Cornwell insists, as he told Linda Richards in a *January* interview, that writing novels "is much better than working."

Cornwell was born in London during World War II; his father was a Canadian airman and his mother a British citizen. Put up for adoption after birth, he was raised by a couple who were members of a strict fundamentalist sect called the Peculiar People. Raised in Essex, Cornwell came of age in a household with prohibitions about all sorts of things: dancing, cigarettes, alcohol, television, doctors, and even toy guns. As with most prohibitions, the last one served only to encourage a secret vice in the young Cornwell—reading about war and great battles of the past. Foremost among these readings were the "Hornblower" books by C. S. Forester. Inspired by these novels, Cornwell tried to enlist in the military several times, but poor eyesight kept him a civilian.

At the age of eighteen Cornwell left home to study theology at London University, graduating in 1967. Then followed a teaching stint for a couple of years. In 1969 he took a job at the British Broadcasting Corporation in London, beginning as a researcher on the *Nationwide* program. He slowly worked his way up through production and direction, and by 1976 had become head of Current Affairs Television for the BBC in Northern Ireland. While in Ulster, he met his wife, Judy Acker, a travel agent on a junket organized by the tourist board of Northern Ireland. Of course, Northern Ireland was the last place in the world anyone would think of taking a vacation at the time, for the country was in the grips of the "Troubles," the religious/political urban warfare that has torn the region apart for decades. One day in 1978 Cornwell saw Acker getting off an elevator, and he determined there and then to marry her. One problem was, however, that Acker, an American, did not want to leave her country.

The year after meeting Acker, Cornwell was promoted to the position as editor of Thames News, with a staff of about two hundred people now under him. As Cornwell told Richards, "that was a classic example of the Peter Principle at work." While he was competent in production and directing, he had no supervisory skills. Still, the pay was good, and by this time he knew that he was going to immigrate to the United States to marry Acker. Since it was becoming apparent that he would not be able to work in television in the United States as he could not get a green card, he stuck with the new position and squirreled away enough money to support him in his new country for a year. That year, Cornwell determined, would be used to try and make an old dream come true. He would sit down and see if he could write a historical novel like those he so admired.

Sharpe Is Born

Cornwell once told a contributor for *Books* that he began writing his own military novels because "I got pissed off with going into bookshops and being confronted only by books on Britain's military defeats. . . . From going into bookshops hoping there'd be a novel about Waterloo or Badajoz, I suddenly hoped there wouldn't be anyone else with the same idea." It was his intent to do for fighting on land what both Forester and author Patrick O'Brien had done for sailors and the navy. Cornwell's year of enforced writing in the United States paid off; within his self-imposed deadline he completed his first manuscript, *Sharpe's Eagle,* set in 1809 during the Talavera Campaign. He sold the novel to Viking and it was published in 1981. What began as a hiatus from television work has since turned into a cottage industry for the prolific Cornwell, who normally writes two novels per year.

The character of Richard Sharpe is something of an Indiana Jones type, a man who works his way up through the ranks from humble beginnings. The

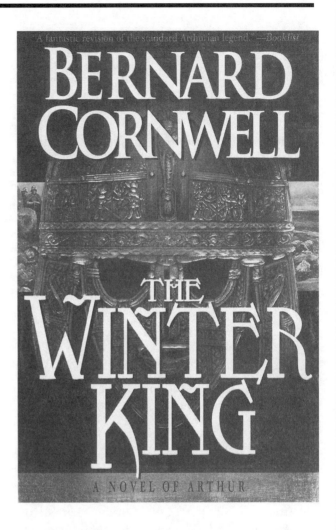

The first of Cornwell's "Warlord" chronicles, this 1996 novel recounts the story of King Arthur and his efforts to keep Britain civilized despite personal tragedy and the treachery of a barbaric court.

novels center on Sharpe's military career in the British Army where he serves under Sir Arthur Wellesley, first duke of Wellington, in the 1800s. Throughout the course of the series readers follow the indomitable Sharpe from private to corporal to sergeant to ensign—for saving Wellington's life at the Battle of Assaye in 1803—and then to lieutenant, captain, major, and lieutenant colonel. Decorated in battle, the tried-and-true Sharpe grows increasingly weary with war. "Sharpe is one of the best fictional creations of recent years," commented Sadler, "and his adventures yield fresh insights into the Napoleonic period. With him the reader re-lives a vanished age, learning the techniques of skirmish and ambush, the handling of the deadly Baker rifle and its fearsome sword-bayonet." Cornwell once described his "Sharpe" novels as "picaresque adventure stories" that are "shamelessly modeled on C. S. Forester's 'Hornblower' series. I have always had a fascination with the Duke of Wellington's army, research on it has been a hobby since my youth, and the Sharpe novels come from that research."

Cornwell quickly hit on a formula for writing his "Sharpe" novels. As he somewhat facetiously explained to Richards, "Now, all a Sharpe fan wants is they go smack into chapter one into a fight. So you kick off with a battle: 15,000 words. That gets the book off to a nice, fast start, lots of dead Frogs (Frenchmen). Introduce plot, all right. Plot begins to snag. Wheel on 40,000 Frogs and start slaughtering them. . . . That lifts the center of the book up, keep it moving, right? Then you finish off the plot in chapter six or seven. And then you've got 40,000, 60,000 words of the battle at the end at which you kill the four villains. Easy. It works every time." Though Cornwell enjoys making such breezy comments in his interviews, claiming that he would not know how to write a contemporary novel, for example, because then he would not have history to crib from, readers and critics alike attest to the fact that the "Sharpe" books are more than mere potboilers.

Each book in the "Sharpe" series focuses on a different battle and, according to Sadler in *Contemporary Popular Writers*, "Each battle is matched with a struggle to outwit an individual enemy who seeks Sharpe's destruction." Commenting further upon the series in *Twentieth-Century Romance and Historical Writers*, Sadler noted: "Without a doubt . . . the peak of Cornwell's achievement is the magnificent sequence of novels featuring his rifleman hero Richard Sharpe, which span the entire period of the Napoleonic Wars, from the viewpoint of the frontline soldier. . . . Cornwell's painstaking research, his sure grasp of authentic period detail, enable him to bring home to the reader the scent and feeling of those vanished times, forcing him to witness afresh the savage butchery of the battles, the squalor and corruption that marks life in the early 19th century."

A *Publishers Weekly* reviewer described *Sharpe's Enemy: Richard Sharpe and the Defense of Portugal, Christmas 1812*, the fifth book in the series, as "colorful, all-action stuff with a strong dash of historical authenticity." Volume ten, *Sharpe's Revenge: Richard Sharpe and the Peace of 1814*, presents "brilliant historic action, adventure, and [a] love story," according to James Dudley in *Library Journal*. After a decade of writing the series, Cornwell's protagonist had made it to the Battle of Waterloo. Reviewing *Sharpe's Waterloo: Richard Sharpe and the Waterloo Campaign: 15 June to 18 June 1815*, Sybil Steinberg

wrote in *Publishers Weekly*: "Readers will thrill to the appearance of Napoleon's army in full panoply, be appalled at the battlefield gore and the robbery of corpses, and hope Cornwell doesn't mean it when he suggests in the epilogue that this may be Sharpe's final appearance." In fact, Cornwell did mean it at the time, but then came the BBC television series adaptation of his book starring Sean Bean that eventually made it to the United States. Cornwell's new publishers pleaded for more "Sharpe" novels so as not to miss this golden egg of free advertising. Cornwell complied, first with *Sharpe's Devil: Richard Sharpe and the Emperor, 1820-1821* and then with prequel titles, three of which are set in India at the turn of the nineteenth century. *Sharpe's Devil*, set both on land and sea, in South America and points between, is a rousing adventure; a contributor for *Publishers Weekly* thought readers "will be dazzled by the rollicking plot, period color and the atavistic thrill of terrific battle scenes right out of a Turner painting."

"I simply try to tell as compelling a story as I possibly can. I don't know if there is any moral. I'm not clever enough to point out morals in my tales. The most important thing you do is the plot. If you are telling a story and elements in the plot are unlikely, you are failing your audience."

—Bernard Cornwell

Sharpe's Battle: Richard Sharpe and the Battle of Fuentes de Orono, May 1811 was also praised by a *Publishers Weekly* reviewer. "Cornwell's superb storytelling and skill at historical recreation are in top form as he masterfully presents carnage, clamor, sting and 'sublime joy' of battle." the critic noted. Colonial India is the setting for *Sharpe's Triumph: Richard Sharpe and the Battle of Assaye, September 1803*, as Cornwell recreates the country and time in "electric prose," according to *Booklist* contributor Brad Hooper. Hooper further commented that the novel is "eminently successful historical fiction." A contributor for *Publishers Weekly* noted Cornwell's "vivid details in descriptions of life in an army camp," and also observed that "best are the battle scenes, laid out clearly." Also set in India is *Sharpe's Fortress: Richard Sharpe and the Siege of Gawilghur, December 1803*, as junior officer Sharpe discovers treason in Her Majesty's forces, making for a "fast-paced historical adventure [that] features plenty of electrifying military action," according to *Booklist* reviewer Margaret Flanagan. Reviewing *Sharpe's Trafalgar: Richard Sharpe and the Battle of Trafalgar, 21 October 1805* in *Booklist,* Hooper noted that the "high standards" Cornwell set for himself at the outset of the series has not diminished "in the least." "The high-seas battle scenes are brilliantly written, and the love scenes . . . tenderly so. That author's fans will eat this one up," Hooper predicted. "As always," added Fred Gervat in *Library Journal,* "Cornwell satisfyingly delivers action, adventure, and a great gallery of villains and heroes, plus the usual beautiful lady." In the eighteenth installment of this bestselling series, *Sharpe's Prey,* Sharpe is in the middle of the 1807 British campaign to destroy the Danish navy anchored in Copenhagen before the French can take their ships and add them to the invasion threat against England. "The traditional military adventure yarn remains alive and well in the capable hands of Cornwell," wrote a reviewer for *Publishers Weekly.* "It's anyone guess how many more are still to come, but Cornwell fans will welcome each and every one."

From U.S. Civil War to King Arthur and Beyond

Cornwell has on occasion taken a break from historical fiction to pen adventure stories set in the present day, such as *Wildtrack, Killer's Wake,* and *Stormchild,* although most reviewers agree these novels are not as successful as his historical fiction. Additionally, he is the author of three historical novels under the pseudonym Susannah Kells: *Crowning Mercy, The Fallen Angels,* and *Coat of Arms.* In *Twentieth-Century Romance and Historical Writers,* Sadler wrote of the pseudonymous works: "Cornwell, as Kells, achieves a compelling vision of both the Civil War and French Revolutionary periods, his powerful and exciting narratives aided by strong characterization, and some very authentic-sounding dialogue. He also manages to convey, in an uncomfortably convincing manner, the almost routine brutality and squalor that are linked with the art and culture of the time, the grim spectacle of a public execution presented with the same visual force as the splendour of a court ball."

The first years of the twenty-first century have witnessed several new historical series by Cornwell, one set during the American Civil War, a second set during the time of England's King Arthur, and a third taking place during the Hundred Years' War. *Rebel, Copperhead, Battle Flag,* and *The Bloody Ground* re-create the grim battles of the U.S. Civil War

through the eyes of Nate Starbuck, a Northern-born son of abolitionist parents who takes up arms for the South, "captivated more by the challenge and peril of war than the righteousness of either side," as *Booklist* contributor Denise Perry Donavin observed. "Wonderful stuff," declared a *Kirkus Reviews* contributor in describing *Rebel.* "Starbuck is a worthy hero, smart enough to be interesting, callow enough to be real. Virginia is a great stage, teeming with Confederate and military politics, and the battle scenes . . . are presented with real mastery. They hurt." Another *Kirkus* reviewer commented: "Why is it that it takes an Englishman to write the most entertaining American military historical novels? Who knows. But it's hard to imagine a more intriguing protagonist than Nate Starbuck." The reviewer concluded that the "Starbuck Chronicles" are "always based on fact, always interesting, often exciting, always entertaining." Reviewing the second novel, *Copperhead,* a *Publishers Weekly* critic maintained that the novelist "surpasses" his achievement in the "Sharpe" books and dubbed the novel "a rollicking treat for Cornwell's many fans." The battle of Antietam—Bull Run—is at the center of the fourth book in the series, *The Bloody Ground.*

A New Take on an Old King

"The genius of Cornwell's narratives about Starbuck and Richard Sharpe," explained *Library Journal* contributor R. Kent Rasmussen, "lies in his ability to place protagonists in such ever deepening personal peril that readers cannot turn away." Cornwell himself had to turn away from the series for a time, when his attentions were drawn by his publisher back to the "Sharpe" novels as well as to a trilogy of books about King Arthur, which the author considers his favorite if not best work. Cornwell said in *Books* that he decided to write about King Arthur because he "wanted to take him out of that romantic mystical land of fable and place him in the very real world where he is most likely to have lived." "To survive at this time and obtain great power," Cornwell continued, "Arthur must have been a brilliant military commander. Previous Arthur novels have concentrated on him as a wise king or great lover, but I see him as a soldier and that's where, of course, my interest in him started."

The author's "Warlord Chronicles" have earned the same sort of favorable notices heaped upon other Cornwell offerings. A *Publishers Weekly* correspondent wrote of *The Winter King:* "Cornwell's Arthur is fierce, dedicated and complex, a man with many problems, most of his own making. . . . Cornwell knows his history—the battle scenes are particularly fine but not once does it get in the way of people of flesh and blood meeting on a darkened field of combat." *Booklist* critic Flanagan noted of this first book in the trilogy that "Cornwell interweaves elements of history, mysticism, and folklore, spinning a fantastic revision of the standard Arthurian legend." Thomas Curwin, reviewing the title in *People Weekly*, also had praise for this first volume in the series, commenting that in "this riveting retelling of the Arthurian legend" Cornwell "skillfully pared the story down to its basic ingredients." The critic concluded: "Without smoke and mirrors, the magic in *The Winter King* is conjured within the human heart, making it all the more wonderful and haunting."

In a review of *Enemy of God*, the second volume in the "Warlord Chronicles," a *Publishers Weekly* contributor declared that, "Writing with brio, Cornwell puts a fresh perspective on these oft-retold events. Realistically gory battles and doomed romantic exploits flavor the narrative, while the strong characterizations bring the men and women behind the legends to vivid life." In this novel Arthur's dream of a unified kingdom seems about to be realized until Lancelot seduces Queen Guinevere and shatters all hopes for peace. "This complex and superbly wrought narrative easily eclipses the more sanitized and tepid version of Arthur's exploits," noted *Booklist* contributor Flanagan. "Readers who have eagerly anticipated the continuation of the . . . [series] will not be disappointed."

Cornwell ends the "Warlord Chronicles" with *Excalibur,* a dramatization of the confrontation between Christianity and the religion of the Druids. There is nothing sweetly Camelot-like about Cornwell's Arthurian tales; this is "the nasty, brutal fifth-century Britain," noted Wilda Williams in *Library Journal*. Cornwell turns the tale into a military story, with Arthur routing the turncoat Lancelot and his Saxon friends. "The action is gripping and skillfully placed," noted a contributor in *Publishers Weekly,* "cadenced by passages in which the characters reveal themselves in conversation and thought, convincingly evoking the spirit of the time." In his interview with Richards, Cornwell voiced regret that the "Warlord Chronicles" came to an end. "I loved them. Best thing I've ever done. . . . And they were fun. They were just fun. I mean, you sat down to write and wrote all day and night. It was glorious."

Stonehenge, a stand-alone title by Cornwell, appeared in 2000. It is set some 4,000 years before, at the dawn of the Bronze Age in Britain, and deals with three brothers whose blood relationship does not stop them from being divided by greed and lust

for power. One brother is a warrior who kills his own father to become leader of the tribe; another is a ruthless sorcerer; and the youngest ultimately builds the temple of Stonehenge at the command of his sorcerer brothers. "This wild tale, rich with sorcery, pagan ritual, greed and intrigue, is Cornwell's most ambitious fiction yet," felt a reviewer for *Publishers Weekly*. Hooper, writing in *Booklist,* also thought Cornwell "rises to the occasion admirably," recreating a world about which so little is known. The result is, Hooper concluded, "total immersion in a place and time."

With *The Archer's Tale*—published in England as *Harlequin*—Cornwell began yet another series, this one set in the fourteenth century at the start of the Hundred Years' War. In the first novel in the series, it is Easter morning in 1343, and a marauding band of Normans, including a mysterious warrior named Harlequin, steal a sacred lance—supposedly the very one used by Saint George to slay the dragon—from a small village church in Hookton on the southern coast of England. Brave young Thomas is the only survivor of the assault, and he vows to avenge the murder of his fellow villagers and also re-capture the sacred lance, which the black-clad Harlequin stole. First, however, Thomas must make his way to France, which he does by joining the army of Kind Edward III as the king is about to invade the continent. He quickly gains a reputation as one of the most accurate of the king's archers, and what began as a simple search for revenge soon becomes a quest for the Holy Grail itself.

The Archer's Tale met with critical praise and eager anticipation for coming volumes. A *Kirkus* reviewer, noting that Cornwell "takes his peerless storytelling to the fourteenth century in the tale of Thomas of Hookton," hoped that a new multi-volume series was in the works. *Booklist* contributor Flanagan also praised the title, calling Cornwell "one of the undisputed masters of historical battle fiction" and maintaining that in *The Archer's Tale* he "spins an irresistible tale of honor and revenge." Flanagan cited the qualities that set Cornwell apart from his competitors as "meticulously developed story lines and razor-sharp characterizations." A contributor for *Publishers Weekly* joined other critics in lauding Cornwell as a "consummate pro when it comes to plying the tried-and-true combination of heroic characters; a fastmoving, action-packed plot; and enough twists and turns to keep the narrative from lapsing into formula." The same critic concluded that *The Archer's Tale* "marks the beginning of a promising new series that brings an intriguing period to life."

If you enjoy the works of Bernard Cornwell, you might want to check out the following books:

Dudley Pope, *Ramage,* 1973.
Rosemary Sutcliff, *Blood and Sand,* 1987.
Jeff Shaara, *Gods and Generals,* 1996.

Bringing intriguing historical periods to life remains Cornwell's bread and butter. While his success has allowed him to establish homes on Cape Cod and in Florida, it is all in a day's work, and Cornwell keeps strict office hours for his writing. "I simply try to tell as compelling a story as I possibly can," he told Missy Daniel in a *Publishers Weekly* profile. "I don't know if there is any moral. I'm not clever enough to point out morals in my tales. The most important thing you do is the plot. If you are telling a story and elements in the plot are unlikely, you are failing your audience."

■ Biographical and Critical Sources

BOOKS

Contemporary Popular Writers, St. James Press (Detroit, MI), 1997, pp. 97-98.
Twentieth-Century Romance and Historical Writers, third edition, St. James Press (Detroit, MI), 1994, pp. 152-53.

PERIODICALS

Booklist, December 15, 1981, p. 537; January 1, 1994, Denise Perry Donavin, review of *Copperhead,* p. 787; May 1, 1995, p. 1550; August, 1997, Margaret Flanagan, review of *Enemy of God,* p. 1876; June 1, 1998, p. 1722; June 1, 1999, Brad Hooper, review of *Sharpe's Triumph,* p. 1741; March 15, 2000, Brad Hooper, review of *Stonehenge,* p. 1292; April 1, 2000, pp. 1444, 1481; October 15, 2000, p. 472; November 15, 2000, Margaret Flanagan, review of *Sharpe's Fortress,* p. 609; March 1, 2001, p. 1295; March 15, 2001, Brad Hooper, review of *Sharpe's Trafalgar,* p. 1332; August 2001, Margaret Flanagan, review of *The Archer's Tale,* p. 2050; December 1, 2001, pp. 663-664.
Books, September-October, 1995, p. 10.
Economist, September 30, 2000, p. 89.

Kirkus Reviews, November 15, 1987, pp. 1592-93; June 15, 1989, p. 785; August 15, 1990, p. 1109; December 15, 1992, p. 1518; November 15, 1993, p. 1407; August 1, 2001, review of *The Archer's Tale,* p. 1046; September 1, 2001, p. 232; September 15, 2001, p. 129.
Library Journal, April 1, 1983, p. 756; May 15, 1996, p. 83; November 1, 1996, p. 122; February 15, 1997, James Dudley, review of *Sharpe's Revenge,* p. 175; April 1, 1997, R. Kent Rasmussen, review of *The Bloody Ground,* p. 144; July, 1997, p. 123; August, 1997, pp. 156-157; June 15, 1998, Wilda Williams, review of *Excalibur,* p. 104; May 15, 1998, p. 147; April 15, 2001, Fred Gervat, review of *Sharpe's Trafalgar,* p. 131; June 1, 2001, p. 248.
Los Angeles Times Book Review, September 10, 1989, p. 10.
Maclean's, June 18, 2001, p. 28.
New York Times Book Review, July 1, 1984, p. 21; March 20, 1988, p. 26; October 7, 1990, p. 39; October 8, 2000, p. 22.
People Weekly, June 10, 1996, Thomas Curwin, review of *The Winter King,* pp. 35-36; August 3, 1998, p. 39.
Publishers Weekly, February 27, 1981, p. 141; April 29, 1983, p. 45; January 13, 1984, review of *Sharpe's Enemy,* p. 62; April 27, 1990, Sybil Steinberg, review of *Sharpe's Waterloo,* p. 54; August 17, 1990, p. 50; August 16, 1991, p. 46; April 13, 1992, review of *Sharpe's Devil,* p. 42; January 25, 1993, review of *Rebel,* p. 80; November 29, 1993, review of *Copperhead,* p. 56; April 24, 1995, review of *Sharpe's Battle,* p. 61; March 11, 1996, review of *The Winter King,* p. 41; June 10, 1996, Missy Daniel, "Bernard Cornwell," pp. 67-68; April 21, 1997, p. 69; June 16, 1997, review of *Enemy of God,* p. 45; June 8, 1998, review of *Excalibur,* p. 52; July 19, 1999, review of *Sharpe's Triumph,* p. 184; March 27, 2000, review of *Stonehenge,* p. 48; October 9, 2000, p. 24; April 16, 2001, review of *Sharpe's Trafalgar,* p. 46; August 6, 2001, review of *The Archer's Tale,* p. 58; December 24, 2001, review of *Sharpe's Prey,* p. 43.
School Library Journal, June, 1999, p. 156.
Times Literary Supplement, August 28, 1981, p. 991; March 29, 1996, p. 24; October 15, 1999, p. 25.
Tribune Books (Chicago, IL), November 18, 1990, p. 7.
Washington Post, December 23, 2001, p. T13.

OTHER

Bernard Cornwell Web site, http://www.bernardcornwell.net/ (March 19, 2002).
Fireandwater.com, http://www.fireandwater.com/ (March 19, 2002), interview with Cornwell.
Januarymagazine.com, http://www.januarymagazine.com/ (March 19, 2002), Linda Richards, "Interview: Bernard Cornwell."*

—*Sketch by J. Sydney Jones*

Kate DiCamillo

Award, and Josette Frank Award from Bank Street College, all 2000, and Newbery Honor Book Award, 2001, all for *Because of Winn-Dixie*; finalist, National Book Award for Young People's Literature, 2001, for *The Tiger Rising*.

■ Personal

Born March 25, 1964, in Merion, PA; daughter of Adolph Louis (an orthodontist) and Betty Lee (a teacher; maiden name, Gouff) DiCamillo. *Education:* University of Florida, B.A., 1987.

■ Addresses

Home—2403 West 42nd St., No. 3, Minneapolis, MN 55410.

■ Career

Writer. The Bookman (a book distributor), Minneapolis, MN, former clerk in children's department.

■ Awards, Honors

McKnight artist fellowship for creative prose, 1998, 2001; Best Book designations from *Publishers Weekly* and *School Library Journal*, Parents' Choice Gold

■ Writings

Because of Winn-Dixie (juvenile novel), Candlewick Press (Cambridge, MA), 2000.
The Tiger Rising (young adult novel), Candlewick Press (Cambridge, MA), 2001.

Contributor of short fiction to periodicals, including *Jack and Jill, Alaska Quarterly Review, Greensboro Review, Nebraska Review,* and *Spider.*

■ Work in Progress

A collection of short stories for adults and a third novel for young readers.

■ Sidelights

"My name is India Opal Buloni, and last summer my daddy, the preacher, sent me to the store for a box of macaroni-and-cheese, some white rice, and two tomatoes and I came back with a dog." Thus begins Kate DiCamillo's 2001 Newbery Honor novel, *Because of Winn-Dixie*, the story of one momentous summer in the life of a ten-year-old Southern girl. "I wrote the story during the worst winter on record in Minnesota when I was missing Florida (where I grew up)," DiCamillo told Shannon Maughan on *Kidsreads.com*. "Also, my apartment building does not allow dogs. But imaginary dogs aren't against the rules. So I made one up to keep me . . . company."

DiCamillo hit the ground running with her debut title, winning awards and reaching best-seller lists.

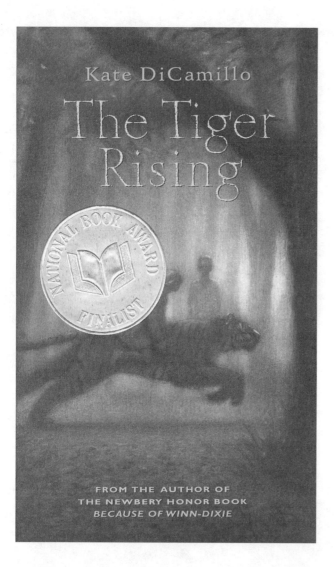

When Rob Horton finds a live, caged tiger that has been seemingly abandoned in the Florida woods, his efforts to care for the beast and deal with a challenging new friendship change his life in Kate DiCamillo's 2001 YA novel.

Her second novel, *The Tiger Rising*, was also well received and was a finalist for the National Book Award in 2001. With two successes under her belt, DiCamillo left her job as a sales clerk in a children's bookshop and determined to devote herself full time to her writing. "I just want to tell more stories," the author told Elizabeth Kennedy on the online *Children's Books*.

A Florida Upbringing

Born near Philadelphia, Pennsylvania in 1964, DiCamillo is the daughter of an orthodontist father and a mother who was a schoolteacher. As the author once noted, "I was a sickly child. My body happily played host to all of the usual childhood maladies—mumps and measles, chickenpox twice, and ear infections—plus a few exotic extras: inexplicable skin diseases, chronic pinkeye, and, most dreaded of all, pneumonia, recurring every winter for the first five years of my life. I mention this because, at the time, it seemed like such a senseless and unfair kind of thing to me, to be sick so often, to miss so much school, to be inside scratching or sneezing or coughing when everybody else was outside playing. Now, looking back, I can see all that illness for what it was: a gift that shaped me and made me what I am. I was alone a lot. I learned to rely on my imagination for entertainment. Because I was always on the lookout for the next needle, the next tongue depressor, I learned to watch and listen and gauge the behavior of those around me. I became an imaginative observer."

The recurring pneumonia in part forced her family—without her father—to move to the warmer climate in central Florida when DiCamillo was five, in hopes that this change would help her physical condition. Her first memories of the South were pleasantly aural: "People talked more slowly and said words I had never heard before," DiCamillo noted on the *Candlewick Press Web site*, "like 'ain't' and 'y'all' and 'ma'am.' The town was small, and everybody knew everybody else. Even if they didn't, they acted like they did. It was all so different from what I had known before, and I fell swiftly and madly in love." DiCamillo also once observed of her childhood in Florida: "There I absorbed the speech patterns and cadences and nuances of life in a small southern town. I did not know it at the time, but Florida (and pneumonia) gave me a great gift: a voice in which to tell my stories."

Stories, indeed, filled DiCamillo's early childhood. Some early favorite titles she read included *The Twenty-one Balloons, The Secret Garden, The Yearling,* and *Ribsey*. But stories of a more personal sort also inform her memories. "When I look back on childhood," DiCamillo once commented, "I remember one moment with great clarity. I was three years old and in the hospital with pneumonia, and my father came to visit me. He arrived in a black overcoat that smelled of the cold outdoors, and he brought me a gift. It was a little, red net bag. Inside it there was a wooden village: wooden church, house, chicken, tree, farmer. It was as if he had flung the net bag out into the bright world and captured the essential elements and shrunk them down and brought them to me. He opened the bag and said, 'Hold out your hands.' I held out my hands. 'No,' he said, 'like this. Like you are going to drink from them.' I did as he said, and he poured the wooden figures, piece by piece, into my waiting hands. Then he told me a story about the chicken and the farmer and the house and the church. Something opened up inside me. There was the weight of the wooden figures in my hands, the smell of my father's overcoat, the whole great world hiding, waiting in the purple dusk outside my hospital room. And there was the story—the story. I think of that moment often. It was another gift of my illness. When I write, I sometimes stop and cup my hands, as if I am drinking water. I try, I want desperately to capture the world, to hold it for a moment in my hands."

DiCamillo attended the University of Florida in Gainesville, where she majored in English and fancied herself a budding writer. There she took a writing class that confirmed her ambition. Given the assignment to describe something in 500 words, DiCamillo wrote about a street musician she saw outside of a grocery store called the Winn-Dixie. When her paper was read in class, the teacher pointed out what the important part of the writing was. As DiCamillo related in her acceptance speech for the 2000 Josette Frank Award, reproduced on the *Bank Street College* Web site, she thought at that moment, "I was a genius! I was born to be a writer!" The teacher went on, however, to note what was special about the paper: "'It's not the writing. . . . There's nothing extraordinary about that.' Not the writing? I sunk lower in my desk." But, DiCamillo recalled, then the teacher pronounced, "'The person who wrote this took the time to actually see the person she was describing. That's what writing is all about. Seeing. It is the sacred duty of the writer to pay attention. To see the world.'" It was a lesson DiCamillo took with her after graduating.

Because of Winn-Dixie

After college DiCamillo moved north, eventually settling in Minneapolis, Minnesota, where she worked at becoming a writer, creating short stories and picture books, and had some success placing stories in literary reviews and journals. In 1998 she was the recipient of a McKnight artist fellowship for writers that helped finance her writing. Meanwhile she supported herself with a day job at a Minneapolis book distributor, The Bookman, where she worked on the children's floor. She worked on her writing daily, producing two pages of manuscript without punctuation or capitalization, just to get the flow. As she told Maughan on *Kidsreads.com*, "My goal is two pages a day, five days a week. I like that Dorothy Parker quote: 'I hate writing, I love having written.' I never want to write, but I'm always glad I have done it."

It was, quite simply, homesickness for Florida that inspired her first juvenile novel, *Because of Winn-Dixie*. "I was missing the sound of Southern people talking," the author noted on the *Candlewick Press Web site*. "And I was missing having a dog." Growing up, DiCamillo had a standard poodle named Minette, which she would dress up in a green tutu, and in college she rescued a dog from the pound. "One night before I went to sleep," DiCamillo explained on her publisher's Web site, "I heard this little girl's voice with a Southern accent say, 'I have a dog named Winn-Dixie.' I just started writing down what India Opal Buloni was telling me." DiCamillo did not work on pure inspiration, however, but studied other middle-grade novels for length. She went through about half of a first draft, revised several times, and then ploughed through the rest of the story.

With a finished manuscript in hand, the next question was how to get it published. Using a contact with Candlewick Press through her work, she got her manuscript—by a long and serendipitous route—onto the desk of Carol LeReau, who saw real promise in the first novel. "She is an incredible editor," DiCamillo told Jennifer M. Brown in a *Publishers Weekly* profile. "It's so amazing to have someone take a chance on you. She has been my shield and armor."

Because of Winn-Dixie appeared in 2000. Winn-Dixie is a big, ugly, and blithely happy dog, and because of his presence in her life, ten-year-old Opal learns elemental truths about her long-gone mother, makes friends in her new hometown, and begins to find her place in the world. She also begin the long and difficult process of letting go of sadness and resentment caused by her mother's abandonment of her and her preacher father seven years earlier. DiCamillo was able to purge some of her own sense of loss with this book, for when she was a young child her own father also left. Opal finds the stray dog one day at the local Winn-Dixie store and when she finally convinces her father to let him keep the mutt, her life takes a decided turn for the better. Newly arrived in the town of Naomi, Florida, the family lives at the Friendly Corners Trailer Park while Opal's dad preaches at the Open Arms Baptist Church. Her father is reluctant to talk of Opal's mother or the reasons for her departure. Both miss the woman more than they can describe. The arrival of Winn-Dixie allows Opal to meet some of the eccentric characters of Naomi, such as librarian Fanny Block, who once fought off a bear in the woods with a copy of *War and Peace;* the ex-con pet-store clerk who plays music for the animals in the store; and the local "witch," Gloria Dump, a woman with sight impairment who sees more with her heart than her eyes. While Opal brings these people together, partly through the intervention of the stray dog, Opal's father also opens up, sharing memories of her departed mother.

Because of Winn-Dixie met with almost universal praise from reviewers. "Scenes of Winn-Dixie raising a ruckus in the church (converted from a grocery store) or racing through their trailer park home in terror of a thunderstorm deftly combine tension and humor," wrote a reviewer for *Publishers Weekly* who concluded "This bittersweet tale of contemporary life in a small Southern town will hold readers rapt." *Booklist*'s Gillian Engberg felt that Opal's "sensitive, believable voice" creates a story "successful in detailing the appealing cast of characters," and maintained that readers "will connect with [Opal's] love for her pet and her open-minded, free-spirited efforts to make friends and build a community." "This well-crafted, realistic, and heartwarming story will be read and reread as a new favorite deserving a long-term place on library shelves," wrote *School Library Journal* contributor Helen Foster James, while a *Horn Book* reviewer noted: "All in all, this is a gentle book about good people coming together to combat loneliness and heartache." Winner of several awards, including the prestigious Newbery Honor, *Remembering Winn-Dixie* got DiCamillo's career off to a rousing start.

The Tiger Rising

DiCamillo followed her fiction debut with a young adult novel that earned as much critical notice as her first book, even becoming a National Book Award finalist. *The Tiger Rising* tells of another youngster with a missing parent. "The story began with the appearance of a single character," DiCamillo explained on her publisher's Web site. "Rob Horton showed up on a short story I wrote and then hung around the house driving me crazy. I fi-

nally asked him what he wanted, and he told me he knew where there was a tiger." Rob, like Opal, and like the author herself, suffers from a missing parent, and the healing power of friendship helps to get him through.

Six months before the book begins, Rob has lost his mother to cancer. His father uproots them from their Jacksonville, Florida home to try for a new start in Lister, Florida. Rob, shut down emotionally, goes through the motions of living, ignoring a strange rash on his legs that a kindly chambermaid tells him is the result of his sadness. Residing at the Kentucky Star Motel, where his father is employed, Rob feels lost and alone. School is not much better; there he faces the usual bullying reserved for new kids. One day Rob discovers a caged tiger in the woods near the motel and finds out that it was given to the owner of the hotel—his father's employer—to pay off a debt. He is soon given responsibility for feeding the creature and feels a close affinity to the tiger. The same day that he discovers the tiger he meets another newcomer to town, Sistine Bailey, on the school bus. She is also friendless and picked on at school, and full of anger that her parents are separating, hoping that her father will come one day and rescue her. The two begin to form a prickly friendship and soon they focus this relationship on the tiger. Rob knows that he has the power to set the animal free—to free his own trapped emotions, in fact. When they do set the animal free, Rob's father is forced to kill it, an act that finally brings son and father closer together.

More somber in tone than DiCamillo's first novel, *The Tiger Rising*, a mixed critical response. Some reviewers complained of the novel's overt symbolism; a *Horn Book* contributor, for example, noted that although the novel "features a well-realized setting and an almost palpable aura of sadness," the "heavy-handed symbolism and sentimentality overwhelm the book's limited characterization and quiet, almost remote, omniscient voice." Emily Herman, reviewing the audio version of the book, also complained of "heavy-handed symbolism [which] leads to an inconclusive climax." For Herman, the tiger in the novel "carries more symbolic weight than the story can plausibly sustain." However, other critics looked beyond the use of symbolism and praised DiCamillo. GraceAnne A. DeCandido, writing in *Booklist,* noted that the author "deftly" blends the suspense and anxiety of getting close to another person after being hurt. "DiCamillo's gorgeous language wastes not a single word," the critic added: "spare and taut her sentences spin out, with the Florida mist rising off them, and unspoken words finally said aloud." Kit Vaughan, writing in

School Library Journal, called *The Tiger Rising* a "multifaceted story with characters who will tug at readers' hearts." Vaughan further remarked that the work is "lush with haunting characters and spare descriptions, conjuring up vivid images. It deals with the tough issues of death, grieving, and the great accompanying sadness, and has enough layers to embrace any reader." And a reviewer for *Publishers Weekly* noted that while this second novel is not as humorous as the first, "it is just as carefully structured, and . . . [DiCamillo's] ear is just as finely tuned to her characters." Concluding the review, the same contributor noted that DiCamillo "demonstrates her versatility by treating themes similar to those of her first novel with a completely different approach. Readers will eagerly anticipate her next work."

If you enjoy the works of Kate DiCamillo, you might want to check out the following books:

Joan Bauer, *Rules of the Road,* 1998.
Sarah Dessen, *Keeping the Moon,* 1999.
Christopher Paul Curtis, *Bud, Not Buddy,* 1999.

Busy at work on a collection of short stories for adults and another young adult novel, DiCamillo continues to mine a rich vein of stories in the world of the commonplace. "What stories are hiding behind the faces of the people that you walk past everyday?" she asked during her Josette Frank Award acceptance speech. "What love? What hopes? What despairs? What I discovered is that every time you look at the world and the people in it closely, lovingly, imaginatively, it changes you. The world, under the microscope of your attention, opens up like a beautiful, strange flower and gives itself back to you in ways you could never imagine."

■ Biographical and Critical Sources

PERIODICALS

Book, May, 2001, p. 80.
Booklist, May 1, 2000, Gillian Engberg, review of *Because of Winn-Dixie,* p. 1665; June 1, 2001, GraceAnne A. DeCandido, review of *The Tiger Rising,* p. 1882; October 15, 2001, p. 428.
Horn Book, July-August, 2000, review of *Because of Winn-Dixie,* p. 455; May-June, 2001, review of *The Tiger Rising,* p. 321.
Plays, May, 2001, p. 69.
Publishers Weekly, February 21, 2000, review of *Because of Winn-Dixie,* p. 88; June 26, 2000, Jennifer M. Brown, "Kate DiCamillo," p. 30; January 15, 2001, review of *The Tiger Rising,* p. 77; April 9, 2001, p. 28; July 9, 2001, p. 22.
School Library Journal, June, 2000, Helen Foster, review of *Because of Winn-Dixie,* p. 143; December, 2000, p. 53; March, 2001, Kit Vaughan, review of *The Tiger Rising,* p. 246; June, 2001, p. 74; August, 2001, Emily Herman, review of *The Tiger Rising* (audio version), p. 90.
Southern Living, August, 2001, p. 48.

OTHER

Bank Street College Web site, http://bnkst.edu/ (February 26, 2002), Kate DiCamillo, "2001 Award Ceremony Acceptance Speeches."
Candlewick Press Web site, http://www.candlewick.com/ (February 26, 2002), "Kate DiCamillo."
Children's Books, http://childrensbooks.about.com/ (February 26, 2002), Elizabeth Kennedy, "2001 Newbery Honor Book Author Kate DiCamillo."
Children's Literature: Meet Authors & Illustrators, http://www.childrenslit.com/ (February 26, 2002).
Kidsreads.com, http://www.kidsreads.com/ (February 26, 2002), Shannon Maughan, "Kate DiCamillo."*

—Sketch by J. Sydney Jones

Marcel Duchamp

■ Personal

Born July 28, 1887, in Blainville, France; died October 2 (some sources say October 1), 1968, in Neuilly, France; immigrated to United States, 1915, naturalized citizen, 1955; son of Eugene (a notary) and Lucie (Nicolle) Duchamp; married Lydie Sarazin-Levassor, 1927 (divorced, 1928); married Alexina Sattler, 1954; children: (second marriage) Paul, Jacqueline, Peter. *Education:* Attended Académie Julian, 1904-05.

■ Career

Artist, writer, consultant, and professional chess player. Worked for printer/engraver in Rouen, France, 1905; cartoonist for *Le Courier français* and *Le Rire*, Paris, France, 1905-10; Bibliotheque Sainte-Genevieve, Paris, librarian, 1913; French Institute of New York, librarian, 1915; co-founder, Society of Independent Artists, New York, NY, 1916; organized, with Katherine S. Dreier and Man Ray, Societé Anonyme (museum), New York, NY, 1920. Guest director, Florine Stettheimer exhibition at Museum of Modern Art, New York, 1946; jury member, Bel Ami International Competition, 1946; consultant to art dealers and collectors. *Exhibitions:* Salon d'Automne, Paris, 1910; Salon des Independents, Paris, 1911; and New York Armory Show, New York, NY, 1913. Work represented in permanent collections, including Museum of Modern Art; Foundation of Contemporary Performance Arts, New York, NY; Guggenheim Museum; Museum of the City of New York; Philadelphia Museum of Art; Seattle Art Museum; Musées de Rouen; Musée National d'Art Moderne, Paris, France; Peggy Guggenheim Foundation, Venice, Italy; National Gallery of Canada; Australian National Gallery; and Staatsgalerie, Stuttgart, Germany. Retrospective exhibits include Pasadena Art Museum, 1963, Gimple fils Ltd., 1964, Tate Gallery, 1966, Galleria Solaria, 1967, Musée National d'Art Moderne, 1967, Wallraf-Richartz-Museum, 1968, Philadelphia Museum of Art, 1966, 1973, 1998, Palazzo Grassi, Venice, 1993, and Pompidou Center, Paris, 2000.

Professional chess player, beginning 1923; member and delegate, Committee of French Chess Federation, Paris, 1931-37; French team captain, First International Chess by Correspondence Olympiad, 1935. Captain's secretary, French Mission for the War, New York, NY.

■ Member

National Institute of Arts and Letters.

■ Awards, Honors

Named Chess Champion by Haute Normandie (France), 1924; winner of Paris Chess Tournament, 1932.

■ Writings

(With V. Halberstadt) *L'opposition et les cases conjugées sont reconciliées* (text on chess), 1932.

Rrose Selavy (collection of puns), 1935.

From the Green Box, translated by George Heard Hamilton, Readymade Press (New Haven, CT), 1957.

Marchand du sel: écrits de Marcel Duchamp, edited by Michel Sanouillet, Le Terrain vague, 1958, published as *The Salt Seller: The Writings of Marcel Duchamp*, edited by Sanouillet and Elmer Peterson, Oxford University Press (New York, NY), 1975.

The Bride Stripped Bare by Her Bachelors, Even, translated from the French by Richard Hamilton and George Heard Hamilton, G. Wittenborn (New York, NY), 1960, 3rd edition, J. Rietman, 1976.

Marcel Duchamp: Schilderijen, tekenigen, ready-mades, documenten (exhibition catalog), Stedelijk van Abbemuseum Eindhoven, 1965.

L'Infinitif, Cordier & Ekstrom (New York, NY), 1966.

Notes and Projects for the Large Glass, edited by Schwarz, Abrams (New York, NY), 1969.

Marcel Duchamp: Grafica e ready-made (exhibition catalog), Galleria civica d'arte moderna, 1971.

Marcel Duchamp Drawings, Etchings for the Large Glass, and Ready-Mades (exhibition catalog), Israel Museum, 1972.

Marcel Duchamp Ready-Made, Regenbogen (Germany), 1973.

(With Elmer Peterson) *Duchamp du signe: Ecrits*, Flammarion (Paris, France), 1975.

Notes, edited by Paul Matisse, Centre Georges Pompidou (Paris, France), 1980.

(With Pierre Cabanne), *Dialogues with Marcel Duchamp*, Da Capo Press (New York, NY), 1988.

The Writings of Marcel Duchamp, edited by Michel Sanouillet, Da Capo Press (New York, NY), 1989.

Duchamp: Great Masters, translated by Alberto Curotto, edited by José Maria Faerna, Abradale Press (New York, NY), 1996.

Contributor to books, including *Marcel Duchamp*, translated by George Heard Hamilton, Grove (New York, NY), 1959; *The Large Glass and Related Works*, Schwarz Gallery, 1967; and *Dadas on Art*, Lucy R. Lippard, editor, Prentice-Hall (Paramus, NJ), 1971. Contributor of articles and poems to journals, including *Arts and Decoration, Manuscripts, Medium, Art News, Arts and Artists, Aspen Magazine, 691, Le Surrealisme au service de la revolution*, and *Plastique*. Editor of *The Blind Man* and *Rong-Wrong* (magazines), 1917; coeditor of surrealist publication *Minotaure*, 1933; founder and editorial adviser, with André Breton and Max Ernst, of *VVV* (magazine), 1940; publisher, with Man Ray, of *New York Dada*.

■ Sidelights

Maverick, innovator, desecrator. These terms and more have been used to describe French artist Marcel Duchamp, a man whose ideas on what does and what does not constitute art have been ultimately more influential than his artwork. Creator of *Nude Descending a Staircase*—perhaps the most famous of all cubist paintings—and inventor of ready-made art, Duchamp was known throughout his life as a resolute challenger of artistic convention. He scrawled a moustache and goatee on a postcard reproduction of the Mona Lisa and called it art; an ordinary ceramic urinal was submitted to a major art exhibition under the title "Fountain"—then sold in the year 2000 for $1.76 million. These sorts of antics foreshadowed the work of later artists, including Andy Warhol, but for Duchamp they were a statement; refusing to accept the standards of the traditional art community, he eschewed line and color for more theoretical and even humorous concerns. As Francis M. Naumann noted of Duchamp on the online *Grove Art*, "The art and ideas of Duchamp, perhaps more than those of any other 20th-century artist, have served to exemplify the range of possibilities inherent in a more conceptual approach to the art-making process. Not only is his work of historical importance—from his early experiments with Cubism to his association with Dada and Surrealism—but his conception of the ready-made decisively altered our understanding of what constitutes an object of art."

"Contradiction formed an important part of the ideological and artistic universe that Duchamp had created for himself," observed Alexander Keneas in the *New York Times*. "Finding scientific laws to be too arbitrary, he formulated his own. 'Why,' he asked, 'must we worship principles which in 50 or 100 years will no longer apply?'" Described as iconoclastic, anarchistic, and nihilistic by his critics and his devotees alike, Duchamp is considered a major influence on the course of modern art. Still, he managed to resist alignment with any one artistic style. In the *New York Times* John Canaday stated: "There is hardly an experimental art movement of [the mid-twentieth century] . . . that cannot trace

Marcel Duchamp's 1911 painting "Apropos of Little Sister" shows the influences of Parisian artists such as Fernand Léger and the reason why the twenty-four-year-old Duchamp was characterized as a "timid cubist."

down through the branches of its family tree to find Marcel Duchamp as its generative patriarch." Still, after only seventeen years of creating art, Duchamp turned his back on painting, spending the second half of his life playing chess. Quitting art was as much of a statement for Duchamp as his artwork itself had been. His was an uncompromising life.

Portrait of the Artist

Born in 1887 in northern France, Duchamp came from a middle-class family, but also a family of artists, although his father was a notary and mayor of Blainville, Normandy. Duchamp's maternal grandfather was a painter of still-lifes and also an engraver; both his older brothers made notable careers as cubists; and his younger sister was a painter and also co-founder of Tabu, a spin-off from the dada group. When he was fifteen, Duchamp painted in the Impressionistic style, as witnessed by a painting from 1902, "Church at Blainville," inspired by reproductions he had seen of the works of Claude

Monet. Completing his schooling in Rouen in 1904, at the age of seventeen, Duchamp left Normandy to join his two brothers, internationally known painter Jacques Villon and acclaimed cubist sculptor Raymond Duchamp-Villon, in Paris. Largely self-taught, Duchamp enrolled at the Académie Julian to study art but left after the first year, enjoying billiards more than his classes. He made a meager living in these years, through contacts from his brothers, selling cartoons for publication in Parisian magazines, including *Le Rire* and *Le Courier français.* Some of these humorous sketches were displayed in the initial Salon des Artistes Humoristes in 1907.

Duchamp's first artistic works, according to *Atlantic* writer Kenneth Baker, were "facile but undistinguished Post-impressionist" paintings. "The Artist's Father," for example, which Duchamp exhibited in the 1910 Salon d'Automne, strongly reflects the influence of Paul Cézanne. Another work from this same time, "Chess Game," shows his brothers and their wives relaxing in the garden of their home in a Paris suburb. The painting does not only incorporate Cezanne's brush-stroke technique, but also displays the vibrant colors of the Fauvist painters. It was at his brothers' home that Duchamp met many of the writers and artists of the day, including critic Guillaume Apollinaire and painter Fernand Léger.

Duchamp as Cubist

Duchamp soon began experimenting with various avant-garde styles and by 1911 "had begun to absorb the impact of Cubism," noted Baker. Writing in the *Nation,* Lawrence Alloway described Duchamp as "a timid Cubist," whose style was "scenic and associative—with genre references, which clearly affiliate[d] him with Cubism's conservatives, not with Picasso and Braque." Baker further remarked that "instead of merely learning the Cubist formula, Duchamp became interested in machine forms and the representation of movement in the static terms of painting." This interest was evident in his 1911 painting "Nude Descending a Staircase," which employed cubism's geometry and subtle tones. Its depiction of spatial movement, achieved with the simultaneous representation of overlapping forms, suggests the influence of Italian futurism and is therefore considered contradictory to the cubist aesthetic.

Exhibited in the 1911 Salon des Independents, "Nude Descending a Staircase" caused such a fury that Duchamp's brothers asked him to withdraw from the show. In 1913 a second version of the painting was the target of ridicule at the New York

Armory show; guards were needed to restrain outraged crowds from damaging the painting, which critics described as "an explosion in a shingle factory" and "a collection of saddlebags." As Keneas explained: "It was neither the nude nor the staircase, apparently, that had provoked them, but the title, painted onto the canvas, which seemed to have little to do with either—and the idea of a nude descending instead of traditionally reclining or standing." Keneas claimed that, for many, the painting represented "the insanity to which modern art had progressed." For Duchamp, however, "Nude Descending a Staircase" was simply "an organiza-

tion of kinetic elements, an expression of time and space through the abstract which is presentation of motion." He was delighted to receive $240 for the painting, which is now part of the permanent collection of the Philadelphia Museum of Art and is valued in the millions.

Writing in *Gardner's Art through the Ages,* Richard G. Tansey and Fred S. Kleiner noted the linkage of "Nude" with the futurists, though Duchamp himself said he had not heard of the futurists when creating the painting. Tansey and Kleiner felt that with this painting Duchamp "sets the dislocated planes of a single figure into a time continuum, suggesting the effect of a primitive motion picture technique. The stuttering rhythm of the bundled, monochromatic planes resembles more the effect produced by a stroboscope." The sway of motion in the painting is represented by arcs made of single lines and of dots in an attempt to portray and analyze successive stages of movement at intervals as the stylized nude moves down the stairs from left to right.

Duchamp thoroughly enjoyed the uproar caused by his painting. "I found it very pleasant," he recalled years later, "because after all my aim was not to please the general public. The scandal was exactly in my program, you might say." Writing in the *New Yorker,* Harold Rosenberg commented on the impact of "Nude Descending a Staircase": "To a greater extent than that of any of his contemporaries, Duchamp's career . . . took place on the stage of public opinion," following the "scandal-success" of the Armory Show.

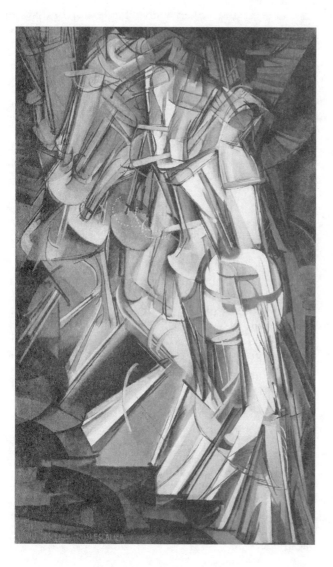

Duchamp's "Nude Descending a Staircase (Number 2)" was exhibited in this second version at 1913's New York Armory show in the hope that it would not cause the same furor as that created by the initial version in Paris two years before.

Artistic Maverick

Duchamp's work continued to attract both praise and criticism, and by late 1913 he was searching for greater freedom of artistic expression than that allowed by either cubism or futurism. He had at this time developed a close friendship with painter Francis Picabia, whom Duchamp felt "had more intelligence than most of our contemporaries." In addition, Keneas remarked, the two "shared each other's sense of iconoclastic wit and absurd humor." Together with writer Apollinaire they were formulating a new concept of art that prefigured the Dada movement; it mocked accepted artistic norms and sought to de-emphasize the artist's hand by using chance and mechanical methods. The nascent movement was partly influenced by the political situation in France. As Canaday suggested, it was perhaps "the insane spectacle of World War I" that ultimately turned Duchamp "away from the rational processes of cubism . . . and led him to the anarchic movement of Dada."

The subject matter of Duchamp's painting at this time became increasingly whimsical and often included strange and purposeless machines, such as the one depicted in "Chocolate Grinder." In an interview with James Johnson Sweeney, reprinted in *Dadas on Art,* Duchamp stated his artistic intention: "I wanted to get away from the physical aspect of painting. . . . I wanted to put painting once again at the service of the mind. And my painting was, of course, at once regarded as 'intellectual literary' painting. It was true I was endeavoring to establish myself as far as possible from 'pleasing' and 'attractive' physical paintings."

For a time he continued to produce drawings and paintings, some of which contain sexual themes with mechanistic bodies. "King and Queen Surrounded by Swift Nudes," which was inspired by pieces and the movements on a chess board, "Virgin," depicting a virgin and bride, "Passage from Virgin to Bride," and "The Bride Stripped Bare by the Bachelors," a drawing later adapted for one of Duchamp's most famous works, all come from this period. "Three Standard Stoppages," a construction of three wooden slats with threads hanging from them, marks Duchamp's move away from traditional art methods of drawing and painting.

Ready-Mades

Duchamp next developed the concept of ready-made art: anything is art if the artist says it is. Thus, commonplace objects could be transformed into art by random selection of the artist. "When he 'chose' this or that object, a coal-shovel for example, it was lifted from the limbo of unregarded objects into the living world of works of art: looking at it made it art," wrote Hans Richter in *Dada: Art and Anti-Art.* Richter viewed the ready-made as "the logical consequence of Duchamp's rejection of art and of his suspicion that life was without a meaning." In the same book Duchamp remarked: "A point that I want very much to establish is that the choice of these 'ready-mades' was never dictated by aesthetic delectation. The choice was based on a reaction of *visual indifference* with a total absence of good or bad taste . . . in fact a complete anaesthesia." His first ready-made appeared in 1913, when "I had the happy idea to fasten a bicycle wheel to a kitchen stool and watch it turn." Thus his first piece of ready-made art bears the title "Bicycle Wheel."

New Yorker art critic Calvin Tomkins commented that with such ideas as ready-made art, Duchamp "quietly undermined the whole notion of serious art and its humorless hierarchies," adding that "Duchamp's humor was subtle and blasphemous." Calling Duchamp "one of the most intelligent artists who ever lived," the critic emphasized that Duchamp's use of chance was not "as a substitute for skill; he was using it as a means of getting away from accepted taste—including his own. He was pursuing . . . the sort of anonymity in which the work itself creates the work."

"The Bride Stripped Bare by Her Bachelors, Even"

Coming to New York City in 1915, Duchamp was preceded by the celebrity of the Armory Show. His wit, charm, and elegance assured him a central position in New York's social and avant-garde artistic circles. While in New York, Duchamp exhibited ready-mades, such as a hardware-store snow shovel titled "In Advance of the Broken Arm." He also continued work on a three-dimensional piece on transparent glass, which he titled "The Bride Stripped Bare by Her Bachelors, Even" or "The Large Glass." Described variously by critics as a masterwork and an insulting hoax, "The Bride . . . " remained unfinished, despite the fact that Duchamp worked on it sporadically until 1923, when it was, according to Baker, "abandoned in a state of 'definitive incompletion.'" Baker noted that, although the work is incomplete, "it continues to be the focus of many dubious interpretations."

Called by Naumann the artist's "most complex and intricate work," the early stages of "The Bride . . . " had been completed on paper and canvas. As Naumann described it, "Mechanomorphic imagery, themes of sexual opposition, references to geometry and physics and a reliance on chance operations and existing objects were all factors in its conception and design." More than nine feet high and constructed of two glass panels, it shows the bride connected by wires to nine uniformed lovers or suitors. Duchamp liked to say that the piece was inspired by a game he had seen at a country fair; others say it is a word play on his own name. Employing cut metal in addition to glass, "The Bride . . . " was a perfect product of its time, combining both dada and surrealist aesthetics.

For years Duchamp collected scraps of paper with jotted notes and sketches regarding "The Bride . . . " and kept them in a large green box "that itself achieved a sort of mythic status in the history of modern art," according to Baker. The contents of the box were later compiled and published in Duchamp's books *From the Green Box, Salt Seller,* and *L'infinitif.* In *Dadas on Art,* editor Lucy R. Lippard called "The Bride . . . " "a pessimistic and ultimately

Completed in 1927, Duchamp's "Door, 11 rue Larrey" reflects the author's interest in perspective as well as his continued promotion of "ready-mades": the transformation of mundane objects into art by shifting their physical context.

nonerotic view of the act of love reduced to a function of entirely detached machines." In Lippard's opinion, *From the Green Box* "constitutes Duchamp's real esthetic legacy": "It shares with [James] Joyce's *Ulysses* a multilateral network of images and ideas, within and without the object resulting from it. Ostensibly about the making of "The Large Glass," *The Green Box* is in fact an admission of the "Glass's" failure to incarnate its own implications. Duchamp himself intended the "Glass" merely to be a 'succinct illustration of all the ideas in the *Green Box*, which would then be a sort of catalogue of those

ideas. In other words, the "Glass" is not to be looked at for itself but only as a function of the catalogue I never made.'"

Rosenberg found similarities between "The Bride . . . " and Rube Goldberg's later machine-composition "The Only Humane Way to Catch a Mouse." "The Bride . . ." he observed, "translates erotic love into a hookup of fanciful mechanical and chemical operations. It is a variant on slapstick comedy, in which human beings act as if their feelings and movements were controlled by wheels, pulleys, and gases."

From Ready-Mades to Dada and Beyond

Duchamp stirred public controversy again in 1917 when he submitted a ready-made porcelain urinal—turned upside down and signed R. Mutt—for exhibition by the Society of Independent Artists, of which he had been a founding member. In Rosenberg's estimation, the act was significant because "Duchamp's denigration of art, his equalizing it with urinals . . . was a matter of principle; he was determined that art should not be overestimated and that the 'art habit' should not produce the reactions of blank solemnity that had once been associated with religion." When the society refused Duchamp's urinal, thereby reversing its policy to accept all entries accompanied by a six-dollar fee, he resigned his membership in protest. Interpreted by the art world as an anti-aesthetic statement, Duchamp's gesture firmly established him as a leader of the international dada movement.

Dada, which began in Zurich, Switzerland during World War I, attacked traditional standards of aesthetics and behavior and stressed both absurdity and chance. By 1919 the movement had reached full bloom in Paris and, as Keneas pointed out, Duchamp became "a hero of the movement . . . without ever taking part in the organized Dada activities." His detachment "seemed only to enhance his prestige." Though he participated only peripherally in Dada, Duchamp sympathized with its "metaphysical attitude," its literary approach, and its basis in nihilism, he told Sweeney. In addition, "Dada was very serviceable as a purgative. And I think I was thoroughly conscious of this at the time and of a desire to effect a purgation in myself."

Artist as Chess Player

After 1918 Duchamp gave up painting completely but continued to produce a variety of collages, sketches, and machine-constructions, much of which he signed Rrose Selavy—the name of the female alter-ego he had created for himself. In 1920 he joined artists Katerine Dreier and Man Ray in founding Societé Anonyme, in New York City, the world's first museum devoted entirely to modern art. Also in that year, Duchamp exhibited his "Mona Lisa," a ready-made aided with mustache and goatee, which he called "L.H.O.O.Q."; roughly translated, the initials stand for "she is hot in the pants."

Three years later, at the age of thirty-six, Duchamp formally retired as an artist and thereby, in the words of Keneas, "carried the vaudeville of esthetic nihilism to its logical conclusion." Explaining his decision, Duchamp expressed regret over what he saw as the commercialization of art for acceptance by the middle class and added: "the whole thing no longer interested me." Further, he told A. L. Chanin in the *New York Times Magazine:* "All good painters have only about five masterpieces to their name. . . . If I've done five good things, it's enough." According to Baker, Duchamp's early retirement made him "the first modern visual artist to make giving up art an important episode in his career." Though many viewed Duchamp's exit as an admirable act, consistent with his philosophy of life and art, "some critics regarded the withdrawal of the Grand Dada as an escape from his own inadequacies as an artist," noted Keneas.

Following retirement Duchamp devoted much of his time to chess playing, an avid interest since his childhood. He found chess to be "purer, socially, than painting," he told Chanin, "for you can't make money out of chess, eh?" Considered by experts to be a good match, Duchamp reached a level of proficiency that allowed him to enter championship competitions. At that point, however, he chose to stop playing in public. Instead he played private games of a Dada-style chess that permitted only illegal moves.

Although he was no longer publicly producing art, Duchamp remained active in the art world as a dealer for other artists, a consultant to collectors, and an organizer of exhibits, including the International Surrealist Exhibition held in Paris in 1938. He also co-founded the surrealist review *VVV* in 1940. Additionally, he continued to study and experiment in perspective and optics, an interest he started as early as 1918. His attempts at generating the effect of depth on a two-dimensional surface progressed through the use of shadow and then by means of intricate mechanical devices. His "Rotary Glass Plates" and "Rotary Demisphere" are early results of these efforts. In the 1930s he experimented with rotary discs which would be played on a record

Decades after ending his career as an active artist, Duchamp created miniature replicas of his works, such as this replica of his first ready-made, "Bicycle Wheel."

player, the spinning of which would give a sensation of depth. Dubbed "Rotoreliefs," these discs were shown at an inventor's fair but did not catch on. In the mid-1930s Duchamp also began to collect miniature reproductions of his work, which he gathered in a suitcase and with which he intended to create a traveling museum of his career, "Boite-en-valise."

Returning to the United States in 1942 to once again flee a European war, Duchamp worked intermittently and in secret over the next two decades on his final large project, "étant donnés," a large, three-dimensional tableau. Through two peepholes in an old Spanish door, the viewer sees a naked woman lying on her back with her legs spread open, holding a glass lantern in one hand. In the background, a waterfall flows. Once again, the enigmatic nature of this piece has attracted a variety of explanations, from a manifestation of private psychology, to tongue-in-cheek humor, and even to a tribute to the artist's former lover Maria Martins, a Brazilian sculptor. As with "The Bride . . .", "étant donnés" was also prefigured with several earlier pieces: "Female Fig Leaf" from 1950, "Objet-Dard," a phallic object from 1951, and "Wedge of Chastity" from 1954. "Étant donné" was placed on display in the Arensberg Collection at the Philadelphia Museum of Art immediately following Duchamp's death in 1968.

The Legacy

Duchamp became a U.S. citizen in 1955, but as Tomkins observed, his "influence on American artists remained marginal until the late fifties, when he was discovered by a generation eager to escape the somewhat suffocating dominance of Abstract Expressionism." Specifically, Tomkins said, the work of artists Robert Rauschenberg and Jasper Johns reflects Duchamp's influence. And Keneas remarked that "if Duchamp did not provide the cure for spiritual malaise he at least offered wit, absurdity and the humor of paradox as anodyne."

With the advent of pop art in the 1960s, interest in Duchamp was revived, and he won public recognition on an international level. The Pasadena Art Museum honored Duchamp in 1963 with his first retrospective exhibition, and in 1966 London's Tate Gallery also staged a large survey exhibit of Duchamp's work. Subsequently, other major institutions, including the Philadelphia Museum of Art and the Metropolitan Museum of Art, followed with extensive showings of Duchamp's work. Ironically, he received recognition from the very type of venerable institution he had mocked with his art. "The Duchampian irony was compounded," Tomkins said, when, at about the same time, "Duchamp's readymades were recreated in multiple sets." The artist expressed his surprise in a letter to Hans Richter: "When I discovered ready mades I thought to discourage esthetics. . . . I threw the bottle-rack and the urinal into their faces as a challenge and now they admire them for their esthetic beauty."

Duchamp's works continue to attract modern audiences, as witnessed by a large-scale exhibition staged at the Philadelphia Museum of Art in 1998-99. Museum curator Bruce Hainley wrote in *Artforum International* that Duchamp "altered so absolutely what and why and how art is (by perverting received notions of what constitutes it, by eroticizing and laughing at it, by making it a joke)." In 2000 the city of Paris paid a tribute to this art revolutionary with a retrospective exhibit at the Pompidou Center. Even mathematicians and scientists also began to reconsider Duchamp's artwork, finding resonances to theorists such as French mathematician Henri Poincaré, for example. Stephen Jay Gould and Rhonda Roland Shearer wrote in *Science* that Duchamp "understood the mathematics of non-Euclidean geometry and higher dimensionality in a far more serious and technical way than any other artist of his time," while Ivars Peterson noted in *Science News* that the "artwork of Marcel Duchamp presents intriguing, yet maddeningly intricate, puzzles."

If you enjoy the works of Marcel Duchamp, you might want to check out the following:

The works of German-French sculptor and painter Hans Arp (1887-1966).
The photography and sculpture of dada artist Man Ray (1890-1976).
The moving sculptures of Alexander Calder (1898-1976).

As Rosenberg emphasized, however, "Duchamp is today by no means an object of unanimous veneration." The artist "did not change the situation of art, but he did explore with the most realistic acuity what art could be, and could not be, in the twentieth century—thus it was possible for the artist to create without falsifying himself." Naumann, however, called Duchamp perhaps "the single most important historical figure to affect the formation and direction of Pop art, Minimalism and conceptual art in the 1960s and 1970s," and argued that his "importance can be judged not only in terms of his artistic influence but also as a harbinger of changes in society at large."

■ Biographical and Critical Sources

BOOKS

Ades, Dawn, and others, *Marcel Duchamp*, Thames & Hudson (London, England), 1999.

Alexandrian, Sarane, *Surrealist Art*, translated from the French by Gordon Clough, Praeger (Westport, CT), 1969.

Cabanne, Pierre, *Dialogues with Marcel Duchamp*, translated from the French by Ron Padgett, Viking (New York, NY), 1971.

Cabanne, Pierre, *Brothers Duchamp: Jacques Villon, Raymond Duchamp-Villon, Marcel Duchamp*, New York Graphic Society (New York, NY), 1976.

Coutts-Smith, Kenneth, *Dada*, Dutton (New York, NY), 1970.

Cummings, Paul, *Dictionary of Contemporary American Artists*, 6th edition, St. Martin's Press (New York, NY), 1994.

D'Harnoncourt, Anne, and Kynaston McShine, editors, *Marcel Duchamp*, Museum of Modern Art (New York, NY), 1974.

Davidson, Susan, and Anne D'Harnoncourt, editors, *Joseph Cornell/Marcel Duchamp . . . Resonance*, Hatje Cantz, 1999.

Hulten, Pontus, editor, *Marcel Duchamp: Work and Life*, MIT Press (Cambridge, MA), 1994.

Kuenzli, Rudolf E., and Francis M. Naumann, editors, *Marcel Duchamp—Artist of the Century*, MIT Press (Cambridge, MA), 1989.

Lippard, Lucy R., editor, *Dadas on Art*, Prentice-Hall (Paramus, NJ), 1971.

Paz, Octavio, *Marcel Duchamp: Appearances Stripped Bare*, Museum of Modern Art (New York, NY), 1974.

Moure, Gloria, *Marcel Duchamp*, Rizzoli International (New York, NY), 1988.

Richter, Hans, *Dada: Art and Anti-Art*, translated from the German by David Britt, H. Abrams (New York, NY), c. 1965.

Schwartz, Arturo, *The Complete Works of Marcel Duchamp*, Delano Greenidge, 2001.

Tansey, Richard G., and Fred S. Kleiner, *Gardner's Art through the Ages*, 10th edition, Harcourt Brace (San Diego, CA), 1996, pp. 1054-1055.

Tomkins, Calvin, *The World of Marcel Duchamp 1887-1968*, Time-Life Books (New York, NY), 1966.

Tomkins, Calvin, *Duchamp: A Biography*, Holt (New York, NY), 1996.

PERIODICALS

Artforum International, October, 1988, pp. 112-119, 120-127; September, 1991, pp. 86-90; summer, 1999, Bruce Hainley, "Joseph Cornell/Marcel Duchamp . . . in Resonance," pp. 150-151; April, 2000, p. 54.

Art in America, December, 1981, pp. 93-116; September, 1993, pp. 72-83; January, 2000, p. 112; April, 2000, p. 153; April, 2001, p. 99.

ARTnews, November, 1968; April, 1983, pp. 17-18; April, 1986, p. 157; April, 1987, pp. 160-161; summer, 1988, p. 89; February, 1999, pp. 98-102; February, 2000, pp. 100-101.

Arts, February, 1992, pp. 13-14.

Atlantic, May, 1974.

Criticism, spring, 1993, pp. 193-119.

Horizon, May-June, 1982.

Interview, April, 1993, p. 60.

Kunstwerk, October, 1968.

Nation, September 7, 1970.

Newsweek, October 14, 1968; September 24, 1973.

New Yorker, February 18, 1974; August 17, 1981, Calvin Tomkins, "The Antic Muse," pp. 80-83; May 2, 1983; Calvin Tomkins, "What the Hand Knows," pp. 13-19; June 21, 1993, Calvin Tomkins, "St. Marcel," pp. 89-92; January 15, 1996, "Dada and Mama," pp. 56-63; November 25, 1996, Calvin Tomkins, "Duchamp and New York," pp. 92-100.

New York Review of Books, March 27, 1997, pp. 22-28.

New York Times, October 3, 1968.

New York Times Magazine, January 22, 1956.

New York Times Book Review, March 3, 1974; December 7, 1975.

Science, November 5, 1999, Stephen Jay Gould and Rhonda Roland Shearer, "Of Two Minds and One Nature," p. 1093; January 7, 2000, p. 41.

Science News, January 1, 2000, Ivars Peterson, "An Artist's Timely Riddles," p. 8.

Spectator, April 10, 1993, pp. 41-42.

Time, October 11. 1968; September 24, 1973; October 26, 1998, p. 102.

Time International, April 17, 2000, p. 67.

OTHER

Grove Art, http://www.groveart.com/ (March 2, 2002), Francis M. Naumann, "Duchamp, (Henri-Robert-)Marcel."

Marcel Duchamp World Community, http://www.marcelduchamp.net/ (March 3, 2002).

Tout Fait: The Marcel Duchamp Studies Online Journal, http://www.toutfait.com/ (March 3, 2002).*

Louise Erdrich

■ Personal

Last name pronounced "Ur-drik"; born June 7, 1954, in Little Falls, MN; daughter of Ralph Louis (a teacher with the Bureau of Indian Affairs) and Rita Joanne (affiliated with the Bureau of Indian Affairs; maiden name, Gourneau) Erdrich; married Michael Anthony Dorris (a writer and professor of Native American studies), October 10, 1981 (died April 11, 1997); children: Reynold Abel (deceased), Jeffrey Sava, Madeline Hannah, Persia Andromeda, Pallas Antigone, Aza Marion, Azure. *Education:* Dartmouth College, B.A., 1976; Johns Hopkins University, M.A., 1979. *Politics:* Democrat. *Religion:* "Anti-religion." *Hobbies and other interests:* Quilting, running, drawing, "playing chess with daughters and losing, playing piano badly, speaking terrible French."

■ Addresses

Home—Minneapolis, MN. *Agent*—c/o Author Mail, HarperCollins, 10 East 53rd St., New York, NY 10022.

■ Career

Writer. North Dakota State Arts Council, visiting poet and teacher, 1977-78; Johns Hopkins University, Baltimore, MD, writing instructor, 1978-79; Boston Indian Council, Boston, MA, communications director and editor of *The Circle*, 1979-80; Charles-Merrill Co., textbook writer, 1980; BirchBark Books, Minneapolis, MN, proprietor, 2000—. Previously employed as a beet weeder in Wahpeton, ND; waitress in Wahpeton, Boston, and Syracuse, NY; psychiatric aide in a Vermont hospital; poetry teacher at prisons; lifeguard; and construction flag signaler. Has judged writing contests.

■ Member

International Writers, PEN (member of executive board, 1985-88), Authors Guild, Authors League of America.

■ Awards, Honors

Johns Hopkins University teaching fellow, 1978; MacDowell Colony fellow, 1980; Yaddo Colony fellow, 1981; Dartmouth College visiting fellow, 1981; First Prize, Nelson Algren fiction competition, 1982, for "The World's Greatest Fisherman"; National Endowment for the Arts fellowship, 1982; Pushcart Prize, 1983; National Magazine Fiction awards, 1983 and 1987; Virginia McCormack Scully Prize for best book of the year dealing with Indians or Chicanos, and National Book Critics Circle Award for fiction, both 1984, *Los Angeles Times Award* for best novel, Sue Kaufman Prize for Best First Novel from American Academy and Institute of Arts and Letters, American Book Award from Before Columbus Foundation, and named among *New York Times Book Review*'s best eleven books of the year, all 1985, all for *Love Medicine*; Guggenheim fellow, 1985-86; *The Beet Queen* was named one of *Publishers Weekly*'s best books, 1986; First Prize, O. Henry awards, 1987; National Book Critics Circle Award nomination; World Fantasy Award for Best Novel, World Fantasy Convention, 1999, for *The Antelope Wife*; National Book Award finalist, for *The Birchbark House*; *Globe & Mail* Top Ten Books of the year, and National Book Award for fiction, finalist, both 2001, both for *The Last Report on the Miracles at Little No Horse*.

■ Writings

NOVELS

Love Medicine, Holt (New York, NY), 1984, expanded edition, 1993.

The Beet Queen, Holt (New York, NY), 1986.

Tracks, Harper (New York, NY), 1988.

(With husband, Michael Dorris) *The Crown of Columbus*, HarperCollins (New York, NY), 1991.

The Bingo Palace, HarperCollins (New York, NY), 1994.

Tales of Burning Love, HarperCollins (New York, NY), 1996.

The Antelope Wife, HarperFlamingo (New York, NY), 1998.

The Last Report on the Miracles at Little No Horse, HarperCollins (New York, NY), 2001.

OTHER

Imagination (textbook), C. E. Merrill, 1980.

Jacklight (poetry), Holt (New York, NY), 1984.

Louise Erdrich and Michael Dorris Interview with Kay Bonetti, (sound recording), American Audio Prose Library, 1986.

Baptism of Desire (poetry), Harper (New York, NY), 1989.

(Author of preface) Michael Dorris, *The Broken Cord: A Family's Ongoing Struggle with Fetal Alcohol Syndrome*, Harper (New York, NY), 1989.

(Author of preface) Desmond Hogan, *A Link with the River*, Farrar, Straus (New York, NY), 1989.

(With Allan Richard Chavkin and Nancy Feyl Chavkin) *Conversations with Louise Erdrich and Michael Dorris*, University Press of Mississippi (Jackson, MS), 1994.

The Falcon: A Narrative of the Captivity and Adventures of John Tanner, Penguin (New York, NY), 1994.

The Blue Jay's Dance: A Birth Year (memoir), HarperCollins (New York, NY), 1995.

Grandmother's Pigeon (children's book), illustrated by Jim LaMarche, Hyperion (New York, NY), 1996.

(And illustrator) *The Birchbark House* (children's book), Hyperion (New York, NY), 1999.

Author of short story "The World's Greatest Fisherman"; contributor to *Resurrecting Grace: Remembering Catholic Childhoods*, Beacon Press (Boston, MA), 2001; contributor to anthologies, including *Norton Anthology of Poetry*; *Best American Short Stories*, 1983 and 1988; and *Prize Stories: The O. Henry Awards*, 1985 and 1987. Contributor of stories, poems, essays, and book reviews to periodicals, including *New Yorker, New England Review, Chicago, American Indian Quarterly, Frontiers, Atlantic, Kenyon Review, North American Review, New York Times Book Review, Ms., Redbook* (with sister Heidi Erdrich under the joint pseudonym Heidi Louise), and *Woman* (with Dorris, under the joint pseudonym Milou North).

■ Adaptations

The Crown of Columbus was optioned for film.

■ Work in Progress

The Master Butcher's Singing Club, a novel.

■ Sidelights

Like William Faulkner and his Yoknapatawpha County, American writer Louise Erdrich has created her own mythical landscape in and around Argus, a fictional Red River Valley reservation town on the Minnesota-North Dakota border, and has also manufactured an eccentric cast of characters who appear and re-appear throughout her many novels set there. These include the Lamartine, Pillager, Morrisey, and Kashpaw families, as well as Father Damien, Nanapush, Dot Adare, Pauline Puyrat, and a score of others who weave in and out of 1984's *Love Medicine* through 2001's *The Last Report on the Miracles at Little No Horse* and beyond. Readers of further titles in Erdrich's loosely connected series, including *The Bingo Palace, The Beet Queen, Tracks,* and *Tales of Burning Love* will recognize and empathize with these old friends, though with *The Antelope Wife* Erdrich branches out to introduce new locations in the region and two new families. "Erdrich's tales are not sequels in the traditional sense," wrote Katie Bacon in *Atlantic Unbound.* "Rather, they are an intricate web of stories, told from different points in time and different points of view, one whose pattern only becomes clear when you step back and view it from a distance."

As a Native American author, Erdrich has also been compared to Richard Wright and James Baldwin for what those writers achieved on behalf of African Americans, as well as to Philip Roth due to his Jewish narratives. Erdrich is credited with bringing Native Americans into mainstream fiction and inspiring an entire generation of new voices in Native-American literature. The daughter of a French-Ojibwe mother and a German-American father, Erdrich explores Native-American themes in her works, with major characters representing both sides of her heritage. She takes a close—sometimes near-horrific, sometimes humorous—look at the meetings of these two cultures, which sometimes clash, sometimes co-mingle. Drawing on her Chippewa/Ojibwe heritage, Erdrich examines the complex relationships—both familial and sexual—between Midwestern Native Americans and their neighboring white communities.

The first in a multi-part series, *Love Medicine* traces two Native-American families from 1934 to 1984 in a unique seven-narrator format through fourteen interconnected stories, and thereby sets the design for further novels with their non-chronological, episodic approach. The novel was extremely well received, earning its author numerous awards, including the National Book Critics Circle Award in 1984. Other novels from Erdrich have been equally well received. As Mark Anthony Rolo, executive director of the Minnesota-based Native American Journalists Association, told John Habich in the Minneapolis, Minnesota *Star Tribune,* "[Erdrich] is the first writer to humanize Indians. She allows their complexities to come out, their contradictions, their faults even."

Storytelling as Cultural Artifact

Erdrich's interest in writing can be traced to her childhood and her heritage. As she told *Writer's Digest* contributor Michael Schumacher, "People in [Native American] families make everything into a story. . . . People just sit and the stories start coming, one after another. I suppose that when you grow up constantly hearing the stories rise, break, and fall, it gets into you somehow." The oldest in a family of seven children, she was born on June 7, 1954, in Little Falls, Minnesota, and raised in Wahpeton, North Dakota. Her Chippewa or Ojibwe grandfather had been the tribal chairman of the nearby Turtle Mountain Reservation, and her parents worked at the Bureau of Indian Falls boarding school. Erdrich once commented on the way in which her parents encouraged her writing: "My father used to give me a nickel for every story I wrote, and my mother wove strips of construction paper together and stapled them into book covers. So at an early age I felt myself to be a published author earning substantial royalties."

Erdrich's mother was born on the Turtle Mountain Chippewa reservation, where her grandfather was tribal chairman, and though she never lived on the reservation, Erdrich visited it often. She told Joseph Bruchac in *Survival This Way: Interviews with American Indian Poets* that she was very close to her grandfather. "He is funny, he's charming, he's interesting." Erdrich also admired the manner in which he could navigate two very different cultures, keeping the old traditions while dealing with the world the Europeans had created. In addition, her grandfather was a wonderful storyteller, instilling a love for story in his young granddaughter. Such traditional storytelling affected Erdrich greatly, and her novels of Chippewa life mimic the varied points of view and time span of the traditional Chippewa story cycle. Erdrich credits also a youth spent without the distraction of television as being influential in her narrative impulse. Most of her early schooling was spent in public schools in Wahpeton, though she also attended a parochial school.

Erdrich entered Dartmouth College in 1972, the year the college began admitting women, as well as the year the Native American studies department was established. The author's future husband and collaborator, anthropologist Michael Dorris, was hired to chair the department. In his class, Erdrich began the exploration of her ancestry that would eventually inspire her novels. Intent on balancing her academic training with a broad range of practical knowledge, she told Miriam Berkley in an interview with *Publishers Weekly,* "I ended up taking some really crazy jobs, and I'm glad I did. They turned out to have been very useful experiences, although I never would have believed it at the time." In addition to working as a lifeguard, waitress, poetry teacher at prisons, and construction flag signaler, Erdrich became an editor for the *Circle,* a Boston Indian Council newspaper. She told Schumacher, "Settling into that job and becoming comfortable with an urban community—which is very different from the reservation community—gave me another reference point. There were lots of people with mixed blood, lots of people who had their own confusions. I realized that this was part of my life—it wasn't something that I was making up—and that it was something I *wanted* to write about." In 1978 the author enrolled in an M.A. program at Johns Hopkins University, where she wrote poems and stories incorporating her heritage, many of which would later become part of her books. She also began sending her work to publishers, most of whom sent back rejection slips.

Years of Collaboration

After receiving her master's degree, Erdrich returned to Dartmouth as a writer-in-residence. Dorris, with whom she had remained in touch, attended a reading of her poetry there and was impressed. A writer himself—Dorris later published the bestselling novel *A Yellow Raft in Blue Water* and receive the 1989 National Book Critics Circle Award for his nonfiction work *The Broken Cord*—Dorris became interested in working with Erdrich and getting to know her better. When he left for New Zealand to do field research and Erdrich went to Boston to work on a textbook, the two began sending their poetry and fiction back and forth with their letters, laying a groundwork for a literary relationship. Dorris returned to New Hampshire in 1980, and Erdrich moved back there as well. The two began collaborating on short stories, including one titled "The World's Greatest Fisherman." When this story won five thousand dollars in the Nelson Algren fiction competition, Erdrich and Dorris decided to expand it into a novel—*Love Medicine*. At the same time, their literary relationship led to a romantic one and in 1981 they were married.

The titles Erdrich and Dorris chose for their novels—such as *Love Medicine* and *A Yellow Raft in Blue Water*—contain rich poetic or visual images and were often the initial inspiration from which their novels were drawn. Erdrich told Schumacher, "I think a title is like a magnet: It begins to draw these scraps of experience or conversation or memory to it. Eventually, it collects a book." Erdrich and Dorris's collaborative process began with a first draft, usually written by whoever had the original idea for the book, the one who would ultimately be considered the official author. After the draft was written, the other person edited it, and then another draft was written; often five or six drafts would be written in all. Finally, the two read the work aloud until they agreed on each word. Although the author had the original voice and the final say, ulti-

mately, both collaborators were responsible for what the work became. This "unique collaborative relationship," according to Alice Joyce in *Booklist,* is covered in *Conversations with Louise Erdrich and Michael Dorris*, a collection of twenty-five interviews with the couple.

Together the couple worked on short stories, poetry, and novels, and had six children together, three of their own and three adopted. One of their children was tragically killed in 1991, causing a major rift in the relationship. That year *The Crown of Columbus* was published, the only novel to actually have both authors' names on it, as well as a book of travel essays, *Route Two*. The marriage continued to unravel, and the couple later separated. Allegations of sexual abuse were leveled at Dorris before his tragic suicide in 1997.

The North Dakota Saga

The 1982 short story "The World's Greatest Fisherman" introduces two of the families that go on to appear in Erdrich's novels of North Dakota. *Love Medicine, The Beet Queen, Tracks, The Bingo Palace, Tales of Burning Love,* and *The Last Report on the Miracles at Little No Horse* encompass the stories of several interrelated families living in and around a reservation in the fictional town of Argus, North Dakota, from 1912 through the 1980s. The novels have been compared to those of Faulkner not only for the creation of this mythical landscape, but also due to the multi-voice narration and non-chronological storytelling the Southern writer employed in works such as *As I Lay Dying*. Erdrich's works, linked by recurring characters who are victims of fate and the patterns set by their elders, are structured like intricate puzzles in which bits of information about individuals and their relations to one another are slowly released in a seemingly random order, until three-dimensional characters—with a future and a past—are revealed. Through her characters' antics, Erdrich explores universal family life-cycles while also communicating a sense of the changes and loss involved in the twentieth-century Native American experience.

Poet Robert Bly, describing Erdrich's nonlinear storytelling approach in the *New York Times Book Review,* emphasized her tendency to "choose a few minutes or a day in 1932, let one character talk, let another talk, and a third, then leap to 1941 and then to 1950 or 1964." The novels' circular format is a reflection of the way in which the works are constructed. Although Erdrich is dealing with a specific and extensive time period, "The writing doesn't start out and proceed chronologically. It never seems to start in the beginning. Rather, it's as though we're building something around a center, but that center can be anywhere." *Love Medicine*, the first in the cycle, appeared in 1984. "With this impressive debut," stated *New York Times Book Review* contributor Marco Portales, "Louise Erdrich enters the company of America's better novelists."

Love Medicine, named for the belief in love potions which is a part of Chippewa folklore, explores the bonds of family and faith that preserve both the Chippewa tribal community and the individuals that comprise it. The novel begins at a family gath-

THE NEW YORK TIMES BESTSELLER
"A PERFECT—AND PERFECTLY WONDERFUL—NOVEL."
—ANNE TYLER

The BEET QUEEN

LOUISE ERDRICH

AWARD-WINNING AUTHOR OF
LOVE MEDICINE and *TRACKS*

Erdrich follows the men and women of Argus in her 1986 novel, which finds the three young Adare children abandoned by their widowed mother and forced to rely on the help of others during the Great Depression of the 1930s.

ering following the death of June Kashpaw, a prostitute. The characters introduce one another, sharing stories about June that reveal their family history and their cultural beliefs. Albertine Johnson, June's niece, introduces her grandmother, Marie, her grandfather, Nector, and Nector's twin brother, Eli. Eli represents the old way, the Native American who never integrated into the white culture. He also plays a major role in *Tracks*, in which he appears as a young man. The story of Marie and Nector brings together many of the important images in the novel, including the notion of "love medicine." As a teenager in a convent, Marie is nearly burned to death by a nun who, in an attempt to exorcize the devil from within her, pours boiling water on Marie. Immediately following this incident, Marie is sexually assaulted by Nector. Marie and Nector are later married, but in middle age, Nector begins an affair with Lulu Lamartine, a married woman. In an attempt to rekindle Nector and Marie's passion, their grandson Lipsha prepares "love medicine" for Nector. But Lipsha has difficulty obtaining a wild goose heart for the potion. He substitutes a frozen turkey heart, which causes Nector to choke to death.

Reviewers responded positively to Erdrich's debut novel, citing its lyrical qualities as well as the rich characters who inhabit it. *New York Times* contributor D. J. R. Bruckner was impressed with Erdrich's "mastery of words," as well as the "vividly drawn" characters who "will not leave the mind once they are let in." Portales, who called *Love Medicine* "an engrossing book," applauded the unique narration technique which produces what he termed "a wondrous prose song."

After the publication of *Love Medicine*, Erdrich told reviewers that her next novel would focus less exclusively on her mother's side, embracing the author's mixed heritage and the mixed community in which she grew up. 1986's *The Beet Queen* deals with whites and half-breeds as well as American Indians, and explores the interactions between these worlds. The story begins in 1932, during the Depression. Mary and Karl Adare's recently widowed mother flies off with a carnival pilot, abandoning the two children and their newborn brother. The baby is taken by a young couple who have just lost their child, while Karl and eleven-year-old Mary ride a freight train to Argus, seeking refuge with their aunt and uncle. When they arrive in the town, however, Karl, frightened by a dog, runs back onto the train and winds up at an orphanage. Mary grows up with her aunt and uncle, and the novel follows her life—as well as those of her jealous, self-centered cousin Sita and their part-Chippewa friend Celestine James—for the next forty years, tracing the themes of separation and loss that began with Mary's father's death and her mother's grand departure.

The Beet Queen was well received by critics, some of whom found it even more impressive than *Love Medicine.* Many noted the novel's poetic language and symbolism; Bly noted that Erdrich's "genius is in metaphor," and that the characters "show a convincing ability to feel an image with their whole bodies." Josh Rubins, writing in the *New York Review of Books,* called *The Beet Queen* "a rare second novel, one that makes it seem as if the first, impressive as it was, promised too little, not too much."

Other reviewers had problems with *The Beet Queen,* but they tended to dismiss the novel's flaws in light of its positive qualities. *New Republic* contributor Dorothy Wickenden considered the characters unrealistic and the ending contrived, but she lauded *The Beet Queen's* "ringing clarity and lyricism," as well as the "assured, polished quality" she felt was missing in *Love Medicine.* Although Michiko Kakutani found the ending artificial, the *New York Times* reviewer called Erdrich "an immensely gifted young writer." "Even with its weaknesses," proclaimed Linda Simon in *Commonweal,* "*The Beet Queen* stands as a product of enormous talent."

After Erdrich completed *The Beet Queen,* she was uncertain as to what her next project should be. The four-hundred-page manuscript that would eventually become *Tracks* had remained untouched for ten years; the author referred to it as her "burden." She and Dorris took a fresh look at it and decided they could relate it to *Love Medicine* and *The Beet Queen.* While more political than her previous novels, *Tracks* also deals with spiritual themes, exploring the tension between ancient Native American beliefs and Christian notions held by Europeans. The novel takes place between 1912 and 1924, before the settings of Erdrich's other novels, and reveals the roots of *Love Medicine's* characters and their hardships. One of the narrators, Nanapush, is the leader of a tribe that is suffering on account of the white government's exploitation. He feels pressured to give up tribal land in order to avoid starvation. While Nanapush represents the old way, Pauline, the other narrator, represents change. The future mother of *Love Medicine's* Marie Lazarre, Pauline is a young half-breed from a mixed-blood tribe "for which the name was lost." She feels torn between her Indian faith and the white people's religion, and is considering leaving the reservation. At the center of *Tracks* is Fleur, a character whom *Los Angeles Times Book Review* contributor Terry Tempest Williams called "one of the most haunting presences in contemporary American literature." Nanapush discovers this

young woman—the last survivor of a family killed by consumption—in a cabin in the woods, starving and mad. Nanapush adopts Fleur and nurses her back to health.

Reviewers found *Tracks* distinctly different from Erdrich's earlier novels, and some felt that it lacks the characteristics that made *Love Medicine* and *The Beet Queen* so outstanding. *Washington Post Book World* critic Jonathan Yardley wrote that, on account of its more political focus, the work has a "labored quality," while Robert Towers stated in *New York Review of Books* that he found the characters melodramatic and the tone overly intense. Katherine Dieckmann, writing in the *Voice Literary Supplement,* affirmed that she "missed [Erdrich's] skilled multiplications of voice," and called the relationship between Pauline and Nanapush "symptomatic of the overall lack of grand orchestration and perspectival interplay that made Erdrich's first two novels polyphonic masterpieces." According to *Commonweal* contributor Christopher Vecsey, however, although "a reviewer might find some of the prose overwrought, and the two narrative voices indistinguishable . . . readers will appreciate and applaud the vigor and inventiveness of the author."

Some reviewers enjoyed *Tracks* even more than the earlier novels. Williams stated that Erdrich's writing "has never appeared more polished and grounded," and added, "*Tracks* may be the story of our time." Thomas M. Disch lauded the novel's plot, with its surprising twists and turns, in the *Chicago Tribune.* The critic added, "Louise Erdrich is like one of those rumored drugs that are instantly and forever addictive. Fortunately in her case you can *just say yes.*"

A Hiatus from Argus

Tracks was the last new North Dakota novel for six years. In 1991 Erdrich and Dorris's jointly authored *The Crown of Columbus* appeared, exploring Native American issues from the standpoint of the authors' own experience rather than that of their ancestors. Marking the quincentennial anniversary of Spanish explorer Christopher Columbus's voyage in a not-so-celebratory fashion, Erdrich and Dorris raise important questions about the meaning of that voyage for both Europeans and Native Americans today. The story is narrated by the two central characters, both Dartmouth professors involved in projects concerning Columbus. Vivian Twostar is a Native-American single mother with eclectic tastes and a teenage son, Nash. Vivian is asked to write an academic article on Columbus from a Native-American perspective and is researching Columbus's diaries. Roger Williams, a stuffy New England Protestant poet, is writing an epic work about the explorer's voyage. Vivian and Roger become lovers, parenting a girl named Violet, but have little in common. Ultimately acknowledging the destructive impact of Columbus's voyage on the Native American people, they each vow to redress the political wrongs symbolically by changing the power structure in their relationship. In the end, as Vivian and Roger rediscover themselves, they rediscover America.

Some reviewers found *The Crown of Columbus* unbelievable and inconsistent, and consider it less praiseworthy than the individual authors' earlier works. However, *New York Times Book Review* contributor Robert Houston appreciated the novel's timely political relevance, noting "moments of genuine humor and compassion, of real insight and sound satire." Other critics also considered Vivian and Roger's adventures amusing, vibrant, and charming.

Erdrich turned to her own experience as a mother of six children for her next work, *The Blue Jay's Dance.* Her first book of nonfiction, *The Blue Jay's Dance* chronicles Erdrich's pregnancy and the birth year of her child. The title refers to a blue jay's habit of defiantly "dancing" towards an attacking hawk, Erdrich's metaphor for "the sort of controlled recklessness that having children always is," noted Jane Aspinall in *Quill & Quire.* Erdrich has been somewhat protective of her family's privacy and has stated the narrative actually describes a combination of her experience with several of her children. Sue Halpern in the *New York Times Book Review* remarked on this difficult balancing act between public and private lives but found that Erdrich's "ambivalence inspires trust . . . and suggests that she is the kind of mother whose story should be told."

Some reviewers averred that Erdrich's description of the maternal relationship is a powerful one; "the bond between mother and infant has rarely been captured so well," commented a *Kirkus Reviews* contributor. While the subject of pregnancy and motherhood is not a new one, Halpern noted that the book provides new insight into the topic: "What makes *The Blue Jay's Dance* worth reading is that it quietly places a mother's love and nurturance amid her love for the natural world and suggests . . . how right that placement is." Although the *Kirkus* reviewer contributor found *The Blue Jay's Dance* to be "occasionally too self-conscious about the importance of Erdrich's role as Writer," others commented positively on the book's examination of the balance between the work of parenting and one's vocation. A *Los Angeles Times* reviewer remarked: "this book is really about working and having children, staying alert and . . . focused through the first year of a child's life."

Erdrich retained her focus on children with her first children's book, *Grandmother's Pigeon.* Published in 1996, it is a fanciful tale of an adventurous grandmother who heads to Greenland on the back of a porpoise, leaving behind grandchildren and three bird's eggs in her cluttered bedroom. The eggs hatch into passenger pigeons, thought to be extinct, through which the children are able to send messages to their missing grandmother. A *Publishers Weekly* reviewer commented, "As in her fiction for adults . . . , Erdrich makes every word count in her bewitching debut children's story."

Another title for young readers, *The Birchbark House,* contains "a title and structure that inescapably recall Laura Ingalls Wilder's family stories," according to a *Horn Book* contributor. Omakayas, a seven-year-old Ojibwe girl, lives on an island in Lake Superior at the time whites are beginning to settle the land and displace the native population. The young girl's days are filled with hard work, but also a love for the old ways, but the whites hover at the frame of the story, their smallpox decimating the natives. "Erdrich is reversing the narrative perspective used in most children's stories about nineteenth-century Native Americans," remarked Mary Harris Russell in the *New York Times Book Review.* "Instead of looking out at 'them' as dangerous curiosities, Erdrich . . . wants to tell about 'us' from the inside." *Booklist* contributor Hazel Rochman also praised this different perspective on an old story: "'Little House' readers will discover a new world, a different version of a story they thought they knew." Indeed, Erdrich has remarked that she consciously inverted the "Little House on the Prairie" books to tell the tale of white settlement of Native American lands from the point of view of the dispossessed.

More Tales from Native America

In 1993 Erdrich revised and expanded *Love Medicine,* adding different perspectives to the tale that deal with different members of the families involved. Then she returned to the descendants of Nanapush with her 1994 novel, *The Bingo Palace.* The fourth novel in the series that began with *Love Medicine, The Bingo Palace* weaves together a story of spiritual pursuit with elements of modern reservation life. Erdrich provides continuity to the series by having the novel primarily narrated by Lipsha Morrisey, the illegitimate son of June Kapshaw and Gerry Nanapush from *Love Medicine.* After working at a Fargo sugar beet factory, Lipsha has returned home to the reservation in search of his life's meaning. He finds work at his uncle Lyman Lamartine's bingo parlor and love with his uncle's girlfriend, Shawnee Ray Toose. Thanks to the magic bingo tickets provided to him by the spirit of his dead mother, June, he also finds modest wealth. The character of Fleur Pillager returns from *Tracks* as Lipsha's great-grandmother. After visiting her, Lipsha embarks on a spiritual quest in order to impress Shawnee and learn more about his own tribal religious rites. Family members past and present are brought together in his pursuit, which comprises the final pages of the novel.

Reviewers' comments on *The Bingo Palace* were generally positive. While Lawrence Thornton in the *New York Times Book Review* found "some of the novel's later ventures into magic realism . . . contrived," his overall impression was positive: "Erdrich's sympathy for her characters shines as luminously as Shawnee Ray's jingle dress." Pam Houston, writing for the *Los Angeles Times Book Review*, was especially taken by the character of Lipsha Morrisey, finding in him "what makes this her most exciting and satisfying book to date." *The Bingo Palace* was also reviewed in the context of the series as a whole. *Chicago Tribune* contributor Michael Upchurch concluded that *The Bingo Palace* "falls somewhere between *Tracks* and *The Beet Queen* in its accomplishment," and added: "The best chapters in *The Bingo Palace* rival, as *Love Medicine* did, the work of Welty, Cheever, and Flannery O'Connor."

Erdrich returned to the character of June Kashpaw in her sixth novel, *Tales of Burning Love*. More accurately, it is the story of June's husband, Jack Mauser, and his five—including June—ex-wives. To begin the tale, Jack meets June while they are both inebriated and marries her that night. In reaction to his inability to consummate their marriage, she walks off into a blizzard and is found dead the next day. His four subsequent marriages share the same elements of tragedy and comedy, culminating in Jack's death in a fire in a house he has built. The story of each marriage is told by the four ex-wives as they are stranded together in Jack's car during a blizzard after his funeral. Again, Erdrich references her previous work in the characters of Gerry and Dot Nanapush, Dot as one of Jack's ex-wives and Gerry as Dot's imprisoned husband.

Reviewers noted Erdrich's masterful descriptions and fine dialogue in this work. According to Penelope Mesic in the *Chicago Tribune*, "Erdrich's strength is that she gives emotional states—as shifting and intangible, as indefinable as wind—a visible form in metaphor." *Times Literary Supplement* contributor Lavinia Greenlaw compared her to both Tobias Wolff—like him "she is . . . particularly good at evoking American small-town life and the space that engulfs it"—as well as Raymond Carver, noting her dialogues to be "small exchanges that . . . map out the barely navigable distance between what's heard, what's meant, and what's said." *Tales of Burning Love* also focuses Erdrich's abilities in depicting the relationship between men and women. Greenlaw continued, "Erdrich also shares Carver's

clear and sophisticated view of the more fundamental distance between men and women, and how that, too, is negotiated." However, Mark Childress in the *New York Times Book Review* commented that while "Jack's wives are vivid and fully realized . . . whenever he's out of sight, he doesn't seem as interesting as the women who loved him."

Explores New Fictional Terrain

While Erdrich covers familiar territory in *Tales of Burning Love*, she seems to be expanding her focus slightly. Roxana Robinson in *Washington Post Book World* remarked, "The landscape, instead of being somber and overcast . . . is vividly illuminated by bolts of freewheeling lunacy: This is a mad Gothic comedy." Or as Verlyn Klinkenborg noted in the *Los Angeles Times Book Review*, "this book marks a shift in . . . [Erdrich's] career, a shift that is suggested rather than fulfilled. . . . there is new country coming into sight, and this novel is her first welcoming account of it."

Part of that "new country" appears in the 1998 novel *The Antelope Wife*, a departure for Erdrich in her adult novels in its focus on new families, the Roys and the Shawanos, living in contemporary Minneapolis. Erdrich follows these families through failed marriages and forced weddings, as well as tragic deaths. As with all of her novels, the plot here also manages to loop back a century to an attack on an Ojibwe village and a child carried off on the back of a dog. Employing techniques of magical realism, Erdrich tells a tale of the saving power of love. In the opening of the book, Private Scranton Roy follows a runaway dog carrying a baby after his cavalry troops have raided the village. Roy literally nurses the baby back to health and raises her as his own until the baby's mother retrieves her. When her mother dies the girl spends time with a herd of antelope and returns to her village with mysterious powers. Now the Antelope Wife of the title, she is enticed to the city where she becomes the link between several generations of white and Native American families. The book "quickly develops into a madrigal," noted Thomas Curwen in the *Los Angeles Times*, "a dreamy chorus of voices that rise at times in harmony and other moments in happy dissonance." Generations later, descendants of that raid now live in Minneapolis, coping with life in a variety of ways: some are homeless, others do the nine-to-five routine. Revolving around Rozin Roy and her husband, Richard Whiteheart Beads, Frank and Klaus Shawano, and the Antelope Wife herself, the book is "vintage Erdrich," according to Barbara Hoffert in *Library Journal*. Hoffert found the novel "absolutely terrific and also a bit disappointing" because "one feels Erdrich has done this all before."

Howard Meredith, reviewing *The Antelope Wife* in *World Literature Today,* voiced similar concerns, noting "the lack of energy that marks this volume." However, Meredith concluded that in spite of such reservations, "Erdrich remains a significant . . . storyteller." Not all reviewers found such weakness in the novel. *Booklist* reviewer Bill Ott wrote that "Erdrich's image-rich prose seduces the reader," while Diana Postlethwaite, writing in the *New York Times Book Review,* remarked that "there is light as well as darkness in this fictional universe, and encountering it offers pain and exhilaration in equal measure." More praise came from Michiko Kakutani in the *New York Times,* who wrote, "Reading *The Antelope Wife* offers a rich taste of the bitter and the sweet. Louise Erdrich looks unflinchingly at the human heart." Curwen concluded, "Richly cadenced, deeply textured, Erdrich's writing has the luster and sheen of poetry, each sentence circling deeper into emotion, motivation and rationale, until love touches not eternity but death, transforming *The Antelope Wife* into a story of longing and longing assuaged, as sustaining as *Love Medicine,* serious, sometimes flawed but altogether passionate."

In 2001 Erdrich returned to the more familiar ground of an Ojibwe reservation in North Dakota for *The Last Report on the Miracles at Little No Horse,* a book that she cited as one of the most difficult to write. Not only were there all the characters and events from previous novels to keep track of, but also Erdrich's ambitions for this novel were large. "I wanted it to be written at the level of a poem," she told Alden Mudge in a *BookPage* interview. "And yet I wanted it to be coherent and have the complexity that it needed. It was hard for me to get there. I threw out huge amounts of paper. I kept the recyclers in business."

In the novel Erdrich reprises a character encountered earlier in her cycle of novels, Father Damien, a Catholic priest. This priest has served the Ojibwe on the remote reservation of Little No Horse, for over half a century, making enormous sacrifices, but also experiencing real joy and contentment. Now, near the end of his life, Father Damien has only one fear: that his true identity will be uncovered. In truth, Father Damien is a woman name Agnes DeWitt who encountered the Father en route to his Indian mission. When he drowned in a flood, Agnes had a mystical experience and decided to assume the priest's identity. She has kept this secret all these years, and now is threatened when a colleague comes to investigate another member of the church, Sister Leopolda, whose piety is under scrutiny. Father Damien alone knows Sister Leopolda's secret, but revealing that might in turn reveal his own secret.

Critical reception to this seventh tale of the North Dakota Ojibwe cycle was laudatory. A reviewer for

Publishers Weekly noted that Erdrich "renders her North Dakota world of the Ojibwe with a lyrical and richly metaphoric prose style." The same contributor further noted the "dozens of comic, tragic and all too-human stories" that are woven into her narrative. *Time* contributor Andrea Sachs called *The Last Report* "enchanting and absorbing," while Ott noted in *Booklist* that it was time to acknowledge Erdrich's cycle of novels as "the pinnacle of recent American fiction," and that *The Last Report* "works beautifully as a reprise of all that has come before." Ott concluded, "This is Erdrich writing at the peak of her powers." Klinkenborg, writing in the *New York Times Book Review,* dubbed the novel "beguiling," and Kakutani in the *New York Times* felt that it was a "deeply affecting narrative . . . by turns comical and elegiac, farcical and tragic." Ron Charles, reviewing the novel in the *Christian Science Monitor,* also had high praise for *The Last Report,* calling it "one of those wonderful books that's as memorable for its parts as it is for its whole." And Curwen, writing in the *Los Angeles Times,* felt the book was "messy, ribald, deeply tragic, preposterous and heartfelt," and that in the final analysis it was a love story. "What shine most brightly through its pages," wrote Curwen, "are Erdrich's intelligence and compassion."

If you enjoy the works of Louise Erdrich, you might want to check out the following books:

N. Scott Momaday, *House Made of Dawn,* 1968.
Leslie Marmon Silko, *Ceremony,* 1977.
Paula Gunn Allen, *Spider Woman's Granddaughters,* 1989.
James Northrup, *Walking the Rez Road,* 1993.

Hard at work on further tales from North Dakota and elsewhere, tales that are universal in their telling, Erdrich seems somewhat amazed still by the length and breadth of her literary creations. "I thought I'd written one story," she told Sybil Steinberg in a *Publishers Weekly* interview. "Then I thought I'd written one book. I never would have imagined that these characters would turn up again and again. But I guess there's some unity of consciousness that underlies your everyday writing that, for me, made going on with these people inevitable." Speaking with Bacon in *Atlantic Un-*

bound, Erdrich summed up her own achievement and her technique thusly: "Primarily . . . I am just a storyteller, and I take . . . [stories] where I find them. I love stories whether they function to reclaim old narratives or occur spontaneously. Often, to my surprise, they do both. I'll follow an inner thread of a plot and find that I am actually retelling a very old story, often in a contemporary setting. I usually can't recall whether it is something I heard, or something I dreamed, or read, or imagined on the spot. It all becomes confused and then the characters take over, anyway, and make the piece their own."

■ Biographical and Critical Sources

BOOKS

Authors and Artists for Young Adults, Volume 10, Gale (Detroit, MI), 1993.

Beacham's Encyclopedia of Popular Fiction, Beacham Publishing (Osprey, FL), Volumes 1, 5, 7, 1996, Volume 11, 1998, Volume 12, 2000.

Bruchac, Joseph, *Survival This Way: Interviews with American Indian Poets*, Sun Tracks/University of Arizona Press (Tucson, AZ), 1987, pp. 73-86.

Contemporary Literary Criticism, Gale (Detroit, MI), Volume 39, 1986, Volume 54, 1989.

Dictionary of Literary Biography, Gale (Detroit, MI), Volume 152: *American Novelists since World War II, Fourth Series*, 1995, Volume 175: *Native American Writers of the United States*, 1997, Volume 206: *Twentieth-Century American Western Writers*, 1999.

Erdrich, Louise, *Tracks*, Harper (New York, NY), 1988.

Erdrich, Louise, *Baptism of Desire*, Harper (New York, NY), 1989.

Jacobs, Connie A., *The Novels of Louise Erdrich*, Peter Lang (New York, NY), 2001.

Pearlman, Mickey, *American Women Writing Fiction: Memory, Identity, Family, Space*, University Press of Kentucky (Lexington, KY), 1989, pp. 95-112.

PERIODICALS

America, May 14, 1994, p. 7.

American Indian Culture and Research Journal, 1987, pp. 51-73; spring, 2001, pp. 107-127, 179-180.

American Literature, September, 1990, pp. 405-422.

Atlantic Monthly, April, 2001, p. 104.

Belles Lettres, summer, 1990, pp. 30-31.

Book, May, 2001, Karen Olson, "The Complicated Life of Louise Erdrich," p. 32.

Booklist, January 15, 1995, Alice Joyce, review of *Conversations with Louise Erdrich and Michael Dorris*, p. 893; March 1, 1998, Bill Ott, review of *The Antelope Wife*, p. 1044; April 1, 1999, Hazel Rochman, review of *The Birchbark House*, p. 1427; January 1, 2000, p. 821; April 1, 2000, p. 1481; December 15, 2000, p. 787; February 15, 2001, Bill Ott, review of *The Last Report on the Miracles at Little No Horse*, p. 1085; October 1, 2001, Joyce Saricks, review of *The Last Report on the Miracles at Little No Horse* (audio version), p. 343.

Chicago Tribune, September 4, 1988, Thomas M. Disch, review of *Tracks*, pp. 1, 6; January 1, 1994, Michael Upchurch, review of *The Bingo Palace*, pp. 1, 9; April 21, 1996, Penelope Mesic, review of *Tales of Burning Love*, pp. 1, 9.

Christian Science Monitor, April 12, 2000, Ron Charles, "Louise Erdrich Finds More Miracles," p. 18.

College Literature, October, 1991, pp. 80-95.

Commonweal, October 24, 1986, Linda Simon, review of *The Beet Queen*, pp. 565, 567; November 4, 1988, Christopher Vecsey, review of *Tracks*, p. 596.

Entertainment Weekly, April 27, 2001, Rebecca Ascher-Walsh, "Past Imperfect," p. 110.

Horn Book, May-June, 1999, review of *The Birchbark House*, p. 329.

Kirkus Reviews, February 15, 1996, review of *The Blue Jay's Dance*, p. 244; April 15, 1996, p. 600.

Library Journal, March 15, 1998, Barbara Hoffert, review of *The Antelope Wife*, p. 92; May 1, 2001, Barbara Hoffert, review of *The Last Report on the Miracles at Little No Horse*, p. 125.

Los Angeles Times, May 17, 1998, Thomas Curwen, "Love Hurts"; April 15, 2001, Thomas Curwen, "The Making of a Saint," p. BR1.

Los Angeles Times Book Review, October 5, 1986, pp. 3, 10; September 11, 1988, Terry Tempest Williams, review of *Tracks*, p. 2; May 12, 1991, pp. 3, 13; February 6, 1994, Pam Houston, review of *The Bingo Palace*, p. 1, 13; May 28, 1995, p. 8; June 16, 1996, Verlyn Klinkenborg, "A Gulliver Shipwrecked on a Coast of Women," pp. 3, 13.

MELUS, summer, 1999, p. 89; fall-winter, 2000, pp. 65, 87.

Nation, October 21, 1991, pp. 465, 486-90.

New Leader, May, 2001, Lynn Sharon Schwartz, "Corporate Sinners and Crossover Saints," p. 35.

New Republic, October 6, 1986, Dorothy Wickenden, review of *The Beet Queen*, pp. 46-48; January 6-13, 1992, pp. 30-40.

Newsday, November 30, 1986.

Newsweek, March 23, 1998, p. 69.

New York Review of Books, January 15, 1987, Josh Rubins, review of *The Beet Queen*, pp. 14-15; November 19, 1988, Robert Towers, review or *Tracks*, pp. 40-41; May 12, 1996, p. 10.

New York Times, December 20, 1984, D. J. R. Bruckner, review of *Love Medicine,* p. C21; August 20, 1986, Michiko Kakutani, review of *The Beet Queen,* p. C21; August 24, 1988, p. 41; April 19, 1991, p. C25; March 24, 1998, Michiko Kakutani, review of *The Antelope Wife,* p. C18; April 6, 2001, Michiko Kakutani, "Saintliness, Too, May Be in the Eye of the Beholder," p. B41.

New York Times Book Review, August 31, 1982, p. 2; December 23, 1984, Marco Portales, review of *Love Medicine,* p. 6; August 31, 1986, Robert Bly, review of *The Beet Queen,* p. 2; October 2, 1988, pp. 1, 41-42; April 28, 1991, Robert Houston, review of *The Crown of Columbus,* p. 10; July 20, 1993, p. 20; January 16, 1994, Lawrence Thornton, review of *The Bingo Palace,* p. 7; April 16, 1995, Sue Halpern, review of *The Blue Jay's Dance,* p.14; May 12, 1996, Mark Childress, review of *Tales of Burning Love,* p. 10; April 12, 1998, Diana Postlethwaite, review of *The Antelope Wife,* p. 6; July 18, 1999, Mary Harris Russell, review of *The Birchbark House,* p. 7; April 8, 2001, Verlyn Klinkenborg, "Woman of Cloth," p. 7.

People, June 10, 1991, pp. 26-27; April 23, 2001, p. 47.

Playboy, March, 1994, p. 30.

Publishers Weekly, August 15, 1986, Miriam Berkley, "Louise Erdrich Interview," pp. 58-59; April 22, 1996, review of *Grandmother's Pigeon,* p. 71; November 1, 1999, p. 58; January 29, 2001, Sybil Steinberg, "PW Talks with Louise Erdrich," p. 64; July 2, 2001, review of *The Last Report on the Miracles at Little No Horse* (audio version), p. 31.

Quill & Quire, August, 1995, Jane Aspinall, review of *The Blue Jay's Dance,* p. 30.

School Library Journal, May, 1999, pp. 122-123.

Time, February 7, 1994, p. 71; April 9, 2001, Andrea Sachs, "A Woman with a Habit," p. 78.

Times Literary Supplement, February 14, 1997, Lavinia Greenlaw, review of *Tales of Burning Love,* p. 21.

Voice Literary Supplement, October, 1988, Katherine Dieckmann, review of *Tracks,* p. 37.

Washington Post Book World, August 31, 1986, pp. 1, 6; September 18, 1988, Jonathan Yardley, review of *Tracks,* p. 3; February 6, 1994, p. 5; April 21, 1996, Roxana Robinson, review of *Tales of Burning Love,* p. 3; April 22, 2001, Ursula K. Le Guin, "Lives of Saint," p. 13.

Western American Literature, February, 1991, pp. 363-364.

World Literature Today, winter, 2000, Howard Meredith, review of *The Antelope Wife,* p. 214.

Writer's Digest, June, 1991, pp. Michael Schumacher, interview with Louise Erdrich, pp. 28-31.

OTHER

Atlantic Unbound, http://www.theatlantic.com/ (January 17, 2001), Katie Bacon, "An Emissary of the Between-World."

BookPage, http://www.bookpage.com/ (February 28, 2002), Alden Mudge, "Louise Erdrich Explores Mysteries and Miracles on the Reservation."

HarperCollins.com, http://www.harpercollins.com/ (February 28, 2002), "Louise Erdrich: Author Bio."

Startribune.com, http://www.startribune.com/ (December 30, 2001), John Habich, "Louise Erdrich: 2001 Artist of the Year."*

Linda Greenlaw

■ Personal

Born in 1962, in Connecticut; daughter of Jim (an information-systems manager) and Martha (a homemaker) Greenlaw. *Education:* Colby College, B.A., 1983.

■ Addresses

Home—Isle au Haut, ME. *Agent*—c/o Hyperion, 114 Fifth Ave., New York, NY 10011.

■ Career

Author and fishing boat captain. Captain of the *Hannah Boden,* a Newfoundland fishing vessel, 1986-97; lobster fisherman, 1997—.

■ Writings

The Hungry Ocean: A Swordboat Captain's Journey, Hyperion (New York, NY), 1999.
The Lobster Chronicles, Hyperion (New York, NY), 2002.

■ Sidelights

Linda Greenlaw has braved 60-foot waves and sleepless nights in her chosen career as a swordfish captain. Furthermore, the thick-skinned Greenlaw is believed to be the only female in her profession in the United States. In her debut as an author, Greenlaw wrote about her experiences on a typical, but difficult, fishing trip on the waters of the Grand Banks. The book, *The Hungry Ocean: A Swordboat Captain's Journey,* published in 1999, details a 30-day trip on Greenlaw's boat, the *Hannah Boden.* Greenlaw and the *Hannah Boden* first caught the public's attention when they were featured in the extremely popular 1997 book *The Perfect Storm,* written by Sebastian Junger. Like Greenlaw's work, *The Perfect Storm* recounted the final days of the *Andrea Gail,* the sister ship to the *Hannah Boden,* before it sank in the same brooding waters of the Grand Banks during a vicious storm in 1991. Greenlaw's work differs in that it relates a more normal fishing venture. In the book Greenlaw describes her endeavor as "the true story of a real, and typical, sword-fishing trip, from leaving the dock to returning." The raw and honest account drew praise from many critics.

Greenlaw was born in Connecticut in the early 1960s, the daughter of Jim and Martha Greenlaw and the second of four children. Jim Greenlaw, an information systems manager, worked for the Bath Iron Works, a shipyard in Maine, while Greenlaw's mother stayed home to care for the children. Greenlaw was raised primarily in Topsham, in the vicinity of Portland, Maine. The family spent their summers in the tiny community of Isle au Haut (population 70) off the New England coast. Green-law was a tomboy, an adventurer, and a born sea-faring girl by her own admission. She loved the outdoors and loved to hunt rabbits; Daniel Boone was her role model. She loved boat rides, too, despite a predisposition for seasickness.

Begins Fishing Career

Growing up near the Maine coast, Greenlaw was drawn to the ocean from an early age. Greenlaw attended Colby College in Waterville, Maine, where she majored in both English and government. During the summer after her freshman year she secured a job as a cook and deckhand on a fishing boat named the Walter Leeman. The owner of the boat, Captain Alden Leeman, was immediately impressed with Greenlaw and never discouraged her enthusiasm. She continued with deckhand work during her free time and during vacations from school. By the time she graduated in 1983, she was determined that her career lay out to sea. In time she accumulated experience in steering the boat and spotting the fish, and she augmented her on-the-job training with trips to the library to learn the details of how the equipment worked and other useful information. She worked with Leeman for nearly ten years and never failed to impress him with her interest and intensity for the job. It was Leeman who installed Greenlaw as a swordfish captain in 1986 when he purchased a second boat, a 65-foot converted shrimper. The boat was old and Leeman himself felt apprehensive about sailing the rig, but Greenlaw appeared unfazed and took command of the boat.

"I have been surprised, even embarrassed, by the number of people who are genuinely amazed that a woman might be capable of running a fishing boat."

—Linda Greenlaw

Male and female alike, those who take to a fishing career are rare individuals. The work requires grit and determination, as swordfish are among the biggest of all of fisherman's prey, and they are swifter than other fish. Small swordfish weigh in the vicinity of 100 pounds, and the larger ones reach 500 pounds. The swordfish boats, called longliners, are approximately 100 feet long. Fishermen employ 40 miles of line to set out 1,000 hooks in 40-foot baited increments called "leaders." Every fish that takes the bait must eventually be pulled into the boat by hand, and that grueling chore, according to Greenlaw, makes the trip worthwhile. She welcomes the invigoration of a one-on-one contest with the fish.

Storms are an occupational hazard; they can send waves soaring to heights of 60 feet, yet Greenlaw never flinched at foul weather according to deckhands. As for monetary remuneration, Greenlaw never worked on salary. She agreed on a wage before she set sail and received a small capital fund prior to castoff, to cover expenses. Profits were split between the owner of the boat and the crew. With overhead averaging $40,000 per trip, profits were rare. According to Greenlaw, her earnings vacillated from $50,000 to $200,000 for any given three-month period when she swordfished.

Greenlaw stands a mere five-foot-three-inches tall, yet by her own admission was undaunted by the difficulty and loneliness of the work. The issue of gender bias in a traditionally male occupation never surfaced in her mind because of the fever-pitch excitement that she realized in the hunt. "Being a woman hasn't been a big deal," Greenlaw wrote in *The Hungry Ocean*. "I never anticipated problems stemming from being female, and never encountered any. I have been surprised, even embarrassed, by the number of people who are genuinely amazed that a woman might be capable of running a fishing boat." It was Greenlaw's parents, more so than her co-workers in fact, who had the most difficulty with her decision to work on the boats. For a time she promised them that she would quit and enroll in law school, but her heart kept her at sea for nearly twenty years.

Greenlaw's life as the only female swordfish captain in the United States came to public attention in 1997 when Sebastian Junger published his book, *The Perfect Storm*. Detailing the once-in-a-hundred-years storm that struck the Newfoundland fishing region in 1991, Junger told of how the *Andrea Gail* sank with six crewmen on board while Greenlaw's ship *Hannah Boden* survived. Junger, also a captain, cited Greenlaw for her seafaring skills. He made an often quoted comment that Greenlaw was, "One of the best captains, period, on the East Coast," and remarked that Greenlaw's swordfish hauls sent market prices plummeting worldwide whenever she docked. Book publishers pursued her to write a personal story of her non-traditional lifestyle. After a bidding war between a number of publishers, Greenlaw agreed to write a book for Hyperion for a $150,000 advance.

Writes Memoir "The Hungry Ocean"

Greenlaw's book details a trip that she made on the *Hannah Boden* with a crew of six. The story, *The Hungry Ocean: A Swordboat Captain's Journey,* described a typical month-long ordeal replete with the real problems that face captains and crew out at sea. Racism, drugs, and insubordination preclude an idyllic experience in even the calmest of waters according to Greenlaw. She effectively described 20-hour workdays onboard the ship, and the trials of living cramped together for 30 days with 50,000 pounds of fish on board. She discussed loyalty and the bravery of selfless shipmates. A *Publishers Weekly* critic commented that Greenlaw's authoritative manner might serve as an inspiration "among personnel managers everywhere." Greenlaw in turn admitted that her crew sometimes called her "ma."

In her book, Greenlaw also described what it is like being female in a male-dominated industry. Even though she had become one of the most successful swordboat captains in the Grand Banks fleet, Greenlaw felt she was often overlooked because of her sex. However, in the book, she writes of her dislike for words such as "fisherwoman." "I am a woman. I am a fisherman. . . . I am not a fisherwoman, fisherlady, or fishergirl. If anything else, I am a thirty-seven-year-old tomboy. It's a word I have never outgrown," the author explained. Greenlaw also discussed the adjustments she made, as well as what she had given up to become a fisherman. "Who cared that I had sacrificed so much for my life adventure? Who knew that I desperately wanted a husband, a house full of children, a boring job?" she wrote.

Yet the main focus of *The Hungry Ocean* is on the month-long trip itself, which the author described as a "slammer." Greenlaw recounted every aspect of the *Hannah Boden*'s voyage, from the type of high-tech equipment used to the importance of a good cook, and even to the expectations and disappointments felt by the crew. Much of the book is devoted to how Greenlaw relates to her all-male crew and the personality conflicts that arise because of the exhausting work and close quarters. Carolyn Fry in *Geographical* noted: "We witness the tensions on board; the difficulties she faces in keeping six men in a confined space away from each other's throats and focused on the task in hand—landing enough swordfish to pay their wages. When the fish remain elusive, we share the crew's disappointment; when the weather and catch is good, we feel triumphant. And we quietly grieve with them for their lost colleagues as the *Hannah Boden* sails close to where the *Andrea Gail* was lost."

Most critics, such as Douglass Whynott of the *New York Times Book Review,* enjoyed Greenlaw's detailed descriptions. "The narrative can be gruesome at times. Catching big fish involves butchery, and here its told in exuberant detail, the slicing and dicing and hooking," Whynott wrote. Whynott went on to call *The Hungry Ocean* "a beautiful book for what it says about the love of the sea." In contrast, a contributor for *Kirkus Reviews* questioned the genuineness of Greenlaw's account, noting that "there is a spit and polish to her writing that feels distant from the subject, not so much overwritten as manufactured." But Brian McCombie of *Booklist* lauded the effort, referring to it as "exciting and gritty."

While *The Hungry Ocean* impressed the critics, it also impressed readers nationwide. An initial printing of 50,000 copies in May of 1999 sold quickly, and by September of that same year the manuscript was in its tenth printing. Greenlaw made personal appearances throughout the year, then switched her sights to fishing for lobster offshore from her residence at Isle au Haut, on her boat, the *Mattie Belle.* She admitted a need to "hug the shore" for a time.

Moves to Isle au Haut

In 2002 Greenlaw published *The Lobster Chronicles,* an account of her life as a lobster fisherman in Maine. Part memoir and part handbook to lobster fishing, the book tells as much about Greenlaw's personal life on the island of Isle au Haut as it does about her work. With only 47 year-round residents, half of whom are Greenlaw's relatives, the island is small and even a bit claustrophobic. Because the book "depicts the foibles and quirks of the independent islanders," as Stephanie Schorow wrote in the *Boston Herald,* Greenlaw was a "little nervous" about it. "I kept my fingers crossed," she told Schorow. "I was so relieved. Everything I've heard has been really positive."

Greenlaw's return to Isle au Haut was stirred by her desire to get reacquainted with her parents, who live on the island, to work close to shore so she can return home every day, and possibly find a husband so she can raise a family of her own. As she told Schorow, "I want what my parents have. I want a companion-slash-mate. I want to have children. It's not something I'm ashamed of. I really don't have any reason to be anything but open and honest about it." But, as Susan Tekulve noted in her review for *Book,* "lobsters are scarce, and eligible men are even more elusive" on Isle au Haut. The critic for *Publishers Weekly* found *The Lobster Chronicles* found that Greenlaw's "self-speculation and uncertainties ... nicely balance her delightfully cocky es-

---

If you enjoy the works of Linda Greenlaw, you might want to check out the following books:

Jon Krakauer, *Into the Wild,* 1996, and *Into Thin Air,* 1997.
Sebastian Junger, *The Perfect Storm,* 1997.
Derek Lundy, *Godforsaken Sea: The True Story of a Race Through the World's Most Dangerous Waters,* 1999.

---

says of island life." Rebecca Brown of *Rebecca's Reads* called the book "a surprisingly absorbing memoir of the life and times of a Maine lobster fisherman who has seen beyond her horizon."

■ **Biographical and Critical Sources**

BOOKS

Greenlaw, Linda, *The Hungry Ocean: A Swordboat Captain's Journey,* Hyperion (New York, NY), 1999.

PERIODICALS

Book, July-August, 2002, Susan Tekulve, review of *The Lobster Chronicles,* p. 82.
Booklist, May 15, 1999, p. 1652; March 15, 2000, Ted Hipple, review of *The Hungry Ocean* audiobook, p. 1396.
Boothbay Register, August 5, 1999, "The Hungry Ocean Author Linda Greenlaw to Visit Sherman's Book Store."
Boston Herald, July 15, 2002, Stephanie Schorow, "Swordfishing Legend Greenlaw Changes Course for Island Life in 'Lobster Chronicles,'" p. 27.
Christian Science Monitor, August 19, 1999, John Bolt, "Master of Her Ship and Her Destiny."
Coastal Living, May-June, 2002, "Lobster Appetizer: An Excerpt from Linda Greenlaw's New Book."
Entertainment Weekly, July 26, 2002, Karen Valby, review of *The Lobster Chronicles,* p. 64.
Geographical, May, 2000, Carolyn Fry, review of *The Hungry Ocean,* p. 92.
Kirkus Reviews, April 15, 1999, p. 598.

Library Journal, May 15, 1999, p. 116; February 1, 2000, Gloria Maxwell, review of *The Hungry Ocean* audiobook, p. 134.
Minerva: Quarterly Report on Women and the Military, spring, 2001, Darlene Iskra, review of *The Hungry Ocean,* p. 39.
National Fisherman, August, 1999.
New York Times Book Review, May 9, 1999, p. 23.
People Weekly, August 30, 1999, Peter Ames Carlin and Tom Duffy, "What's My Line?: One of Few Women to Ever Captain a Swordfish Boat, Linda Greenlaw Hooks Readers with a Memoir of the Deep," p. 69.
Publishers Weekly, January 12, 1998, Judy Quinn, "A 'Perfect Storm' Spinoff, of Sorts," p. 17; April 12, 1999, review of *The Hungry Ocean,* p. 62; July 19, 1999, Daisy Maryles, "Storming the Charts," p. 84; August 2, 1999, review of *The Hungry Ocean* audiobook, p. 27; September 6, 1999, Daisy Maryles, "Gone Fishin'," p. 23; May 6, 2002, review of *The Lobster Chronicles,* p. 44; July 8, 2002, Charlotte Abbott, "Catching Lobster Lovers in Their Natural Habitat," p. 18.
Women's Review of Books, October, 1999, Meg Daly, "In the Boys' Club," p. 23.
Yachting, July, 2000, Kenny Wooton, "'Perfect' Postscript: Flawed Practice," p. 13.

OTHER

American and International Authors Index, http://www.bestselling-books.com/ (February 21, 2001), "About Linda Greenlaw."
CBS News Online, http://www.cbsnews.com/ (February 21, 2001), "Woman in the Eye of the Storm."
Habitat Media Web site, http://www.habitatmedia.org/ (July 25, 2002), interview with Linda Greenlaw.
Keppler Associates Speakers Bureau, http://www.kepplerassociates.com/ (February 21, 2001).
Rebecca's Reads Web site, http://rebeccasreads.com/ (July 25, 2002), Rebecca Brown, review of *The Lobster Chronicles.*
Sportsjones: The Daily Online Sports Magazine, http://www.sportsjones.com/ (February 21, 2001), Jeff Merron, review of *The Hungry Ocean.*
USA Today Online, http://www.usatoday.com/ (February 21, 2001), "On the High Seas: Linda Greenlaw."*

John Grisham

Personal

Born February 8, 1955, in Jonesboro, AR; son of a construction worker and a homemaker; married Renee Jones; children: Ty, Shea (daughter). *Education:* Mississippi State University, B.S., University of Mississippi, J.D. *Religion:* Baptist.

Addresses

Home—Charlottesville, VA. *Agent*—Jay Garon-Brooke Associates, Inc., 101 West 55th St., Suite 5K, New York, NY 10019.

Career

Writer. Admitted to the Bar of the State of Mississippi, 1981; lawyer in private practice in Southaven, MS, 1981-90. Served in Mississippi House of Representatives, 1984-90.

Writings

NOVELS

A Time to Kill, Wynwood Press (New York, NY), 1989.

The Firm, Doubleday (New York, NY), 1991.
The Pelican Brief, Doubleday (New York, NY), 1992.
The Client, Doubleday (New York, NY), 1993.
John Grisham (collection), Dell (New York, NY), 1993.
The Chamber, Doubleday (New York, NY), 1994.
The Rainmaker, Doubleday (New York, NY), 1995.
The Runaway Jury, Doubleday (New York, NY), 1996.
The Partner, Doubleday (New York, NY), 1997.
The Street Lawyer, Doubleday (New York, NY), 1998.
The Testament, Doubleday (New York, NY), 1999.
The Brethren, Doubleday (New York, NY), 2000.
A Painted House, Doubleday (New York, NY), 2001.
Skipping Christmas, Doubleday (New York, NY), 2001.
The Summons, Doubleday (New York, NY), 2002.

Also author of screenplays *The Gingerbread Man* (under pseudonym Al Hayes), and *Mickey.*

Adaptations

The Firm was adapted as a film directed by Sydney Pollack and starring Tom Cruise, Gene Hackman, and Jeanne Tribblehorn, Paramount Pictures, 1993; *The Pelican Brief* was adapted as a film directed by Alan J. Pakula and starring Julia Roberts and Denzel Washington, 1994; *The Client* was adapted as a film directed by Joel Schumacher and starring Susan Sarandon and Tommy Lee Jones, 1994; *The Chamber* was adapted as a film directed by James

Foley and starring Chris O'Donnell and Gene Hackman, 1996; *A Time to Kill* was adapted as a film directed by Joel Schumacher and starring Matthew McConaughey and Sandra Bullock, 1996; *The Rainmaker* was adapted as a film directed by Francis Ford Coppola and starring Matt Damon and Claire Danes, 1997.

■ Sidelights

The author of fourteen back-to-back bestsellers, many of which have been turned into blockbuster movies, John Grisham can count his revenues and copies sold of his legal thrillers in the hundreds of millions. Translated into more than thirty languages, Grisham was one of the major success stories in publishing during the 1990s. As Malcolm Jones noted in *Newsweek*, Grisham was "the best-selling author" of the decade with his formula of "David and Goliath go to court," and the success of his books has helped to make legal thrillers one of the most popular genres among U.S. readers. Jones further commented, "As part of an elite handful of megaselling authors that includes Stephen King, Danielle Steele, Michael Crichton and Tom Clancy, Grisham has literally taken bookselling to places it's never been before—not just to airport kiosks but to price clubs and, most recently, online bookselling." Grisham's best-sellerdom even extends to countries where the legal system is completely different than that in the United States. "He sells to everyone," Jones continued, "from teens to senior citizens, from lawyers in Biloxi to housewives in Hong Kong."

When Grisham began writing his first novel, he never dreamed that he would become one of America's best-selling novelists. Yet the appeal of his legal thrillers such as *The Firm, The Pelican Brief, The Client, The Rainmaker,* and *The Summons,* among others, has been so great that initial hardcover print runs of his novels number in the hundreds of thousands and the reading public regularly buys millions of copies of his books. The one-time lawyer now enjoys a celebrity status that few writers will ever know. "We think of ourselves as regular people, I swear we do," Grisham was quoted as saying of himself and his family by Keli Pryor in *Entertainment Weekly.* "But then someone will drive 200 miles and show up on my front porch with books for me to sign. Or an old friend will stop by and want to drink coffee for an hour. It drives me crazy." As he told Jones, "I'm a famous writer in a country where nobody reads."

Hardscrabble Youth

As a youth, Grisham had no dreams of becoming a writer, although he did like to read. Born in Jonesboro, Arkansas in 1955, he was the son of a construction-worker father and a mother who was a homemaker for the family. His father traveled extensively in his job, and the Grisham family moved many times. Each time the family took up residence in a new town, Grisham would immediately go to the public library to get a library card. "I was never a bookworm," he maintained in an interview for *Bookreporter.com.* "I remember reading Dr. Seuss, the Hardy Boys, *Emil and the Detectives,* Chip Hilton, and lots of Mark Twain and Dickens." Another constant for Grisham was his love of baseball, something he has taken with him into adulthood. One way he and his brothers would gauge the quality of each new hometown was by inspecting its little league ballpark. In 1967 the family moved to a permanent home in Southaven, Mississippi. There, Grisham enjoyed greater success in high school athletics than he did in English composition, a subject in which he earned a D grade. Although he had determined to become a professional baseball player, it seemed to others that Grisham's dreams were larger than his reach. "My athletic ability did nothing but invite taunts," he told *Bookreporter.com.* "I was an indifferent student and an athlete with delusions of adequacy, dreams of adulation."

After high school graduation Grisham enrolled at Northwest Junior College in Senatobia, Mississippi, where he remained for a year, playing baseball for the school team. Transferring to Delta State University in Cleveland, Mississippi, he continued with his baseball career until he realized that he was not going to make it to the big leagues. Transferring to Mississippi State University, Grisham studied accounting with the ambition of eventually becoming a tax attorney. By the time he earned his law degree from the University of Mississippi, however, his interest had shifted to criminal law, and he returned to Southaven to establish a practice in that field.

Lawyer, Legislator, Writer

Although his practice was successful, Grisham grew restless in his new career. He switched to the more lucrative field of civil law and won many cases, but the sense of personal dissatisfaction remained. Hoping to somehow make a difference in the world, he entered politics with the aim of reforming his state's educational system. Running as a Democrat, he won a post in the state legislature; four years later, he was reelected. After a total of seven years in public office, Grisham became convinced that he would never be able to cut through the red tape of government bureaucracy in his effort to improve Mississippi's educational system and resigned his post in 1990. "I served for seven years in the Mississippi

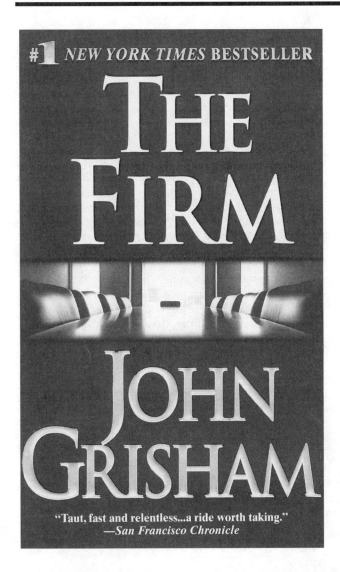

#1 *NEW YORK TIMES* **BESTSELLER**

THE FIRM

JOHN GRISHAM

"Taut, fast and relentless...a ride worth taking."
—*San Francisco Chronicle*

John Grisham burst onto the literary scene with this 1991 novel about an ambitious young attorney who joins a high-powered law firm with clients of questionable integrity.

House of Representatives," Grisham told Benjamin Svetkey in an interview for *Entertainment Weekly*, "almost two terms, then I quit. You have to serve about twenty years there before you have any clout. The chamber was full of these old moss-backs who'd been there forever. So I just said, I can't do this. I'm still a junkie when it comes to politics—I can't help but follow it—but I never want to serve in office again."

While working in the legislature, Grisham continued to run his law office. His first book, *A Time to Kill,* was inspired by a scene he saw one day in court, when a preadolescent girl testified against her rapist. "I felt everything in those moments," Gr-

isham told Pryor. "Revulsion, total love for that child, hate for that defendant. Everyone in that courtroom wanted a gun to shoot him." Unable to get the story out of his mind, be began to wonder what would happen if the girl's father had killed his daughter's assailant. Soon he had the core of a book dealing with a black father who shoots the white man who raped his daughter. "I never felt such emotion and human drama in my life," Grisham disclosed to *People*. "I became obsessed wondering what it would be like if the girl's father killed that rapist and was put on trial. I had to write it down."

Writing his first novel, let alone publishing it, was no easy task for Grisham. "Because I have this problem of starting projects and not completing them, my goal for this book was simply to finish it," he revealed to *Publishers Weekly* interviewer Michelle Bearden. "Then I started thinking that it would be nice to have a novel sitting on my desk, something I could point to and say, 'Yeah, I wrote that.' But it didn't consume me. I had way too much going on to make it a top priority. If it happened, it happened." Working sixty- to seventy-hour weeks between his law practice and political duties, Grisham rose at five in the morning to write an hour a day on his first novel, thinking of the activity as a hobby rather than a serious effort at publication.

Finishing the manuscript in 1987, Grisham next had to look for an agent. He was turned down by several before finally receiving a positive response from Jay Garon. Agent and author encountered a similarly difficult time trying to find a publisher; 5,000 copies of the book were finally published by Wynwood Press and Grisham received a check for $15,000. He purchased 1,000 copies of the book himself, peddling them at garden-club meetings and libraries and giving many of them away to family and friends. Ironically, *A Time to Kill* is now rated by some commentators as the finest of Grisham's novels. Furthermore, according to Pryor, "Those first editions are now worth $3,900 each," and after being republished, "the novel Grisham . . . couldn't give away has 8.6 million copies in print and has spent 80 weeks on the best-seller lists."

Corners Market on Legal Thrillers

Despite the limited initial success of *A Time to Kill,* Grisham was not discouraged from trying his hand at another novel. The second time around he decided to follow guidelines set forth in a *Writer's Digest* article for plotting a suspense novel. The result was *The Firm,* the story of a corrupt Memphis-based law firm established by organized crime for purposes of shielding and falsifying earnings. Recruited to the practice is Mitchell McDeere, a promising Harvard law school graduate who is overwhelmed by the company's apparent extravagance. After learning of his employers' uncompromising methods, including relentless surveillance of its employees and their families, McDeere grows increasingly alarmed—and curious. When his criminal bosses discover that McDeere has been indulging his curiosity, he becomes an instant target of both the firm and the authorities monitoring the firm's activities. Agents from both the Central Intelligence Agency and the Federal Bureau of Investigation pressure McDeere to function as a spy within the firm. When he runs afoul of the ostensible good guys, McDeere finds himself in seemingly endless danger.

Grisham was not as motivated when writing *The Firm* as he had been when composing *A Time to Kill,* but with his wife's encouragement he finished the book. Before he even began trying to sell the manuscript, he learned that someone had acquired a bootlegged copy of it and was willing to give him $600,000 to turn it into a movie script. Within two weeks, Doubleday, one of the many publishers that had previously rejected *A Time to Kill,* offered Grisham a contract.

Upon *The Firm*'s publication, several reviewers argued that Grisham had not attained a high art form, although it was generally conceded that he had put together a compelling thriller. *Los Angeles Times Book Review* critic Charles Champlin wrote that the "character penetration is not deep, but the accelerating tempo of paranoia-driven events is wonderful." Chicago *Tribune Books* reviewer Bill Brashler offered similar praise, proclaiming that *The Firm* reads "like a whirlwind." The novel was listed on the *New York Times* bestseller list for nearly a year and sold approximately ten times as many copies as its predecessor. By the time the film version was released, there were more than seven million copies of *The Firm* in print. This amazing success gave Gr-

A young woman dying of leukemia (Claire Danes) seeks the help of a young attorney (Matt Damon) in battling an insurance company denying payment for her treatments in the film adaptation of Grisham's 1995 novel *The Rainmaker*.

isham the means he needed to build his dream house, quit his law practice, and devote himself entirely to writing.

In a mere 100 days, Grisham wrote his follow-up to *The Firm*. Another legal thriller, *The Pelican Brief* tells the story of a brilliant, beautiful female law student named Darby Shaw. When two U.S. Supreme Court justices are murdered, Shaw postulates a theory as to why the crimes were committed. Just telling people about her idea makes her gravely vulnerable to the corrupt law firm responsible for the killings. Soon she is running for her life—all the while bravely continuing to investigate the conspiracy. In reviewing *The Pelican Brief*, some critics complained that Grisham had followed the premise of *The Firm* far too closely. John Skow reflected this opinion in his review for *Time*: "The Pelican Brief . . . is as close to its predecessor as you can get without running *The Firm* through the office copier."

In addition to some criticism, Grisham also received praise for creating another exciting story. Frank J. Prial, writing in the *New York Times Book Review*, observed that despite some flaws in *The Pelican Brief*, "Grisham has written a genuine page-turner. He has an ear for dialogue and is a skillful craftsman." Made into a film starring Denzel Washington and Julia Roberts, *The Pelican Brief* enjoyed success comparable to *The Firm*, selling millions of copies.

In just six months, Grisham put together yet another bestseller titled *The Client*. This legal thriller focuses on a young boy who, after learning a sinister secret, turns to a motherly lawyer for protection from both the mob and the FBI. Like *The Firm* and *The Pelican Brief*, the book drew lukewarm reviews but became a bestseller and a major motion picture. For a time in the spring of 1993, after *The Client* came out and *A Time to Kill* was republished, Grisham was in the rare and enviable position of having a book at the top of the hardcover bestseller list and books in the first, second, and third spots on the paperback bestseller list.

In *Entertainment Weekly*, Grisham acknowledged that his second, third, and fourth books were formula-driven. He described his recipe for a bestseller in the following way: "You throw an innocent person in there and get 'em caught up in a conspiracy and you get 'em out." He also admitted to rushing through the writing of *The Pelican Brief* and *The Client*, resulting in "some damage" to the books' quality. Yet he also complained that the critical community treats popular writers harshly. "I've sold too many books to get good reviews anymore," he told Pryor. "There's a lot of jealousy, because [reviewers] think they can write a good novel or a best-seller and get frustrated when they can't. As a group, I've learned to despise them."

Slows the Pace

With his fifth novel, Grisham departed from his proven formula and proceeded at a more leisurely pace. Not only did he take a full nine months to write *The Chamber*, a book in which the "good guys" and "bad guys" are not as clearly defined as in his previous efforts, but the book itself, at almost five hundred pages, takes time to unravel its story line. The novel tells the tale of Ku Klux Klansman Sam Cayhall, who is on death row for the murder of two young sons of a Jewish civil rights attorney. After languishing in prison for years, Cayhall is surprised by the arrival of his estranged grandson, Adam Hall. Hall, an attorney, sets out to reverse his grandfather's death sentence, even though he considers Sam to be the family demon.

The novel is a careful study of a family's history, an examination of the relationship between lawyer and client, and a description of life on death row. It is "a curiously rich milieu for a Grisham novel," according to *Entertainment Weekly* critic Mark Harris, "and it allows the author to do some of his best writing since [*A Time to Kill*.]" Skow credited Grisham with producing a thought-provoking treatise on the death penalty. In *Time* Skow noted that *The Chamber* "has the pace and characters of a thriller, but little else to suggest that it was written by the glib and cheeky author of Grisham's legal entertainments. His tough first novel, the courtroom rouser *A Time to Kill*, is a closer match. . . . Grisham may not change opinions with this sane, civil book, and he may not even be trying to. What he does ask, very plainly, is an important question: Is this what you want?" A reviewer for the London *Sunday Times* stated that "Grisham may do without poetry, wit and style, and offer only the simplest characterisation. The young liberal lawyer may be colourless and the spooky old prisoner one-dimensional; but there is no doubt that this ex-lawyer knows how to tell a story." While *The Chamber* was less obviously commercial than his previous three books, Grisham had little trouble selling the movie rights for a record fee. The movie, starring Chris O'Donnell and Gene Hackman, was released in 1996.

Grisham's 1995 novel, *The Rainmaker*, features a young lawyer, Rudy Baylor, recently graduated from law school, who finds himself desperate for a job when the small firm he had planned to work for is bought out by a large, prestigious Memphis firm that has no use for him. After going to work for Bruiser Stone, a shady lawyer with underworld clients, Baylor finds himself averting an FBI raid on Stone's firm while also trying to pursue a lawsuit brought by a terminally ill leukemia patient against an insurance company that has refused to pay for

Gene Hackman and Chris O'Donnell star in the 1996 film adaptation of *The Chamber*, adapted from Grisham's novel about a man who attempts to clear the name of his grandfather, a member of the Ku Klux Klan convicted of murder.

her treatment. While some reviewers again directed harsh criticism at Grisham for his "pedestrian prose" and "ridiculously implausible" plot—in the words of *New York Times* critic Michiko Kakutani—others praised the novel. Garry Abrams, for instance, writing in the *Los Angeles Times Book Review*, commended the author's "complex plotting," noting: "In his loping, plain prose, Grisham handles all his themes with admirable dexterity and clarity." The book was made into a motion picture starring Matt Damon and Claire Danes and released in 1997.

Grisham also garnered surprisingly warm critical comments for 1996's *The Runaway Jury*. Set in a Mississippi gulf coast town, the novel features a legal showdown between several large tobacco companies—"Big Tobacco," in Grisham's parlance—and the widow of a man who died of lung cancer after smoking heavily for three decades. At issue in the trial are the makeup and actions of the jury. Big Tobacco hires the ruthless Rankin Fitch to influence the jury in subtle ways to ensure that it will acquit

the tobacco companies of any wrongdoing, but Fitch finds himself challenged unexpectedly by the mysterious Nicholas Easter, who gets himself appointed to the jury. Along with his girlfriend, Marlee, Easter appears to have even greater influence over the actions of the jury than Fitch does. Writing in the *New York Times*, Christopher Lehmann-Haupt remarked that Grisham's "prose continues to be clunky, the dialogue merely adequate and the characters as unsubtle as pushpins." But the critic also felt that "the plot's eventual outcome is far more entertainingly unpredictable" than Grisham's previous novels, and he declared that Grisham "for once . . . is telling a story of genuine significance."

Grisham continued his streak of phenomenally popular novels with 1997's *The Partner*, about a law-firm partner who fakes his own death and absconds with ninety million dollars. In pursuit are his former partners and a shady defense contractor who had planned to split the millions, which were generated by a fraudulent claim. With the help of a mysterious Brazilian named Eva Miranda, the fugitive figures out an ingenious scheme to hide the money but is unable to avoid the pursuit of his enemies. Discussing his less-than-virtuous protagonist, Grisham told Mel Gussow of the *New York Times,* "I wanted to show that with money you can really manipulate the system. You can buy your way out of trouble." *Philadelphia Inquirer* reviewer Robert Drake called *The Partner* "a fine book, wholly satisfying, and a superb example of a masterful storyteller's prowess captured at its peak."

Lawyers with a Twist

With *Street Lawyer* Grisham once again presents a young lawyer on the fast track who has a life-altering experience. Michael Brock, a young lawyer on the rise, is taken hostage, along with eight other attorneys, at his upscale firm by a homeless man who identifies himself simply as Mister. A police sniper ends the standoff, killing Mister and leaving Michael troubled. He soon discovers that Mister was one of many evicted from apartments with the aid of Michael's law firm; further investigations show that the same eviction resulted in the deaths of a mother and her four small children. Ultimately Michael's social conscience kicks in and he quits his cushy job to go after his now-former law firm.

The fast pace and moral stance of the novel attracted a chorus of praise. Reviewing *Street Lawyer* in *Entertainment Weekly,* Tom De Haven noted that "success hasn't spoiled John Grisham. Instead of churning out rote legal thrillers, his court reporting keeps getting better." De Haven further noted that Grisham, while not having the "literary genius" of John Steinbeck, "does share with him the conscience of a social critic and the soul of a preacher." Cynthia Sanz similarly reported that Grisham "has forsaken some of his usual suspense and fireworks in favor of an unabashedly heart-tugging portrait of homelessness." However, Sanz further noted that the author does not sacrifice his "zippy pacing" to do so. Praise did not only appear in the popular press. "In a powerful story," wrote Jacalyn N. Kolk in the *Florida Bar Journal,* "John Grisham tells it like it is on both sides of the street." Kolk felt that this "entertaining" novel "may stir some of us [lawyers] to pay more attention to the world around us."

The Testament provides another departure from the usual Grisham formula. As a reviewer for *Publishers Weekly* noted, "Grisham confounds expectations by sweeping readers into adventure in the Brazilian wetlands and, more urgently, into a man's search for spiritual renewal." Grisham has firsthand experience of Brazil, having traveled there often and once even helping to build houses for the poor. His novel eschews the legal wrangling and courtroom suspense his readers have come to expect. Instead, in this tale he proves he "can spin an adventure yarn every bit as well as he can craft a legal thriller," according to *Newsweek* reviewer Jones. In the book, billionaire Troy Phelan, an elderly eccentric, leaves his wealth to his illegitimate daughter, Rachel Lane, a missionary in Brazil. Nate O'Reilly, a dissipated alcoholic who is also a top attorney in Washington, D.C., is dispatched by his firm to track down Rachel. But Nate has no idea what he is in for: fierce storms, a plane crash, hunger, dangerous animals, and dengue fever all confront him. Meanwhile, back home Phelan's other children scheme to get the will set aside. In Brazil Nate finds Rachel and through her integrity and serenity turns away from his old gods of power and booze. The reviewer for *Publishers Weekly* felt that while the storytelling is not "subtle," Grisham's use of the suspense novel to "explore questions of being and faith puts him squarely in the footsteps of Dickens and Graham Greene." The same reviewer concluded that *The Testament* is "sincere, exciting, and tinged with wonder." Speaking with Jones, Grisham remarked, "The point I was trying to make with Nate was that if you spend your life pursuing money and power, you're going to have a pretty sad life."

Lawyers and judges of a much different ilk populate Grisham's eleventh novel, *The Brethren.* Incarcerated in a minimum-security federal prison, three former judges meet daily in the law library, writing briefs and handling cases for other inmates. But they are also fine-tuning a scam of quietly epic proportions. Soliciting closeted gay males with ads run in magazines, they then turn around and blackmail the respondents. Things are going fine until they catch the wrong fish—a congressman on his way to the White House with very strong connections in the CIA. The congressman's powerful supporters do not want to see their man destroyed, and thus the hunt is on for the blackmailers. Noting that Grisham veered away from his usual David-and-Goliath scenario in *The Brethren,* a reviewer for *Publishers Weekly* still felt that "all will be captivated by this clever thriller that presents as crisp a cast as he's yet devised, and as grippingly sardonic yet bitingly moral a scenario as he's ever imagined." Writing in *Entertainment Weekly,* De Haven also commented on the novel's cast of ne'er do wells, noting that "if you can get past [Grisham's] creepy misanthropy, he's written a terrifically entertaining story."

Mainstream Fiction

With his 2001 novel, *A Painted House,* initially serialized in *The Oxford American*—a small literary magazine Grisham co-owns—the author did the unthinkable for his fans: he wrote a book with no lawyers. "It's a highly fictionalized childhood memoir of a month in the life of a 7-year-old kid, who is basically me," Grisham explained to *Entertainment Weekly*'s Benjamin Svetkey. *Book*'s Liz Seymour called the novel "genre-busting," and "the unsentimental story of a single harvest season in the Arkansas Delta as seen through the eyes of the seven-year-old son and grandson of cotton farmers." Though the tale may be without lawyers, it is not without conflict and incident, including trouble between the migrant workers young Luke Chandler's family brings in for the cotton harvest. The plot includes a couple of murders and an illegitimate birth for starters, and a tornado that threatens to destroy the Chandler livelihood. A reviewer for *Publishers Weekly* noted that Grisham's "writing has evolved with nearly every book," and though the "mechanics" might still be visible in *A Painted House,* there are "characters that no reader will forget, prose as clean and strong as any Grisham has yet laid down and a drop-dead evocation of a time and place that mark this novel as a classic slice of Americana."

Some critics differed. Writing in *Booklist,* Stephanie Zvirin called into question the merits of Grisham's coming-of-age novel: "The measured, descriptive prose is readable, to be sure, and there are some truly tender moments, but this is surface without substance, simply an inadequate effort in a genre that has exploded with quality over the last several years." As usual with a Grisham novel, however, there was a divergence among critical voices. What Zvirin found "inadequate," *Entertainment Weekly* contributor Bruce Fretts described as a "gem of an autobiographical novel." Fretts further commented, "Never let it be said this man doesn't know how to spin a good yarn." And reviewing *A Painted House* in *Time*, Jess Cagle criticized the slow pace of the book, but concluded that Grisham's "compassion for his characters is infectious, and the book is finally rewarding—a Sunday sermon from a Friday-night storyteller."

A modern Christmas tale replaces courtroom antics in center stage in *Skipping Christmas,* when accountant Luther Krank convinces his wife in a Scrooge-like manner to skip the usual Christmas and go on a Caribbean cruise instead. They will miss all the shopping, office parties, card-swapping, and other cumbersome events of the season . . or so they think. At the last minute, a telephone call changes their plans. "Hilarity ensues," noted *Library Journal* reviewer Samantha J. Gust, "but the poignant conclusion is unforgettable." Gust found *Skipping Christmas* further proof of Grisham's "ability to tell a story without a courtroom in sight." Reviewing the same title in *Publishers Weekly,* a contributor thought that though Grisham's story "lacks magic," the "misanthropy in this short novel makes a good antidote to more cloying Christmas tales, and the book is fun to read."

#1 *NEW YORK TIMES* **BESTSELLER**

THE BRETHREN

JOHN GRISHAM

"TERRIFIC STORYTELLING BY ONE OF THE MASTERS OF THE GAME."—*USA TODAY*

In this 2000 novel a trio of incarcerated former judges hatch a plan to make millions of dollars while still behind prison walls.

Returns to Legal Thrillers

With his 2002 title, *The Summons,* Grisham answered the summons of his millions of fans and returned to his lawyer roots. The book marked not only his return to thrillers, but also to Ford County, Mississippi, which was the setting for *A Time to Kill.* Ray

If you enjoy the works of John Grisham, you might want to check out the following books:

David Morrell, *The Covenant of the Flame*, 1991.
Scott Turow, *Pleading Guilty*, 1993.
David Baldacci, *Last Man Standing*, 2001.

Atlee is a forty-three-year-old professor of law at the University of Virginia. Still reeling from a recent divorce, he receives a letter from his dying father to come to the family home in Mississippi for a final reckoning. Estranged from this cranky but supposedly incorruptible former judge, Atlee is reluctant to make the trip, but does so only to discover his father already dead and several million dollars in cash waiting at the house. Atlee's black-sheep brother, who also received a summons, arrives later. Ray has one question: Where did all this money come from? Ray has little time to ask questions, however, as his brother goes missing and a gang of thugs pursues him even at his father's funeral. Reviewing the book in *Entertainment Weekly*, Svetkey was not impressed, finding *The Summons* "not all that tough to put down" and with "few shocking surprises." Nonetheless, shortly after publication *The Summons* topped the list of hardcover best sellers, selling well over 100,000 copies in its first week of publication alone.

In little more than a decade Grisham realized greater success than most writers enjoy in a lifetime. Despite such success, the former lawyer and politician remains realistic about his limitations, and believes that a time may come when he will walk away from writing just as he previously abandoned both law and politics. In his interview with Bearden, he compared writers to athletes and concluded: "There's nothing sadder than a sports figure who continues to play past his prime." However, beginning his second decade as a novelist Grisham seemed far from that point, his imagination still swirling with new book ideas. "They drop in from all directions," he told Svetkey. "Some gestate for years and some happen in a split second. They'll rattle around in my head for a while, and I'll catch myself mentally piecing it together. How do I suck the reader in, how do I maintain the narrative tension, how do I build up to some kind of exciting end? A lot of ideas don't work out. I have a lot of great setups that I can never finish. Right now I have about ten ideas I'm working out on paper. Some of those will work, some won't."

When not working on new books, Grisham takes time out to go on mission trips with his church group as well as indulge in his major pastime: baseball. He has built a six-field ballpark on his Virginia estate that has hosted hundreds of little league players. His dreams of becoming a major league baseball player may have faded, but his love for the sport has not.

■ Biographical and Critical Sources

BOOKS

Contemporary Literary Criticism, Volume 84, Gale (Detroit, MI), 1995, pp. 189-201.

PERIODICALS

Book, January, 2001, Liz Seymour, "Grisham Gets Serious," pp. 34-36.

Booklist, February 1, 1993, p. 954; September 15, 2000, p. 259; February 1, 2001, Stephanie Zvirin, review of *A Painted House,* p. 1020.

Christianity Today, October 3, 1994, p. 14; August 9, 1999, p. 70.

Christian Science Monitor, March 5, 1993, p. 10.

Detroit News, May 25, 1994, p. 3D.

Entertainment Weekly, April 1, 1994, Keli Pryor, "Over 60 Million Sold!," pp. 15-20; June 3, 1994, Mark Harris, "Southern Discomfort," p. 48; July 15, 1994, p. 54; July 29, 1994, p. 23; February 13, 1998, Tom De Haven, review of *The Street Lawyer,* pp. 64-65; February 4, 2000, Tom De Haven, "Law of Desire," p 63; February 11, 2000, Benjamin Svetkey, "Making His Case," pp. 63-64; February 9, 2001, Bruce Fretts, "Above the Law," pp. 68-69; February 15, 2002, Benjamin Svetkey, "Trial and Errors," pp. 60-61.

Florida Bar Journal, June, 1998, Jacalyn N. Kolk, review of *The Street Lawyer,* p. 115.

Forbes, August 30, 1993, p. 24; January 8, 2001, p. 218.

Globe & Mail (Toronto, Ontario, Canada), March 30, 1991, p. C6.

Kirkus Reviews, February 1, 2001.

Library Journal, August, 2000, p. 179; March 1, 2001, p. 131; September 1, 2001, p. 258; December, 2001, Samantha J. Gust, review of *Skipping Christmas,* pp. 170-171.

Los Angeles Times, December 25, 2001, p. E4; February 26, 2002, p. E3.

Los Angeles Times Book Review, March 10, 1991, Charles Champlin, "Criminal Pursuits," p. 7; April 5, 1992, p. 6; April 4, 1993, p. 6; May 14, 1995, Garry Abrams, review of *The Rainmaker,* p. 8.

National Review, April 6, 1998, pp. 51-52.

New Republic, August 2, 1993, p. 32; March 14, 1994, p. 32; August 22, 1994, p. 35.

Newsday, March 7, 1993.

New Statesman, June 9, 1995, p. 35.

Newsweek, February 25, 1991, p. 63; March 16, 1992, p. 72; March 15, 1993, pp. 79-81; December 20, 1993, p. 121; February 19, 1999, Malcolm Jones, "Grisham's Gospel," p. 65.

New York, August 1, 1994, pp. 52-53.

New Yorker, August 1, 1994, p. 16.

New York Times, March 5, 1993, p. C29; July 29, 1994, p. B10; April 19, 1995, Michiko Kakutani, review of *The Rainmaker,* pp. B1, B9; April 28, 1995, p. C33; May 23, 1996, Christopher Lehmann-Haupt, review of *The Runaway Jury,* p. C20; March 31, 1997, Mel Gussow, review of *The Partner,* p. B1; February 4, 2002, p. B1; February 5, 2002, p. B7.

New York Times Book Review, March 24, 1991, p. 37; March 15, 1992, Frank J. Prial, "Too Liberal to Live," p. 9; October 18, 1992, p. 33; March 7, 1993, p. 18; December 23, 2001, p. 17; February 24, 2002, p. 13.

People Weekly, April 8, 1991, pp. 36-37; March 16, 1992, pp. 43-44; March 15, 1993, pp. 27-28; June 27, 1994, p. 24; August 1, 1994, p. 16; March 2, 1998, Cynthia Sanz, review of *The Street Lawyer,* p. 37; February 12, 2001, p. 41; February 18, 2002, p. 41.

Philadelphia Inquirer, March 23, 1997, Robert Drake, review of *The Partner.*

Publishers Weekly, February 22, 1993, Michelle Bearden, "PW Interviews: John Grisham," pp. 70-71; May 30, 1994, p. 37; May 6, 1996, p. 71; February 10, 1997; February 1, 1999, review of *The Testament,* p. 78; January 10, 2000, p. 18; January 31, 2000, review of *The Brethren,* p. 84; January 22, 2001, review of *A Painted House,* p. 302; October 29, 2001, p. 20; November 5, 2001, review of *Skipping Christmas,* p. 43; February 18, 2002, p. 22.

Southern Living, August, 1991, p. 58.

Sunday Times (London, England), June 12, 1994, review of *The Chamber,* p. 1.

Time, March 9, 1992, John Skow, "Legal Eagle," p. 70; March 8, 1993, p. 73; June 20, 1994, John Skow, review of *The Chamber,* p. 67; August 1, 1994; February 26, 2001, Jess Cagle, review of *A Painted House,* p. 72.

Tribune Books (Chicago, IL), February 24, 1991, Bill Brashler, review of *The Firm,* p. 6; September 8, 1991, p. 10; February 23, 1992, p. 4; February 28, 1993, p. 7.

Voice Literary Supplement, July-August, 1991, p. 7.

Wall Street Journal, March 12, 1993, p. A6.

Washington Post, January 29, 2002, p. C3.

OTHER

Bookreporter.com, http://www.bookreporter.com/ (March 3, 2002), "Author Profile: John Grisham."

John Grisham Web site, http://www.jgrsham.com/ (March 1, 2002).

University of Mississippi Web site, http://www. olemiss.edu/ (March 3, 2002), "John Grisham."*

Dan Gutman

Personal

Born October 19, 1955, in New York, NY; son of Sid Gutman (in advertising) and Adeline (a homemaker; maiden name, Wernick) Berlin; married Nina Wallace (an illustrator), September 25, 1983; children: Sam, Emma. *Education:* Rutgers University, B.A., 1977, M.A., 1979.

Addresses

Home and office—224 Euclid Ave., Haddonfield, NJ 08033. *Agent*—Mitch Rose, 799 Broadway, New York, NY 10003.

Career

Video Review Publications, coeditor of *Electronic Fun*, 1982-83; Carnegie Publications, founder and editor-in-chief of *Computer Games*, 1983-84; freelance writer, 1984—.

Member

National Writers Union, Society of Children's Book Writers and Illustrators, Society for American Baseball Research.

Awards, Honors

Sequoyah Book Award, and Nutmeg Children's Book Award, both 1999, Volunteer State Book Award, 2000, and Iowa Children's Choice Award, and Maud Harte Lovelace Award, both 2001, all for *The Million-Dollar Shot*; Keystone Book Award, 2000, for *Jackie and Me*; California Young Reader Medal, 2001, for *Honus and Me*; Nevada Young Readers' Award, 2001, for *Virtually Perfect*.

Writings

The Greatest Games, Compute Books (Greensboro, NC), 1985.

I Didn't Know You Could Do THAT with a Computer!, Compute Books (Greensboro, NC), 1986.

It Ain't Cheatin' if You Don't Get Caught, Penguin (New York, NY), 1990.

(Editor) Douglas J. Hermann, *SuperMemory*, Rodale Press (Emmaus, PA), 1991.

Baseball Babylon, Penguin (New York, NY), 1992.

Baseball's Biggest Bloopers, Viking (New York, NY), 1993.

Baseball's Greatest Games, Viking (New York, NY), 1994.

World Series Classics, Viking (New York, NY), 1994.

Banana Bats and Ding-Dong Bells, Macmillan (New York, NY), 1995.

They Came from Centerfield, Scholastic (New York, NY), 1995.

Taking Flight, Viking (New York, NY), 1995.

Ice Skating, Viking (New York, NY), 1995.

Gymnastics, Viking (New York, NY), 1996.

The Way Baseball Works, Simon & Schuster (New York, NY), 1996.

The Kid Who Ran for President, Scholastic (New York, NY), 1996.

The Pitcher Who Went out of His Mind, Scholastic (New York, NY), 1997.

The Catcher Who Shocked the World, Scholastic (New York, NY), 1997.

The Green Monster in Left Field, Scholastic (New York, NY), 1997.

The Shortstop Who Knew Too Much, Scholastic (New York, NY), 1997.

Honus and Me, Avon (New York, NY), 1997.

The Million-Dollar Shot, Hyperion (New York, NY), 1997.

Katy's Gift, Running Press (Philadelphia, PA), 1998.

Virtually Perfect, Hyperion (New York, NY), 1998.

(Adaptor) *Cal Ripken, Jr.: My Story,* Dial (New York, NY), 1999.

Jackie and Me, Avon (New York, NY), 1999.

Funny Boy Meets the Airsick Alien from Andromeda, Hyperion (New York, NY), 1999.

The Kid Who Became President, Scholastic (New York, NY), 1999.

Joe DiMaggio, Aladdin (New York, NY), 1999.

(As Herb Dunn) *Jackie Robinson,* Aladdin (New York, NY), 1999.

Funny Boy versus the Bubble-brained Barbers from the Big Bang, Hyperion (New York, NY), 2000.

Funny Boy Meets the Chit-chatting Cheese from Chattanooga, Hyperion (New York, NY), 2000.

Landslide! A Kid's Guide to the U.S. Elections, Simon & Schuster (New York, NY), 2000.

Babe and Me, HarperCollins (New York, NY), 2000.

Johnny Hangtime, HarperCollins (New York, NY), 2000.

The Million-Dollar Kick, Hyperion (New York, NY), 2001.

The Secret Life of Dr. Demented, Pocket Books (New York, NY), 2001.

The Edison Mystery, Simon & Schuster (New York, NY), 2001.

Qwerty Stevens, Stuck in Time with Benjamin Franklin, Simon & Schuster (New York, NY), 2002.

Shoeless Joe and Me, HarperCollins (New York, NY), 2002.

Author of "I Didn't Know You Could Do THAT with a Computer!" a self-syndicated column, 1983—, and a monthly column in *Success.* Contributor to periodicals, including *Esquire, Writer's Digest, Newsweek, Village Voice, Discover, Science Digest, Psychology Today, USA Today,* and *Home Office Computing.*

■ Work in Progress

Mickey and Me, a further installment in Gutman's baseball card time-slip series.

■ Sidelights

The author of almost forty books in a little over a decade of writing, Dan Gutman has written on topics from computers to baseball. Beginning his freelance career as a nonfiction author dealing mostly with sports for adults and young readers, Gutman has concentrated on juvenile fiction since 1995. His most popular titles include the time-travel sports book *Honus and Me* and its sequels, and a clutch of baseball books, including *The Green Monster from Left Field.* From hopeful and very youthful presidential candidates to stunt men, nothing is off limits in Gutman's fertile imagination. As he noted on his author Web site, since writing his first novel, *They Came from Centerfield,* in 1994, he has been hooked on fiction. "It was fun to write, kids loved it, and I discovered how incredibly rewarding it is to take a blank page and turn it into a WORLD."

Gutman was born in New York City in 1955, but moved to Newark, New Jersey the following year and spent his youth there. "It was pretty uneventful," Gutman wrote on his Web site, "until June 1, 1968, when I came home from a Little League game and found that my dad had suddenly abandoned my mom, my sister Lucy, and me. It was pretty traumatic, as you can imagine, but we all survived."

Gutman went to college at Rutgers University, graduating in 1977 with a degree in psychology. He went on to graduate school, but, as he noted on his Web site, "After spending a few unhappy years . . . I decided that psychology was not for me. What I really wanted to do, I wanted to write humor, like Art Buchwald or Erma Bombeck." In 1980, he moved to New York City and started working toward his goal, publishing humorous essays in a small newspaper and in children's humor magazines. His attempts at writing magazine articles proved as unsuccessful as his efforts at penning screenplays. Fortunately, books were part of the mix for the budding freelancer. "I thought I had some good book ideas," Gutman noted, "but publishers weren't interested. I received hundreds of rejection letters. It was very frustrating, but I was determined and persistent. I felt I had some ability as a writer, but I didn't know where to direct it."

With the rising popularity of the video game Pac-Man in the early 1980s, Gutman started the magazine *Video Games Player.* "This was the first (and only) job I ever had," Gutman remarked on his Web site. The magazine prospered, changing its name after a couple of years to *Computer Games.* An added bonus to this job was that Gutman met his wife through the magazine; she was hired as an illustrator and they married in 1983. Slowly, Gutman became known in the trade as a computer expert. "This was astonishing to me, because I knew next to nothing about computers (I still don't)." But other publications were desperate for writers on computers, and Gutman's status as editor of *Computer Games* carried some weight. Soon he had a syndicated column in the Philadelphia *Inquirer* and the Miami *Herald.* "I felt like a fraud the whole time," Gutman confessed. When *Computer Games* went out of business in 1985, Gutman became a full-time freelance writer, penning articles on computers, but also on a wider range of subjects, from psychology to sports, placing his articles in a variety of national publications. "I was gaining confidence as a writer," Gutman recalled, "but I still hadn't found the type of writing I really wanted to do."

Turns Hand to Book-Length Topics

In 1987 Gutman decided to focus on sports articles, writing for *Discovery* about the physics behind the spitball, scuffball, and corked bats. This article in turn led to an adult baseball book, *It Ain't Cheatin' if You Don't Get Caught.* This book's modest success prompted Gutman to write other adult sports titles, including *Baseball Babylon,* a history of scandals in the sport. In 1992, with a twelve-year-old son in the house, Gutman decided to try his hand at writing for children. What followed were some more baseball books, as well as books on other sports such as gymnastics and ice skating. Reviewing one of these early titles, *Baseball's Greatest Games,* in *Booklist,* Carolyn Phelan commented that Gutman's "ability to re-create dramatic moments, his flair for telling details and quotations, and his staccato reporting of plays makes the book quite readable." Further praise came from Chris Sherman in a *Booklist* review of *World Series Classics,* a book, Sherman thought, that "should appeal to all baseball lovers, reluctant readers or not." Reviewing Gutman's *Ice Skating* in *Booklist,* Sherman noted that the author "packs in more than enough information for report writers and presents it in a thoroughly entertaining, enthusiastic style." Likewise in a review of *Gymnastics,* Sherman noted in *Booklist* that Gutman's "tone throughout is breezy and enthusiastic."

The success of these early titles kept Gutman focused on nonfiction sports books for young readers, but eventually he decided to give fiction a try. His first novel, *They Came from Centerfield,* blends base-

In Dan Gutman's 1996 novel twelve-year-old Judson Moon decides to get a first-hand look at the democratic process by running for president of the United States.

ball and alien invasion and was quickly sold to Scholastic publishers. In the book, aliens visit Earth and threaten to destroy it unless a group of kids teach them how to play baseball. With this first fiction title under his belt, Gutman was off and running.

With *The Kid Who Ran for President* Gutman takes the adult worry about a candidate who might be too old to run for president and flips it on its head. How young is too young to be president? Twelve-year-old Judson Moon means to find out, starting a campaign that has kids across the country sending him campaign contributions. These same kids refuse to clean their rooms or do their homework until their parents pass a constitutional amendment getting rid of the age restriction for president. In a *Booklist* review, Phelan felt that "this first-person novel is an entertaining romp through the political process." A contributor for *Publishers Weekly* also lauded the book, writing that "the author pulls off a feat as impressive as Judd's victory: he actually makes his hero a credible 12-year-old." The same reviewer called the book a "snappy, lighthearted farce." Gutman reprised the formula in his 1999 sequel, *The Kid Who Became President*, in which Judson Moon, now thirteen, becomes president. Sara Nelson, writing in *Family Life*, felt that the "cross-cultural tidbits here are gems."

Branching Out

With 1997's *Honus and Me* Gutman hit on a winning combination, though editors were at first reluctant to grasp it. The book went to a number of publishers over several years before a sympathetic editor saw the potential in this time-slip sports story. While cleaning out an old woman's attic, twelve-year-old Joe Stoschak finds a mint-condition baseball card from 1909. It is, in fact, the most valuable baseball card in the world, the Honus Wagner T-206. Honus, a baseball great, soon plays a part in the book, as Joe, wondering if he should return the card (worth $450,000) to its rightful owner, is transported back in time by rubbing the card. Back in 1909, Honus helps Joe not only with his moral quandary, but also with his baseball swing. Reviewers and readers alike found the book a winner. A contributor for *Publishers Weekly* called the juvenile novel a "joyfully entertaining yarn" and concluded that for sports fans "who like a snappy plot along with the play-by-play, this novel hits at least a triple." *Booklist* reviewer Ilene Cooper dubbed the book a "peppy, pleasing offering" that will "delight young baseball fans" and even non-sports readers who will "enjoy the fantasy elements."

Further titles dealing with Joe and other magical baseball cards followed, initiated by Gutman's enthusiastic editor. *Jackie and Me* takes Joe back to 1947 to go on an adventure with Jackie Robinson during his rookie season with the Brooklyn Dodgers, experiencing in person the racial prejudice which this African-American ball player had to overcome. In *Babe and Me* Joe time-travels to 1932 with his father to see firsthand whether or not the great Babe Ruth called his legendary home run in the third game of the World Series before he hit the ball. With *Shoeless Joe and Me*, Joe travels back to 1919 in hopes of preventing the Black Sox Scandal and saving the reputation of the great "Shoeless Joe" Jackson.

Reviewers responded positively to Gutman's time-slip books. Karen Hutt, reviewing *Jackie and Me* in *Booklist*, felt fans "will enjoy the baseball action,

which is enhanced by historical photos of Robinson's rookie year." In a review of *Babe and Me*, Gillian Engberg in *Booklist* noted that Gutman "weaves a delightfully improbable fantasy from actual events" to create a novel full of "action," "rich baseball lore, and the sense of adventure." A reviewer for *Publishers Weekly* thought that Gutman's account of the World Series as well as Joe's own relationship with his father in *Babe and Me* "are equally skillful." And in a *Booklist* review of *Shoeless Joe and Me*, Phelan called the book a "not-quite believable, but still highly enjoyable time-travel adventure."

> "When I visit a school I inspire the kids, the kids inspire me, and I even get paid for it! Finally . . . I figured out what my career should be—writing fiction for kids and visiting schools. For the first time I felt that I was doing something I was good at, something that was fun, creatively rewarding, and appreciated by an audience."
>
> —Dan Gutman

From baseball, Gutman turns to basketball and soccer in two novels, *The Million-Dollar Shot* and *The Million-Dollar Kick*. When Eddie Ball wins a poetry contest, he gets a chance to win a million dollars by shooting a free throw during half-time at an NBA game. Along the way to the novel's exciting climax, Gutman takes time out to describe Eddie's relationships with his widowed mother, with his friend, Annie, a black girl in his trailer park, and with Annie's father who once lost his own chance to play professional basketball and now wants to see Eddie succeed. Other plot complications include a mysterious individual who is pulling pranks on Eddie in hopes of shaking him before his big free throw. *Booklist*'s Lauren Peterson found *The Million-Dollar Shot* "a solidly written story that will appeal to a larger audience than most sports novels do." Gutman noted on his Web site, "Many kids have told me this is my best book."

With *The Million-Dollar Kick*, Gutman does for soccer what he did for basketball in *The Million-Dollar Shot*. Whisper Nelson, a seventh grader in Oklahoma City, enters a slogan-writing contest and gets the chance to win a million dollars with a single shot against the goalkeeper of the local team. Whisper is Gutman's first female main character. A reviewer for *Publishers Weekly* found *The Million-Dollar Kick* to be a book that would appeal to "reluctant players and soccer fans alike," while *Booklist* contributor Anne O'Malley noted that Gutman "captures Whisper's pain and dry wit beautifully in this strong story about a teen getting through tough times." "This is an exciting sports story with a compelling message about individuality and self-reliance, as well as a touch of romance," commented Elaine E. Knight in a *School Library Journal* review of *The Million-Dollar Kick*.

Gutman has also produced many non-sports novels. *Virtually Perfect* is a story about the son of a movies special-effects expert who creates what Gutman calls a "vactor" or a virtual actor on a computer. When the boy, Yip, feeds the vactor enough intelligence, it comes through the screen and begins to exist in the real world like a real kid. Yip's failure to program a proper conscience in the vactor brings strong consequences, however. "Gutman taps out a smoothly diverting "What if?' tale," wrote a contributor for *Publishers Weekly*. "Its breezy dialogue and quick pace give this caper the scent of a smartly written sitcom; readers will supply the laugh track."

With *Johnny Hangtime,* which Gutman counts among his best books, the novelist deals with another aspect of films: the Hollywood stuntman. In this book the stuntman is thirteen-year-old Johnny Thyme, who does all the stunts for teen idol Ricky Corvette, a miserable person in real life but a hero in his guise as a movie star. Trouble is, Johnny has to do his stunts in secret so that fans do not know Ricky is not doing them. This in turn gets Johnny into trouble at school, as he cannot get involved in any activities that might injure him. Things come to a climax in a stunt involving Niagara Falls, where Johnny's father was supposedly killed. Tim Wadham, reviewing *Johnny Hangtime* in *School Library Journal*, had reservations about the realism of the plot in which a young teen would be allowed to do such stunts, but concluded: "Still, there are some laugh-out-loud moments, and the action will appeal to readers wanting high-interest, low-reading-level material."

Other non-sports stories deal with the adventures of Qwerty Stevens. In *The Edison Mystery* thirteen-year-old Qwerty goes into the backyard after a fight with his mother. Digging, he finds what he thinks is an early phonograph once belonging to inventor Thomas Edison who had his workshop in the vicinity. However, the device is actually a machine that sends Qwerty off to Spain and then to Edison's lab where the inventor is busy working on the first light bulb. In search of her brother, Qwerty's sister soon turns up in 1879, and the united siblings quickly realize they are stuck in the past if Edison can't somehow send them home. "The story is chock-full of interesting tidbits about Edison's life," wrote Lisa Prolman in *School Library Journal*, "and provides a good glimpse of life in the 19th century." Prolman further commented, "Overall, this is an entertaining novel that should draw fans of time-travel stories." Gutman reprised this idea with his *Qwerty Stevens, Stuck in Time with Benjamin Franklin*, in which the Edison machine sends him back to Philadelphia on July 4, 1776.

If you enjoy the works of Dan Gutman, you might want to check out the following books:

W. P. Kinsella, *Shoeless Joe*, 1982.
William Sleator, *The Duplicate*, 1988.
Stephen Manes, *An Almost Perfect Game*, 1995.

Gutman maintains a busy speaking schedule, visiting schools across the country and presenting a program which uses sports as a theme to get students excited about reading and writing. "This has been the most satisfying thing I've done in my career," Gutman reported on his Web site. "When I visit a school I inspire the kids, the kids inspire me, and I even get paid for it! Finally . . . I figured out what my career should be—writing fiction for kids and visiting schools. For the first time I felt that I was doing something I was good at, something that was fun, creatively rewarding, and appreciated by an audience. Kids often tell me that my books make them laugh. This is funny to me, because writing humor was what I wanted to do when I got started back in 1980! It just took me a while to figure out the best way to do it."

■ Biographical and Critical Sources

PERIODICALS

Booklist, June 1, 1994, Carolyn Phelan, review of *Baseball's Greatest Game,* p. 1792; September 15, 1994, Chris Sherman, review of *World Series Clas-*

sics, p. 134; June 1, 1995, pp. 1768-1769; October 1, 1995, Chris Sherman, review of *Ice Skating*, pp. 300-301; May 1, 1996, Chris Sherman, review of *Gymnastics*, p. 1500; July, 1996, p. 1795; November 1, 1996, Carolyn Phelan, review of *The Kid Who Ran for President*, p. 498; April 15, 1997, Ilene Cooper, review of *Honus and Me*, pp. 1428-1429; October 1, 1997, Lauren Peterson, review of *The Million-Dollar Shot*, p. 329; June 1, 1998, p. 1766; February 1, 1999, Karen Hutt, review of *Jackie and Me*, p. 974; June 1, 1999, p. 1822; September 1, 1999, p. 132; February 1, 2000, Gillian Engberg, review of *Babe and Me*, p. 1023; July, 2001, p. 2029; October 1, 2001, p. 342; November 15, 2001, Anne O'Malley, review of *The Million-Dollar Kick*, p. 571; January 1, 2002, Carolyn Phelan, review of *Shoeless Joe and Me*, p. 857.

Book Report, March-April, 1994, p. 58; November-December, 1994, p. 60; September-October, 1995, p. 62; March-April, 1996, p. 56; November-December, 1996, p. 58.

Family Life, February 1, 2001, Sara Nelson, review of *The Kid Who Became President*, p. 93.

New York Times Book Review, April 1, 1990, p. 16; April 5, 1992.

Publishers Weekly, November 11, 1996, review of *The Kid Who Ran for President*, p. 76; February 10, 1997, review of *Honus and Me*, p. 84; April 6, 1998, review of *Virtually Perfect*, p. 79; January 31, 2000, review of *Babe and Me*, p. 108; August 27, 2001, review of *The Million-Dollar Kick*, p. 86.

School Library Journal, March, 1993, p. 210; June, 1994, p. 155; November, 1994, pp. 125-126; August, 1995, p. 152; December, 1995, p. 117; August, 1996, pp. 155-156; November, 1996, p. 106; December, 1997, p. 124; August, 1998, p. 163; March, 1999, pp. 209-210; February, 2000, p. 120; January, 2001, Tim Wadham, review of *Johnny Hangtime*, p. 130; August, 2001, Lisa Prolman, review of *The Edison Mystery*, p. 182; December, 2001, Elaine E. Knight, review of *The Million-Dollar Kick*, p. 134.

OTHER

Dan Gutman: Children's Book Author, http://www.dangutman.com/ (March 4, 2002).*

Lillian Hellman

▪ Personal

Born June 20, 1906, in New Orleans, LA; died of cardiac arrest, June 30, 1984, in Martha's Vineyard, MA; daughter of Max Bernard (a businessman) and Julia (Newhouse) Hellman; married Arthur Kober (a writer), December 30, 1925 (divorced, 1932). *Education:* Attended New York University, 1922-24, and Columbia University, 1924.

▪ Career

Playwright and author. Horace Liveright, Inc. (publisher), New York, NY, manuscript reader, 1924-25; theatrical playreader in New York, NY, 1927-30; Metro-Goldwyn-Mayer, Hollywood, CA, scenario reader, 1930-31; worked as part-time playreader for producer Harold Shulman, New York, NY, beginning 1932. Taught or conducted seminars in literature and writing at Yale University, 1966, and at Massachusetts Institute of Technology and Harvard University. Director of plays in New York, NY, including *Another Part of the Forest*, 1946, and *Montserrat*, 1949. Narrator, Marc Blitzstein Memorial Concert, New York, NY, 1964.

▪ Member

American Academy of Arts and Letters, American Academy of Arts and Sciences (fellow), Dramatists Guild (member of council), American Federation of Television and Radio Artists.

▪ Awards, Honors

New York Drama Critics Circle Award, 1941, for *Watch on the Rhine*, and 1960, for *Toys in the Attic*; Academy Award nominations for screenplays *The Little Foxes*, 1941, and *The North Star*, 1943; honorary M.A. from Tufts University, 1950; Antoinette Perry ("Tony") Award nominations, for book of a musical, 1957, for *Candide* and for best play, 1960, for *Toys in the Attic*; Brandeis University Creative Arts Medal in Theater, 1960-61; LL.D. from Wheaton College, 1961, Douglass College of Rutgers University, Smith College, and New York University, all 1974, Franklin and Marshall College, 1975, and Columbia University, 1976; Gold Medal for drama from National Institute of Arts and Letters, 1964; National Book Award in Arts and Letters, 1969, for *An Unfinished Woman*, and nomination, 1974, for *Pentimento: A Book of Portraits*; elected to Theatre Hall of Fame, 1973; MacDowell Medal, 1976.

▪ Writings

(Editor and author of introduction) Anton Chekhov, *Selected Letters*, Farrar, Straus (New York, NY), 1955, reprinted, 1984.

(Editor and author of introduction) Dashiell Hammett, *The Big Knockover* (selected stories and short novels), Random House (New York, NY), 1966, published in England as *The Dashiell Hammett Story Omnibus,* Cassell, 1966.

An Unfinished Woman (memoirs; also see below), Little, Brown (Boston, MA), 1969, reprinted, Macmillan (London, England), 1987.

Pentimento: A Book of Portraits (memoirs; also see below), Little, Brown (Boston, MA), 1973.

Scoundrel Time (memoirs; also see below), introduction by Garry Wills, Little, Brown (Boston, MA), 1976.

Three (contains *An Unfinished Woman, Pentimento: A Book of Portraits, Scoundrel Time,* and new commentaries by author), Little, Brown (Boston, MA), 1979.

Maybe: A Story (memoirs), Little, Brown (Boston, MA), 1980.

(With Peter S. Feibleman) *Eating Together: Recollections and Recipes,* Little, Brown (Boston, MA), 1984.

PLAYS

The Children's Hour (first produced in New York, NY, at Maxine Elliott's Theatre, November 20, 1934; also see below), Knopf (New York, NY), 1934, acting edition, Dramatists Play Service (New York, NY), 1953, reprinted, 1988.

Days to Come (first produced in New York, NY, at Vanderbilt Theatre, December 15, 1936; also see below), Knopf (New York, NY), 1936.

The Little Foxes (three-act; first produced in New York, NY, at National Theatre, February 15, 1939; also see below), Random House (New York, NY), 1939, acting edition, Dramatists Play Service (New York, NY), 1942, Viking (New York, NY), 1973.

Watch on the Rhine (three-act; first produced on Broadway at Martin Beck Theatre, April 1, 1941; also see below), Random House (New York, NY), 1941, limited edition with foreword by Dorothy Parker, privately printed, 1942, acting edition, Dramatists Play Service (New York, NY), 1944, reprinted, 1986.

Four Plays (contains *The Children's Hour, Days to Come, The Little Foxes,* and *Watch on the Rhine*), Random House (New York, NY), 1942.

The Searching Wind (two-act; first produced in New York, NY, at Fulton Theatre, April 12, 1944; also see below), Viking (New York, NY), 1944.

Another Part of the Forest (three-act; first produced at Fulton Theatre, November 20, 1946; also see below), Viking (New York, NY), 1947, reprinted, 1973.

Montserrat (two-act; adapted from Emmanuel Robles's play; first produced at Fulton Theatre, October 29, 1949; also see below), Dramatists Play Service (New York, NY), 1950.

The Autumn Garden (three-act; first produced in New York, NY, at Coronet Theatre, March 7, 1951; also see below), Little, Brown (Boston, MA), 1951, revised acting edition, Dramatists Play Service (New York, NY), 1952.

The Lark (adapted from Jean Anouilh's play *L'Alouette;* first produced on Broadway at Longacre Theatre, November 17, 1955; also see below), Random House (New York, NY), 1956, acting edition, Dramatists Play Service (New York, NY), 1957.

(Author of book) Leonard Bernstein, *Candide: A Comic Opera Based on Voltaire's Satire* (first produced on Broadway at Martin Beck Theatre, December 1, 1956; also see below), Random House (New York, NY), 1957.

Toys in the Attic (three-act; first produced Off-Broadway at Hudson Theatre, February 25, 1960; also see below), Random House (New York, NY), 1960, acting edition, Samuel French (New York, NY), 1960.

Six Plays (contains *Another Part of the Forest, The Autumn Garden, The Children's Hour, Days to Come, The Little Foxes,* and *Watch on the Rhine*), Modern Library (New York, NY), 1960, limited edition with illustrations by Mark Bellerose, Franklin Library, 1978.

My Mother, My Father and Me (adapted from Burt Blechman's novel *How Much?;* first produced on Broadway at Plymouth Theatre, April 6, 1963; also see below), Random House (New York, NY), 1963.

Collected Plays (contains *The Children's Hour, Days to Come, The Little Foxes, Watch on the Rhine, The Searching Wind, Another Part of the Forest, Montserrat, The Autumn Garden, The Lark, Candide, Toys in the Attic,* and *My Mother, My Father and Me*), Little, Brown (Boston, MA), 1972.

Also author of unpublished and unproduced play, *Dear Queen.*

SCREENPLAYS

(With Mordaunt Shairp) *Dark Angel,* United Artists, 1935.

These Three (based on *The Children's Hour*), United Artists, 1936.

Dead End, United Artists, 1937.

The Little Foxes (based on her play), RKO, 1941.

The North Star, a Motion Picture about Some Russian People (released by RKO, 1943; later released for television broadcast as *Armored Attack*), introduction by Louis Kronenberger, Viking (New York, NY), 1943.

The Searching Wind, Paramount, 1946.

The Chase, Columbia, 1966.

OTHER

Pentimento: Memory as Distilled by Time (sound recording), Center for Cassette Studies, c. 1973.

Lillian Hellman: The Great Playwright Candidly Reflects on a Long Rich Life (sound recording), Center for Cassette Studies, c. 1977.

Conversations with Lillian Hellman, edited by Jackson R. Bryer, University Press of Mississippi (Jackson, MS), 1986.

Contributor of plays to anthologies, including *Four Contemporary American Plays,* Random House (New York, NY), 1961; *Six Modern American Plays,* Random House (New York, NY), 1966; and *A Treasury of the Theatre: Modern Drama from Oscar Wilde to Eugene Ionesco,* Simon & Schuster (New York, NY), 1967. Contributor of sketches to "Broadway Revue," produced in New York, NY, 1968; contributor of articles to *Collier's, New York Times, Travel and Leisure,* and other publications.

Hellman's manuscripts are collected at the University of Texas at Austin.

■ Adaptations

Marc Blitzstein adapted *The Little Foxes* as an opera, *Regina,* in 1949. *Another Part of the Forest* was filmed by Universal in 1948; *The Children's Hour* was adapted as a film starring Deborah Kerr and Shirley MacClain; *Toys in the Attic* was adapted for film by United Artists, 1963. Television adaptations include *Montserrat,* 1971, and *The Lark.* A section of Hellman's memoir *Pentimento* was adapted into the film *Julia* and released in 1977. In 1986, William Luce wrote a one-woman play, *Lillian,* based on Hellman's life; the production ran briefly in New York City.

■ Sidelights

She has been called one of the most influential female playwrights of the twentieth century; the voice of social consciousness in American letters; the theatre's intellectual standard-bearer—and yet Lillian Hellman always prided herself on avoiding easy labels. At the time of her death in 1984, the author/playwright could claim more long-running Broadway dramas—five—than could renowned American writers like Tennessee Williams, Edward Albee, and Thornton Wilder. Ironically, though, Hellman was

perhaps best remembered by a later generation of Americans for posing in a mink coat in an advertisement titled "What Becomes a Legend Most?" Pamela Monaco recognized this cult of celebrity in her essay in *Dictionary of Literary Biography,* noting that biographies, stage plays, and even a television movie have been created about Hellman since her death. Such interest, Monaco wrote, "at times seems to eclipse interest in her drama." However, Monaco went on to comment, "her contributions to the American stage cannot be ignored. Her unflinching examination of individuals' actions and their consequences, her fully realized characters speaking realistic dialogue, and her ability to bring her characters to a climactic confrontation epitomize Hellman's dramaturgy." In plays such as *The Children's Hour, The Little Foxes, Watch on the Rhine, The Searching Wind, Another Part of the Forest,* and *Toys in the Attic* Hellman explored controversial themes from lesbianism to fascism, as well as examined the stifling effects of greed and avarice in family relations.

Born in turn-of-the-twentieth-century New Orleans to a struggling shoe merchant and his upper-middle-class wife, Hellman had a childhood that was far from ordinary. Both parents were descendants of German Jews who came to the United States in the mid-1800s. Her mother's family, the Newhouses, were wealthy and well connected; through them Hellman's father, Max, got the money he needed to open a shoe company. Hellman's maternal grandmother, Sophie, was the family matriarch and left a strong impression on her impressionable young granddaughter. Family meals at the Newhouse domicile were boring for Hellman, the talk focusing on money and possessions and punctuated by frequent snipes at Max Hellman's lower-class background. Equally influential for Hellman was the relationship she had with her distant, refined mother, which relationship haunted Hellman well into adulthood. "So far apart were the temperaments of mother and daughter—for Hellman was always a spirited, independent child—that only after her mother had been dead for five years did [Hellman] realize how much she had loved her," maintained Carol MacNicholas in the *Dictionary of Literary Biography.*

Though born in the South, Hellman did not receive a typical Southern sensibility. As Katherine Lederer noted in her *Lillian Hellman,* "Although [Hellman] spent enough time in the South during these years to be knowledgeable about its manners, traditions, and customs, it would be more accurate to describe her background as urban-Jewish." When Hellman was five years old, her father's partner ran off with the firm's funds and bankrupted him. The Newhouses had relocated to New York, and Hellman's family followed suit, her father becoming a travel-

Lillian Hellman's award-winning play *The Children's Hour* focuses on the way the lives of two dedicated school teachers are destroyed by prejudices fed by a young girl's spiteful innuendo.

ing salesman. The family continued to spend half of each year in New Orleans, a strange living arrangement that had the young Hellman living in relative luxury on West Ninety-fifth Street in New York, and in New Orleans staying in a boarding house run by her father's sisters. The rooming house later became the inspiration for Hellman's 1951 play, *The Autumn Garden*. Such a living arrangement played havoc with Hellman's education; she was never an enthusiastic student, attending New York's Wadleigh High School, and then New York University and Columbia for several years.

From Manuscript Reader to Playwright

By the age of nineteen Hellman had left college to work as a manuscript reader for a New York City publishing firm. For the ambitious Hellman, the benefits of working in publishing ran beyond five o'clock. "After working hours, [the publishers'] parties gave Hellman her firsthand acquaintance with the adventurous, often reckless life of the literary world of the 1920s," MacNicholas noted. "The bohemian life appealed to the young woman who was just advancing into her own twenties; she enjoyed the glamour of the writer's world and nurtured the impulse to find excitement in whatever she did."

For Hellman that impulse led her into an early marriage to press agent Arthur Kober, and career jumps into playreading and book reviewing. Following her husband to Paris, Hellman made side trips to Germany, where in 1929 she witnessed an embryonic Nazi movement that became her first exposure to anti-Semitism. Anti-Semitism is a theme that would later emerge in her plays *Watch on the Rhine* and *The Searching Wind*. Meanwhile, during her Paris sojourn, she published her first works of fiction, two short stories published in the *Paris Comet*, an English-language periodical edited by her husband. By 1930 the Kobers had moved to Hollywood, where Hellman read scripts for Metro-Goldwyn-Mayer. It was there, too, that she met the mystery novelist/screenwriter Dashiell Hammett.

Sensing that her marriage to Kober was failing, Hellman turned to Hammett, best known for the stylish suspense novel *The Thin Man*—some critics believe Hammett based his suave detectives Nick and Nora Charles on himself and Hellman—and he became her lover and mentor. Hammett encouraged Hellman's first produced play, *The Children's Hour*, in 1933. Based on a true story that happened in Scotland, the play is "about the way scandalmongering can ruin people's lives, [and] focuses on two young women, Karen Wright and Martha Dobie, who have set up a private boarding school," explained MacNicholas. "Their prospects for a happy and secure future are shattered when one of their pupils, Mary Tilford, a spoiled and vicious problem child, tells her grandmother, . . . a pillar of local society, about an abnormal sexual relationship between Karen and Martha." *The Children's Hour* caused a sensation in its time, not merely for its controversial subject matter, but also for its writer's obvious talent. Banned in Boston, Chicago, and London and refused a viewing by the Pulitzer committee, the play still earned strong reviews from New York critics. "So far as sheer power and originality are concerned, [Hellman's] play is not merely the best of the year but the best of many years past," wrote J. W. Krutch in *Nation*. Monaco noted that *The Children's Hour* "reveals the elements that helped categorize her as a writer of melodrama or of the well-made play," and further commented that the sensation stirred up by the lesbian theme "drew attention away from Hellman's primary concern, an issue that appeared in almost all of her plays: the damage that a single lie can do to multiple lives. For Hellman, the interest is not in who tells the lie or why, but in examining the consequences." One of Hellman's most popular plays, *The Children's Hour* had the longest run, with 691 performances in New York, and earned her $125,000, a large sum during the Great Depression. When *The Children's Hour* was denied a major award or prize because of its subject matter, the slight encouraged independent-minded theater critics to band together to form the Drama Critics' Circle to award its own prize for drama.

Golden Age of American Drama

Hellman's success attracted Hollywood, and she was hired by Samuel Goldwyn in 1935 as a screenwriter for $2,500 a week. Her first screen adaptation was of the play *The Dark Angel*, and she also adapted her own play, *The Children's Hour* as *The Three,* in which a heterosexual love triangle replaces lesbianism. Hellman continued to write for Hollywood off and on throughout her career, but it is with her plays for the theater that she gained real prominence. Hellman in fact ushered in an era, from the late 1930s through the late 1940s, of classic dramas that helped shape a golden age of American theatre.

There was a stutter step, however, before such a golden age came to fruition. While in Hollywood, she worked on her next play, *Days to Come,* which opened on Broadway in 1936 and closed within a week. As Monaco wrote, the play "suffers from too many plots. None of the characters is fully developed, and the last act suffers because too many conflicts have to be resolved." The story of a factory owner calling in strike breakers, *Days to Come* earned Hellman criticism from both ends of the political spectrum, some calling it Marxist propaganda, and others chiding it as a lesson in middle-class morality.

For her next play, such criticism was stilled. Researching the material for several years and rewriting it nine times, Hellman brought *The Little Foxes* to Broadway in 1939. Perhaps the playwright's best-known work, it is an excoriating look at the rivalries and disloyalty among a turn-of-the-twentieth-century Southern family, an exploration of how the wealthy Hubbard clan in an unnamed Alabama town schemes to keep itself rich and powerful at the expense of both outsiders and each other. In this tale, "William Marshall, a visiting Chicago businessman, has displayed a willingness to establish a local cotton mill to be controlled by the

Hubbards if they can raise enough money to buy fifty-one percent of the new company," as MacNicholas explained. "An intense power struggle ensues, dividing the family into two camps: the powerful and cruel Hubbard siblings (Regina and her two brothers, Ben and Oscar), and those brought into the family by marriage (Horace, Regina's husband; Alexandra, their fair-minded daughter; and Birdie, Oscar's wife)." By the second act every Hubbard is out for him- or herself. When Regina's husband, Horace, refuses to invest in the deal, the Hubbards take matters into their own hands and "borrow" the money from his safety-deposit box. When Horace learns of the theft, he confronts his wife, but dies of a heart attack as Regina ignores his pleas for his heart medicine. Now Regina demands from her brothers that she be cut in on the deal. She now has the wherewithal to leave for Chicago, but not before her daughter, Alexandra, having learned the truth of her mother's deceptions, decides to leave the family forever.

The Little Foxes, both in its stage and film incarnations, was a popular and critical success. Some critics took its theme of greed as a parable for the rise of the industrial South; others saw the play as Hellman's look back at the turmoil within her own family. Monaco noted the similarities between *The Little Foxes* and the earlier *The Children's Hour.* "The 'good' and 'bad' characters are clearly marked," Monaco wrote, "and evil succeeds because decent people do not try to prevent it." Opening at the National Theater in New York on February 15, 1939, the play ran for 410 performances, with critics drawing parallels to the work of Ibsen and Chekhov. A film version of *The Little Foxes* appeared in 1941, a musical version, *Regina,* in 1949, and "it continues," as Monaco noted, "to be Hellman's most revived play."

In 1946, seven years after *The Little Foxes* premiered, Hellman produced what today is known as a prequel titled *Another Part of the Forest.* This play takes a look at the Hubbard clan two decades before audiences met them in *The Little Foxes.* "Twenty years does not transport them to the age of innocence; their evil natures are already well cultivated," noted Richard Moody in his *Lillian Hellman: Playwright.* The mixed reviews heaped on *Another Part of the Forest* focused on critics' speculation that Hellman had packed too much melodrama into the play. Moody found that the follow-up work did "not match the earlier play in concentrated power. [Hellman] has followed too many paths. If fewer crises had been packed into the two days [in which the story takes place], if the voices had been less strident, . . . [then the characters] might have become more fully realized, and our hearts might have become more committed." For all its structural faults, though, Moody called *Another Part of the Forest* "a strong and exciting play."

In between *The Little Foxes* and *Another Part of the Forest* Hellman premiered the political drama *Watch on the Rhine.* This 1941 production focuses on a Washington family and the war refugees they harbor. Among the boarders are a Rumanian count and his American wife, as well as an anti-Nazi German. Fear and prejudice follow the characters, resulting in tragedy. Except "for those who suffered through the Hitler years," remarked Moody, "the fierce impact of the play in 1941 cannot be fully sensed. If it appears melodramatic now, it appeared melodramatic then, but with a difference: the world was boiling with melodrama. Cruelty and villainy were not figments of the playwright's imagination, and it was almost impossible for a writer to tell us anything we didn't already know or to dramatize atrocities more effectively than events had already dramatized them." Hellman "knew that her fiction must do more than demonstrate the strange and awful truth that screamed from the front pages of every daily paper," he added. A critic of the day, Rosamond Gilder of *Theatre Arts,* called *Watch on the Rhine* "more faulty in structure" than *The Children's Hour* and *The Little Foxes,* and also noted that Hellman, "whose hallmark has been an almost brutal cynicism, who has excelled in delineating mean, ruthless and predatory types, [here indulges] in a tenderness, an emotionalism that borders on the sentimental." As Monaco noted, the critical reaction to this timely play-coming only months after Pearl Harbor, was strongly positive. "Most critics hailed the play as Hellman's best to date," Monaco wrote. "Some called it the best war play of its time. Overall, Hellman created more likable characters, and even her villain, Teck, is more pathetic than evil." Running for 378 performances, the play won for Hellman the Drama Critics' Circle Award. Her partner, Hammett, wrote the movie version.

By the early 1940s Hellman and Hammett were solidly a couple, though they remained unmarried. Together they had purchased a 130-acre property, Hardscrabble Farm, in New York State that remained Hellman's primary residence until the early 1950s. In 1942 Hammett enlisted in the U.S. Armed Forces and went to the Aleutians; Hellman went back to Hollywood where she wrote the screenplay for *The North Star* and also began work on her new play, *The Searching Wind.* A blend of politics and a domestic situation, the message of the play, according to Monaco, is that "when decent people ignore their political responsibilities, fascism spreads." The same year it opened in New York, 1944, Hellman made her second visit to Russia, spending two weeks on the Warsaw front with the Russian army.

By the late 1940s Hellman's involvement in leftist politics was beginning to get her into trouble in strongly anti-Communist America. Blacklisted in Hollywood, she would not write another movie script until the 1960s. Called before the House Un-American Activities Committee in 1952, Hellman steadfastly refused to provide names of supposed Communists she might know. Her principles cost her dearly, for she was deprived of steady income from Hollywood, and also lost Hardscrabble Farm, having to sell it to pay legal fees and the back taxes the government suddenly discovered she owed.

Plays of the 1950s and 1960s

The 1950s saw Hellman writing three play adaptations—*Montserrat, The Lark,* and *Candide,* the last a musical—plus an original work, *The Autumn Garden.* Monaco described *The Autumn Garden* as "a departure from her earlier plays." Set in 1949, the play has no political overtones, but instead tells of "the middle-age despair of a group of people brought together on vacation at the home of Constance Tuckerman, who has opened her house as a summer resort in order to keep it." Assembling a cast of eccentric characters, Hellman lets them play against one another in the hothouse environment of this house. Reviewers noted, as Monaco explained, "the Chekhovian mood, the lack of villains and melodrama, and the Hellman trademark of sharp dialogue."

It wasn't until 1960, however, that the playwright had her next important original drama produced. *Toys in the Attic* examines the psychological effects of sudden wealth on a poor family. One of Hellman's best plays, according to Moody, *Toys in the Attic* "achieves the magnitude and human revelation that have always been the mark of serious drama." The plot revolves around two sisters, Carrie and Anna Berniers, who have devoted their lives to their ne'er-do-well younger brother, Julian. They find that he has married a wealthy but neurotic woman, and when Julian returns home to visit, he brings both his bride and fistfuls of cash, which he distributes indiscriminately. "The sudden reversal of fortune is too shocking to accept, and Carrie is convinced that her brother has gone crazy," noted MacNicholas.

With *Toys in the Attic,* Hellman "picked up the sword of judgment many playwrights of the period [had] laid aside and [wielded] it with renewed vigor," said John Gassner in his book *Dramatic Soundings: Evaluations and Retractions Culled from Thirty Years of Dramatic Criticism.* Gassner also viewed "the special merit of Lillian Hellman's work

Vanessa Redgrave and Jane Fonda star in *Julia,* the 1977 film adaptation of Hellman's autobiographical *Pentimento.*

that dreadful things are done by the onstage characters out of affectionate possessiveness, rather than out of ingrained villainy. Although the author's corresponding view of life is ironic and is trenchantly expressed, there is no gloating over human misery, no horror-mongering, no traffic with sensationalism in *Toys in the Attic.*" The play won Hellman her second Drama Critics' Circle Award and ran for 556 performances. The following year, Hellman's longtime partner, Hammett, died.

Toys in the Attic was Hellman's last major play; she produced one more drama, *My Mother, My Father and Me,* an adaptation of Burt Blechman's novel *How Much?* that ran only briefly in 1963. From 1969 on she was well regarded as the author of a quartet of books recounting events in her life. From the beginning of her public life, the writer's left-leaning politics were intertwined with her career. As MacNicholas pointed out, "The origins of [Hellman's]

liberalism are traced to her childhood: on the one hand, she witnessed her mother's family increase their fortunes at the expense of Negroes; on the other, she admired the dignity and tough-mindedness of her black nurse Sophronia. Dashiell Hammett, of course, was a radical who shared and influenced much of her life in the 1930s and 1940s."

Hellman the Memoirist

With Hellman's first book of memoirs, *An Unfinished Woman,* the author took an unconventional approach to traditional autobiography, as Moody described it. "Only in the first third of the book does she allow chronology to govern her narrative. After that she swings freely among her remembrances of places, times, and people—all intimately observed, all colored with some special personal involvement."

The word "pentimento" describes a phenomenon in art wherein a painting fades to the point that one can see the rough sketches and previous drafts through the surface of the finished work. The word also serves as the title of Hellman's second book of memoirs, a look at the friends and relations that fueled Hellman's adult years. This book garnered much critical notice, most notably for its sophisticated writing style. "It is now apparent that *An Unfinished Woman* was the beginning—a try-out, if you will, and more hesitant than arrogant—of a new career for Lillian Hellman," declared *New York* critic Eliot Fremont-Smith. "*Pentimento: A Book of Portraits* . . . is its realization." Fremont-Smith also called the work one of "extraordinary richness and candor and self-perception, and triumph considering the courage such a book requires, a courage that lies, [the author] shows by example, far deeper than one is usually inclined to accept."

Muriel Haynes, in a *Ms.* review, dubbed *Pentimento* "a triumphant vindication of the stories the author threw away in her twenties because they were 'no good.' These complex, controlled narratives profit from the dramatist's instinct for climax and immediate, sharp characterization; but they have an emotional purity her plays have generally lacked." Less impressed was *London Magazine* reviewer Julian Symons, who said that the memoir "is not, as American reviewers have unwisely said, a marvel and a masterpiece and a book full of perceptions about human character. It is, rather, a collection of sketches of a fairly familiar kind, which blend real people known to history and Lillian Hellman . . . with people known only by their Christian names in the book, who may be real or partly fictionalized." By far the best known section of the book is "Julia," the story of Hellman's friendship during the 1930s with a rich young American woman working in the European underground against the Nazis. The story was adapted into the popular film *Julia* in 1977.

In *Pentimento*, as in her other books, Hellman was occasionally criticized by the press for presenting her facts unreliably, "bending" the truth to support her views. Paul Johnson, reviewing the memoir in the *Spectator*, cited an article casting doubt on whether or not "Julia" actually existed. "What [Boston University's Samuel McCracken] demonstrates, by dint of checking Thirties railway timetables, steamship passenger lists, and many other obscure sources, is that most of the facts Hellman provides about 'Julia's' movement and actions, and indeed her own, are not true." Johnson further suggested that what Hellman had been presenting all along is a left-wing apologia for World War II and the McCarthy era that followed.

Hellman, though no Stalinist, had in fact rebelled against the anti-communist investigations during the postwar era. In one of her most memorable statements, she informed the House Un-American Activities Committee (HUAC) that she had no intention of cutting her conscience to fit that year's fashion. Her book *Scoundrel Time* is based on the story of "the sixty-seven minutes that [the author] spent before the [HUAC] in Washington in 1952, of what preceded the hearings, and what its consequences were," according to *Listener* critic David Hunt. Even though Hellman was "scrupulously specific in what she [said] in *Scoundrel Time*, carefully limiting her text to what she herself experienced, thought, said, and did, this memoir nevertheless applies directly to the essential experience of her time—in other words, to history," noted Bruce Cook in a *Saturday Review* article. "There are a couple of good reasons for this. First, and probably most important, is that this is a work of *literary* quality. As with . . . *An Unfinished Woman* and *Pentimento*, *Scoundrel Time* is a triumph of tone. No writer I know can match the eloquence of her ah-what-the-hell as she looks back over the whole sorry spectacle and tells with restraint and precision just what she sees." *Scoundrel Time*, in the opinion of *New York Times Book Review* contributor Maureen Howard, "is not a confessional book. Hellman has seldom told more than her work required. . . . [HUAC figureheads] are sketched in, and she gives us the details of her own bewildering sadness during those hard times. . . . Her stories are guarded and spare by design." *Ms.* critic Vivian Gornick shared this view, calling *Scoundrel Time* "a valuable piece of work. The kind of work that stands alone, untouched, in the midst of foolish criticism and foolish praise alike."

Among the Hellman memoirs, the playwright's last work, *Maybe: A Story*, represents the most obvious tie between fact and fiction. *New Republic* critic Maggie Scarf, who couldn't decide if the book was a novelized autobiography or an autobiographical novella, called "monumental despair" the "true subject of *Maybe*. For Lillian Hellman has gone swimming in the waters of time and memory and found herself adrift in a vast sea of unreliability—the shore of solid information . . . seems to recede each time she believes she has the true details in sight." The narrative covers the life of Sarah Cameron, "a woman whom Hellman knew very slightly but over a long period of time," according to Scarf, who explained that "Sarah may or may not have taken Lillian Hellman's first lover away from her." "Absorbing as this autobiographical material is, it does not compensate, in my opinion, for the emptiness at the heart of the book," noted Robert Towers in a *New York Times Book Review* piece. "Miss Hellman fails to bring Sarah Cameron into existence as even a remotely comprehensible woman. The evidence is so scattered, so inconsistent, so blurred by time and alcohol, that we are left with a wraith too insubstantial to evoke even a sense of mystery, much less to support a valid point about the ultimate unknowability of figures in our past."

To Gornick, writing in the *Village Voice,* Hellman's digressions into her past seem unworthy of the author's talent. "The association between Hellman and Sarah herself has no substance whatever; it's all fragments and fancy speculations and peripheral incidents and mysterious allusions that seem only to provide the writer with an excuse to call up once again Hammett and the drinking years, the aunts in New Orleans, making movies for Sam Goldwyn. The effort to surround Sarah with metaphoric meaning is strained and painfully obvious." Walter Clemons, in a *Newsweek* review, saw the inconsistencies in *Maybe* in another way: "Her nonstory, for that is what her tale of Sarah turns out to be, is a tricky, nervy meditation on the fallibility of memory, the failure of attention, the casual aplomb of practiced liars, the shivery unpredictability of malice." Clemons also praised Hellman's sharp voice, given her advanced years and alcoholic history.

Even as she moved into her seventies, Hellman remained a vibrant force in the public eye. She fueled this reputation in 1980 when she sued her contemporary, Mary McCarthy—author of *The Group*—after McCarthy told Dick Cavett on his talk show that she found Hellman an overrated and dishonest writer. Hellman sought damages in excess of 1.7 million dollars for "mental pain and anguish"; the suit, however, died when she did, on June 30, 1984, following several years of emphysema and diminishing eyesight. She left an estate worth four million dollars, most of which was divided into two funds: the Lillian Hellman Fund to provide grants in the arts and sciences and the Dashiell Hammett Fund, which provides for similar grants but which focuses on political, social, and economic beliefs consistent with the Marxist Hammett.

Maybe was Hellman's last major published work; a cookbook, co-written with longtime friend Peter Feibleman, came out shortly after her death. The news of Hellman's passing brought out a string of testimonials from notable writers, including these words by *Newsweek*'s David Ansen: "In her 60s, looking back on her life in her memoirs, Hellman found her indelible voice. The gallery of portraits in *Pentimento*—especially 'Julia'—are unforgettable: whether they prove to be as much fiction as fact, as some have accused, cannot diminish their power and glamour. She may have called herself 'unfinished,' but a more appropriate title would have been 'An Unmellowed Woman'. . . . The Hellman anger arose from her clear-eyed view of social

---

If you enjoy the works of Lillian Hellman, you might want to check out the following:

The plays of Eugene O'Neill, including *Long Day's Journey into Night.*
The works of Tennessee Williams, including *The Glass Menagerie.*
The plays of Edward Albee, including *Who's Afraid of Virginia Woolf?*

---

injustice and strong moral convictions, and she remained true to her passion throughout her rich and tumultuous life. Not for her the modernist halftones of alienation and equivocation. The fire within her lit up the cultural landscape; its heat will be deeply missed." Monaco noted that Hellman would be remembered for the controversy surrounding *The Children's Hour* and the truthfulness of her memoirs. "Most of all, however," Monaco concluded, "she will be remembered for her contributions to the American stage. Hellman always resented being called the "first great American female playwright,' for as she said, O'Neill is not remembered as a great American male playwright. Yet, her entry into a male-dominated profession and her ability to become a force on the American stage helped the next generation of women playwrights find a place."

■ Biographical and Critical Sources

BOOKS

Adler, Jacob H., *Lillian Hellman,* Vaughn, 1969.

Authors in the News, Gale (Detroit, MI), Volume 1, 1976, Volume 2, 1976.

Contemporary Literary Criticism, Gale (Detroit, MI), Volume 2, 1974, Volume 4, 1975, Volume 8, 1978, Volume 14, 1980, Volume 18, 1981, Volume 33, 1985, Volume 44, 1987, Volume 52, 1989.

Dictionary of Literary Biography, Gale (Detroit, MI), Volume 7: *Twentieth-Century American Dramatists,* 1981, pp. 275-295, Volume 228: *Twentieth-Century American Dramatists,* 2000, pp. 96-115.

Dictionary of Literary Biography Yearbook: 1984, Gale (Detroit, MI), 1985.

Falk, Doris V., *Lillian Hellman,* F. Ungar (New York, NY), 1978.

Feibleman, Peter, *Lilly: Reminiscences of Lillian Hellman,* Morrow (New York, NY), 1988.

Gassner, John, *Dramatic Soundings: Evaluations and Retractions Culled from Thirty Years of Dramatic Criticism,* Crown (New York, NY), 1968.

Griffin, Alice, and Geraldine Thorsten, *Understanding Lillian Hellman,* University of South Carolina Press (Columbia, SC), 1998.

Lederer, Katherine, *Lillian Hellman,* Twayne (Boston, MA), 1979.

Mellen, Joan, *Hellman and Hammett: The Legendary Passion of Lillian Hellman and Dashiell Hammett,* HarperCollins (New York, NY), 1996.

Melnick, Ralph, *The Stolen Legacy of Anne Frank: Meyer Levin, Lillian Hellman, and the Staging of the Diary,* Yale University Press (New Haven, CT), 1997.

Moody, Richard, *Lillian Hellman: Playwright,* Bobbs-Merrill (Indianapolis, IN), 1972.

Turk, Ruth, *Lillian Hellman, Rebel Playwright,* Lerner (Minneapolis, MN), 1995.

Wright, William, *Lillian Hellman: The Image, the Woman,* Simon & Schuster (New York, NY), 1986.

PERIODICALS

Back Stage, May 2, 1997, p. 43; November 3, 2000, p. 46.

Chicago Tribune, March 30, 1980.

Listener, November 18, 1986, David Hunt, review of *Scoundrel Time.*

London Magazine, August-September, 1974, Julian Symons, review of *Pentimento.*

Modern Drama, spring, 1996, pp. 16-30.

Ms., January, 1974, Muriel Haynes, review of *Pentimento;* August, 1976, Vivian Gornick, review of *Scoundrel Time.*

Nation, May 22, 1935, J. W. Krutch, review of *The Children's Hour.*

New Republic, August 2, 1980, Maggie Scarf, review of *Maybe;* August 13, 1984; July 29, 1996, p. 42.

Newsweek, June 2, 1980, Walter Clemons, review of *Maybe.*

New York, September 17, 1973, Eliot Fremont-Smith, review of *Pentimento.*

New Yorker, May 19, 1997, p. 100.

New York Review of Books, June 10, 1976.

New York Times, November 13, 1980; August 26, 1984.

New York Times Book Review, September 23, 1973; April 25, 1976, Maureen Howard, review of *Scoundrel Time;* June 1, 1980, Robert Towers, review of *Maybe.*

Saturday Review, April 17, 1976, Bruce Cook, review of *Scoundrel Time.*

Spectator, July 14, 1984, Paul Johnson.

Theatre Arts, June, 1941, Rosamund Gilder, review of *Watch on the Rhine.*

Time, May 19, 1980.

Variety, October 29, 2001, pp. 35-36.

Village Voice, May 19, 1980, Vivian Gornick, review of *Maybe.*

Washington Post, May 19, 1980.

■ Obituaries

PERIODICALS

Chicago Tribune, July 1, 1984.

Los Angeles Times, July 1, 1984.

Newsweek, July 9, 1984, David Ansen.

New York Times, July 1, 1984.

Washington Post, July 1, 1984.*

Spike Jonze

■ Personal

Born Adam Spiegel, c. 1969, in St. Louis, MO (one source says Rockville, MD); married Sofia Coppola, June 26, 1999.

■ Addresses

Office—c/o Satellite Films, 941 North Mansfield Ave., Los Angeles, CA 90038.

■ Career

Director, actor, and writer. *Freestylin'* magazine, Torrance, CA, staff writer, late 1980s; freelance photographer for *Freestylin'*, *Trans World Skateboarding*, *BMX Action*, and *Homeboy* magazines, c. late 1980s-early 1990s; director of videos, beginning early 1990s; directed first professional video, "100 Percent," for Sonic Youth, 1992; has also directed videos for the Beastie Boys, Björk, the Breeders, Fatboy Slim, Ween, and Weezer; director of commercials for Lee Jeans, Levi's, Wrangler, among others. Editor of *Dirt* magazine, 1991; co-publisher of *Grand Royal* magazine, 1997. Director of *Hi-Octane* (television series), Comedy Central, 1994; (and producer) *Las Nueve Vidas de Paco—The Chocolate Movie* (short film), 1995; *Amarillo by Morning* (documentary short), 1997; *How They Get There* (short film), 1997; *Being John Malkovich* (feature film) USA Films, 1999; and *Adaptation,* Columbia, 2002. Film appearances include *Mi Vida Loca,* 1993; *The Game,* 1997; *Three Kings,* 1999; *Being John Malkovich,* 1999; and *Keep Your Eyes Open,* 2002. Television appearances include *MTV Movie Awards,* 2000; and *MTV Video Music Awards,* 2001. Cinematographer, *Bed, Bath, and Beyond,* 1996; and *Free Tibet,* 1998. Producer of television programs *Jackass,* 2000; and *Human Nature,* 2001.

■ Awards, Honors

New York Film Critics Circle Award for best first film, Venice Film Festival FIPRESCI Award, and Online Film Critics Society Award for best debut, all 1999, Deauville Film Festival critics award, Independent Spirit Award, Sierra Award, Las Vegas Film Critics Society grand special prize, Florida Film Critics Circle Award, and Academy Award nomination for best director, all 2000, and Bodil Award nomination, ALFS Award, and London Film Critics Circle Award for Director of the Year, 2001, all for *Being John Malkovich;* Broadcast Film Critics Association Award for breakthrough artist, 2000.

■ Writings

Beastie Boys: Sabotage (video), 1994.

Las Nueve Vidas de Paco—The Chocolate Movie (short film), 1995.

(And creator) *Jackass* (television series), MTV, 2000.

Contributor to magazines.

■ Work in Progress

The Curious Case of Benjamin Button, based on a short story by F. Scott Fitzgerald, for Paramount Pictures.

■ Sidelights

Director Spike Jonze shot into the mainstream with his first feature film, *Being John Malkovich*. Though the sleeper hit nabbed the director an Oscar nomination, it was not typical Hollywood fare. It is a quirky fantasy about a man who comes upon a room in his office building that leads into the mind of the eponymous character. This was the perfect project for Jonze, whose oddball wit and unconventional way of looking at the world helped make the project a success. Jonze cut his directorial teeth on music and commercial videos for years before graduating to feature length films, ads, and clips that reflect a decidedly subversive view on the accepted way of doing things. He cast the rock group Beastie Boys as 1970s detectives for one video, and dropped the group Weezer into the 1950s via an episode of the television series *Happy Days* in another. "Whenever newspaper and magazine articles are written about . . . Jonze, the word 'hip' almost always pops up somewhere in the story," wrote Alona Wartofsky in a *Washington Post* profile of the director. Wartofsky further commented that this is a prospect Jonze finds deeply horrifying.

Born around 1969, Jonze's real name is Adam Spiegel. Beyond that, much of his early life is a mystery, as the director provides differing accounts of his past and is known to assume various alter egos. As Ethan Smith noted in *New York*, "He avoids interviews, cancels press conferences, and routinely fabricates information about his past. In a recent British television profile, he presented himself as a Corvette-driving loudmouth dressed in a tank top and a do-rag."

Various sources, though, claim that Jonze and a sibling grew up in Bethesda, Maryland. Smith reported that Jonze's parents divorced when he was young; his mother, Sandy Granzow, works in communications for the World Bank while his father, Arthur Spiegel III, runs an international health-care consulting firm. Though Jonze denies it, several sources say that he is an heir to the $3 billion-a-year Spiegel mail order catalog fortune. Karen Schoemer in *Newsweek*, however, noted that "he's only distantly related."

Ever since he was young, Jonze was an avid skateboarder and loved freestyle bike riding. In junior high and high school, he worked at a dirt-bike shop. The owner there, Jay Metzler, told Smith in *New York*, "For all intents and purposes, the kid kind of raised himself. He was basically a ward of the Rockville BMX store." It was there he earned the nickname "Spike" because he would often arrive at work unshowered with his hair sticking up. The shop was legendary among bike enthusiasts and often received visits from out-of-town professional cyclists. Jonze enjoyed picking them up at the airport in a chauffeur uniform as a joke.

In high school Jonze took up photography and started submitting work and writing letters to the Torrance, California-based *Freestylin'* magazine, a periodical devoted to BMX culture. They offered him a job as a staff writer, so the day after his high school finals, Jonze left for the West Coast. For two years he and friend Mark Lewman lived in a townhouse on the same block as the magazine's offices and rode their skateboards to work each day. Eventually Jonze began taking photographs for *Trans World Skateboarding*, *BMX Action*, and *Homeboy*, as well as for *Freestylin'*.

After the BMX craze died down and *Freestylin'* closed up shop, Jonze and Lewman were hired in 1991 to run *Dirt*, a magazine for teenage boys that was the counterpart to *Sassy*. It only survived a few issues, but in the meantime Jonze's reputation for photography and videos was growing. His first video project, *Video Days*, is a twenty-minute handheld tape of a skateboarding team performing tricks. Jonze's work in this film is unique among videographers in several aspects. First, he skates alongside the team for some of the shots, providing some unique angles. Also, he introduces a wacky sense of humor, mainly by setting the visuals to the Jackson Five song "I Want You Back" instead of using the typical thrash-punk or speed-metal soundtrack.

From Skater to MTV Video Guru

Before long, *Video Days* was legendary around the Southern California music and skate scene. After the band Sonic Youth caught sight of it, they hired Jonze to co-direct their "100 Percent" video, along with Tamra Davis, wife of Mike D of the Beastie Boys. During production of that video, Jonze met his future wife, Sofia Coppola, daughter of film director Francis Ford Coppola. Singer Kim Gordon told Schoemer in *Newsweek*, "They'd hang out together, but it was almost like the he's-too-nice syndrome. I was like, 'Show her your dark side!' We'd go to Thrifty's and try to find sunglasses for him." Jonze and Coppola remained friends for several years before becoming romantically involved.

Subsequently, director Peter Care hired Jonze as a cameraman, and helped him land a job directing for Satellite Films, owned by Polygram. Soon Jonze was shooting videos for cutting-edge groups like Weezer, Ween, and the Breeders. In the 1994 Weezer video "Buddy Holly," he uses computer imaging to place the band into an episode of the television sitcom *Happy Days*.

Also in 1994 Jonze created the noteworthy "Sabotage" video for the Beastie Boys. It was shot as a hilarious takeoff on corny 1970s cop shows and features the rap trio in fake mustaches, Afro wigs, aviator sunglasses, and sleazy polyester outfits. His 1995 video for Björk's "It's oh So Quiet" recalls 1930s film choreographer Busby Berkley's over-the-top dance routines. For the band Daft Funk's "Da Funk," Jonze produced a faux cinema vérité fantasy involving a dog-headed man named Charlie who walks along Second Avenue in Manhattan. For R.E.M. he produced a karaoke-like sequence in "Crush with Eyeliner," which has Japanese youths posing as the band. For Wax's "California," he turned the quick-cutting image of rock video on its head, producing instead a one-image video with slow-motion images of a man on fire running. Puff Daddy's performance of "It's All about the Benjamins" incites a senior prom audience to wake from their sleepwalking state and do serious damage to their school.

Jonze really began to make his name with the video "Praise You" for British deejay Fatboy Slim. Co-directed with Roman Coppola, now his brother-in-law, the video was shot like an amateur home video, featuring the fictional Torrance Community Dance Group performing in front of a movie theater one evening. A real audience gathers and the theater manager even provides an unplanned finale, storming out and turning off the music. "Praise for You" won an MTV Video Award for best direction and breakthrough video. However, when Jonze took the stage to accept the award, he arrived in character as Richard Koufey, the bearded, rhythmless leader of

A sea of John Malkoviches haunts the main character in *Being John Malkovich*, director Spike Jonze's offbeat 1999 comedy starring John Cusack, Cameron Diaz, and, of course, Malkovich himself.

the fictional Torrance Community Dance Group from his video. He proceeded to perform with his "community dancers" on the show, even amusing the audience with a dance solo and a cartwheel. "Spike's the most innovative funny guy out there," commented Fatboy Slim label director David Levine to Wartofsky. "He's a genius. He puts a completely different twist on artists. His videos take away all the vanity and hoopla of 'Hey, I'm a rock star.' He just makes these funny, great little films." Jonze noted to Wartofsky that he enjoys doing music videos. "It's fun. In general, I put the song on at home or driving around and just listen to it over and over again, and write down random ideas and then see which ones I like most when I look back over the list or which ones may fit together."

Jonze eventually began to branch out into commercials, heading up the somewhat surreal Lee Jeans spots featuring the doll Buddy Lee. He also directed a Levi's ad inspired by emergency-room drama shows; it includes a team of doctors singing Soft Cell's "Tainted Love" as an EKG monitor keeps time. In another Levi's ad, Jonze came up with the idea of demonstrating the toughness of the material by having a man dragged behind a van; Jonze himself is the man being dragged. More hands-on treatment shows up in Jonze's ad for Nissan's Frontier truck. A man is snoozing in a recliner, completely unaware of the machinations of his Australian shepherd, who manages the chair and its occupant out of the living room and onto the city streets for a chilling and daredevil ride down hilly streets, narrowly missing vehicles on the way, to come to a stop in front of a Nissan dealership. As Wartofsky pointed out, the ad required three types of recliners: "electric-powered, gas-powered and gravity-powered." Jonze himself was again involved in the ad as more than director; he took a course in demolition driving so that he could drive one of the vehicles that almost runs into the speeding recliner. "Spike's work stands out," executive producer Steve Neely told Wartofsky. "Which is hard to do with eight million commercials out there. He's very conceptual, and when he gets involved in a project, he likes to involve Spike in them, creatively speaking—which is a big positive."

Breaks into Feature Films

Meanwhile, Jonze was yearning to break into feature films. In 1993 he did so with a bit part in Allison Anders' *Mi Vida Loca—My Crazy Life.* Working in television, he directed some segments of Comedy Central's 1994 series *Hi-Octane,* starring, produced, and written by Sofia Coppola. His first hoped-for directorial project, however—an adaptation of the children's book *Harold and the Purple Crayon*—ran into several behind-the-scenes roadblocks and its production was canceled. One fringe benefit of that production, however, was meeting director and writer David Russell, who became a fast friend and later invited Jonze to take part in his 1999 film, *Three Kings.*

Meanwhile, Jonze worked on several short films, such as *Las Nueve Vidas de Paco—The Chocolate Movie, How They Get There,* about how a shoe ended up at the side of the road, and *Amarillo Morning,* the last two of which were screened at Sundance Film Festival. In 1997 he had another acting part, this time in David Fincher's *The Game,* and in 1998, his work as a cinematographer made the big screens with the arrival of *Free Tibet,* his filming of the 1996 Tibetan Freedom Festival.

1999 proved to be a break-out year for Jonze in several respects. He landed a role in Russell's *Three Kings,* co-starring George Clooney, Mark Wahlberg, and Ice Cube. In it, he plays Conrad Vig, a racist Gulf War soldier who is plotting with his fellow soldiers to steal millions from Iraqi leader Saddam Hussein. This role was much higher profile than his earlier forays into acting, and it also allowed Jonze to do some stunt work, which was a long-held dream for him. "Spike will try anything," Russell told Anne E. Musumeci of *Harper's Bazaar.* "I knew he'd be into playing a guy who could be crazy vicious as well as extremely sweet." Musumecci felt that Jonze's performance "is impressive and deeply menacing." Also in 1999 Jonze and Coppola were married at the Coppola's Napa Valley vineyard with no less than Tom Waits crooning "Here Comes the Bride." And in the fall of that same year Jonze scored his biggest coup to date as director of the off-the-wall *Being John Malkovich,* produced by Michael Stipe of the band R.E.M.

Being John Malkovich

Jonze worked on *Being John Malkovich* for over three years. With a screenplay penned by Charlie Kaufman, it is a surrealist romp hitting on themes of gender, identity, and love and starring John Cusack as out-of-work puppeteer Craig Schwartz who—working as a filer—discovers a portal into the mind of actor John Malkovich. Craig stumbles across this portal behind a filing cabinet in the office building where he works on the 7 1/2th floor. The floor is appropriately only half as tall as other floors, causing workers to walk in a perennially stooped position. Craig and a coworker, played by Catherine Keener, end up selling "rides" into Malkovich's brain that last fifteen minutes, until the thrill-seeker is unceremoniously dumped from the sky into a ditch next to the New Jersey Turnpike. A purposely de-glamorized Cameron Diaz plays Craig's wife, who gets involved in a strange love triangle with Keener's character and Malkovich while attempting to nurse her pet chimp through a psychic trauma.

Crucial to the project from the outset was, of course, the cooperation of Malkovich. When first starting to work on the project, Jonze and Kaufman had no idea if the actor would agree to appear in the film. "We tried to think who we could get if John didn't say yes," Jonze told Wartofsky. "Charlie [Kaufman] and I sat down and made a list, but we never came up with anybody that really excited us. There was the first choice and then there was like a hundred fiftieth choices and nothing in between." But they kept working "in blind faith," hoping for the best. In the end, Francis Ford Coppola talked Malkovich into taking part in the film.

Critical response to the movie was either glowing or perplexed. Some viewers just did not "get" the movie, but those who did gave it high marks. Stephen Hunter, writing in the *Washington Post,* called *Being John Malkovich* the year's "most inventive film and one of the most purely enjoyable." Hunter called the film a "document of pure surrealism" that does not "take place in a dream universe but in our own." Also writing in the *Washington Post,* Desson Howe dubbed the movie a "brilliantly inventive fantasy" that "fuses weird to wonderful." Howe concluded that *Being John Malkovich* is "so full of creativity, so subversive, so alive" that it makes the prospect of further collaborations between Jonze and Kaufman "delicious." Janet Maslin, reviewing the movie in the *New York Times,* felt it was an "irresistible first feature by the stellar video director, Spike Jonze." Maslin noted that while Jonze's film was not the first to explore the prospect of getting inside the head of another person, it "is definitely the most fun." Writing in the *Wall Street Journal,* Joe Morgenstern forgave what he considered "lapses and longueurs," which "seems to be located at the intersection of Lewis Carroll, Marcel Duchamp and MTV," because for much of the time the film left the critic "agog at the surreal carryings-on, and gaga over the Dada." Kenneth Turan added more praise in his *Los Angeles Times* review, noting that Jonze "displays the same kind of unexpected delight in playing with reality that he used in music videos and celebrated commercials."

For *Nation* contributor Stuart Klawans, the film was not only entertaining, but also thought-provoking. "If [*Being John Malkovich*] doesn't leave you self-defeated by laughter, you should begin . . . to hear a small, insistent voice in your head, which will ask a lot of questions. What if celebrity, that most

Jonze leaves his directing chair to take a starring role in the 1999 film *Three Kings,* which finds a team of unscrupulous American servicemen tempted by the riches of the region they were sent to protect.

American of virtues, exists next door to nonentity? How come people fall in love with an 'inner self' but get picky about its wrappings?" Brian D. Johnson, reviewing the movie in *Maclean's*, also noted the mix of genres in the movie, commenting that it's "one funny movie," but also one that explores "the passageway between artistic failure and success." Johnson concluded that Jonze "pulls all the right strings to dance the high wire between art and entertainment." *Newsweek* critic David Ansen added to the chorus of praise, commenting that Jonze "has made a deliciously one-of-a-kind surrealist farce."

Being John Malkovich earned Jonze an Academy Award nomination in 2000 for best director, thus boosting his reputation even further. In addition he was honored with awards ranging from the New York Film Critics Circle Award, to the Venice Film Festival, the Online Film Critics Society, the Deauville Film Festival, and the Florida Film Critics Circle Award. He also received a Broadcast Film Critics Association Award for breakthrough artist for his work on *Being John Malkovich* as well as for his role in *Three Kings*.

If you enjoy the works of Spike Jonze, you might want to check out the following films:

Brazil, directed by Terry Gilliam, 1985.
Fight Club, directed by David Fincher, 1999.
Black Hawk Down, directed by Ridley Scott, 2001.

Since the success of his debut feature, Jonze has continued with the mix of video, ads, and movies that sustained his early career. He created a memorable post-apocalypse spot for Nike in 2000 titled "The Morning After," and was brought onboard Al Gore's presidential campaign to film a short documentary about the candidate behind the scenes. Shot with a hand-held camera, the film was intended to make Gore more user-friendly. Writing in the *New York Times* about that effort, Caryn James called Jonze a "master of meticulous films that create the illusion of looseness, and he used the intimacy of hand-held cameras, and smooth editing that looked tossed together, to recreate the Gore image." In 2001 Jonze returned to his video roots with a music video

for Fatboy Slim's "Weapon of Choice," with actor Christopher Walken performing a graceful dance on screen. "Brilliantly funny" is how Wartofsky described the video in the *Washington Post.* Jonze's work in feature films also progressed, with two films: *Adaptation,* based on the novel *The Orchid Thief* and written for the screen by Kaufman, and *The Curious Case of Benjamin Button,* based on a short story by F. Scott Fitzgerald. In the former movie, Kaufman and Jonze once again create a surreal blend, telling a story within a story involving a screenwriter's attempt at adapting *The Orchid Thief* for film. Jonze's years as an underground icon may have ended, but his eclectic blend of creativity is only just beginning.

■ Biographical and Critical Sources

PERIODICALS

Cineaste, spring, 2000, p. 72.
Entertainment Weekly, March 17, 1995, p. 33; November 5, 1999, p. 49; December 24, 1999, p. 46; October 19, 2001, p. 52.
Harper's Bazaar, November, 1999, Anne E. Musumecci, "Being Spike Jonze," p. 146.
Interview, October, 1999, p. 210.
Los Angeles Times, November 20, 1997, p. E3; October 29, 1999, Kenneth Turan, review of *Being John Malkovich,* p. 1; August 18, 2000, p. 26; September 30, 2000, p. 2.
Maclean's, November 15, 1999, Brian D. Johnson, "Lost in the Fun House," p. 152.
Nation, October 25, 1999, p. 42; November 22, 1999, Stuart Klawans, "Just a Cannes Job?," p. 32.
Newsweek, October 18, 1999, Karen Schoemer, "Being Spike Jonze," p. 74; November 1, 1999, David Ansen, "Get Inside His Head," p. 85.
New York, October 25, 1999, Ethan Smith, "Spike Jonze Unmasked," p. 44.
New York Times, May 7, 1995, Patrick Phillips, "Boy Wonder Gets the Purple Crayon"; October 1, 1999, Janet Maslin, "A Portal Leading to Self-Parody," p. 10; August 18, 2000, Caryn James, "The Lighter Side of the Candidate," p. A20; October 8, 2000, p. 2; September 2, 2001, p. 4.
Ottawa Sun, November 12, 1999, p. 47.
People, July 19, 1999, p. 79.
Shoot, November 26, 1999, p. 8; March 24, 2000, p. 36.
Time, November 1, 1999, p. 108.
Variety, September 6, 1999, p. 61.
Wall Street Journal, October 29, 1999, Joe Morgenstern, review of *Being John Malkovich,* p. W1.

Washington Post, October 24, 1999, Alona Wartofsky, "A Jonze for Inventiveness," p. G1; October 29, 1999, Desson Howe, "The Incredible Brilliance of 'Being,'" p. N41, Stephen Hunter, "'John Malkovich': A Mind of Its Own," p. C1; August 5, 2001, Alona Wartofsky, "The Walken Shtick, Creepy . . . and Cool," p. G1.

OTHER

Hollywood.com, http://www.hollywood.com/ (March 6, 2002), "Celebrity Biography: Spike Jonze."

Virgen.net, http://www.virgin.net/ (September 3, 2000), Chris Roberts, "Keeping up with the Jonze: Spike Jonze Interview."*

Frida Kahlo

The Letters of Frida Kahlo: Cartas Apasionadas, selected and edited by Martha Zamora, Chronicle Books (San Francisco, CA), 1995.

■ Personal

Full name, Magdalena Carmen Frida Kahlo y Calderon; born July 6, 1907, in Coyoacan, Mexico; died, July 13, 1954, in Coyoacan, Mexico; daughter of Guillermo (a photographer) and Matilde (Calderon) Kahlo; married Diego Rivera (an artist), 1929 (marriage ended 1939), remarried, 1940.

■ Career

Artist. *Exhibitions:* Held one-woman shows in Mexico City, Mexico, 1953, New York, NY, and Paris, France. Paintings included in permanent collections, including the Frida Kahlo Museum and the Dolores Olmedo Patino Museum, both in Mexico City.

■ Writings

The Diary of Frida Kahlo: An Intimate Self-Portrait, introduction by Carlos Fuentes, essay and commentaries by Sarah M. Lowe, Abrams (New York, NY), 1995.

■ Sidelights

Twentieth-century Mexican painter Frida Kahlo often commented, "I never painted dreams. I painted my own reality." Some critics and biographers argue that such a reality was more a surreal nightmare than reality or dream, for many of Kahlo's two hundred paintings are self-portraits, dealing directly with her battle to survive a horrific accident when she was eighteen years old. As her biographer, Hayden Herrera, noted in *Grove Art*, the self-portraits "are a kind of exorcism by which she projected her anguish on to another Frida, in order to separate herself from pain and at the same time confirm her hold on reality." Her primitive style and elements of fantasy are immediately recognizable, as is her black-haired subject with the full eyebrows grown almost into one. Blending European influences such as surrealism with distinct Latin-American iconography, Kahlo was praised by surrealists such as Andre Breton, and by her husband, Diego Rivera, during her lifetime. She had three solo exhibitions before her death in 1954, garnering a large reputation in the Latin-American art world. Since that time, her reputation has grown to international proportions, fueled during the 1970s and early 1980s by a spate of biographies and critical works about the artist and reinforced in the 1990s with publication of her diaries and letters. Despite the success she achieved as an artist, and her acquaintance with many notable figures of her day—including Leon Trotsky—Kahlo suffered immense psychological and physical pain for much of her life. The artist, who was stricken with polio at the age of six, also experienced continual back pain and underwent several operations as a result of injuries sustained in the accident when she was a teenager. Often, she was forced to paint while lying on her back.

Kahlo was born three years before the Mexican Revolution, during which the people rejected the dictatorship of Porfirio Diaz and triggered a period of rapid and dramatic social and economic transformation in Mexico and a revival of Mexico's native cultural roots. Out of this re-discovered tradition grew the muralist style that influenced so much of Mexican art during Kahlo's lifetime. Born in 1907—she would later say 1910 in order to have her birth coincide with the revolution—in a suburb of Mexico City, Kahlo was the daughter of a well-respected photographer, Guillermo Kahlo, who immigrated to Mexico from Germany at age nineteen. Kahlo's mother, Matilde Calderon, was of Spanish and Indian descent and largely uneducated. The child spent much of her life in the house, Casa Azul, which Guillermo Kahlo built shortly before his daughter's birth. Her parents were vastly different in temperament: the father a creative, boundary-pushing artist, and the mother more conservative, a devout Catholic and a proud housekeeper. Kahlo was more drawn to her father, who encouraged his daughter's creative energy. Her relationship with her mother, who suffered from depression after the loss of an infant son, was more distant and cool.

One of six daughters, Kahlo was an essentially happy and free-spirited child until she suffered a mild case of polio when she was six or seven. The polio left her with a withered right leg and her foot turned outward. The resulting limp caused her pelvis and spine to become twisted as Kahlo grew and also inspired taunts from her schoolmates. Kahlo's father helped to nurse her back to health and later encouraged her to play sports—not a typical activity for young girls at the time—in order to overcome her disability. Entering the National Preparatory School in 1922, she quickly became the class prankster, and was known for the traditional costumes she liked to wear in support of the spirit of the revolution. Indigenous jewelry, brightly colored native clothing, and braided hair worn atop her head in the style of Oaxaca natives were her preferred dress. When she was sixteen, she met painter Diego Rivera, who came to her preparatory school to decorate the walls of the auditorium. She quickly developed a crush on this internationally famous muralist, over twenty years her senior, and would spend entire afternoons watching him paint. Kahlo soon reported to her friends that she intended to have his baby one day.

All such dreams faded as a result of the incidents of September 17, 1925. That day Kahlo was badly injured when an electric trolley crashed into the side of the bus she was riding home from school. The collision split the bus in half and drove a piece of iron into Kahlo's pelvis and back, breaking them in several places. Other injuries included a fractured collarbone and ribs, as well as a shattered right leg and foot. The effects of this accident plagued Kahlo the rest of her life: she lived in pain most of the time; she was permanently crippled in the right leg; and she could never bear children. Over the course of her life, Kahlo would have more than thirty operations, most of them on her spine and her right foot.

Despite the chronic pain she suffered throughout her adult life as the result of a tragic accident, Frida Kahlo completed many canvases prior to her untimely death in 1954.

Painting as Therapy

During her long convalescence, Kahlo turned to painting as an emotional outlet. Self-taught, Kahlo produced her first self-portrait to give to a boyfriend of the time. As Melissa Chessher noted in a cover story for *American Way,* "Like all the self-portraits that followed, the painting was a gift meant to join the artist and a loved one, a kind of talisman against Frida's constant fear that people wouldn't remember her, that she was unloved." A couple of years later, Kahlo began showing her work to Rivera. She was anxious for his criticism, as she had begun incorporating some of his motifs in her own work: a deliberately primitive style, simplified areas of bright color, and subject matter taken from the archaeology and folk art of Mexico. Yet her own contribution to an emerging style was a surrealist blend of fantasy and fable, as well as her use of animals in the paintings, in particular monkeys and dogs. Rivera was impressed by the young woman's talent and encouraged her to continue. Soon the relationship turned amorous and the couple was married in 1929.

For Rivera, this was his third marriage, and it was never a conventional relationship. Rivera had extramarital affairs—including one with Kahlo's own sister—and Kahlo retaliated by having affairs with both men and women. Their marriage lasted for ten years, and it was during that turbulent decade and into the 1940s that Kahlo painted some of her best-known work. Some of these paintings, such as 1931's "Frida and Diego," record the vicissitudes of her marriage to Rivera, the second of two damaging accidents in her life, as she often said. In this painting Rivera is shown as the great master painter while Kahlo, dressed in her usual long-skirted Mexican outfit, is the nurturing wife of the artist. When they divorced in 1939, she produced "The Two Frida's," in which, as Herrera noted in *Grove Art,* "her heart is extracted and her identity split." The painting, Herrera explained, "conveys her desperation and loneliness at the time of their divorce."

Other paintings of the time, such as "The Broken Column," recall the injuries she received in the bus crash. In this self-portrait, Kahlo's naked body is strapped with bands and also pierced with nails. Her torso is split in half, the broken column of the title. "Moving from Rivera's jazzy black dancer series to Kahlo's *The Broken Column* is like stepping out of a warm tropical rain into a bone-chilling blizzard of pain," wrote Jeff Spurrier in *Connoisseur.* One other self-portrait of the time, "The Wounded Deer," continues this theme of being impaled: her head is grafted onto the body of a doe which is pierced with arrows. However, despite such injuries, the deer still stands tall. Such images were little less than what reality itself provided for Kahlo: even with her numerous operations, nothing could stop the bone deterioration, and she often "lived in braces, surgical corsets and wheelchairs, paraphernalia she transformed on canvas with a macabre vibrancy," as R. Z. Sheppard noted in *Time.* Thus, physical and emotional pain became Kahlo's main subject matter. Influenced by Rivera, Kahlo was, clearly, no mere clone. She developed her own distinctive style, a "hybrid of classical, modern, and Mexican folk art," as Sheppard noted. "She was an impressive colorist and a meticulous technician." Among her admirers in the art world were Pablo Picasso, Wassily Kandinsky, Andre Breton, and Rivera himself, who claimed Kahlo had a bigger talent than his own.

In the midst of their stormy relationship, Rivera and Kahlo formed the center of an intellectual group in Mexico that included artists and politicians of the day, mostly from the left, for Kahlo and Rivera both firmly believed in international communism. Kahlo's "Self-Portrait Dedicated to Leon Trotsky" attests in part to this circle of acquaintances; Kahlo had one of her many affairs with that Russian revolutionary. In 1932 Rivera was commissioned to produce murals for the Detroit Institute of Arts, and the couple lived in the United States for a time. While there Kahlo miscarried a pregnancy, and later she confronted this painful experience in the painting "Henry Ford Hospital." As Chessher described the painting, "[Kahlo] lies nude in a hospital bed with a pool of blood beneath her and a large tear falling from her eye. Her stomach is swollen, and veinlike red ribbons stretch from her hand." These connect to six images, including a small Rivera portrait, a likeness of the miscarried fetus, an iron vise, a snail, an orchid, and pelvic bones. As Spurrier commented, "Like all Kahlo surrealistic images, it is haunting and hypnotic, powerful far beyond its physical size." Indeed, most of Kahlo's canvasses were relatively small in size; the artist herself was only five feet tall. This was in sharp contrast to Rivera's massive murals and his equally massive body at over six feet in height and weighing three hundred pounds.

The Final Years

Though Kahlo and Rivera divorced in 1939, they remarried, at Rivera's insistence, the following year. However, Kahlo had conditions for this remarriage:

Kahlo, posing alongside her painting *Las dos Fridas*, a 1939 dual portrait of the artist.

they would have no sexual intercourse and Kahlo would support herself financially with proceeds from her art. In the 1940s, at Rivera's urging, Kahlo taught art students at her studio. Throughout these years her health continued to decline; while numerous operations confined her to bed for months on end, her international reputation continued to grow and her paintings were shown in exhibitions in Europe and New York, often linked with the Surrealists. Ultimately Frida rejected this classification.

Toward the end of her life, she was finally granted her first solo show in her native country. The prospect of this helped to bring her out of what was becoming an increasingly depressed state as a result of her physical problems. However, by the time of

the exhibition, Kahlo was once again bed-ridden and her many fans feared she would miss her own opening. But at the last minute she arrived by ambulance and was set up in a four-poster bed at the gallery to receive the will wishes of visitors.

Her exhibit in Mexico was one of the last high points in Kahlo's life, for several months later doctors had to amputate her right leg due to gangrene. Increasingly the artist had to rely on painkillers to get her through the day. Life was becoming more of a burden than a joy to her. As she noted in the diary she kept of this period, "I hope the exit is joyful—and I hope never to come back." She continued to paint until the end; her final painting was of a watermelon, titled "Long Live Life," "both a salute to life and an acknowledgment of death's imminence," according to Herrera. Kahlo's last public appearance was at a demonstration protesting the CIA-sponsored overthrow of Guatemala's leftist President Jacobo Arbenz. She died a week later, on July 13, 1954, just a week short of her forty-seventh birthday. Though the cause of her death was reported at the time to be a pulmonary embolism, many now agree that Kahlo took her own life, most probably with an overdose of painkillers. At her funeral, attended by hundreds in Mexico City, Kahlo created a final stir. Just as her body was passing into the crematorium, the sudden heat from the open furnace doors caused her body to sit upright, and, as Herrera described the scene in his biography, *Frida*, "her blazing hair stood out from her face in an aureole." Sheppard commented in *Time*, "She was a woman who knew how to make an entrance and an exit."

The Legacy

By the 1970s Kahlo's fame had taken on worldwide dimensions. Fueled by a resurgence of feminism and a willingness in the art world to look seriously at her harsh messages, Kahlo became something of a cult figure, with buttons, T-shirts, and the full panoply of spin-off items on sale with her likeness. Herrera's 1983 biography also did much to increase such popularity. In 1984 the Mexican government also formally recognized Kahlo's work as important to the country's national heritage. A sure sign of her arrival were the prices her works now fetched at auction houses. In 1977, at the first auction of one of her paintings at Sotheby's, for example, the sale price was only $19,000, below even the low estimate. Less than two decades later Sotheby's sold another of her paintings for $3.2 million, at that time the highest ever paid for a painting by a Latin-American artist and for a female artist. Television specials and films followed. In 2002 the movie *Frida* was released, directed by Julie Taymor and starring Salma Hayek as Kahlo, and Alfred Molina, Geoffrey Rush, and Edward Norton, among other internationally celebrated actors.

In 1995 two more books were published in conjunction with this rediscovery of Kahlo. The first was her long-secreted diary, which had been stored in a bank vault in Mexico City for several years. Administrators of the Rivera estate had previously allowed only a select few, such as Kahlo's biographers, limited access to her writings. In 1994, however, the estate put the diary up for auction, and the art-book publisher Abrams was the highest bidder for the

pages Kahlo wrote during the last ten years of her life. The diary was reproduced in the 1995 book *The Diary of Frida Kahlo: An Intimate Self-Portrait*. Kahlo's sketches, often accompanied by captions and her written musings on a variety of introspective topics, form the book's core; it also contains an introductory chapter by Mexican critic and author Carlos Fuentes. Deborah Solomon, reviewing *The Diary of Frida Kahlo* for the *New York Times Book Review*, noted that it "is less pure diary than a hybrid creature mixing drawings and watercolors with casual prose-poems," and remarked that Kahlo's art seems to yield more clues to the artist herself than does the journal. Amanda Hopkinson, writing in *New Statesman*, also drew attention to the fact that this is not a typical artist's notebook nor a record of Kahlo's daily activities. "Instead," wrote Hopkinson, "its integration of text and image depends as much on visual as verbal puns, on mutual nourishment between profound emotions and often playful jottings." Donna Seaman in *Booklist* had a more

An eerie portrait of Kahlo completed in 1949 shows her harboring thoughts of noted Mexican muralist Diego Rivera, her husband.

straightforward reaction to the diary, calling it "a remarkable and precious book." A contributor for *Publishers Weekly* found the work "haunting," and a "testament to Kahlo's resilience and courage." And reviewing the *Diary* in *Art in America*, Jill Johnson felt it "is a very special publishing event." Johnson particularly commented on "'automatic' writing in various scripts, hues, moods, and degrees of clarity or messiness, both of thought and execution, along with riots of color and spontaneous, seemingly childlike bursts of imagery evolved from accidents, doodles and improvisation . . . [that] make this book a visual delight." Johnson concluded that Kahlo's *Diary* "is a gorgeous phoenix; it adds to the luster of her posthumous life as an artist."

If you enjoy the works of Frida Kahlo, you might want to check out the following:

The works of Italian photographer Tina Modotti (1846-1942).
The murals of Mexican artist Diego Rivera (1886-1957).
The works of surrealists like Marcel Du-Champ (1887-1968) and Joan Miró (1893-1983).

Seaman and Solomon also reviewed *The Letters of Frida Kahlo: Cartas Apasionadas*, also published in 1995. The eighty letters chosen by Martha Zamora include letters that the artist wrote as a teenager to her first boyfriend, as well as later missives she sent to family, friends, and even to her doctors. The documents provide a portrait of a woman who was perhaps not as dark and brooding as her paintings may have suggested; critics note that in many of them Kahlo writes profusely and affectionately of Rivera. Still, Solomon found something lacking. "All in all, Kahlo's letters and diaries are most revealing in their very lack of revelation," she observed in her *New York Times Book Review* piece. "They have the odd effect of dulling the edge of her originality, allowing her to command center stage while providing no hint of how or why she got there." Seaman in *Booklist*, however, found that Kahlo's "frank, affectionate and energetic letters play in revealing counterpoint to her wrenching mythic paintings." Likewise, a contributor for *Publishers Weekly* thought that these "candid letters . . . flesh out [Kahlo's] image with revealing personal glimpses."

■ Biographical and Critical Sources

BOOKS

Dictionary of Hispanic Biography, Gale (Detroit, MI), 1996.

Drucker, Malka, *Frida Kahlo: Torment and Triumph*, University of New Mexico Press (Albuquerque, NM), 1995.

Frida Kahlo Masterpieces, W. W. Norton, (New York, NY), 1994.

Garza, Hedda, *Frida Kahlo*, Chelsea House (New York, NY), 1993.

Grimberg, Salomon, *Lola Alvarez Bravo, the Frida Kahlo Photographs*, Art Publishers (New York, NY), 1991.

Herrera, Hayden, *Frida: A Biography of Frida Kahlo*, Harper & Row (New York, NY), 1983.

Herrera, Hayden, *Frida Kahlo: The Paintings*, Harper-Collins (New York, NY), 1991.

Lozan, Luis-Martin, editor, *Frida Kahlo*, Little, Brown (Boston, MA), 2001.

Tibol, Raquel, *Frida Kahlo: An Open Life*, translated by Elinor Randall, University of New Mexico Press (Albuquerque, NM), 1993.

Zamora, Martha, *Frida Kahlo: I Painted My Own Reality*, Chronicle Books (San Francisco, CA), 1995.

PERIODICALS

American Way, December 1, 1990, Melissa Chessher.

Art in America, March, 1996, Jill Johnson, review of *The Diary of Frida Kahlo*, pp. 31-32; September, 2001, p. 168.

ARTnews, April, 1996, pp. 91-92.

Booklist, October 1, 1995, Donna Seaman, review of *The Letters of Frida Kahlo* and *The Diary of Frida Kahlo*, p. 244.

Connoisseur, August, 1990, Jeff Spurrier, "The High Priestess of Mexican Art," pp. 66-72.

Frontiers, spring, 1993, pp. 165-189.

Hispanic, July, 1993, pp. 23-26.

Latin American Research Review, summer, 1997, pp. 243-257.

Library Journal, May 15, 1994, p. 72; January, 1996, pp. 81-82; January, 2002, p. 49.

New Statesman, November 17, 1995, Amanda Hopkinson, review of *The Diary of Frida Kahlo*, p. 39.

New York Times, August 10, 1994, p. C9.

New York Times Book Review, November 19, 1995, Deborah Solomon, review of *The Letters of Frida Kahlo* and *The Diary of Frida Kahlo*, p. 12.

People Weekly, February 12, 1996, p. 83.

Publishers Weekly, February 20, 1995, p. 118; August 28, 1995, review of *The Letters of Frida Kahlo*, p. 96; October 9, 1995, review of *The Diary of Frida Kahlo*, p. 72.

School Arts, January, 1996, pp. 22-26.

Time, March 28, 1983, R. Z. Sheppard, review of *Frida*, p. 68.

Vogue, April, 1983, pp. 152-153.

OTHER

Frida Pages, http://www/fridakahlo.it/ (March 6, 2002).

Grove Art, http://www.groveart.com/ (March 6, 2002), Hayden Herrera, "Kahlo (y Calderon), (Magdalena Carmen) Frida."

World of Frida Kahlo, http://www.members.aol.com/fridanet/ (March 6, 2002).*

Joy Kogawa

■ Personal

Born June 6, 1935, in Vancouver, British Columbia, Canada; daughter of Gordon Goichi (a minister) and Lois (a kindergarten teacher; maiden name, Yao) Nakayama; married David Kogawa, May 2, 1957 (divorced, 1968); children: Gordon, Deidre. *Education:* Attended University of Alberta, 1954, Anglican Women's Training College, 1956, Conservatory of Music, 1956, and University of Saskatchewan, 1968.

■ Addresses

Home—P.O. Box 2950, Station D., Ottawa, Ontario, Canada.

■ Career

Office of the Prime Minister, Ottawa, Ontario, Canada, staff writer, 1974-76; freelance writer, 1976-78; University of Ottawa, writer-in-residence, 1978; freelance writer, 1978—.

■ Member

League of Canadian Poets, Writers Union of Canada.

■ Awards, Honors

Books in Canada First Novel Award, 1981, and Canadian Authors Association Book of the Year Award, Before Columbus Foundation American Book Award, and American Library Association notable book citation, all 1982, all for *Obasan*; Periodical Distributors Best Paperback Fiction Award, 1983; Order of Canada, 1986.

■ Writings

NOVELS

Obasan, Lester & Orphen Dennys (Toronto, Ontario, Canada), 1981, David Godine (Boston, MA), 1982.

Naomi's Road (juvenile fiction), Oxford University Press (Toronto, Ontario, Canada), 1986.

Itsuka (sequel to *Obasan*), Viking Canada (Toronto, Ontario, Canada), 1992, Anchor Books (New York, NY), 1993.

The Rain Ascends, Knopf (Toronto, Ontario, Canada), 1995.

POETRY

The Splintered Moon, University of New Brunswick (St. John, New Brunswick, Canada), 1967.

A Choice of Dreams, McClelland & Stewart (Toronto, Ontario, Canada), 1974.

Jericho Road, McClelland & Stewart (Toronto, Ontario, Canada), 1977.

Woman in the Woods, Mosaic Press (Oakville, Ontario, Canada), 1985.

The Edible Woman, Goose Lane Editions, 2000.

A Song of Lilith, illustrated by Lilian Broca, Raincoast Books, 2000.

Contributor of poems to magazines, including *Canadian Forum, West Coast Review, Queen's Quarterly, Quarry, Prism International,* and *Chicago Review.*

■ Sidelights

"Every book I've written has changed me," noted Canadian poet and novelist Joy Kogawa to *Anglican Journal*'s Sue Careless. "The journey of the pen is a transforming one because when you use the pen as a pick axe as deeply as you can, it will bring up the most amazing jewels, not only of memory but of insight and understanding, and it will transform you." Author of juvenile fiction, adult novels, and poetry, Kogawa is best known for her novel *Obasan*, a fictionalization of her own experiences as a Japanese Canadian during World War II, and for its sequel, *Itsuka.* She is also the author of the 1995 novel *The Rain Ascends,* about child abuse, and of the children's book *Naomi's Road.* Her several volumes of poetry, written before and after her novels, such as *The Splintered Moon, A Choice of Dreams, Jericho Road,* and *Woman in the Woods,* have "the hallmark of great poetry," according to a critic for *Contemporary Women Poets.* "It elicits a sense of wondering surprise at unexpected combinations of words or at clinching assonances that suggest emotions without spelling them out. Her poems manage to tell stories without ever slipping into the narrative mode." The same critic went on to comment that even when confronted by the "most blatant injustices, [Kogawa] usually remains detached enough to instill humor in her indictment." Although said of her poetry, such a judgment can be passed on Kogawa's prose works as well. In addition to pursuing her career as a writer, Kogawa has turned her attention to political work on behalf of Japanese Canadian citizens and the underprivileged.

Born in Vancouver, Canada, in 1935, Kogawa lived in that city until World War II. Her father, Gordon Nakayama, was a minister and her mother a kin-

Canadian writer Joy Kogawa's 1981 autobiographical novel parallels its author's own experiences after her family was interned in a camp for people of Japanese ancestry during World War II.

dergarten teacher and musician. The family was torn apart in 1941 when they, along with thousands of other Japanese Canadians and Japanese Americans on the west coast of Canada and the United States, were evacuated and sent to internment camps in the interior. The Canadian government feared subversive acts by recent immigrants and even by those who, like Kogawa, were born in Canada. In addition to being interned, these people also lost their property and possessions, all confiscated by the government. Held long after the war ended, these people were forced to permanently resettle away from the coastal regions. Kogawa was first sent to a camp in central British Columbia and later removed even further east, to a camp in Coaldale, Alberta. There the well-educated family worked as field laborers throughout the war. Kogawa's mother never recovered from the shock of such a displacement.

After the war Kogawa studied education at the University of Alberta, taught for a year in elementary education, and then returned to the university to study music. In 1957 she moved to Toronto, where she married and had two children. Two years later she began writing both poetry and stories.

From Poetry to a First Novel

By 1964 Kogawa had published her first short story; three years later came her first poetry collection publication, *The Splintered Moon.* The following year she and her husband divorced and she devoted more time to her writing. In 1974 she took a job as staff writer for the prime minister of Canada, and the same year published her second volume of poetry, *A Choice of Dreams.* Already Kogawa's major theme was becoming apparent: exploring the crime of the Japanese Canadian removal and examining the culture of her own origins. Most of the poems in the second collection report her impressions on the several months she spent with relatives in Japan, traveling to the graves of her ancestors, trying to make sense of the chaos of Tokyo's rush hour, even dealing with the horror of Hiroshima with a degree of humor. Poems such as "Day of the Bride," in which she refers to the attempts of Japanese girls to look Western or like "Caucasian mannequins," such as "Gift Giving and Obligation," and "Hiroshima Exit," all provide a poet's eye-view of the new Japan and of the difficulty of cultural identity, return, and acceptance.

Kogawa's third collection, *Jericho Road,* moves to more personal topics, such as a bitter dissection of marriage in "The Wedlocked" or an evocation of the grief of dislocation in "Poem for Wednesday": "but it's dark here Wednesday / never comes my hands uprooted my / hands crumbling I'll put down this / empty no longer with me river this / white breeze in a soundless / forest without trees." As the contributor to *Contemporary Women Poets* noted of this poem, the "heart-rending dislocation of grief is reflected in the dislocation of syntax." Biblical allusions also abound, and the Japanese roots are less visible here, except for the poem "On Hearing Japanese Haiku."

Thus, before turning to fiction Kogawa was a "seasoned poet," wrote Gurleen Grewal in *Feminist Writers.* Gary Willis likewise commented in *Studies in Canadian Literature* that Kogawa's first three vol-

umes of poetry are filled with "lyric verse" and poems that often "express feelings that emerge from a narrative context that is only partly defined." Kogawa explained to Janice Williamson in *Sounding Differences: Conversations with Seventeen Canadian Women Writers* that her poems often arise out of her dreams: "The practice of poetry . . . ," she said, "is the sweeping out of debris between the conscious and the unconscious."

Obasan

In 1981 came Kogawa's fist novel, *Obasan,* and with that debut novel, wrote Grewal in *Feminist Writers,* "Kogawa proved herself to be among the finest of feminist-humanist writers." To tackle the subject of her family's internment, the writer knew she could not depend on poetry alone; in order to capture the true thrust of the story she would need the breadth of the novel. "Through protagonist Naomi Nakane's recollection of her painful childhood," wrote Grewal, "*Obasan* lays bare the inter-generational pain of Japanese Canadians affected by the Canadian government's relocation and internment of its citizens during World War II."

Obasan was the first Canadian novel to deal with the internment of 20,000 of its citizens of Japanese heritage. The novel focuses on thirty-six-year-old Naomi. She and brother Stephen were separated from their loving parents during World War II. Their mother, visiting relatives in Japan, was not allowed to return to Canada, and their father was shipped to a labor camp. Naomi and Stephen were sent to a frontier town along with their Uncle Isamu and aunt, or obasan, of the title. When their parents never returned, they were raised by their aunt and uncle in a house filled with silence. One of the mysteries of Naomi's childhood was yearly pilgrimages. As a child, Naomi continually asked "Why do we come here every year?" and as an adult, Naomi has lost the ability to communicate; as Kogawa writes, she is a victim of "the silence that will not speak." *Obasan* explores Naomi's search for the answer to her childhood question and shows her long-awaited acknowledgment of, as Grewal noted, "life's imperative to heal."

At the beginning of the novel Naomi's uncle has just died, and the rest of the novel, wrote Erika Gottleib in *Canadian Literature,* "takes shape as a mourner's meditation during a wake, a framework well suited to the novel's central metaphor of a spiritual journey." Urged by another relative, her Aunt Emily, an activist seeking justice for internment victims, Naomi relives her past, thus enabling her to learn about the secrets long held by her family. Naomi reviews documents about the Japanese internment to understand what happened to her and her family. And at the end of the novel, Naomi learns the truth that has been kept from her, that her mother suffered and died in Nagasaki, a victim of the "other holocaust," as Grewal called it. Naomi, through her examination of the past and her examination of the truth, at last is free and learns to speak again.

Throughout the course of the novel Naomi realizes her estrangement from mainstream Canadian society as well as from traditional Japanese culture. Kogawa explores the differences of these two groups. Willis commented of *Obasan*, "[it is] expressive of a sensibility that wishes to define, in relation to each other, Japanese and Canadian ways of see-

ing, and even to combine these divergent perceptions in an integrated and distinctive vision." In one scene, Naomi muses on carpentry: "There is a fundamental difference in Japanese workmanship—to pull with control rather than push with force." The contrast between the "restrained" Japanese and the "forceful" Canadians is also apparent in the difference between the Issei—those born in Japan—and the Nisei—those born abroad, as represented by Naomi's two aunts. Neither of their models works for Naomi who "like Kogawa," wrote Willis, "has roots in both traditions." By the end of the her own exploration, "Naomi blends a Japanese attention to silence with a Western attention to words. Indeed, it is this blending that gives rise to the distinctive beauties and subtleties of *Obasan*."

Kogawa enriches her text with documentation of this era of Canadian history. *Obasan* ends with the widely ignored memorandum sent by the Cooperative Committee on Japanese Canadians to the Canadian government in 1946, pointing out that the deportation of Japanese Canadians was "wrong and indefensible" and "an adoption of the methods of Nazism." Kogawa also includes among Aunt Emily's diaries and notes "a series of chilling nonfictional official papers and newspaper accounts," pointed out Edmund M. White in the *Los Angeles Times Book Review*. These elements serve to emphasize what White called "systematic outrages inflicted by the Canadian government on its own citizens [that] echo the Nazi treatment of the Jews." Edith Milton in the *New York Times Book Review* wrote that *Obasan* "grows into a quietly appalling statement about how much hatred can cost when it is turned into a bureaucratic principle." White also found that "the novel, in turn, shares some of the tone of *The Diary of Anne Frank* in its purity of vision under the stress of social outrage."

Obasan's political implications have been noted by many critics, including Grewal, who wrote, "this beautifully crafted novel with its moving resonances has done invaluable service to its varied readers. It has opened necessary dialogue; it has healed." Yet *Obasan* always remains, according to Milton, "a tour de force, a deeply felt novel, brilliantly poetic in its sensibility." Willis noted that the message of Kogawa's poetry is more fully realized in *Obasan*, "an imaginative triumph over the forces that militate against expression of our inmost feelings." White further remarked that the novel has "a magical ability to convey suffering and privation, inhumanity and racial prejudice, without losing in any way joy in life and in the poetic imagination."

JOY KOGAWA
Author of OBASAN

ITSUKA

"Profoundly political, exquisitely intimate, *Itsuka* reverberates with longing and hope."
— The Canada Times

Kogawa's 1992 novel finds protagonist Naomi Nakane—from *Obasan*—working to force the Canadian government to return the property of Japanese-Canadians confiscated during World War II.

For this debut novel, Kogawa won *Books in Canada*'s First Nobel Award as well as the Book of the Year Award from the Canadian Authors Association. A remarkable inauguration of a fiction career, in ways *Obasan* worked against Kogawa's more recent fiction, for reviewers continually compared her new books with that impressive debut. The novel was influential in more than an artistic manner, for it helped spur the fight to redress the wrongs to the Japanese Canadian community, which brought about a government-level apology in 1988. "*Obasan* is a much-needed, public corrective to official versions that down-play or rationalize the mistreatment of Japanese Canadians during and after the war," according to Ruth Y. Hsu in *Amerasia Journal*. Since its publication, the novel has continued to garner critical respect and response, earning entire chapters in some critical studies and comparisons to John Okada's groundbreaking 1957 novel, *No-No Boy,* and to Jeanne Wakatsuki Houston's 1973 work, *Farewell to Manzanar.* Hsu noted that the historic significance of Kogawa's text was one of the reasons for the novel's continuing popularity, but another "continuing resonance that *Obasan* finds with readers can be understood not simply as its capacity to tell a more complete story for a particular racial group, but also in its ability to underscore how the very process of narration is often implicated in power structures that disenfranchise certain groups."

More Poetry and a Juvenile Novel

Following the success of her first novel, Kogawa became involved in the movement in Canada to redress the wrongs done to Japanese Canadians. Her busy years of organization work kept her from longer novels for a time. In 1985 she came out with another collection of poetry, *Woman in the Woods,* something of a return to the aesthetic considerations of *Jericho Road,* dealing with violence and grief, but also maintaining a lighter tone. The "insight found [in *Woman in the Woods*]," wrote Frank Manley in *Books in Canada,* "is enlightening." He also lauded its "passion for life" along with "its ability to say volumes with only a few words."

In 1987 she published her first juvenile novel, *Naomi's Road,* a reworking of some of the material from *Obasan* told from Naomi's perspective as a young girl going through her dislocation first to the interior of British Columbia and then to a farm in Alberta. At this camp Naomi makes friends with the white daughter of a family who lives nearby. Reviewing *Naomi's Road* in *Canadian Materials,* Fran Newman felt it was a "joy," and personally "delighted in the whole book." Newman also felt that

Kogawa "lovingly and effectively described" the Japanese way of life, and created characters "as delicate as rice paper drawings."

Returns to Novels

Kogawa returned to the characters she developed in *Obasan* in 1992 with *Itsuka.* Sandra Martin noted in *Quill and Quire* that "Kogawa is not so much writing a sequel as reclaiming themes and characters from *Obasan.*" In *Itsuka* Naomi goes to Toronto in the 1980s where she works on a multicultural journal and takes her first lover, Father Cedric, a French-Canadian priest. With his help, Naomi turns to activism in her desire to win redress for the victims of Canada's internment policies, as Kogawa herself did. In *Itsuka,* which means "someday," the political and erotic plots become intertwined. Other personal stories also come to the fore, including Naomi's strained relationship with her brother, now a concert violinist, and her relationship with her Aunt Emily and her cause. The book, using a similar technique as *Obasan,* closes with an apology from the Canadian government in which it admits to instituting policies "influenced by discriminatory attitudes" toward Japanese Canadians and also to its own "unjust" actions.

Grewal maintained that *Itsuka* allows "the reader to witness Naomi's growth and personal fulfillment" and that it "openly bears the message of hope and trust implicit in *Obasan.*" Yet Martin compared *Itsuka* unfavorably to the first novel, finding that "Kogawa seems too close to the partisan squabbling that accompanies any such [political] movement. She hasn't yet absorbed the facts and translated them into fiction." Janice Kulyk Keefer, writing in *Books in Canada,* also admitted to "a certain disappointment" with the book, one centering on "the absence in *Itsuka* of the kind of poetically charged language and intensity of perception that give *Obasan* its extraordinary power and beauty." But Keefer also realized that "it would be wrong to fault *Itsuka* for not being *Obasan Revisited.*" She further commented, "What Kogawa has done in her new novel is to move into a different kind of imaginative territory, exposing the politics of multiculturalism that has in may ways abetted rather than eradicated the racism that she presents as an institutionalized aspect of Canadian life." This opinion was also shared by Kathryn Barnwell, writing in *Canadian Forum,* who found the "highly poetic and allusive style of *Obasan*" missing in *Itsuka.* Barnwell felt it was Kogawa's intention to document the process of

Kogawa's 2000 poetic *A Song of Lilith*, based on the creation story from the Bible, features artwork by Lilian Broca.

that Kogawa's intention with *Itsuka* was in part didactic, Hutcheon concluded that the "personal warmth, commitment, and generosity that characterize the dedication of the book . . . are what make the reader as student, for the most part, happy to listen her to the author as teacher."

With her 1995 novel *The Rain Ascends*, Kogawa leaves behind the thorny subject of Japanese-Canadian identity and redress for an even pricklier topic: child sexual abuse. As such, Kogawa's novel explores yet another hidden atrocity, something else people had too long been silent about. Millicent Shelby, the Anglo-Canadian daughter of Anglican priest Charles Barnabass Shelby, has kept a secret all her life. Growing up in her small Alberta town, Millicent led a favored existence. Her father was revered for his good works until other clergy got wind of his predilection for young boys. Forty years later, Millicent still keeps the secret, single and middle-aged, and living with her widowed father at his new congregation in British Columbia. Millicent now wrestles with the problem of whether her father's good works outweigh his bad one; with whether or not she should end the silence. Millicent comes down on the side of silence, while the minister's daughter-in-law, Eleanor, insists that he must face the consequences of his actions. In this dialectic, the novel resembles to an extent *Obasan*, with the two aunts who look at the idea of redress from different viewpoints. "The novel itself is thus testimony to the instability of the speaking/silence polarity," wrote Arnold E. Davidson in a *Canadian Literature* review of *The Rain Ascends*. Davidson went on to point out that the father's sins are not the main subject of the novel. Rather it is the "daughter's anguished response to her father and . . . the ambiguous ways that she has been and continues to be his victim" that takes center stage. Davidson felt *The Rain Ascends* "is an ambitious novel" and that in many ways it was "impressive," but it was also "disappointing," especially in comparison to the high-water mark set by *Obasan*. However, as Davidson concluded, it "is still a novel well worth reading." Reviewing the book in *Books in Canada*, Allan Casey found it to be a "fascinating, troubling, and compassionate exploration of the dark side of human sexuality." A reviewer for *Maclean's* regretted Kogawa's tendency, toward the end of the novel, to "sermonize," but felt "she should be forgiven, for in the process she forces contemplation of profound, if unpleasant, moral questions." A contributor to *Quill and Quire* also drew attention to the moral lesson in Kogawa's novel, noting how "the need to know the unspeakable truth draws us through the pages as it does Millicent." The same reviewer had

redress and reconciliation, and concluded, "We should be grateful to the Japanese Canadian community for insisting that this national wound be acknowledged, and healed." Writing in *Canadian Literature*, Linda Hutcheon found much to ponder in *Itsuka*. "In one of the most daring and challenging connections in the novel," Hutcheon noted, "the dispersal of the Japanese during and after the war becomes a metaphor for the fragmentation of Canada as a whole." The critic also felt that Naomi grows during the course of the narrative: "Through the novel, [Naomi] moves, slowly and self-consciously, from passivity that is almost a form of paralysis to action—on two levels at once. As she learns to fear love and sexuality less . . . and to trust her own body and emotions, she can liberate her political along with her private passions." Allowing reservations about the quality of fiction in *The Rain Ascends,* but concluded that Kogawa's "theme is crucial: as in *Obasan* and *Itsuka,* she reminds us once again that if we are to go on being human, truth matters."

If you enjoy the works of Joy Kogawa, you might want to check out the following books:

Jeanne Wakatsuki Houston, *Farewell to Manzanar,* 1973.

Yoshiko Uchida, *Journey Home,* 1978, and *Journey to Topaz,* 1985.

Lawson Fusao Inada, *Legends from Camp,* 1992.

In all Kogawa's best work, she forces the reader to look at tough truths, to face the unspeakable and, by breaking the silence, to begin the process of healing. As Martin noted, "Through her poetry, her sublime novel *Obasan,* her children's story *Naomi's Road,* and . . . *Itsuka,* Kogawa has written poignantly about how innocent and loyal Japanese Canadian were stripped of their home and their possessions, interned, and dispersed." Grewal discerned a more universal message in Kogawa's work: an emphasis on "compassion and arduous work of healing." "I think pain is brain food, it makes the brain stretch," Kogawa told Hsu. "So people who are willing to go though that, not for self-glory but out of caring about the world, what they offer is valuable. It's sort of like a guide for the rest of us."

■ Biographical and Critical Sources

BOOKS

Cheung, King-Kok, *Articulate Silences: Hisaye Yamamoto, Maxine Hong Kingston, Joy Kogawa,* Cornell University Press (Ithaca, NY), 1993.

Contemporary Literary Criticism, Volume 78, Gale (Detroit, MI), 1994.

Contemporary Women Poets, St. James Press (Detroit, MI), 1998.

Feminist Writers, St. James Press (Detroit, MI), 1996.

Hogan, Robert, and others, editors, *Memory and Cultural Politics: New Essays in American Ethnic Literatures,* Northeastern University Press (Boston, MA), 1996.

Kogawa, Joy, *A Choice of Dreams,* McClelland & Stewart (Toronto, Ontario, Canada), 1974.

Kreiswirth, Martin, and Mark A. Cheetham, editors, *Theory between the Disciplines: Authority/Vision/Politics,* University of Michigan Press (Ann Arbor, MI), 1990, pp. 213-229.

Ling, Amy, and others, editors, *Reading the Literatures of Asian America,* Temple University Press (Philadelphia, PA), 1992.

Pearlman, Mickey, editor, *Canadian Women Writing Fiction,* University Press of Mississippi (Jackson, MS), 1993.

Williamson, Janice, *Sounding Differences: Conversations with Seventeen Canadian Women Writers,* University of Toronto Press (Toronto, Ontario, Canada), 1993.

PERIODICALS

Amerasia Journal, spring, 1996, Ruth Y. Hsu, "A Conversation with Joy Kogawa," pp. 199-217.

Anglican Journal, May, 1998, p. 14; July, 1998, Sue Careless, "Author (Joy Kogawa) on Journey of Self-Discovery," p. 14.

Booklist, January 1, 1994, p. 806.

Books in Canada, May, 1986, Frank Manley, review of *Woman in the Woods,* pp. 43-44; April, 1992, Janice Kulyk Keefer, review of *Itsuka,* p. 35; November, 1995, Allan Casey, "Dagger Descends, Rain Ascends," p. 11.

Canadian Children's Literature, Volume 49, 1988, pp. 51-53; winter, 1996, pp. 34-46.

Canadian Forum, February, 1982, pp. 39-40; December, 1992, Kathryn Barnwell, "Sharing Brokenness," pp. 38-39.

Canadian Literature, summer, 1986, Erika Gottlieb, review of *Obasan,* pp. 34-53; spring, 1988, pp. 58-66, 68-82; autumn-winter, 1989, pp. 251-253; winter, 1990, pp. 41-57; spring, 1993, Linda Hutcheon, "Someday," pp. 179-181; spring, 1994, p. 12; spring, 1996, pp. 11-36; autumn, 1997, Arnold E. Davidson, "A Daughter's Dilemma," pp. 115-118, 148-150; spring, 1999, pp. 101-119.

Canadian Materials, Volume 15, number 1, 1987, Fran Newman, review of *Naomi's Road.*

Feminist Studies, summer, 1990, pp. 288-312.

Globe & Mail, September 29, 2001.

Horn Book, October, 1982, p. 553.

Kunapipi, Volume 16, number 1, 1994.

Los Angeles Times Book Review, July 11, 1982. Edmund M. White, review of *Obasan,* p. 3.

Maclean's, July 13, 1981, p. 54; November 6, 1995, review of *The Rain Ascends,* p. T7.

MELUS, fall, 1985, pp. 33-42; winter, 1999, pp. 93-106.

Mosaic, spring, 1988, pp. 215-226; September, 2000. p. 35.

New Yorker, June 14, 1982, p. 134.

New York Times Book Review, September 5, 1982, Edith Milton, review of *Obasan,* pp. 8-9; March 13, 1994, p. 18.

Publishers Weekly, April 2, 1982, p. 67; March 18, 1988, p. 87.

Quill & Quire, March, 1992, Sandra Martin, review of *Itsuka,* p. 57; December, 1995, review of *The Rain Ascends,* p. 30.

School Library Journal, May, 1988, p. 98.

Studies in Canadian Literature, Volume 12, number 2, Gary Willis, 1987, pp. 239-249.

World Literature Today, winter, 1992, pp. 56-58.

OTHER

Texts by Joy Kogawa, http://quarles.unbc.edu/ (March 10, 2002).

Voices from the Gaps, http://voices.cla.umn.edu/ (March 9, 2002), "Joy Kogawa."*

Joyce McDonald

1984-89; Betterway Publications, Inc., editor, 1989-90; Drew University, Madison, NJ, adjunct lecturer, 1989-2000; East Stroudsburg University, East Stroudsburg, PA, assistant professor of English, 1990-96.

■ Personal

Born August 4, 1946, in San Francisco, CA; daughter of Eugene William (a police lieutenant) and Mayme (a homemaker; maiden name, Beilstein) Schanbacher; married Hubert (Mac) McDonald (a department chair and instructor at the Chubb Institute). *Education:* University of Iowa, B.A., 1972, M.A., 1974; Drew University, Ph.D., 1994.

■ Addresses

Home—Warren County, NJ. *Agent*—Tracey Adams, McIntosh & Otis, Inc., 353 Lexington Ave., New York, NY 10016.

■ Career

Charles Scribners Sons, New York, NY, production assistant, 1976-78; Springer-Verlag, New York, NY, production editor, 1978-80; freelance editor/copyeditor, 1980-84; McDonald Publishing Company, Inc./Shoe Tree Press, NJ, publisher and editor,

■ Member

Society of Children's Book Writers and Illustrators, Authors Guild, Rutgers University Council on Children's Literature.

■ Awards, Honors

Children's Choice Book designation, International Reading Association/Children's Book Council, 1989, for *Mail-Order Kid;* Children's Book of the Year honors, Child Study Children's Book Committee, 1997, for *Comfort Creek;* "Books in the Middle" Outstanding Titles of the Year, *Voice of Youth Advocates,* Books for the Teen Age citation, New York Public Library, Top Ten Best Books for Young Adults, American Library Association (ALA), ALA'S 100 Best Books for Teens (1966-2000), and Best Children's Books of the Year citation, Children's Book Committee, all 1998, all for *Swallowing Stones;* Books for the Teen Age citation, New York Public Library, for *Shadow People;* ALA Best Book for Young Adults, Edgar Alan Poe Award nominee, Mystery Writers of America, and New York Public Library Books for the Teen Age citation, all 2002, all for *Shades of Simon Gray.*

■ Writings

Mail-Order Kid (juvenile novel), G. P. Putnam's Sons (New York, NY), 1988.

Homebody (picture book), illustrated by Karl Swanson, G. P. Putnam's Sons (New York, NY), 1991.

Comfort Creek (juvenile novel), Delacorte Press (New York, NY), 1996.

Swallowing Stones (young adult novel), Delacorte Press (New York, NY), 1997.

The Stuff of Our Forebears: Willa Cather's Southern Heritage (literary criticism), University of Alabama Press (Tuscaloosa, AL), 1998.

Shadow People (young adult novel), Delacorte Press (New York, NY), 2000.

Shades of Simon Gray (young adult novel), Delacorte Press (New York, NY), 2001.

■ Work in Progress

Reinventing Sylvia (working title), a young adult novel; *A Hip-Hop Happening* (working title), a picture book; and *Now I Wake* (working title), a middle grade novel dealing with racial issues.

■ Sidelights

"I've always been a little off balance when it comes to books," wrote author Joyce McDonald on her Web site. "I love everything about them. Not just the words, but the way books feel in my hands and the way they smell." McDonald's many and varied careers attest to this love: she worked several years for a publishing house in Manhattan, operated her own small publishing house, owned and managed a bookstore, published a children's literary magazine, taught literature and writing at the university level, and now is a full-time writer for young readers. Words and books are indeed the breath of life of McDonald, whose novel-length writing credits include *Mail-Order Kid, Comfort Creek, Swallowing Stones, Shadow People,* and *Shades of Simon Gray,* as well as a picture book, *Homebody,* and a literary history of renowned author Willa Cather titled *The Stuff of Our Forebears.*

McDonald told an interviewer for *Amazon.com,* "Everything I read and experience influences my writing. Sometimes I feel like a sponge, just soaking up everything in sight. Often stories I read in newspapers will pique my interest. News stories give us

In Joyce McDonald's 1997 novel, teens Michael MacKenzie and Jenna Ward suffer the aftereffects of an accident that leaves Jenna's father dead.

limited facts. Often I'm left with the question why? If it's an interesting story, I find my imagination wants to fill in the blanks."

Filling in the Blanks

"I didn't set out to be a writer," McDonald noted on her Web site. "My plans were for the big screen. I adored movies. As a kid I was always slipping in and out of imagined roles loosely based on characters in my favorite movies." One such movie was *Snow White,* which she saw as a four year old and whose evil queen and her shape-changing "still creeps me out," as McDonald noted.

Books were another early passion. "I have always had a passion for books," McDonald once commented. "I grew up in a house where books lined shelves in almost every room. Each night my mother would read to me before I went to bed. We continued this ritual until I was almost eight and certainly old enough to read for myself. To this day, I still read for a few hours every night, curled up under my cozy covers, with a cup of herbal tea nearby. Needless to say, most of my professional life has been devoted to books through one means or another."

Born in San Francisco, California, McDonald grew up in Chatham, New Jersey, the daughter of a father who was a policeman and mother who was a homemaker. With three younger brothers, McDonald grew up in a boisterous family, but found her own activities revolved increasingly around books. Soon she was not only reading them, but also creating them. McDonald has noted that she can not recall a time when she wasn't inventing stories, either to tell to friends or to "publish." As she told the interviewer for *Amazon.com*, "As a child I had an overactive imagination. Daydreaming was a favorite pastime. During school hours, I would often write stories or draw pictures when I was supposed to be working on assignments."

"My first book," she once recalled, "was far from an elaborate production: eight pages of tediously hand-printed words and smudged crayon illustrations tenuously held together by a small safety pin. (We didn't own a stapler.) I was six years old." Unfortunately, her teachers were more interested in her penmanship ("my worst subject," McDonald admits) than in her creativity with words. Nonetheless, McDonald continued to write and illustrate her own works throughout elementary school. "I rarely shared these early endeavors with anyone, except my mother or grandmother. I remember the first time I experienced the delicious feeling of encountering a receptive audience. When I was seven, my mother took one of my stories and typed it into legible form—my handwriting was atrocious even at that early stage—then passed it along to a friend of hers who was an elementary school teacher. What is particularly memorable for me is the image I hold of my mother sitting at the kitchen table hunting out the keys of my father's old portable Smith Corona typewriter. She didn't know how to type, so it must have taken her hours. Yet it may well have been one of the most important things she ever did for me, because her message was loud and clear. She liked what I had written. Validation! There's nothing more intoxicating to a struggling writer (even one who's only seven years old)."

With this encouragement, McDonald was off and running as a writer. "There was no stopping me after that. If I wasn't writing stories, I was telling them. The recipients of these early attempts at developing plot and character were neighborhood friends who sat around looking tolerant while I poured out monster and ghost stories filled with blood and gore. Yes, blood and gore. After all, these kids were a tough audience. I did what I had to do to hold their interest. It was one of my first lessons in storytelling. No matter how well crafted, how deeply philosophical, how delightfully metaphorical a story might be, if it didn't entertain, it was a flop."

By the time she was ten, McDonald had decided to tackle her first novel, leaving out the illustrations this time. "It was the middle of winter and every day I'd run home from school, head for the desk in my bedroom, and work on my book, appropriately titled "Very Cold Days," about a large, boisterous family. By age eleven, I had taught myself how to type on the same old Smith Corona my mother used, and the stories and plays kept coming, although not quite as frequently during my high school years. I was much more interested in spending time with my friends." In high school, McDonald was fortunate to have an English teacher, Miss Miles, who encouraged her students to do some creative writing—namely, write a short story. "One of my best memories is of Miss Miles reading my story out loud to the class. She had selected my story and one other. And for the second time in my life, I felt the validation of an audience. My peers and my teacher 'liked' my work."

Despite her interest in writing, McDonald started college as an art major. "I'm not at all sure why, but I suspect it was because it never occurred to me that writing was something people did for a living. Writing was simply a way of life, something very much linked to my survival, like eating or breathing. It wasn't until I later majored in English at the University of Iowa and had the opportunity to take fiction courses with such talented writers as Stuart Dybek, that I began to think of writing as a possible career." But there were no straight lines in McDonald's academic career. Her first two years were spent in a junior college where she studied art. Then she took some time off to travel in Europe, living a summer in Ireland, and also traveling, working, and studying in England and Spain. Thereafter, she returned to full-time college at the University of Iowa, earning her bachelor's in English in 1972, and her master's in 1974.

The City Lights

After graduating with a master's degree in English, McDonald moved to New York City, the location of most of the country's major publishing houses, to

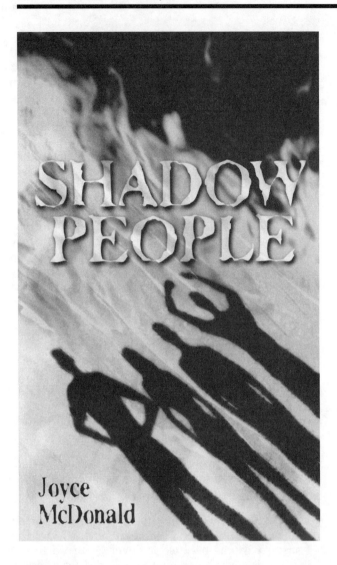

Four confused teens find an outlet for their frustration in group violence until a young girl falls in love with one of the gang's members.

ingway, F. Scott Fitzgerald, and Marjorie Kinnan Rawlings had entered. The same offices where they met with their famous editor, Max Perkins. I was in heaven."

During her years in publishing McDonald continued to write her own adult novels and short stories, although nothing was ever published. "As discouraging and painful as it was to receive rejection letters, I kept at it. Looking back, I realize now that these were my apprentice years. And all writers must endure them if they are to learn and grow." McDonald would use the experience she gained in the publishing industry much later, when she started her own small publishing company specializing in children's books.

McDonald stayed at Scribners for two years, then moved on to the textbook and academic book publisher Springer-Verlag for a couple more years, before going freelance as a copyeditor. By this time she was married, and from 1984 to 1989 ran her own small publishing company and also published a literary magazine that showcased the work of young writers. Children's books had become a fascination for McDonald. "For years, whenever I went to the library," McDonald once explained, "I found myself gravitating toward the children's section. To this day I can't explain it, but on these excursions I would always find myself coming home with an armload of children's books. I still do. This seemingly harmless pastime eventually spilled over into my professional life. I not only began to publish the works of New Jersey children's authors, but also tried my hand at writing books for children. And with thirteen nieces and nephews, I have rarely been at a loss for material, although I also draw from my own childhood experiences as well as those of my husband."

look for a job. "One of my dreams had been to work in the publishing industry," McDonald once commented. "So despite warnings from several well-meaning friends who told me it was virtually impossible to 'break in' to the industry unless you knew someone (which I didn't), I continued to 'pound the pavement' for several weeks, leaving my resume with receptionists at all the publishing houses I wanted to work for." Her perseverance paid off; McDonald was offered an entry-level position at Charles Scribner's Sons. "Scribners was still a family-owned business in those days. The first time I walked into the editorial offices, all my romanticized images of the publishing world came with me. This was the same building Ernest Hem-

From Editor/Publisher to Writer

With help from a professional writers' group, her writing acquired the polish it needed. In 1988 McDonald's first book, *Mail-Order Kid*, was published. "*Mail-Order Kid* began as a simple magazine story that I had submitted to *Highlights* for one of their contests," McDonald once noted. "When it was returned, I stuffed it away in a filing cabinet. But the idea behind the story—the relationship between a ten-year-old boy and his adopted six-year-old Korean brother—continued to intrigue me. Over several months the characters grew in my imagination, taking on lives of their own. But I knew I needed something more to make the story work. That 'something more' came from my brother Jack's experience. Several years ago, he ordered a red fox from a company in Florida. Needless to say, our parents knew nothing about this purchase until a cage, harboring a small, frightened fox, appeared on our doorstep one afternoon. The fox, uprooted from its natural environment, seemed the perfect metaphor for the confused and frightened Tae Woon, who suddenly finds himself in a strange country with a resentful brother."

Mail-Order Kid is the story of Flip Doty, a fifth grader who is not pleased with the fact that his parents decided to adopt a six-year-old Korean boy into their formerly one-child home. Brother Todd is an embarrassment to Flip, eating fireflies and taking off his clothes in the middle of Woolworth's. If his parents can get a kid brother for him through the mail, Flip doesn't see any reason he can't get a red fox the same way. However, the pet fox, Vickie, wreaks havoc at home. About to lose his beloved pet, Flip begins to see parallels between the fox and his new brother, as each try to adapt to a new situation. The novel was praised by *School Library Journal* contributor Nancy P. Reeder as "a well-written story with a pertinent message." Reeder also found the main characters to be "well developed and realistic." In *Booklist* Phillis Wilson noted that McDonald "balances humorous escapades with touching moments" of acceptance by Flip for both his brother and the fox that must be returned to the wild.

McDonald's first picture book, *Homebody*, was published in 1991. "Like its predecessor," McDonald once commented, "this book takes place in a rural setting, much like the area my husband and I live in, an area not far from the Delaware Water Gap which is rich in beauty and teeming with wildlife. I love animals, especially cats (we have several), so it seemed natural that my next book would be about a cat (the 'Homebody' of the story) and a dog. The animals are abandoned by their owners who leave their rundown, rented house in the middle of the night to avoid paying the rent. The new owner plans to repair the house and then sell it. He eventually takes the dog home with him, but has no idea that there is a cat hiding on the property. The gray cat is not about to reveal her presence, or to leave, 'Because home was home, and that was that.' The story is actually a fictionalized account of a similar quiet drama which I watched unfold over several months not far from my home." Illustrated by Karl Swanson, *Homebody* was cited as a story of "abandonment and compassion" by *School Library Journal* contributor Virginia Opocensky, who praised the book as "a good choice for reading aloud and discussing the story's message of concern."

Meanwhile, McDonald had begun her second career as a college professor by embarking on a Ph.D. program at Drew University. Time constraints forced her to sell her publishing business, "yet somewhere between course work, comprehensive exams, writing my dissertation, and teaching, I did squeeze in time to write another children's book." *Comfort Creek,* a children's novel about the Ellerbee family's fall onto hard times, was published in 1996. "Many of the background details in the novel are based on stories that my husband, who was born and raised in Florida, had shared with me over the years," McDonald explained.

In the novel the family breadwinner loses his job when the mining company he works for goes bankrupt. His wife leaves him and their three children to pursue her dream of becoming a country and western singer. All of this makes sixth grader Quinnella Ellerbee disgruntled, and she has to learn to take control of the changes that other people—namely her parents—have caused in her life. Michael Cart praised the work, noting in *Booklist* that "an unusual setting and the realistic handling of economic and environmental issues . . . strengthen this engaging story." Praising narrator Quinn as "a spunky character with a uniquely honest voice that readers are sure to like," Jacqueline Rose wrote in *Voice of Youth Advocates* that readers of Comfort Creek "will be moved by the ending in which a father and daughter heal their damaged relationship." Elizabeth S. Watson commented in *Horn Book* that all the characters "are believably drawn, with consistent and authentic dialogue," and that Quinn's voice "both leads and supports the other elements perfectly." And writing in *School Library Journal,* Cyrisse Jaffee called the novel a "well-written, evocative, and insightful story with an emotionally satisfying conclusion."

Young Adult Novels

McDonald worked as an adjunct lecturer and assistant professor at two different colleges throughout much of the 1990s, but the pull of books was always strong for her. In 1997 she published her first young adult novel, *Swallowing Stones*. Told through the alternating viewpoints of seventeen-year-old Michael MacKenzie and fifteen-year-old Jenna Ward, the novel explores the repercussions of a single, presumably harmless, act on a web of interconnected lives. Michael's attempts to hide the evidence of a gun shot which inadvertently kills Jenna's father, result in a tangled net of deception and lies that become increasingly more complex as the book progresses. "The story is based on a tragic shooting accident that took place in my hometown several years ago," McDonald said, "an incident that had continued to haunt me. And, as with all my books, the story began with hearing the character's voice in my mind." "This mesmerizing story largely derives its power from the respect McDonald demonstrates for these teens and their emotions," Joel Shoemaker noted in *School Library Journal,* adding that the story will have readers "turning the page to find out what happens next." "McDonald has crafted a gem," Brooke Selby Dillon wrote in *Book Report,* with "believable and empathetic characters; fascinating minor characters, who defy stereotypes; poetic, haunting, yet easily accessible language; a touch of mysticism; and a finely threaded theme." A contributor for *Publishers Weekly* similarly felt that readers "will quickly become absorbed in this electrifying portrait of fear and deception," while *Booklist*'s Frances Bradburn concluded, "McDonald masterfully moves both teens to an inevitable, if somewhat nebulous, final confrontation, as Michael appears to accept the consequences of his actions."

"With the publication of *Swallowing Stones* I finally came to accept that my writing is as important to me now as it was in my formative years, perhaps even more so," the author once commented. "It is no longer just an activity I do in my spare time, especially since 'spare time' is a rare commodity these days. So I have limited my teaching to only one fiction writing course a year, and spend almost all my days writing. With each new book, I find myself testing new themes and challenging myself with more complex characters and plots.

"My life so far has tended to be a series of sometimes unexpected digressions. But as serendipitous as it has been, that rambling route has somehow taken me to the places I needed to be to become the writer I am today. I still continue to write scholarly articles and most recently a book, *The Stuff of Our Forebears: Willa Cather's Southern Heritage.* I suspect many of my colleagues in the academic profession wonder why I spend time writing children's fiction when I could be pursuing more scholarly work. But I can't imagine a more satisfying or rewarding way to spend my days."

McDonald published her next young adult novel, *Shadow People,* in 2000. In the novel, four seemingly different teenagers are thrown together when they meet by chance—or fate—at a deserted camping grounds. They are joined by invisible bonds of anger, frustration, and loneliness, and form a gang, the Lords of Destruction. Apart from each other, they are fairly ordinary teens, but together and in the dark of night, they are drawn to violence. These four include Gabriel, whose family has moved to

Praised for its suspense, McDonald's 2001 novel finds an ancient evil reconstituted after high school student Simon Gray crashes his car into a centuries-old tree and strange things begin to happen.

the country from New York after his brother was killed by robbers; Lydia, who comes from a family that practices survivalist training; Alec, the oldest of the quartet and a kid who has been in and out of trouble for years; and Hollis, a computer geek and mastermind of the gang. A random act of vandalism soon escalates to more and more violent crimes. Eventually they blow up a building, inadvertently killing a homeless person in the act. These four soon cross paths with Gem, a classmate who falls in love with Gabriel. The question at the heart of this novel, is if solid Gem will offer Gabriel a way out of the cycle of violence, or be drawn into it herself. When Gabriel finally decides to leave the group, Gem becomes the target for the others. Barbara Jo McKee, writing in *School Library Journal,* called *Shadow People* a "chilling story" with "well drawn" characters and a "surprise ending [that] is true to our justice system." *Booklist*'s Debbie Carton felt that the novel is "unrelenting in its dark vision," and that the "dark, brooding story line builds to a horrifying climax, with the sickening knowledge that the guilty will go unpunished." Similarly, a reviewer for *Publishers Weekly* felt that "McDonald's chilling premise and credible depiction of the gang dynamic—propelled by fear—will keep the pages turning."

In her 2001 title, *Shades of Simon Gray*, McDonald puts a "supernatural spin on her latest tale of teenage malfeasance," according to *Booklist*'s John Peters. Simon Gray, a seemingly model teenager, crashes his car into the Liberty Tree in the middle of his small New Jersey town, and now lies in a coma. But was this an accident or attempted suicide? As Simon's body remains in the hospital bed, his spirit returns to the site of his accident. The Liberty Tree is also known as the Hanging Tree, and in his supernatural travel, Simon meets up with Jessup Wildemere, hanged from that tree in 1798 for murder. Meanwhile, an investigation at school has uncovered a computer hacking scheme that gives students access to tests. Now three graduating seniors hope that Simon has destroyed all evidence of their computer break-in before his accident. Simon has, in fact, been used by one of the seniors—Devin, who got him into the illicit project by playing on his obvious affection for her. At the same time, Simon's connection with the ghost of Jessup leads him to understand that this historical person was unjustly accused and executed. This truth finally prods Simon out of his coma and back into the daylight, and though the computer hackers are never caught, they do discover the error of their ways, all of them coming out of the experience better persons.

"The author blends elements of ghost story, thriller, and (unrequited) romance in this spooky tale from a guilty conscience," wrote Lauren Adams in a *Horn Book* review of *Shades of Simon Gray*. Vicki Reutter, writing in *School Library Journal*, found that McDonald's "juggling of numerous plot elements is interesting and will appeal to mystery fans," though she also felt that the supernatural elements in the story "feels imposed and unnecessary." A critic for *Kirkus Reviews*, however, praised McDonald both for writing and for plotting: "Written with considerable narrative skill, the supernatural elements are so cleverly integrated that the ending is both satisfying and convincing." This same reviewer concluded, "A page-turning plot, good characterization, and very convincing setting will have this suspenseful thriller driving up library circulation." And a contributor for *Publishers Weekly* observed that Simon "is a thoughtful, interesting character," and that McDonald "paints an eerie, electric atmosphere of menace that lingers past the final page."

If you enjoy the works of Joyce McDonald, you might want to check out the following books:

Lois Duncan, *I Know What You Did Last Summer*, 1973.
Robert Cormier, *We All Fall Down*, 1991.
Trudy Krisher, *Kinship*, 1997.

McDonald is hard at work on books in all three of the genres she has worked in earlier: picture book, juvenile novel, and young adult novel. "I love being totally immersed in a new story," McDonald told Debbi Michiko Florence in a *Justkidink* interview, "caught up in the lives of my characters. When the writing is going well, I can't wait to sit down at my computer every day. When I'm between books, I sometimes feel at loose ends. Writing gives my life structure."

■ Biographical and Critical Sources

PERIODICALS

American Literature, September, 1999, pp. 592-593.
Booklist, June 1, 1988, Phillis Wilson, review of *Mail-Order Kid*, p. 1676; November 15, 1996, Michael Cart, review of *Comfort Creek*, p. 588; October 15, 1997, Frances Bradburn, review of *Swallowing Stones*, pp. 397-398; February 15, 1999, p. 1084; November 15, 2000, Debbie Carton, review of *Shadow People*, p. 634; January 1, 2002, John Peters, review of *Shades of Simon Gray*, p. 842.
Book Report, November-December, 1996, pp. 41-42; November-December, 1997, Brooke Selby Dillon, review of *Swallowing Stones*, pp. 37-38.
Bulletin of the Center for Children's Books, June, 1988, pp. 211-212; February, 1997, pp. 213-214.
Horn Book, January-February, 1997, Elizabeth S. Watson, review of *Comfort Creek*, p. 62; January-February, 2002, Lauren Adams, review of *Shades of Simon Gray*, pp. 80-81.
Journal of American Studies, April, 2000, pp. 183-184.
Kirkus Reviews, September 15, 2001, review of *Shades of Simon Gray*, p. 1362.
Publishers Weekly, November 25, 1996, review of *Comfort Creek*, pp. 75-76; September 22, 1997, review of *Swallowing Stones*, p. 82; August 23, 1999, p. 61; December 11, 2000, review of *Shadow People*, p. 85; October 1, 2001, review of *Shades of Simon Gray*, p. 62.

School Library Journal, May, 1988, Nancy P. Reeder, review of *Mail-Order Kid,* p. 98; January, 1992, Virginia Opocensky, review of *Homebody,* p. 93; November, 1996, Cyrisse Jaffee, review of *Comfort Creek,* p. 108; September, 1997, Joel Shoemaker, review of *Swallowing Stones,* p. 71; November, 2000, Barbara Jo McKee, review of *Shadow People,* p. 148; November, 2001, Vicki Reutter, review of *Shades of Simon Gray,* pp. 161-162.

Tribune Books (Chicago, IL), September 22, 1991, p. 5.

Voice of Youth Advocates, October, 1996, Jacqueline Rose, review of *Comfort Creek,* p. 212; December, 1997.

OTHER

Amazon.com, http://www.amazon.com/ (March 11, 2002), "Amazon.com Talks to Joyce McDonald."

Book Page, http://www.bookpage.com/ (March 11, 2002), James Neal Webb, review of *Shades of Simon Gray.*

Justkidink, http://www.geocities.com/justkidink/ (April 12, 2002) Debbi Michiko Florence, "An Interview with Young Adult Novelist Joyce McDonald."

Joyce McDonald, Author, Books for Teens and Young Readers, http://www.joycemcdonald.com/ (March 11, 2002).*

William Nicholson

■ Personal

Born 1948, in England; married Virginia Bell (a writer), 1988; children: three. *Education:* Christ's College, Cambridge University, B.A. (English literature), 1970.

■ Addresses

Home—Sussex, England. *Agent*—PFD, Drury House, 34-43 Russell Street, London WC2B 5HA, England.

■ Career

Author, screenwriter, and director. British Broadcasting Corporation, director and producer of documentary films; executive producer, *Everyman*, 1979-82, *Global Report*, 1983-84, and *Lovelaw*, 1985-86. Director, *Firelight*, Carnival/Wind Dancer, 1997.

■ Awards, Honors

British Association of Film and Television Artists (BAFTA) Award for Best Television Play, 1985, for *Shadowlands*; BAFTA nomination for Best Single Drama, 1987, Banff Festival award for Best Drama, 1988, for *Sweet as You Are*; BAFTA Award for Best Television Drama, 1987, New York Film Festival award for Best Television Film, 1987, and ACE Award for Best Picture, 1988, all for *Life Story*; Best Play of 1990, *Evening Standard*, for *Shadowlands*; Oscar nomination for Best Screenplay, and BAFTA Award nomination for Best Adapted Screenplay, both 1994, both for *Shadowlands*; Emmy nomination for Outstanding Writing for a Miniseries or Special, 1997, for *Crime of the Century*; Special Jury Prize, San Sebastian International Film Festival, 1997, for *Firelight*; Sierra Award nomination for Best Original Screenplay, 2000, and BAFTA Award nomination for Best Original Screenplay, and Oscar nomination for Best Original Screenplay, both 2001, all for *Gladiator*; Gold Award, Nestles Smarties Awards, 2000, and Blue Peter Book of the Year, 2001, all for *The Wind Singer*.

■ Writings

NOVELS

The Seventh Level, New American Library (New York, NY), 1979.
The Wind Singer (Book one of "The Wind on Fire" Trilogy), Hyperion (New York, NY), 2000.
Slaves of the Mastery (Book two of "The Wind on Fire" Trilogy), Hyperion (New York, NY), 2001.
Firesong (Book three of "The Wind on Fire" Trilogy), Hyperion (New York, NY), 2002.

TELEPLAYS

Martin Luther, Heretic, BBC-TV.
Shadowlands (also see below), BBC-TV, 1985.
New World, BBC-TV, 1986.
The Vision, BBC-TV, 1986.
Life Story (also titled *Double Helix* and *Life Force*), BBC-TV, 1987.
Sweet as You Are, BBC-TV, 1987.
The March, BBC-TV, 1990.
A Private Matter, Longbow Productions/HBO, 1992.
Crime of the Century, HBO, 1996.

STAGE PLAYS

Shadowlands, produced at Queen's Theatre, London, England, 1989.
Map of the Heart, produced at Globe Theatre, London, England, 1991.
Katherine Howard, produced at Chichester Festival Theatre, Chichester, England, 1998.
The Retreat from Moscow, produced at Minerva Theatre, Chichester, England, 1999.

SCREENPLAYS

Sarafina!, Distant Horizon/BBC, 1992.
Shadowlands (adapted from his teleplay), Savoy/ Spelling International, 1993.
Nell, Polygram, 1994.
(And director) *First Knight,* Columbia Pictures, 1995.
Firelight, Carnival/Wind Dancer, 1997.
The Legend of Grey Owl, Beaver Productions, 1999.
Gladiator, Dreamworks, 2000.

■ Work in Progress

Screenplays for *American Caesar,* Universal, *Fertig,* Columbia, and *Bewitched,* Columbia.

■ Sidelights

William Nicholson is a prolific English screenwriter, playwright, and television and film director twice nominated for Oscars: once for his script of *Shadowlands,* about the late-in-life love of British philosopher C. S. Lewis, and again for his screenplay for the 2000 blockbuster *Gladiator.* Other movies from Nicholson's pen include *Sarafina!, Nell, First Knight,*

and *Firelight,* the last which he also directed. Television credits include the Home Box Office presentations *A Private Matter* and *Crime of the Century,* while for the British Broadcasting Corporation (BBC) he has scripted award-winning dramas including *Life Story, Sweet as You Are,* and *The March.* Nicholson took everyone by surprise, however, with *The Wind Singer,* published in 2000, as he turned his hand to young adult fiction in a futuristic first book of "The Wind on Fire" trilogy that earned him a prestigious Nestle Smarties Gold Award. Subsequent volumes in the trilogy are *Slaves of the Mastery* and *Firesong.* "I still love working as a screenwriter on films," Nicholson told Jo-Anna Wildman in a *booktrusted. com* interview, "but it is a collaborative medium where you do not have complete control and have to give a lot of consideration to finances and budgets. I wanted to work on a project where I could let my imagination carry me wherever it will."

Anthony Hopkins and Joseph Mazello star in *Shadowlands,* a film biography of British author, educator, and theologian C. S. Lewis that was written by William Nicholson.

Born in 1948, Nicholson grew up in Sussex and Gloucestershire, England. His childhood was full of books, as he told Wildman. "I read a great deal when I was a child. My favorites were the 'William' books by Richard Crompton and I collected them avidly, reading and re-reading them time and time again. We lived in a small town with a second hand bookshop and I would go there every Saturday morning to see if they had any more William books in that week." Science fiction, comics, and detective stories rounded out Nicholson's early reading tastes, and by the time he was a teenager these were added to by the James Bond books.

"My first novel was at age sixteen," Nicholson told *Achuka* interviewer Lisette Menage, "and strongly influenced by the James Bond books, it was called 'The World, the Flesh and the Devil.'" Nicholson further commented that he loved the process of writing that first novel and felt it was truly fantastic "until it was finished and of course I realised it was garbage." Another youthful fantasy novel was influenced by Franz Kafka and dealt with a man who longs for a child and soon becomes pregnant. "It was all very deadpan and I was writing about the practical difficulties involved." Nicholson was encouraged by his mother in these efforts, telling him that his fantasy and his early poems were indications of great things to come. These poems were mostly written for the school magazine, which he edited.

Educated at Downside School, Nicholson went on to Christ's College, Cambridge, where he majored in English literature. It was during these years that he began his life-long aversion to tests as the ultimate measurement of a student's worth. Successful at such exams himself, he still felt the gross unfairness of such an arbitrary measure. Upon graduation from Cambridge, Nicholson soon found employment at the BBC.

Jodie Foster stars in *Nell*, Nicholson's screenplay adaptation of Mark Handley's play about a young woman who is discovered living alone in the woods, her only previous human interaction having been with her now-long-dead mother.

Work in Television

By the mid-1970s Nicholson had worked his way up to making documentaries, and over the next decade made more than forty of them for the BBC. During this time he was also executive producer of several series. His first major success was for the television drama *Shadowlands*, his take on the romance between the writers C. S. Lewis and the American Joy Gresham. In the drama, Lewis—the author of religious studies as well as the classic juvenile novel *The Lion, the Witch and the Wardrobe*—is a stodgy, crusty old bachelor shaken out of his staid ways by the brash young American poet whom he subsequently marries. When Gresham then slowly dies of cancer, Lewis is confronted with the very pain he has so eloquently written of in his religious studies, the chiseling effect of God testing us, and his faith is shaken to the roots. Winner of a British BAFTA Award for best television play, the drama starred Claire Bloom as Gresham and Joss Ackland as Lewis.

Four years later, Nicholson turned this television drama into a successful stage play that was produced in both London and New York. Reviewing the New York production, *Time*'s William A. Henry III noted that the play "does work," and that Nicholson "finds a wealth of delicate metaphor in

Sean Connery stars as King Arthur in the 1995 Nicholson-coauthored film *First Knight*.

the imagery of the title, a reference to Lewis' assertion that true life is inner . . . and what happens on earth [is] a mere shadow existence." The play further develops the contradictions in Lewis's life, and how the death of his wife both confirmed the power of the Almighty but also made him look elsewhere for consolation. Lewis in part found this consolation in turning from Christian theological writing to children's fables, such as *The Lion, the Witch, and the Wardrobe*. Writing in *Back Stage*, David Sheward felt the play "brilliantly" fulfills the promise of "an evening of some mental challenge," and further noted that "Nicholson's play effectively chronicles Lewis's journey in the shadowlands which become all too painfully real for him." The literary quality of the play was also noticed by other reviewers. "Rarely does biography lend itself to a lofty theme with the eloquence of 'Shadowlands,' William Nicholson's exquisitely literate tear-jerker," wrote critic Philip Brandes in the *Los Angeles Times*. Nicholson has continued to make forays into the live theater throughout his career.

Meanwhile, still working in television, Nicholson turned out a string of successes for the BBC. In the award-winning *Sweet as You Are* he tells the tale of a heterosexual couple whose life is turned upside down when one of the couple develops AIDS. With *Life Story*, also known as *Double Helix*, he scripts the story of the researchers who ultimately found and began to map DNA. His 1990 drama, *The March*, is a story set in the future about a group of people who set off from a refugee camp in Africa to search for food in Europe.

Nicholson's first teleplay for the U.S. market, *A Private Matter*, was presented on HBO and caused a critical stir, taking on the controversial subject of abortion. Taken from a real-life incident, the drama tells the story of Sherri Finkbine, a Phoenix television personality who hosted a kid's show. The time is 1962, before the dangers of the drug Thalidomide were widely known. Pregnant with her fifth child, Finkbine takes the sedative only to later discover that her baby will surely be born with birth defects. Finkbine and her husband, played by Sissy Spacek and Aidan Quinn, determine to travel to have an abortion. Before this, however, Finkbine—under the promise of anonymity—talks to a local news reporter about her Thalidomide experience, hoping to save other women the same tragedy. When her name is leaked, a scandal ensues. Finkbine is immediately fired from her job, as is her school-teacher husband, and the community turns against them. Ken Tucker, writing in *Entertainment Weekly,* noted that the "writer's job is a tough one—he must be faithful to the facts of this case and work in arguments on both sides of the abortion issue, as well as create vivid, sympathetic characters." Tucker went on to observe that *A Private Matter* "deals with abortion as forth-rightly as any entertainment programming I've seen." Reviewing the show in *Los Angeles Times,* Ray Loynd also called attention to Nicholson's writing, noting that he "has drawn a passive but vitally complex heroine" for this drama which is "a timely, urgent, dramatic statement, all the more effective because it's a first-rate production." Writing in the *Washington Post,* Tom Shales also felt that Nicholson's script "is well paced and conscientious," though the critic did feel Nicholson had difficulties "coming up with a climax." Several years later, Nicholson went on to earn an Emmy nomination for his 1996 original HBO movie *The Crime of the Century,* which chronicles the famous Lindbergh kidnaping trial.

Credits on the Big Screen

Nicholson's first big-screen writing came in his co-adaptation of the South African stage musical *Sarafina!,* about a group of teenagers protesting apartheid and starring Whoopi Goldberg. Reviewing the movie version in the *Washington Post,* Rita Kempley found problems with this adaptation, noting that despite some high points, "mostly this political musical strikes a jarring chord." Kempley described *Sarafina!* As an "awkwardly enthusiastic cross between a township 'Fame' and a kid's 'Cry Freedom.'"

More successful by far was Nicholson's adaptation of his own television drama and stage play *Shadowlands* for the 1993 movie directed by Richard Attenborough and starring Anthony Hopkins and Debra Winger. Covering much the same ground as the earlier television drama and play, the movie was filmed on location in Oxford and won Nicholson an Oscar nomination for his script. Generally enthusiastic reviews greeted this strongly emotional film. *Shadowlands,* according to Desson Howe, writing in the *Washington Post,* "isn't just a three-hankie tear-jerker. You'll need a bulk of linen to stay dry through this romance between Anthony Hopkins and Debra Winger. Yet this dramatized account of the C. S.

Lewis-Joy Gresham affair is more than manipulative." Howe further noted that the movie is an "engaging encounter between adults," but it also deals with "lost childhoods, questions of God, intellect versus emotion, pain versus pleasure and other far-reaching themes." While some critics noted that the film adaptation takes some of the complexity out of the stage play, most agreed on its power. A reviewer for *Time* called both the movie itself and the performances by the main stars "strong, unsentimental, exemplary."

Nicholson next turned his attention to the script for *Nell,* the story of a mountain girl raised away from civilization who develops her own language. Adapted from a play by Mark Handley, the movie starred Jodie Foster as the nature girl, Liam Neeson, and Natasha Richardson. Critics generally agreed that the story follows well-traveled lines, some comparing it to Werner Herzog's *The Mystery of Kaspar Hauser* and others to *Forrest Gump.* As Richard Corliss noted in a *Time* review, the movie "illustrates the familiar movie moral that wounded creatures are powerful ones with powerful lessons to teach those who would presume to educate them." Corliss concluded that the film would probably not have been made without Foster producing it, but commented "It's the worthiest kind of vanity production, welcome in any movie season."

From speech problems, Nicholson turned his hand to the Lancelot legend in *First Knight,* with Richard Gere as the wayward knight, Julia Ormond as Guinevere, and Sean Connery as King Arthur. The viewing public and most critics had little enthusiasm for this movie, which *Newsweek*'s Jeff Giles wrote "disappoints in a lot of ways." The worst of these, according to Giles is that "the movie simplifies the famous love triangle almost beyond recognition." John Simon of *National Review* noted that the film is "an earnestly dull attempt that even enlisted the screenwriting talents of William Nicholson, albeit to scant avail."

More successful was Nicholson's film *Firelight,* his debut movie directing stint, adapted from his own screenplay. The story of a poor Swiss governess who is paid to bear a child for a wealthy English aristocrat and then disappear, it is a romantic story at its base. Charles, the aristocrat in question, has a wife, but she has been paralyzed and in a coma for two years from a riding accident. An arrangement is made whereby Charles and Elisabeth, the Swiss woman, meet at an inn in Normandy and spend three nights together in hopes of getting Elisabeth pregnant. In the event of a birth, the agreement is that Elisabeth will deposit the child near Charles's estate. But motherly love finally overcomes her, and she spends years tracking down Charles—whose name she does not know—finally taking a job with his sister-in-law as the new governess in order to be close to her own child. Such proximity renews the passion the two felt for each other during their earlier tryst. Reviewing the film in *Washington Post*, Michael O'Sullivan called it "emotionally and visually sophisticated," and a movie that ignites the familiar fare [of love] with a scorchingly honest exploration of such difficult issues as guilt, pretense, sacrifice, feminism, mercy-killing and the velvet handcuffs that link a mother with her own flesh and blood." Stanley Kaufmann, reviewing the movie in *New Republic*, felt it was a "hybrid: a Victorian drama written, so to speak, today." Kaufmann further noted it "has a heart-tugging, twisty plot." And Lisa Nesselson praised the movie in *Variety*, calling the film a "keenly thesped costumer made resonant by contemporary concerns including surrogate motherhood, strict vs. permissive parenting and the moral speedbumps of euthanasia." Nesselson further noted, "William Nicholson follows a

distinguished docu career at the BBC and a solid track record in penning TV dramas with this deceptively reserved but affecting widescreen debut." Nicholson also wrote scripts for *Grey Owl*, directed by Attenborough and starring Pierce Brosnan, and for the hit *Gladiator*, for which he won a second Oscar nomination.

Finds Inspiration in Young Adult Novels

With his successful television and screen career going at full steam, it was quite a surprise when Nicholson came out with his first young adult novel in 2000, *The Wind Singer*, the first of a trilogy. Better, yet, the novel was not only good, but an instant success with young readers, a book that won him the prestigious Nestle Smarties Prize. "I love writing for Hollywood, but there is far more checking and agreeing involved and you have to be far more organised," Nicholson told Menage in partial expla-

Nicholson both directed and authored the screenplay for the 1997 film *Firelight*, starring Sophie Marceau as a governess who agrees to bear her employer's child.

Nicholson contributed his writing talents to the 2000 blockbuster film *Gladiator*, starring Russell Crowe as a Roman Legionnaire-turned-slave.

nation for this artistic change of hats. "With *Wind Singer* I was able to let rip, I didn't know where I would go or what would come up. I let it be wild and free and then hammered it into shape. There is a tendency for fantasy to get boring, you have to create good characters and let them take you there."

The Wind Singer tells the timeless, dystopian tale of the city of Aramanth, where family ratings determine the privileges as well as the housing under a color-coded caste system. In this society, testing is all-important; young children learn from an early age to jump through these academic hoops or fall by the wayside. In the end it is the High Examination that determines one's class. The twins Kestrel and Bowman Hath live in this walled city-state, and their family does not agree with the exam system that determines one's future. Instead they hark back to the days of legend when the Wind Singer, an odd sculpture in the center of town, sent out beautiful sounds and the people of the town lived in har-

mony with one another. However, long ago, the key to the Wind Singer was stolen by Lord Morah during a war.

When the youngest in the Hath family, two-year-old Pinpin, fails her first exams, Kestrel dares to criticize the system. Such criticism can not be allowed. The chief examiner labels her a "wild child" and sends her to Special Teaching, a place from which she is never to escape. Her father also suffers for this, banished to a Residential Study Course. Kestrel vows to save Aramanth and return the harmonies of Wind Singer by finding its key. Bowman joins forces with his sister in this endeavor, and they are joined by their friend Mumpo, a silly and rather thick schoolmate. Together they escape from Aramanth and with the help of an old map set off on a quest to find the key to Wind Singer. Their quest brings them into danger at every turn, dealing with the evil Morah, the Mudpeople, the zombie-like Old Children, bloodthirsty desert tribes, and also the Zars, part of Morah's army and programmed to kill. The trio of unlikely heroes comes through all these adventures and ultimately they are able to restore the voice to Wind Singer and break the evil spell of Morah.

Critical praise met publication of *The Wind Singer* in England, though it was more muted with the novel's U.S. publication. A reviewer for *Publishers Weekly* felt that this "imaginative debut YA novel . . . starts out tantalizingly, but eventually neglects its internal logic." However the same reviewer felt that perhaps such seeming inconsistencies "will be explained in subsequent installments." *Booklist*'s GraceAnne A. DeCandido considered the description of the caste system somewhat "heavyhanded," but also that the "background is well delineated." She also praised the use of supporting characters, in particular the "comic relief" supplied by Mumpo. "A thrilling denouement leaves the way clear for the rest of the saga." John Peters, reviewing the title in *School Library Journal*, felt that "fans of such barbed journey tales . . . will enjoy the social commentary." Fuller praise came from Audrey Marie Danielson, writing in *KidsReads.com*, who noted that Nicholson "has skillfully created a fantasy world that also encompasses his view of our contemporary educational system."

Many other reviewers also responded to Nicholson's criticism of the exam system. "Some people have said that *The Wind Singer* is a satire on the educational system," Nicholson noted to Wildman, "but it is actually an attack on any system where a narrow set of test results are applied. I don't like simple measurements as tags. . . . The main attack in the book in on conformism amongst children. I think that groups of any kind can be very dangerous as you are forced to do something, even if you don't want to, just to gain respect and fit in." Nicholson further commented that he wanted the reader to "derive strong satisfaction from two things, first the destruction of the exam system and second the coming together of the Hath family after the terrors they have been through."

Nicholson takes his tale forward five years in the second volume of the trilogy, *Slaves of the Mastery*. Here the twins are fifteen, of marrying age in Aramanth. Since the restoration of the Wind Singer, the city-state has become kinder but also weaker. It soon proves to be a perfect target for the ruthless soldiers of the Mastery, who easily storm and burn the city, taking its people into slavery. Led by Marius Ortiz, the Mastery keep brutal control over their subjects. If anyone disobeys, a member of the community is burned before their eyes in a metal cage. Kestrel alone has escaped the Mastery. Find-

ing herself on her own, she seeks revenge. First, however, she must find her brother, Bowman, following his call telepathically across the desert. On her way, she meets Sisi, a spoiled child engaged by her parents to Ortiz. Soon Sisi and Kestrel become fast friends, and Kestrel opens the young girl's eyes to the world around her. Bowman, meanwhile, has been training his mind telekinetically, learning the secrets of the mysterious Singer people, and has been taken on by Ortiz as a "truth teller." Mumpo has also been busy learning the killing dance, the manaxa, of the Mastery, and killing the champion of the city in a contest. Finally the twins team up to fight the Mastery and bring their people out of slavery. "Despite its length," wrote DeCandido in *Booklist*, "this reads quickly, and . . . it has some splendid battle scenes." Eva Mitnick, writing in *School Library Journal*, had high praise for the novel, noting that *Slaves of the Mastery* is a "masterful sequel." Mitnick added that "political intrigue, magical power, and quiet humor will keep the pages turning . . . but at the heart of this tale is an exploration of slavery, freedom, and destiny." Mitnick also applauded Nicholson's cast of characters, every one of whom "is compelling and full of life." Nicholson completes his trilogy with the 2002 title *Firesong*.

If you enjoy the works of William Nicholson, you might want to check out the following:

Philip Pullman's "His Dark Materials" fantasy series.
Spartacus, a film starring Kirk Douglas, 1960.
The Governess, a film starring Minnie Driver, 1998.

The versatile Nicholson may continue to write further young adult novels; he also has several films in production. A common thread runs through all his work, whether in television, film, or books: a willingness to take chances, to examine the givens in society, and to blend an intellectual approach with entertaining story lines. The worlds of C. S. Lewis and the Hath family are not that distant as seen through the clear gaze of this British storyteller.

■ Biographical and Critical Sources

BOOKS

International Motion Picture Almanac, 1996 edition, Quigley Publishing (New York, NY), 1996.

PERIODICALS

Back Stage, November 23, 1990, David Sheward, review of *Shadowlands,* p. 36; February 10, 1995, p. 34.

Booklist, October 15, 2000, GraceAnne A. DeCandido, review of *The Wind Singer,* p. 438; October 15, 2001, GraceAnne A. DeCandido, review of *Slaves of the Mastery,* p. 389.

Bookseller, December 7, 2001, p. 36.

Christian Science Monitor, December 16, 1994.

Commonweal, January 28, 1994, pp. 22-23.

Entertainment Weekly, June 19, 1992, Ken Tucker, review of *A Private Matter,* pp. 56-58.

Los Angeles Times, June 20, 1992, Ray Loynd, "TV Review: A Mother's Abortion Ordeal," p. 1; July 7, 1995, Philip Brandes, "'Shadowlands' Pulls on the Heartstrings," p. 27; September 4, 1998, p. 10; September 5, 1998, p. 10; February 24, 2000, p. C52; May 3, 2001, p. F52.

Maclean's, January 17, 1994, Brian D. Johnson, review of *Shadowlands,* p. 61.

Magpies, July, 2002, Helen Purdie, review of *Firesong,* pp. 18-19.

Nation, January 7, 1991, pp. 27-28.

National Review, February 7, 1994, pp. 72-73; February 6, 1995, pp. 72-74; August 14, 1995, John Simon, review of *First Knight,* pp. 55-57.

New Republic, February 7, 1994, p. 26; October 12, 1998, Stanley Kaufmann, review of *Firelight,* pp. 30-31.

Newsweek, July 10, 1995, Jeff Giles, review of *First Knight,* p. 56.

New Yorker, December 19, 1994, p. 108.

Publishers Weekly, August 28, 2000, review of *The Wind Singer,* p. 84; November 19, 2001, p. 70.

School Library Journal, December, 2000, John Peters, review of *The Wind Singer,* p. 146; December, 2001, Eva Mitnick, review of *Slaves of the Mastery,* p. 141.

Time, November 19, 1990, William A. Henry III, review of *Shadowlands* (play), p. 106; December 27, 1993, review of *Shadowlands* (movie), p. 72; December 12, 1994, Richard Corliss, review of *Nell,* p. 92.

Variety, December 13, 1993, p. 38; September 29, 1997, Lisa Nesselson, review of *Firelight,* pp. 61-62.

Washington Post, June 20, 1992, Tom Shales, "TV Previews: 'Private Matter,' Public Nightmare," p. B1; September 25, 1992, Rita Kempley, "Reviews: The Spirit of 'Sarafina!,'" p. B7; August 17, 1993, p. C9; January 7, 1994, Desson Howe, "Illuminating 'Shadowlands,'" p. N34; September 4, 1998, Michael O'Sullivan, "Intense and Illuminating 'Firelight,'" p. N37.

OTHER

Achuka, http://achuka.com/ (March 10, 2002), Lisette Menage, "William Nicholson Interview."

Booktrusted.com, http://www.booktrusted.com/ (March 10, 2002), Jo-Anna Wildman, *"The Wind Singer* by William Nicholson: Interview."

Hollywood.com, http://www.hollywood.com/ (March 10, 2002), "William Nicholson."

IndieWIRE, http://www.indiewire.com/ (March 10, 2002), Anthony Kaufman, "Inside the Studio Beast: William Nicholson Directs 'Firelight.'"

KidsReads.com, http://www.kidsreads.com/ (March 10, 2002), Audrey Marie Danielson, review of *The Wind Singer.**

—Sketch by J. Sydney Jones

Jill Paton Walsh

■ Personal

Born April 29, 1937, in London, England; daughter of John Llewellyn (an engineer) and Patricia (Dubern) Bliss; married Antony Edmund Paton Walsh (a chartered secretary), August 12, 1961 (separated); children: Edmund Alexander, Margaret Ann, Helen Clare. *Education:* St. Anne's College, Oxford, Dip. Ed., 1959, M.A. (honors; English). *Religion:* "Skepticism." *Hobbies and other interests:* Photography, gardening, cooking, carpentry, reading.

■ Addresses

Home—72 Water Lane, Histon, Cambridge CB4 4LR, England.

■ Career

Enfield Girls Grammar School, Middlesex, England, English teacher, 1959-62; writer, 1962—. Whittall Lecturer, Library of Congress, Washington, DC, 1978. Visiting faculty member, Center for the Study of Children's Literature, Simmons College, Boston, 1978-86. Founder, with John Rowe Townsend, of Green Bay Publishers, 1986.

■ Member

Society of Authors (member of Management Committee), Children's Writers Group.

■ Awards, Honors

Book World Festival award, 1970, for *Fireweed;* Whitbread Prize (shared with Russell Hoban), 1974, for *The Emperor's Winding Sheet; Boston Globe-Horn Book* Award, 1976, for *Unleaving;* Arts Council creative writing fellowship, 1976-77, and 1977-78; Universe Prize, 1984, for *A Parcel of Patterns;* Smarties Prize Grand Prix, 1984, for *Gaffer Samson's Luck;* Best Book, *School Library Journal,* 1992, for *Grace;* shortlist, Booker Prize, 1994, for *Knowledge of Angels;* fellow, Royal Society of Literature, 1996; Phoenix Award, 1998, for *A Chance Child;* Commander of the British Empire.

■ Writings

JUVENILE FICTION

Hengest's Tale, illustrated by Janet Margrie, St. Martin's Press (New York, NY), 1966.

The Dolphin Crossing, St. Martin's Press (New York, NY), 1967.

Fireweed, Macmillan, 1969, Farrar, Straus (New York, NY), 1970.

Goldengrove (see also below), Farrar, Straus (New York, NY), 1972.

Toolmaker, illustrated by Jeroo Roy, Heinemann (London, England), 1973, Seabury Press (New York, NY), 1974.

The Dawnstone, illustrated by Mary Dinsdale, Hamish Hamilton (London, England), 1973.

The Emperor's Winding Sheet, Farrar, Straus (New York, NY), 1974.

The Huffler, Farrar, Straus (New York, NY), 1975, published as *The Butty Boy,* illustrated by Juliette Palmer, Macmillan (London, England), 1975.

Unleaving (see also below), Farrar, Straus (New York, NY), 1976.

Crossing to Salamis (first novel in trilogy; also see below), illustrated by David Smee, Heinemann (London, England), 1977.

The Walls of Athens (second novel in trilogy; also see below), illustrated by David Smee, Heinemann (London, England), 1977.

Persian Gold (third novel in trilogy; also see below), illustrated by David Smee, Heinemann (London, England), 1978.

Children of the Fox (contains *Crossing to Salamis, The Walls of Athens,* and *Persian Gold*), Farrar, Straus (New York, NY), 1978.

A Chance Child, Farrar, Straus (New York, NY), 1978.

The Green Book, illustrated by Joanna Stubbs, Macmillan (London, England), 1981, illustrated by Lloyd Bloom, Farrar, Straus (New York, NY), 1982, published as *Shine,* Macdonald (London, England), 1988.

Babylon, illustrated by Jenny Northway, Deutsch (London, England), 1982.

A Parcel of Patterns, Farrar, Straus (New York, NY), 1983.

Lost and Found, illustrated by Mary Rayner, Deutsch (London, England), 1984.

Gaffer Samson's Luck, illustrated by Brock Cole, Farrar, Straus (New York, NY), 1984.

Torch, Viking (New York, NY), 1987.

Birdy and the Ghosties, illustrated by Alan Marks, Macdonald (London, England), 1989.

Can I Play Farmer, Farmer?, Bodley Head (London, England), 1990.

Can I Play Wolf?, Bodley Head (London, England), 1990.

Can I Play Jenny Jones?, Bodley Head (London, England), 1990.

Can I Play Queenie?, Bodley Head (London, England), 1990.

Grace, Viking (New York, NY), 1991.

When Grandma Came (picture book), illustrated by Sophie Williams, Viking (New York, NY), 1992.

Matthew and the Sea Singer, Farrar, Straus (New York, NY), 1993.

Pepi and the Secret Names (picture book), Lee & Shepard (New York, NY), 1995.

Thomas and Tinners, illustrated by Alan Marks, Farrar, Straus (New York, NY), 1995.

Connie Came to Play (picture book), Viking (New York, NY), 1995.

When I Was Little Like You (picture book), Viking (New York, NY), 1997.

ADULT FICTION

Farewell, Great King, Coward McCann (New York, NY), 1972.

Five Tides (short stories), Green Bay Publications (Cambridge, England), 1986.

Lapsing, Weidenfeld & Nicolson (London, England), 1986, St. Martin's Press (New York, NY), 1987.

A School for Lovers, Weidenfeld & Nicolson (London, England), 1989.

The Wyndham Case (detective novel), St. Martin's Press (New York, NY), 1993.

Knowledge of Angels, Houghton Mifflin (Boston, MA), 1994.

A Piece of Justice: An Imogen Quy Mystery, St. Martin's Press (New York, NY), 1995.

Goldengrove Unleaving (includes *Goldengrove* and *Unleaving*), Black Swan (London, England), 1997.

The Serpentine Cave, St. Martin's Press (New York, NY), 1997.

(Contributor) Dorothy Sayers, *Thrones, Dominations,* St. Martin's Press (New York, NY), 1998.

A Desert in Bohemia, St. Martin's Press (New York, NY), 2000.

OTHER

(With Kevin Crossley Holland) *Wordhoard: Anglo-Saxon Stories,* Farrar, Straus (New York, NY), 1969.

(Editor) *Beowulf* (structural reader), Longman (London, England), 1975.

The Island Sunrise: Prehistoric Britain, Deutsch (London, England), 1975, published as *The Island Sunrise: Prehistoric Culture in the British Isles,* Seabury Press (New York, NY), 1976.

Some of Paton Walsh's manuscripts and papers may be found in the Kerlan Collection, University of Minnesota, Minneapolis.

■ Adaptations

Gaffer Samson's Luck was adapted to audio in 1987; *Torch* was adapted for a BBC serial film; *Knowledge of Angels* was adapted to audio in 1996 by Isis Audio; *A Parcel of Patterns* was adapted to audio in 1996 by Listening Library.

■ Sidelights

Author of over thirty books for young readers and a dozen titles for adults, Jill Paton Walsh is noted for her works which deal realistically with life, death, and maturation. While her novels vary widely in terms of genre and style, Judith Atkinson of *Twentieth-Century Children's Writers* noted, "The most immediately attractive features of these novels . . . are their absorbing plots and believable settings." Sheila Egoff declared in *Thursday's Child* that, "Of [the many] skilled and sensitive writers [for young people], [Paton] Walsh is the most formally literary. Her writing is studded with allusions to poetry, art and philosophy that give it an intellectual framework unmatched in children's literature." Paton Walsh's works examine eras and topics such as life, death, and honor in Anglo-Saxon England (*Hengest's Tale* and *Wordhoard*), Victorian child labor in England (*A Chance Child*), growing up in World War II England (*The Dolphin Crossing* and *Fireweed*), life in the Early Stone Age (*Toolmaker*), and loyalty in the midst of destruction in fifteenth-century Byzantium (*The Emperor's Winding Sheet*). She has also written several novels that center on the Cornish coast, where she spent part of her childhood, as well as award-winning adult novels such as *Knowledge of Angels* and *A Desert in Bohemia* that feature not only penetrating and gripping plot lines, but also philosophical inquiry and subtle characterizations.

Paton Walsh was born Gillian Bliss, a member of a loving family living in suburban London, in 1937. However, she entered the world only with difficulty, being a breech birth. Pulled violently from the womb, her right arm was permanently damaged, and there was fear that there might have been brain damage, as well, an anxiety exacerbated by the fact that Paton Walsh did not begin speaking until she was well over two years old. However, when she began, the toddler spoke full sentences. As she wrote in an essay for the *Something about the Author Autobiography Series* (*SAAS*), "Looking back, I am not surprised that I was chary of talking until I had got the grammar straight in my head, for my entire family made a nonstop game . . . of pedantically correcting each others' speech for the most minuscule errors of form or usage." Her first words, in response to a neighbor's inquiry as to her daily routine, were, "Normally I play with bricks."

Her parents soon realized that their child would possess unimpeded intelligence, but continued to limit her physical activities. Her response when told that she would be unable to do a certain thing was to try it, succeed, and infer from the experience that she was much more able-bodied than her family and doctors thought. "This has left me with a life-

In Jill Paton Walsh's 1969 YA novel, two British teens flee both their families and their London homes after that city is bombed by German pilots during the blitzkrieg of 1940.

long disposition to have a shot at things," Paton Walsh wrote in *SAAS*. "Confronted with a difficult task, as constructing a built-in wardrobe, making a ballgown, or writing a publishable book, I am still inclined to tackle it, reflecting that if someone else can do it, I probably can. This is arrogant, of course, but it often proves true. . . . If I had been contented to do only what the doctors told my parents I would be able to do, I would have led a very narrow life!" Though she was sometimes discouraged from some activities, Paton Walsh's childhood was devoid of any prejudices or special treatment based on her status as a girl. In a family interested in academic accomplishments, the criteria for achievement were the same for Paton Walsh and her sister as for their brothers.

Her father was an engineer, one of the earliest experimenters with television, and he and his wife actively stimulated their children to enjoy learning. "For the whole of our childhoods," Paton Walsh wrote in her *SAAS* entry, "I, and my brothers and sister—I am the eldest of four—were surrounded by love and encouragement on a lavish scale. . . . And to an unusual degree everyone was without prejudices against, or limited ambitions for, girls. As much was expected of me as of my brothers." Paton Walsh's early years were spent during the dangers of World War II, an experience that she later chronicled in some of her novels. "For five crucial years of my childhood—from the year I was three to the year I was eight—the war dominated and shaped everything around me," Paton Walsh explained in *SAAS*, "and then for many years, until well into my teens, postwar hardships remained."

How will Creep's brother ever find him now?

An abused and unwanted boy dubbed Creep finds himself transported to a coal-mining town of the late nineteenth century after he stows away on an English canal boat in Paton Walsh's 1978 title.

The family endured all the usual hardships suffered by tens of thousands of other British families during the war. "I do not know if there was a plan of evacuation there when the war began, which my parents did not join in, or if Finchley [where she lived] did not seem a likely target," she continued in *SAAS*. Finally her mother's stepfather, upset by a bombing raid, moved the family to his place in Cornwall, in the far west of England. Although Jill's mother soon returned with her younger children to her husband in London, Jill herself remained in Cornwall for the next five years, returning to her family only after her grandmother suffered a fatal heart attack. "I left St. Ives when I was just eight," Paton Walsh explained in *SAAS*. "A part of me is still rooted on that rocky shore, and it appears again and again in what I write." With the death of her grandmother, Paton Walsh left the safe and comfortable world she had known and stepped directly into wartime London. "That first night back," she recalled, "I lay awake listening to the clanging sounds, like dustbins rolling round the night sky, made by German rockets falling somewhere a little distance off." Part of the harsh realities of the times was that everyone wore identification discs on his or her wrist in case of bombings.

"The children I talk to nowadays are very interested in the Second World War," Paton Walsh remarked in her *SAAS* essay. "They think it must have been a time of excitement and danger, whereas it was actually dreadfully boring." Wartime restrictions and shortages meant that normal childhood activities—movies, radio, and even outdoor play—were severely limited. "I remember, in short, a time of discomfort and gloom, and, above all, upheaval." Part of the upheaval was caused by her mother's relatives, who had been wealthy colonists in Southeast Asia before the war, and who returned to England, newly impoverished, to live with her family. Because they had their own ideas of proper female behavior, Paton Walsh wrote, she never knew "whether it was good and clever to give voice to my opinions, or pushy and priggish; not knowing from one day to the next what sort of behavior would be expected of me." "Yet in the long run," Paton Walsh concluded, "I have benefitted greatly from all this. I protected myself. I learned not to care what other people think. I would say what I liked, read what I was interested in, go on my own way, and ignore what the invading hoards of aunts and uncles thought, about me, or about anything else."

Paton Walsh attended a Catholic girl's school in North Finchley, whose environment was quite different from the liberality of her home life. "The nuns who taught me were suspicious of me," she declared in her *SAAS* entry. "They liked girls who worked very hard, not those who found it easy." When Paton Walsh left the school, it was to take a place at Oxford University. "I enjoyed myself vastly at Oxford, made friends, talked late into the night, and even worked sometimes, and work included lectures by both C. S. Lewis and J. R. R. Tolkien. The subject of the lectures and tutorials was always literature or philology—we wouldn't have dared ask those great men about their own work!—but the example they set by being both great and serious scholars, and writers of fantasy and books for children was not lost on me."

From Teacher to Homemaker to Author

By the time Paton Walsh completed her degree, she was engaged to a man she had met at school. She obtained a teaching position, but soon discovered that she disliked being a teacher. "I didn't teach long," she explained in her *SAAS* entry. "I got married in my second year as a teacher, and eighteen months later was expecting a child." The life of a housewife, however, did not suit her either: "I was bored frantic. I went nearly crazy, locked up alone with a howling baby all day and all night. . . . As plants need water and light, as the baby needed milk, I needed something intellectual, cheap, and quiet." So, she said, "I began to write a book. It was a children's book. It never occurred to me to write any other kind."

"Until the moment I began to write I did not know that I was a writer," Paton Walsh commented in *SAAS.* The book she began to work on in those days, she noted, "was, unfortunately, a dreadfully bad book. It had twelve chapters of equal length, with a different bit of historical background in each one." Eventually Kevin Crossley Holland, an editor with Macmillan, explained to Paton Walsh that to publish this particular book might be a bad idea. He then offered her an option on her next work. "I set to work joyfully on *Hengest's Tale,*" she recalled, "a gory epic retold out of fragments of *Beowulf,* and I stopped work only for a fortnight—between chapter three and chapter four—when my second child, my daughter Margaret, was born. *Hengest's Tale* was my first published book. And I have never forgotten the difference it made to be able to say, to others, certainly, but above all, to myself, 'I am a writer.'" "Blood, blades, and betrayals are the hallmarks of this story of Hengest the Jute, invader and settler of fifth century Kent," Arthur T. Leone noted in the *New York Times Book Review.* The story is based on the legend of Hengest and fellow warrior Horsa,

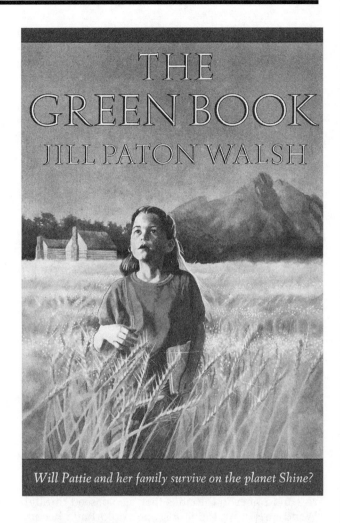

THE GREEN BOOK
JILL PATON WALSH

Will Pattie and her family survive on the planet Shine?

Taking place on a near-future Earth, this 1981 novel finds Pattie and her family fleeing the dying planet and moving to the planet Shine, only to find new difficulties in their new home.

who conquered British King Vortigern and settled in Kent. *Horn Book* reviewer Paul Heins described *Hengest's Tale* as "a memorable historical narrative."

Writing of Paton Walsh's technique in her historical fiction, *Dictionary of Literary Biography* contributor Rosanne Fraine Donahue observed that the author "makes the past relevant through likable and credible characters: the protagonist in conflict with and alienated from the adult world is a universal and timeless subject. The world the protagonist experiences may differ from that of the reader, but Paton Walsh evokes recognition from her reader while at the same time maintaining historical authenticity." Donahue further commented, "Believing that to write historical novels one must be as good at history as any historian, Paton Walsh has produced works that are both historically and psychologically true. She is mindful of the distinction between historical fiction and historical fact and operates in the realm of the possible while never crossing over into the false."

While Paton Walsh's second child, Margaret, was born during her work on *Hengest's Tale,* her third daughter, Helen Clare, had arrived by the time she started work on *Fireweed.* Paton Walsh's experiences during World War II prompted her to write *The Dolphin Crossing* and *Fireweed,* her second and third books. Since she was so young when the war began, Paton Walsh set out to research the war, reading everything she could find in newspapers and magazines to supplement her memory. *The Dolphin Crossing* and *Fireweed* "tell of friendships between upper-class and working-class teenagers," Louise L. Sherman observed in *School Library Journal.* The relationships developed in each book are the result of wartime evacuations. Two boys from differing social classes become friends and set sail for Dunkirk in *The Dolphin Crossing.* In *Fireweed,* a boy and girl run away from their evacuation sites to return to London, then band together to survive the blitz. "A haunting, truly impressive novel," Ellen Lewis Buell declared in a *Book World* review of *Fireweed.*

A Chance Child and *The Huffler* resulted from a holiday cruise through England's canals. While most of the trip provided views of beautiful countryside, Paton Walsh was struck by the ugliness of the factories and mines in the cities they also passed through. Wondering how the landscape could have become so blighted and abused, Paton Walsh set out to research the Industrial Revolution. As research for *A Chance Child,* Paton Walsh ventured into an operating coal mine. Once again she wore an identifying numbered disc on her wrist. A waif named Creep is the principal character of *A Chance Child,* which focuses on child labor in the mines, mills, and factories of the Victorian era. An abused child himself, Creep runs away from home, climbs aboard a rickety canal boat, and finds himself carried back in time to the nineteenth-century. From accounts of real children Paton Walsh found in old reports, the author recounts the beatings, accidents, and deaths that were a common consequence of nineteenth-century child labor. "Tenderly and carefully, Jill Paton Walsh adds horror to horror, painting a foul darkness against which the stunted limbs of the children gleam with a lurid pallor," Jane Langton commented in the *New York Times Book Review.* Naomi Lewis, writing in the *Observer,* found *A Chance Child* "an eerie, memorable novel."

Paton Walsh's childhood home in St. Ives provided the setting for *Goldengrove* and *Unleaving,* the author's "most ambitious and popular works," according to Donahue. Both have at their center a loss, and also speak of adolescent memory and emotion. Inspired in part by the Gerard Manley Hopkins poem "Spring and Fall," the two novels take their titles from that poem's second line: "Margaret are you grieving, / Over Goldengrove unleaving?" Both titles are about a teenager, Madge, who enters the precipitous stage of adolescence the summer she learns that her cousin Paul, with whom she has spent every vacation at her grandmother's Goldengrove, is actually her brother. In *Unleaving,* Madge, now grown up, inherits Goldengrove and along with it the "reading group" to whom the house has been rented for the summer. Friendship and love develop between Madge and Patrick, the son of one of the professors inhabiting the house. "*Unleaving* loses everything in a synopsis," Elizabeth S. Coolidge wrote in *Washington Post Book World,* "for its significance lies in what the characters think and feel, not in what they do." While death and its effects on each of the characters is the central theme of *Unleaving,* it is "in no way a gloomy book, but one that leaves the reader with a warm and optimistic view of humankind," Coolidge concluded. "[Paton] Walsh doesn't tidy up the blight for which man was born," Alice Bach noted in the *New York Times Book Review.* "She's too wise to attempt answers about growing, living, dying, ethical choices. She exalts the mystery, the unknowing itself."

Setting as Inspiration

Paton Walsh noted in *SAAS* that most of her stories begin with a place. While some are memories, others result from trips for pleasure or research. Her first adult novel, *Farewell, Great King,* features details of the Greek countryside; the children's stories *The Emperor's Winding Sheet* and *Children of the Fox* also are infused with realistic settings by trips to Greece and Turkey. In *The Emperor's Winding Sheet,* Paton Walsh "brilliantly projects the dying splendor of Constantinople and the agony of its fall," a *Kirkus Reviews* contributor noted. Young Piers Barber ventures from his Bristol home to the far-off land, where he becomes the protector of Emperor Constantine. *Children's Book Review*'s C. S. Hannabuss found that, like *The Dolphin Crossing,* "war is used dramatically; it is a place full of real terrors, and not tied down with wishy-washy abstractions about courage and endurance." With the trio of novels, *Crossing to Salamis, The Walls of Athens,* and *Persian Gold,* gathered in *Children of the Fox,* Paton Walsh returns to a historical figure she dealt with in her first adult title, Themistokles and his struggle with Persia. "In all three of the stories, the actions of Themistokles are historically accurate," wrote Donahue, "but the emphasis in each is on the [fictional] child" who is added to the historical mix.

One story that diverged from Paton Walsh's pattern of writing about places was *A Parcel of Patterns*, inspired by an account of the devastation the Plague brought to the village of Eyam that was told to her by her partner and fellow author, John Rowe Townsend. The story does, however, share another similarity with Paton Walsh's previous works: it features a group of ordinary people behaving courageously in a time of need. When Paton Walsh first heard of the villagers, who banded together to quarantine themselves from other villages in an effort to prevent the disease's spread, she was reminded of the acts of bravery, great and small, that she witnessed in the air raid shelters of her childhood London. Especially prominent is her recollection of the neighborhood milkman who had a knack for calming people and encouraging them to work together during the raids, but who became simply Mike the milkman the next morning. She confided that Mike also appears to some degree in the wartime accounts of *Fireweed* and *The Emperor's Winding Sheet*.

The title's "parcel of patterns," a bundle of dressmaking diagrams, is what the Plague brings to Eyam in 1665. When the villagers realize they are infected, they agree to quarantine themselves for the sake of their neighbors. Supplies are delivered to the town boundaries; vinegar-soaked money is left as payment. The story's narrator, Mall, relates the villagers' efforts to prevent others from coming into contact with them, including Thomas, the man she loves. When Thomas refuses to stay away, Mall finds a way to make him believe she has died; Thomas's grief leads him to join the villagers to die as well. "This is a most dreadful, moving story, and it is related . . . with a quiet, unerring restraint which will disturb and possess the reader long after the frenzy aroused by a sensational approach would have died away," Neil Philip asserted in the *Times Educational Supplement*.

Paton Walsh's inspiration for the 1984 *Gaffer Samson's Luck* was once again a place, this time the cottage that she and her husband bought in a desolate area near Cambridge known as the Fens. When young James arrives in his new village, he finds friendship not among the other youths but with an elderly neighbor, Gaffer Samson. When Samson is hospitalized, he sends James to find his "piece of luck," which he buried seventy years earlier in the marshes. James's quest to find the item leads him to a confrontation with the leader of the village gang. In a *School Library Journal* review, Cynthia K. Leibold predicted that "this eloquent story of friendship and responsibility will prove a rewarding adventure for persistent readers."

From the contemporary world, Paton Walsh turns to the distant past and the science fiction future in a trio of novels. *Toolmaker* goes back to Stone Age England in a story about a young boy, Ra, and his battle for survival. *The Green Book*—a "small masterpiece," according to *Horn Book*'s Gregory Maguire—tells the tale of a community that immigrates to a distant planet before Earth begins to fall apart. And with *Torch*, Paton Walsh presents a primitive postnuclear future society in which two teens are entrusted with the last Olympic torch and charged with delivering it to the Games. Having no idea what or where the Games are, the pair nevertheless set out to fulfill their obligation. The Games they eventually find, however, are now played for evil purposes, such as selecting slaves and identifying weak children for death. In a *School Library Journal* review, Christine Behrmann found the book "a rewarding challenge to readers who will not emerge with answers but rather an added ability to ask some important questions," while a *Kirkus Reviews* contributor described *Torch* as "a richly textured novel with a strong theme concerning the value to society—in any age—of cooperation and choices freely made."

Paton Walsh employed her research skills again in *Grace,* based on the true story of the 1838 rescue of nine shipwreck victims by Grace Darling and her father, a lighthouse keeper. Having lived peacefully and simply before the rescue, Grace finds unbearable the constant attention she receives after the rescue. Even worse, many of the mainland townspeople accuse Grace of attempting the rescue for monetary gain: rescuers traditionally received a generous reward for their efforts, and Grace had in effect taken money from the lifeboat crew by doing their job. While others recognized Grace's heroism, the uproar was nonetheless too much for her, and she died four years later. "Paton Walsh has brought [Grace] back to life for today's readers in a way that is completely engrossing," Connie C. Rockman declared in *School Library Journal*.

Readers of All Ages

Throughout the 1990s Paton Walsh tended to save her longer tales for the adult titles which have been a part of her repertoire. Writing for children during that decade was largely confined to shorter fiction and picture books. For example, her 1992 title, *When Grandma Came*, is a picture book about a well-traveled grandmother who considers her grandchild to be her "greatest treasure," according to Joan M. Hildebrand in *Childhood Education*. Hildebrand further dubbed this book a "beautifully cadenced story for young children." *Pepi and the Secret Names* is another picture book, this one telling the tale of Pepi, whose father is commissioned to decorate the tomb

Recounting actual events, Paton Walsh relates the problems that befell lighthouse keeper daughter Grace Darling after she and her father rescued a ship's crew cast adrift off the British coast in the early nineteenth century.

of Prince Dhutmose. The girl supplies living models for her father, by convincing various wild creatures to pose for him. In part a puzzle book involving hieroglyphic signs for the names of the animals, this picture book is a "valuable addition to classroom units to ancient Egypt," wrote *Booklist*'s Kay Weisman.

A further picture book, *Connie Came to Play,* deals with sharing. *Booklist*'s Stephanie Zvirin felt that the pictures are "perfectly attuned to the spare, subtle rendering of a familiar childhood situation," while *Horn Book*'s Hanna B. Zeiger noted that this "gentle story presents a peaceful and innovative solution to the common childhood problem of sharing toys." Paton Walsh's 1997 picture book effort, *When I Was*

Little Like You, focuses on a grandmother's reminiscences with her young granddaughter. A reviewer for *Publishers Weekly* found this to be a "quiet tale," and *Booklist*'s Helen Rosenberg likewise thought it was a "simple story."

The *New York Times Book Review*'s Barbara Wersba admired Paton Walsh's ability to capture the fears and emotions of childhood, something she believes many adults have forgotten. "Jill Paton Walsh, however, has not forgotten—and I am rather in awe of her," Wersba reflected. "She writes as though she were still twelve years old, choking back angry tears." Paton Walsh attributes her affinity for writing children's literature to her own childhood experiences. "The epoch in life in which people first meet a crisis, in which they first begin to define themselves, their own needs, feelings, opinions, is the epoch which they will always feel the most important," she stated in *SAAS.* "The upheavals and changes and conflicts which the war brought to my life mean that for me childhood is the important and interesting stage of life."

While most of her work has been in the realm of children's fiction, Paton Walsh has also written several well-received adult novels. *Lapsing* presents "an unusual, fastidiously focused tale of a spiritual journey to disillusionment by a bright, deeply committed young Roman Catholic woman," a *Kirkus Reviews* contributor noted. A mutual attraction develops between Tessa and Father Theodore; Tessa marries in an unsuccessful effort to resolve the conflict. *Publishers Weekly* reviewer Diane Roback found *Lapsing* "an arresting novel, nuanced and clever."

In *The Wyndham Case* and *A Piece of Justice,* Paton Walsh "dipped her toe in the sleuthing pond," according to Yvonne Nolan, writing in *Publishers Weekly,* "with a quaintly old-fashioned, quintessentially English creation, nurse and amateur sleuth Imogen Quy." A reviewer for *Publishers Weekly* felt that in *The Wyndham Case* Paton Walsh "produces a clear, sequential mystery, unmuddied by extraneous elements." The same contributor praised the writing for "precision, grace and a lovely sense of place." Reviewing the second Imogen Quy mystery, another reviewer for *Publishers Weekly* called the book "brisk and neatly plotted." The popularity of these mysteries convinced the Dorothy Sayers estate that Paton Walsh was the writer to finish one of Sayers's manuscripts, *Thrones, Dominations,* and Paton Walsh's "collaborative" effort was a resounding success. "Sayers fans will relish the cooperative sleuthing of Peter [Wimsey] and Harriet and the self-effacing Bunter as [Paton] Walsh deftly captures and subtly updates the spirit of the series, endowing the iconic characters with additional depth and complexity," wrote a contributor for *Publishers Weekly*. Reviewing the same novel in *Commonweal*, Elizabeth Bartelme reported that "Jill Paton Walsh has . . . stitched together Dorothy Sayers's work with her own contribution to make a coherent whole. . . . Walsh has taken an unfinished manuscript and produced a most effective exit work for the writer who was arguably the preeminent mystery novelist of our time."

More serious in tone and intent are other more literary novels for adults and also for mature teen readers, including the 1994 *Knowledge of Angels,* shortlisted for the prestigious Booker Prize in England, *The Serpent Cave* from 1997, and her ambitious novel from 2000, *A Desert in Bohemia.* In the first-named title, "religious faith and belief inform this novel about a wolf girl, an atheist and a devout theologian," wrote Nolan. It is the theologian's fervent hope that he can use the wild girl to try and convince the atheist that the belief in God is innate in all humans, even those unlearned. Set in the fifteenth century, the novel focuses on Palinor, a wealthy engineer washed up on a European island run by the cardinal-prince Severo. When Palinor announces that he is an atheist, Severo sends him to a monk to be converted; atheism is an offense punishable by death on the island. At the same time, Severo has heard of a wild girl, Amara, raised by wolves, who has been found on the island. He sends her to a convent hoping the nuns there can discover if this feral creature has ever felt God's presence. These two plot lines ultimately converge in the attempted conversion of Palinor. A novel of ideas, this book was praised by critics on both sides of the Atlantic, though in her home country Paton Walsh had to self-publish the work. A reviewer for *Publishers Weekly* noted that "sonorous prose, a polyphonic interweaving of themes and a diverse cast of characters from all rungs of society leaven an often didactic tale which addresses timeless issues." Similarly, *Booklist*'s Ilene Cooper observed that in this "intricately conceived and marvelously executed story, [Paton] Walsh looks at faith through a kaleidoscope," ultimately forcing readers to "keep twisting the lens for themselves."

A Desert in Bohemia is a novel ten years in the making, set in the fictional Czech land called Comenia, and following the course of Eastern European politics through the last half of the twentieth century. The author follows nine characters over the decades from 1945, and the end of the Nazi occupation, through the decades of Soviet control, up to the independence of 1990. The book opens with a young woman narrowly escaping a Nazi massacre and finding refuge in an empty castle, where she discovers an abandoned baby. The story proceeds to follow Eliska and this baby through the communist takeover and her marriage to the peasant Jiri, who welcomes the Soviets and the new society. Other characters include Michael, an aristocrat whose family once owned the abandoned castle and who escapes to Austria from the Red partisans. His friend Frantisek likewise escapes to England. "Questions of identity haunt these uprooted characters," noted a reviewer for *Publishers Weekly,* and ultimately the novel asks the difficult question about what one must do to survive in an immoral world. The same critic felt that Paton Walsh's "lucid and graceful prose style" informs this novel of ideas, calling it a "signal achievement" with "a cunningly orchestrated plot, a relentlessly chilling atmosphere and indelible character portraits." *Library Journal*'s Patricia Gulian felt the novel was "beautifully written," while *School Library Journal*'s Penny Stevens noted

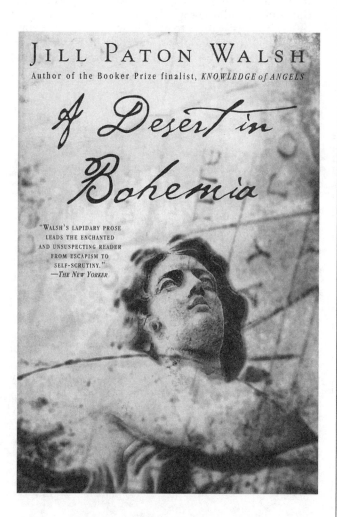

JILL PATON WALSH

Author of the Booker Prize finalist, *KNOWLEDGE of ANGELS*

A Desert in Bohemia

"WALSH'S LAPIDARY PROSE LEADS THE ENCHANTED AND UNSUSPECTING READER FROM ESCAPISM TO SELF-SCRUTINY."
—*THE NEW YORKER*

In the days following World War II, Eliska emerges from hiding and makes her new home in an abandoned castle, where she is joined by others who must make the transition to a new way of life in central Europe.

that the strengths of this "thought-provoking book are the philosophical discussions on free will, and communism versus capitalism." Stevens also felt that "teens will appreciate the points of view of the various characters and gain a deeper understanding of the political movements that exist in Eastern Europe."

Writing, for Paton Walsh, is not so much about self-expression as it is the harnessing of such inner creativity to a higher truth. "If you want to express yourself," Paton Walsh told Nolan, "you need the services of a lover or a psychiatrist; if you want to express a book, you might conceivably manage it. . . . You can't deduce the personality of the potter from the pots. It's a thing you've made and offered to somebody else for their use, and, believe me, a novel is like that. It's a made thing and ought not to contain a direct self-expression of the writer. It ought to be an object crafted out of a passion for the subject and a knowledge of the audience. If you put self-expression into it, you're writing a certain kind of thing, which is current but very self-indulgent. It's too personal; it won't do as a model of art."

If you enjoy the works of Jill Paton Walsh, you might want to check out the following books:

Vivien Alcock, *The Stonewalkers*, 1983.
Katherine Paterson, *Lyddie*, 1991.
Iain Lawrence, *The Wreckers*, 1998.

"As time has gone by," Paton Walsh concluded in her *SAAS* entry, "I have won the friendship of many other writers and readers and book-lovers. I feel lucky in this, beyond my deserts. . . . A writer is what I shall be as long as there is a daydream in my head, and I have strength to sit up and type."

■ Biographical and Critical Sources

BOOKS

Children's Literature Review, Volume 2, Gale (Detroit, MI), 1976.
Contemporary Literary Criticism, Volume 35, Gale (Detroit, MI), 1985.

Dictionary of Literary Biography, Volume 161: *British Children's Writers since 1960,* Gale (Detroit, MI), 1996, pp. 245-257.
Egoff, Sheila A., *Thursday's Child: Trends and Patterns in Contemporary Children's Literature,* American Library Association, 1981.
St. James Guide to Young Adult Writers, second edition, St. James Press (Detroit, MI), 1999.
Something about the Author Autobiography Series, Volume 3, Gale (Detroit, MI), 1987, pp. 189-203.
Twentieth-Century Young Adult Writers, St. James Press (Detroit, MI), 1994.

PERIODICALS

Booklist, February 15, 1994, Ilene Cooper, review of *Knowledge of Angels,* p. 1062; April 15, 1995, Kay Weisman, review of *Pepi and the Secret Names,* p 1501; August, 1995, p. 1932; January 1, 1996, Stephanie Zvirin, review of *Connie Came to Play,* p. 849; March 15, 1997, p. 1253; October 1, 1997, p. 309; November 15, 1997, Helen Rosenberg, review of *When I Was Little Like You,* p. 568.
Book World, May 17, 1970, Ellen Lewis Buell, review of *Fireweed,* p. 3.
Childhood Education, spring, 1993, Joan M. Hildebrand, review of *When Grandma Came,* p. 174.
Children's Book Review, summer, 1974, C. S. Hannabuss, review of *The Emperor's Winding Sheet,* p. 71.
Christian Century, June 3, 1998, pp. 585-587.
Commonweal, May 8, 1998, Elizabeth Bartelme, review of *Thrones, Dominations,* pp. 26-28.
Entertainment Weekly, December 19, 1997, p. 73; March 13, 1998, pp. 68-69.
Horn Book, August, 1967, Paul Heins, review of *Hengest's Tale,* p. 478; May-June, 1996, Hanna B. Zeiger, review of *Connie Came to Play,* pp. 327-328; January-February, 1997, pp. 85-86; November-December, 2000, Gregory Maguire, review of *The Green Book,* p. 682.
Kirkus Reviews, May 1, 1974, review of *The Emperor's Winding Sheet,* pp. 490-491; October 1, 1987, review of *Lapsing,* p. 1419; March 1, 1988, review of *Torch,* p. 371.
Library Journal, November 1, 1997, p. 118; January, 1998, p. 147; September 1, 1999, p. 252; November 1, 2000, Patricia Gulian, review of *A Desert in Bohemia,* p. 138.
New Statesman, October 31, 1986, p. 31; February 20, 1998, p. 47.
New Statesman and Society, August 19, 1994, p. 39.
New Yorker, November 27, 1989, p. 142.
New York Times Book Review, April 9, 1967, Arthur T. Leone, review of *Hengest's Tale,* p. 26; November 5, 1972, Barbara Wersba, "The Damage Called

Growing Up," p. 6; August 8, 1976, Alice Bach, review or *Unleaving,* p. 18; June 17, 1979, Jane Langton, review of *A Chance Child,* pp. 24-25; June 16, 1985, p. 30; June 14, 1992, p. 31; March 15, 1998, p. 16; February 4, 2001, p. 21; February 4, 2002, p. 20.

Observer (London, England), December 10, 1978, Naomi Lewis, "Castles Dangerous," p. 38.

Publishers Weekly, October 16, 1987, Diane Roback, review of *Lapsing,* p. 70; July 12, 1993, review of *The Wyndham Case,* p. 72; January 10, 1994, review of *Knowledge of Angels,* p. 41; March 13, 1995, review of *Pepi and the Secret Names,* p. 69; June 19, 1995, review of *A Piece of Justice,* p. 52; January 13, 1997, p. 36; November 17, 1997, review of *When I Was Little Like You,* p. 60; January 5, 1998, review of *Thrones, Dominations,* p. 62; October 9, 2000, review of *A Desert in Bohemia,* p. 71; November 27, 2000, Yvonne Nolan, "Jill Paton Walsh—Novel Ideas Along the Cam," p. 48.

School Library Journal, February, 1985, Cynthia K. Leibold, review of *Gaffer Samson's Luck,* p. 80; May, 1988, Christine Behrmann, review of *Torch,* p. 111; July, 1992, Louise L. Sherman, "In the Homes of Strangers: The World War II Evacuation of British Children in Children's Literature," p. 42; June, 2001, Penny Stevens, review of *A Desert in Bohemia,* p. 184.

Times Educational Supplement, January 13, 1984, Neil Philip, "A Terrible Beauty," p. 42; November 11, 1994, p. R2.

Times Literary Supplement, March 29, 1985, p. 349; November 29, 1985, p. 1358; November 28, 1986, p. 1347; November 22, 1991, p. 24; January 31, 1997, p. 21; September 22, 2000, p. 21.

Washington Post Book World, May 2, 1976, Elizabeth S. Coolidge, "Two Modern English Morality Tales," p. L13.

OTHER

Jill Paton Walsh's Home Page, http://www.greenbay.co.uk/ (March 18, 2002).*

Ezra Pound

gland, editor, 1917-19; *Dial*, Paris correspondent, 1922; founder and editor of *Exile*, 1927-28; radio broadcaster in Rome until 1945; arrested by U.S. Army, 1945, and charged with treason; declared insane and unfit to stand trial for his life; committed to St. Elizabeth's Hospital, Washington, DC, until 1958.

■ Personal

Born October 30, 1885, in Hailey, ID; died November 1, 1972, in Venice, Italy; buried in San Michele Cemetery on the island of San Giorgio Maggiore, Italy; son of Homer Loomis (a mine inspector, then assayer) and Isabel (Weston) Pound; married Dorothy Shakespear, 1914; lived with Olga Rudge for twelve years; children: Omar Shakespear, Mary Rachewilz. *Education:* Attended University of Pennsylvania, 1901-03; Hamilton College, graduated, 1905; University of Pennsylvania, M.A., 1906.

■ Awards, Honors

Honorary degree from Hamilton College, 1939; Bollingen Library of Congress Award, 1949, for *The Pisan Cantos;* Academy of American Poets fellowship, 1963; *Dial* Award for distinguished service to American letters.

■ Career

Writer, poet, and critic. Wabash College, Crawfordsville, IN, lecturer in French and Spanish, 1906; Regent Street Polytechnic Institute, London, England, teacher of literature; *Poetry*, Chicago, IL, London correspondent, 1912-19; associated with H. L. Mencken's *Smart Set*; W. B. Yeats's unofficial secretary in Sussex, England, 1913-16; unofficial literary executor for Ernest Fenollosa, London, 1914; member, editorial staff, *Mercure de France, Egoist,* and *Cerebralist;* founder, with Wyndham Lewis, of Vorticist magazine *BLAST!*, 1914; *Little Review,* London, En-

■ Writings

POETRY

A Lume Spento (also see below), privately printed by A. Antonini (Venice, Italy), 1908.

A Quinzaine for This Yule, Pollock (London, England), 1908.

Personae, Elkin Mathews (London, England), 1909.

Exultations, Elkin Mathews (London, England), 1909.

Provencal, Small, Maynard (Boston, MA), 1910.

Canzoni, Elkin Mathews (London, England), 1911.

Ripostes of Ezra Pound, S. Swift (London, England), 1912, Small, Maynard (Boston, MA), 1913.

Personae and Exultations of Ezra Pound, [London, England], 1913.

Canzoni and Ripostes of Ezra Pound, Elkin Mathews (London, England), 1913.

Lustra of Ezra Pound, Elkin Mathews (London, England), 1916, Knopf (New York, NY), 1917.

Quia Pauper Amavi, Egoist Press (London, England), 1918.

The Fourth Canto, Ovid Press (London, England), 1919.

(And translations) Umbra, Elkin Mathews (London, England), 1920.

Hugh Selwyn Mauberley, Ovid Press (London, England), 1920.

Poems, 1918-1921, Boni & Liveright (New York, NY), 1921.

A Draft of XVI Cantos, Three Mountains Press (Paris, French), 1925.

Personae: The Collected Poems of Ezra Pound, Boni & Liveright (New York, NY), 1926.

Selected Poems, edited and with an introduction by T. S. Eliot, Faber & Gwyer (London, England), 1928, Laughlin (New York, NY), 1957.

A Draft of the Cantos 17-27, John Rodker (London, England), 1928.

A Draft of XXX Cantos, Hours Press (Paris, France), 1930, Farrar & Rinehart (New York, NY), 1933.

Homage to Sextus Propertius, Faber (London, England), 1934.

Eleven New Cantos: XXXI-XLI, Farrar & Rinehart (New York, NY), 1934, published as A Draft of Cantos XXXI-XLI, Faber (London, England), 1935.

(Under pseudonym The Poet of Titchfield Street) Alfred Venison's Poems: Social Credit Themes, Nott (London, England), 1935.

The Fifth Decade of Cantos, Farrar & Rinehart (New York, NY), 1937.

Cantos LII-LXXI, New Directions (New York, NY), 1940.

A Selection of Poems, Faber (London, England), 1940.

The Pisan Cantos (also see below), New Directions (New York, NY), 1948.

The Cantos of Ezra Pound (includes The Pisan Cantos), New Directions (New York, NY), 1948, revised edition, Faber (London, England), 1954.

Selected Poems, New Directions (New York, NY), 1949.

Personnae: The Collected Poems of Ezra Pound, New Directions (New York, NY), 1950, published as Personnae: Collected Shorter Poems, Faber (London, England), 1952, new edition published as Collected Shorter Poems, Faber (London, England), 1968.

Seventy Cantos, Faber (London, England), 1950.

Section Rock-Drill, 85-95 de los Cantares, All'Insegna del Pesce d'Oro (Milan, Italy), 1955, New Directions (New York, NY), 1956.

Thrones: 96-109 de los Cantares, New Directions (New York, NY), 1959.

The Cantos (1-109), new edition, Faber (London, England), 1964.

The Cantos (1-95), New Directions (New York, NY), 1965.

A Lume Spento, and Other Early Poems, New Directions (New York, NY), 1965.

Selected Cantos, Faber (London, England), 1967.

Drafts and Fragments: Cantos CX-CXVII, New Directions (New York, NY), 1968.

Collected Early Poems of Ezra Pound, New Directions (New York, NY), 1976.

From Syria: The Worksheets, Proofs, and Text, edited by Robin Skelton, Copper Canyon Press (Port Townsend, WA), 1981.

Diptych Rome-London (includes Hugh Selwyn Mauberley), New Directions (New York, NY), 1994.

Early Poems, Dover (Mineola, NY), 1996.

PROSE

The Spirit of Romance, Dent (London, England), 1910, New Directions (New York, NY), 1952, revised edition, P. Owen (London, England), 1953.

Gaudier-Brzeska: A Memoir Including the Published Writings of the Sculptor and a Selection from His Letters, John Lane (London, England), 1916, New Directions (New York, NY), 1961.

(With Ernest Fenollosa) Noh; or, Accomplishment: A Study of the Classical Stage of Japan, Macmillan (London, England), 1916, Knopf (New York, NY), 1917, published as The Classic Noh Theatre of Japan, New Directions (New York, NY), 1960.

Pavannes and Divisions, Knopf (New York, NY), 1918.

Instigations of Ezra Pound, Together with an Essay on the Chinese Written Character by Ernest Fenollosa, Boni & Liveright (New York, NY), 1920.

Indiscretions, Three Mountains Press (Paris, France), 1923.

(Under pseudonym William Atheling) Antheil and the Treatise on Harmony, Three Mountains Press (Paris, France), 1924, published under his own name, P. Covici (New York, NY), 1927, 2nd edition, Da Capo (New York, NY), 1968.

Imaginary Letters, Black Sun Press (Paris, France), 1930.

How to Read, Harmsworth (London, England), 1931.

ABC of Economics, Faber (London, England), 1933, New Directions (New York, NY), 1940, 2nd edition, Russell (London, England), 1953.

ABC of Reading, Yale University Press (New Haven, CT), 1934, new edition, Faber (London, England), 1951.

Make It New, Faber (London, England), 1934, Yale University Press (New Haven, CT), 1935.

Social Credit: An Impact (pamphlet), Nott (London, England), 1935.

Jefferson and/or Mussolini, Nott (London, England), 1935, Liveright (New York, NY), 1936.

Polite Essays, Faber (London, England), 1937, New Directions (New York, NY), 1940.

Culture, New Directions (New York, NY), 1938, new edition published as *Guide to Kulchur*, New Directions (New York, NY), 1952.

What Is Money For?, Greater Britain Publications, 1939, published as *What Is Money For?: A Sane Man's Guide to Economics*, Revisionist Press, 1982.

Carla da Visita, Edizioni di Lettere d'Oggi (Rome, Italy), 1942, translation by John Drummond published as *A Visiting Card*, Russell (London, England), 1952, published as *A Visiting Card: Ancient and Modern History of Script and Money*, Revisionist Press, 1983.

L'America, Roosevelt e le cause della guerra presente, Edizioni Popolari (Venice, Italy), 1944, translation by John Drummond published as *America, Roosevelt and the Causes of the Present War*, Russell (London, England), 1951.

Introduzione alla natura economica degli S.U.A., Edizioni Popolari (Venice, Italy), 1944, translation by Carmine Amore published as *An Introduction to the Economic Nature of the United States*, Russell (London, England), 1958.

Oro e Lavoro, Tip. Moderna (Rapallo, Italy), 1944, translation by John Drummond published as *Gold and Work*, Russell (London, England), 1952.

Orientamenti, Edizioni Popolari (Venice, Italy), 1944.

"If This Be Treason . . . " (four original drafts of Rome radio broadcasts), privately printed, Olga Rudge, 1948.

The Letters of Ezra Pound, 1907-1941, edited by D. D. Paige, Harcourt (New York, NY), 1950.

Patria Mia, R. F. Seymour (Chicago, IL), 1950, published as *Patria Mia and The Treatise on Harmony*, Owen (London, England), 1962.

Literary Essays of Ezra Pound, edited and with an introduction by T. S. Eliot, New Directions (New York, NY), 1954.

Lavoro ed Usura, All'Insegna del Pesce d'Oro, 1954.

Brancusi, [Milan, Italy], 1957.

Pavannes and Divagations, New Directions (New York, NY), 1958.

Impact: Essays on Ignorance and the Decline of American Civilization, edited and with an introduction by Noel Stock, Regnery (Washington, DC), 1960.

EP to LU: Nine Letters Written to Louis Untermeyer, edited by J. A. Robbins, Indiana University Press (Bloomington, IN), 1963.

Pound/Joyce: The Letters of Ezra Pound to James Joyce, edited by Forrest Read, New Directions (New York, NY), 1967.

Selected Prose, 1909-1965, edited by William Cookson, New Directions (New York, NY), 1973.

Ezra Pound and Music: The Complete Criticism, edited by R. Murray Schafer, New Directions (New York, NY), 1977.

"Ezra Pound Speaking": Radio Speeches of World War II, edited by Leonard W. Doob, Greenwood Press (Westport, CT), 1978.

Letters to Ibbotsom, 1935-1952, National Poetry Foundation (Orono, ME), 1979.

Ezra Pound and the Visual Arts, edited by Harriet Zinnes, New Directions (New York, NY), 1980.

Letters to John Theobald, Black Swan Books (London, England), 1981.

Pound-Ford, the Story of a Literary Friendship: The Correspondence between Ezra Pound and Ford Madox Ford and Their Writings about Each Other, New Directions (New York, NY), 1982.

Ezra Pound and Dorothy Shakespear: Their Letters, 1909-1914, New Directions (New York, NY), 1984.

Pound-Lewis: The Letters of Ezra Pound and Wyndham Lewis, New Directions (New York, NY), 1985.

Selected Letters of Ezra Pound and Louis Zukofsky, New Directions (New York, NY), 1987.

Pound the Little Review: The Letters of Ezra Pound to Margaret Anderson, New Directions (New York, NY), 1988.

A Walking Tour in Southern France: Ezra Pound among the Troubadors, edited with an introduction by Richard Sieburth, New Directions (New York, NY), 1992.

The Letters of Ezra Pound to Alice Corbin Henderson, edited by Ira B. Nadel, University of Texas Press (Austin, TX), 1993.

Ezra Pound and James Laughlin: Selected Letters, edited by David Gordon, Norton (New York, NY), 1994.

Ezra Pound and Senator Bronson Cutting: A Political Correspondence, 1930-1935, University of New Mexico Press (Albuquerque, NM), 1995.

Pound/Cummings: The Correspondence of Ezra Pound and E. E. Cummings, edited by Betty Ahearn, University of Michigan Press (Ann Arbor, MI), 1996.

Pound/Williams: Selected Letters of Ezra Pound and William Carlos Williams, edited by Hugh Witemeyer, New Directions (New York, NY), 1996.

Machine Art and Other Writings: The Lost Thought of the Italian Years (essays), edited by Maria Luisa Ardizzone, Duke University Press (Durham, NC), 1996.

Ezra and Dorothy Pound: Letters in Captivity, 1945-1946, edited by Omar Pound and Robert Spoo, Oxford University Press (New York, NY), 1998.

I Cease Not to Yowl: Ezra Pound's Letters to Olivia Rossetti Agresti, edited by Demetres P. Tryphonopoulos and Leon Surette, University of Illinois Press (Urbana, IL), 1998.

TRANSLATOR

The Sonnets and Ballate of Guido Cavalcanti, Small, Maynard (Boston, MA), 1912, published as *Ezra Pound's Cavalcanti Poems* (includes "Mediaevalism" and "The Other Dimension"), New Directions (New York, NY), 1966.

(Contributor of translations) *Selections from Collection Yvette Guilbert,* [London, England], 1912.

Cathay, Elkin Mathews (London, England), 1915.

Certain Noh Plays of Japan, Cuala Press (Churchtown), 1916.

Twelve Dialogues of Fontenelle, 1917.

Remy de Gourmont, *The Natural Philosophy of Love,* Boni & Liveright (New York, NY), 1922.

Confucius, *To Hio: The Great Learning,* University of Washington Bookstore (Seattle, WA), 1928.

Confucius: Digest of the Analects, Giovanni Scheiwiller, 1937.

Odon Por, *Italy's Policy of Social Economics, 1930-1940,* Istituto Italiano D'Arti Grafiche (Rome, Italy), 1941.

(Translator into Italian, with Alberto Luchini) *Ta S'eu Dai Gaku Studio Integrale,* [Rapallo, Italy], 1942.

Confucius, *The Great Digest* [and] *The Unwobbling Pivot,* New Directions (New York, NY), 1951.

Confucius, *Analects,* Kasper & Horton (New York, NY), 1951, published as *The Confucian Analects,* P. Owen (London, England), 1956, Square $ Series, 1957.

The Translations of Ezra Pound, edited by Hugh Kenner, New Directions (New York, NY), 1953, enlarged edition published as *Translations,* New Directions (New York, NY), 1963.

The Classic Anthology, Defined by Confucius, Harvard University Press (Cambridge, MA), 1954.

Richard of St. Victor, *Pensieri sull'amore,* [Milan, Italy], 1956.

Enrico Pea, *Moscardino,* All' Insegna del Pesce d'Oro (Milan, Italy), 1956.

Sophocles, *Women of Tiachis* (play; produced in New York at Living Theatre, 1960), Spearman, 1956, New Directions (New York, NY), 1957.

Rimbaud, All' Insegna del Pesce d'Oro (Milan, Italy), 1957.

(With Noel Stock) *Love Poems of Ancient Egypt,* New Directions (New York, NY), 1962.

EDITOR

(And contributor) *Des Imagistes* (anthology; published anonymously), A. & C. Boni (New York, NY), 1914.

(And contributor) *Catholic Anthology, 1914-1915,* Elkin Mathews (London, England), 1915.

Passages from the Letters of John Butler Yeats, Cuala Press, 1917.

Ernest Hemingway, *In Our Time,* Three Mountains Press (Paris, France), 1924.

The Collected Poems of Harry Crosby, Volume Four, Torchbearer, (Paris, France), 1931.

Guido Cavalcanti, *Rime,* Marsano (Genoa, Italy), 1932.

Profiles (anthology), [Milan, Italy], 1932.

(And contributor) *Active Anthology,* Faber (London, England), 1933.

Ernest Fenollosa, *The Chinese Written Character as a Medium for Poetry,* Square $ Series, 1935.

(With Marcella Spann) *Confucius to Cummings: An Anthology of Poetry,* New Directions (New York, NY), 1964.

OTHER

The Cambridge Companion to Ezra Pound, edited by Ira B. Nadel, Cambridge University Press (New York, NY), 1998.

Contributor to *British Union Quarterly, Townsman, Hudson Review, National Review, New Age* (under the pseudonym Alfred Venison), and other periodicals. Also author of score for "Le Testament," a ballet and song recital based on the poem by François Villon, 1919-21, first produced in Spoleto, Italy, 1965; *Villon* (opera), c. early 1920s, portions produced in Paris, 1924, and broadcast on BBC-Radio, 1931 and 1962; *Cavalcanti* (unfinished opera); and several short pieces for the violin.

■ Sidelights

Visionary, literary pioneer, traitor, poseur, genius. All of these terms have been used at one time or another to describe Ezra Pound, considered one of the major literary figures of the twentieth century. A controversial figure within modern poetry, Pound has also been one of its most important contributors. His *Cantos,* a half-century attempt at codifying his chaotic world in verse, is considered one of the premier achievements of modernism, indeed of poetry from any age, yet one of the least-read "great" poems in the English canon. In an introduction to the

Literary Essays of Ezra Pound, T. S. Eliot declared that Pound "is more responsible for the twentieth-century revolution in poetry than is any other individual." Four decades later, Donald Hall reaffirmed this appraisal in *Remembering Poets*, noting that "Ezra Pound is the poet who, a thousand times more than any other man, has made modern poetry possible in English."

The importance of Pound's contributions to the arts and to the revitalization of poetry early in the twentieth century has been widely acknowledged; yet in 1950, Hugh Kenner could claim in his groundbreaking study *The Poetry of Ezra Pound*, "There is no great contemporary writer who is less read than Ezra Pound." Pound never sought, nor had, a wide reading audience; his technical innovations and use of unconventional poetic materials often baffled even sympathetic readers. Early in his career he aroused controversy because of his aesthetic views; later he was equally controversial because of his political views in espousing the fascism of Italian dictator Mussolini and creating broadcast propaganda for the enemy of the United States during World War II. For the greater part of the twentieth century, however, Pound devoted his energies to advancing the art of poetry and maintaining his aesthetic standards in the midst of extreme adversity. A noted literary critic, Pound was also a tireless supporter of other artists and writers, championing the publication of such twentieth-century greats as James Joyce, Robert Frost, William Butler Yeats, T. S. Eliot, Ernest Hemingway, and a bevy of others. Ironically, his deeds—both grandiose and ridiculous—may well live longer than his words, for Pound himself felt that his monumental verse cycle in the *Cantos* was ultimately a failure.

Wendy Stallard Flory summed up Pound's achievement in *Dictionary of Literary Biography*: "Ezra Pound's influence on the development of poetry in the twentieth century has unquestionably been greater than that of any other poet. No other writer has written as much poetry and criticism or devoted as much energy to the advancement of the arts in general. Nor has any writer been the focus of so much heated controversy. More widely recognized than any other writer by his poet-contemporaries for his influence on their work, he has at the same time been the most widely and bitterly condemned by critics. Opinions about Pound run the gamut from uncritical adulation to vituperative hatred."

American Roots

Pound saw himself as the result of two powerful American traditions: of the colonial period on his

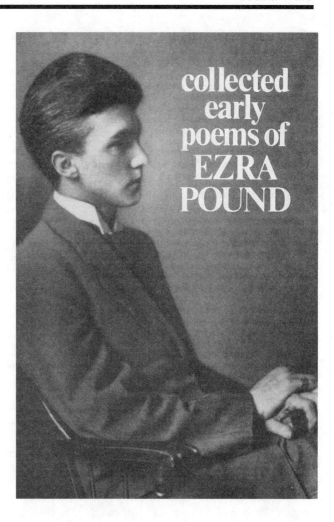

Pound's early work, which begins with 1908's *A lume spento* and includes a number of shorter works penned before World War I, were available only in limited editions prior to their publication by New Directions in 1976.

mother's side, distantly related to the poet Henry Wadsworth Longfellow, and of the pioneering spirit of the country on his father's side. Pound's grandfather on that side, Thaddeus Pound, was one of those examples of rugged individualism who owned a lumber company, opened rail lines, founded a bank, and was even a governor of Wisconsin and a United States Congressman. Pound himself was something of a pioneer, born on the frontier in Hailey, Idaho, on October 30, 1885. His father, Homer Pound, ran the local land office; his mother, Isabel Weston Pound, of more genteel birth than Homer, was no fan of the frontier. She was more suited to the East, and in 1887 she won her way with the family moving to New York City, one step ahead of the Great Blizzard of that year in the West. The Pounds stayed in New York for a time, then settled at grandfather

Thaddeus's farm in Wisconsin for a year before moving to Philadelphia, where Homer took a position as assistant assayer at the United States Mint.

Pound grew up in Philadelphia, attending the Chelten School, founded by the suffragette Annie Heacock, then the Cheltenham Military Academy, and later the Cheltenham Township High School. Europe held a fascination for the young Pound ever since his first trip there in 1898, with an aunt, when he spent three months in England, France, Belgium, Germany, Switzerland, and Italy. Not quite sixteen, he entered the University of Pennsylvania in 1901, studying English under Felix Schelling. A second trip to Europe in 1902 reinforced his earlier impressions; he knew that he would eventually need to spread his wings to that continent to learn what he could from the European tradition.

Back at the University of Pennsylvania, Pound became friends with William Carlos Williams, himself destined to be a well-known poet; their friendship would last until Williams's death in 1963. In 1903, Pound transferred to Hamilton College, where he earned his undergraduate degree in 1905. He studied Anglo-Saxon, French, Italian, Spanish, and even Provencal at Hamilton, studies that "helped to turn his literary enthusiasms in a direction that would have a decisive influence on his poetry, criticism, and translations," according to Flory. It was while he was a student that he hit on the idea of his *Cantos*, talking with one of his professors. He decided that he would begin this poem as a descent into the underworld by Odysseus, but in a form "that would imitate Anglo-Saxon prosody," Flory wrote. Another early and lasting influence on Pound was his religious upbringing; he read the Bible regularly as a teenager and also paid close attention to the sermons delivered at his local church. Romance was never far from his mind, either. An early relationship with Hilda Doolittle, later known as the poet H.D., led to an engagement, though it was later broken off.

Graduating from Hamilton, Pound returned to the University of Pennsylvania for graduate studies in Romance languages, immersing himself in Latin literature and the Italian Renaissance. In 1906-07 he earned a fellowship to research the plays of the Spaniard Lope de Vega, and did much of this study at the British Museum and at Madrid's National Library. Earning his master's degree, he took a teaching post at Wabash College in Indiana in 1907, but ultimately lost the position in part because he allowed an actress to spend the night in his lodgings. It was time to explore less provincial surroundings.

Pound in London

In his article "How I Began," collected in *Literary Essays*, Pound claimed that as a youth he had resolved to "know more about poetry than any man living." In pursuit of this goal, he settled in London from 1908 to 1920, where he carved out a reputation for himself as a member of the literary avant-garde and a tenacious advocate of contemporary work in the arts. Through his criticism and translations, as well as in his own poetry, particularly in his *Cantos*, Pound explored poetic traditions from different cultures ranging from ancient Greece, China, and the continent, to current-day England and America. In *The Tale of the Tribe* Michael Bernstein observed that Pound "sought, long before the notion became fashionable, to break with the long tradition of Occidental ethnocentrism." In his efforts to develop new directions in the arts, he also promoted and supported such writers as James Joyce, T. S. Eliot and Robert Frost. The critic David Perkins, writing in *A History of Modern Poetry*, summarized Pound's enormous influence: "The least that can be claimed of his poetry is that for over fifty years he was one of the three or four best poets writing in English"; and, Perkins continued, his "achievement in and for poetry was threefold: as a poet, and as a critic, and as a befriender of genius through personal contact." In a 1915 letter to Harriet Monroe, Pound himself described his activities as an effort "to keep alive a certain group of advancing poets, to set the arts in their rightful place as the acknowledged guide and lamp of civilization."

First, however, Pound spent a few months in Venice. Arriving in Italy in 1908 with only eighty dollars, Pound spent eight dollars to have his first book of poems, *A Lume Spento*, printed in June, 1908, in an edition of one hundred copies. An unsigned review appearing in the May, 1909, *Book News Monthly* (collected in *Ezra Pound: The Critical Heritage*) noted, "French phrases and scraps of Latin and Greek punctuate his poetry. . . . He affects obscurity and loves the abstruse." William Carlos Williams wrote to Pound, criticizing the bitterness in the poems; Pound objected that the pieces were dramatic presentations, not personal expressions. On October 21, 1909, he responded to Williams, "It seems to me you might as well say that Shakespeare is dissolute in his plays because Falstaff is . . . or that the plays have a criminal tendency because there is murder done in them." He insisted on making a distinction between his own feelings and ideas and those presented in the poems: "I catch the character I happen to be interested in at the moment he interests me, usually a moment of song, self-analysis, or sudden understanding or revelation. I paint my man as I *conceive* him," explaining that "the sort of thing I do" is "the short so-called dramatic lyric." Pound continued to explore the possibilities of the dramatic lyric in his work, later expanding the technique into the character studies of *Homage to Sextus Propertius* and *Selwyn Mauberley* and of the countless figures who people the *Cantos.*

Pound carried copies of *A Lume Spento* to distribute when he moved to London later that year; the book convinced Elkin Mathews, a London bookseller and publisher, to bring out Pound's next works: *A Quinzaine for This Yule, Exultations* and *Personae.* Reviews of these books were generally favorable, as notices collected in *The Critical Heritage* reveal: Pound "is that rare thing among modern poets, a scholar," wrote one anonymous reviewer in the December, 1909 *Spectator,* adding that Pound has "the capacity for remarkable poetic achievement." British poet F. S. Flint wrote in a May, 1909 review in the *New Age,* "we can have no doubt as to his vitality and as to his determination to burst his way into Parnassus." Flint praised the "craft and artistry, originality and imagination" in *Personae,* although several other unsigned reviews pointed out difficulties with Pound's poems.

His first major critical work, *The Spirit of Romance,* was, Pound said, an attempt to examine "certain forces, elements or qualities which were potent in the medieval literature of the Latin tongues, and are, I believe, still potent in our own." The writers he discussed turn up again and again in his later writings: Dante, Cavalcanti, and Villon, for example. Pound contributed scores of reviews and critical articles to various periodicals such as the *New Age,* the *Egoist,* the *Little Review* and *Poetry,* where he articulated his aesthetic principles and indicated his literary, artistic, and musical preferences, thus offering information helpful for interpreting his poetry. In his introduction to the *Literary Essays of Ezra Pound,* T. S. Eliot noted, "It is necessary to read Pound's poetry to understand his criticism, and to read his criticism to understand his poetry." His criticism is important in its own right; as David Perkins pointed out in *A History of Modern Poetry,* "During a crucial decade in the history of modern literature, approximately 1912-1922, Pound was the most influential and in some ways the best critic of poetry in England or America." Eliot stated in his introduction to Pound's *Literary Essays* that Pound's literary criticism was "the most important contemporary criticism of its kind. He forced upon our attention not only individual authors, but whole areas of poetry, which no future criticism can afford to ignore."

Imagism to Vorticism

Around 1912 Pound helped to create the movement he called "Imagism," which marked the end of his early poetic style. In remarks first recorded in the March, 1913 *Poetry* and later collected in his *Literary Essays* as "A Retrospect," Pound explained his new literary direction. Imagism combined the creation of an "image"—what he defined as "an intellectual and emotional complex in an instant of time" or an "interpretative metaphor"—with rigorous requirements for writing. About these requirements, Pound was concise but insistent: "1) Direct treatment of the 'thing' whether subjective or objective 2) To use absolutely no word that did not contribute to the presentation 3) As regarding rhythm: to compose in sequence of the musical phrase, not in sequence of a metronome." These criteria meant 1) To carefully observe and describe phenomena, whether emotions, sensations, or concrete entities, and to avoid vague generalities or abstractions. Pound wanted "explicit rendering, be it of external nature or of emotion," and proclaimed "a strong disbelief in abstract and general statement as a means of conveying one's thought to others." 2) To avoid poetic diction in favor of the spoken language and to condense content, expressing it as concisely and precisely as possible. 3) To reject conventional metrical forms in favor of individualized cadence. Each poem, Pound declared, should have a rhythm "which corresponds exactly to the emotion or shade of emotion to be expressed."

The original Imagist group included just Pound, his old friend from America H. D. (Hilda Doolittle), Richard Aldington, F. S. Flint, and William Carlos Williams. American poet Amy Lowell also adopted the term, contributing one poem to the 1914 anthology *Des Imagistes,* edited by Pound. In following years, Lowell sponsored her own anthologies that Pound thought did not meet his Imagist standards; and wishing to dissociate himself from what he derisively called "Amygism," he changed the term "Image" to "Vortex," and "Imagism" to "Vorticism." Writing in the *Fortnightly Review* of September 1, 1914, Pound expanded his definition of the image: "a radiant node or cluster, it is what I can, and must perforce call a VORTEX, from which, and through which, and into which ideas are constantly rushing." As a much more comprehensive aesthetic principle, Vorticism also extended into the visual arts and music, thus including such artists as the Englishman Wyndham Lewis and Henri Gaudier-Breska, a French sculptor.

Pound's contributions to translation and his rapid critical and poetic development during the Vorticist years are reflected in *Cathay,* translations from the Chinese. In a June, 1915 review in *Outlook,* reprinted in *The Critical Heritage,* Ford Madox Ford declared it "the best work he has yet done;" the poems, of "a supreme beauty," revealed Pound's "power to express emotion . . . intact and exactly." Sinologists criticized Pound for the inaccuracies of the translations; Wai-lim Yip, in his *Ezra Pound's Cathay,* admitted, "One can easily excommunicate Pound from the Forbidden City of Chinese studies"; yet he believed that Pound conveyed "the central concerns of the original author" and that no other translation "has assumed so interesting and unique a position as *Cathay* in the history of English translations of Chinese poetry." In *The Pound Era,* Kenner pointed out that *Cathay* was an interpretation as much as a translation; the "poems paraphrase an elegiac war poetry. . . . among the most durable of all poetic responses to World War I." Perhaps the clearest assessment of Pound's achievement was made at the time by T. S. Eliot in his introduction to Pound's *Selected Poems;* he called Pound "the inventor of Chinese poetry for our time" and predicted that *Cathay* would be called a "magnificent specimen of twentieth-century poetry" rather than a translation.

Champion of Literature and Art

Another important facet of Pound's literary activity was his tireless promotion of other writers and artists. He persuaded Harriet Monroe to publish T. S. Eliot's "The Love Song of J. Alfred Prufrock," calling it in a 1914 letter to Monroe "the best poem I have yet had or seen from an American." In 1921 he edited Eliot's *The Waste Land* (published 1922), possibly the most important poem of the modernist era. In a circular (reprinted in Pound's *Letters*) for Bel Esprit, the well-intentioned but ill-fated scheme to help support artists in need, Pound described the poetic sequence of Eliot's poem as "possibly the finest that the modern movement in English has produced." Eliot in turn dedicated the poem to "Ezra Pound, *il miglior fabbro*" (the better craftsman), and in his introduction to Pound's *Selected Poems* (1928) declared, "I sincerely consider Ezra Pound the most important living poet in the English language."

Pound was also an early supporter of the Irish novelist James Joyce, arranging for the publication of several of the stories in *Dubliners* (1914) and *A Portrait of the Artist as a Young Man* (1916) in literary magazines before they were published in book form. Forrest Read, in his introduction to *Pound/Joyce: The Letters of Ezra Pound to James Joyce,* reported that Pound described Joyce to the Royal Literary Fund as "*without exception* the best of the younger prose writers." Read declared that Pound "got Joyce printed" and "at critical moments Pound was able to drum up financial support from such varied sources as the Royal Literary Fund, the Society of Authors, the British Parliament, and the New York lawyer John Quinn in order to help Joyce keep writing." Richard Sieburth in *Instigations: Ezra Pound and Remy de Gourmont* noted, "Ever concerned about the state of Joyce's health, finances, and masterpiece-in-progress, Pound prevailed upon him to quit Trieste for Paris, thus setting in motion one of the major forces that would make Paris the magnet of modernism over the next decade. When Joyce and family arrived in Paris in July, Pound was there to help them settle: he arranged for lodgings, and loans . . . and introduced Joyce . . . to the future publisher of *Ulysses* (1922), Sylvia Beach."

Other writers Pound praised while they were still relatively unknown included D. H. Lawrence, Robert Frost, H. D., and Ernest Hemingway. In his *Life of Ezra Pound,* Noel Stock recalled that in 1925, the first issue of *This Quarter* was dedicated to "Ezra Pound who by his creative work, his editorship of several magazines, his helpful friendship for young and unknown . . . comes first to our mind as meriting the gratitude of this generation." Included among the tributes to Pound was a statement of appreciation from Ernest Hemingway: "We have Pound the major poet devoting, say, one-fifth of his time to poetry. With the rest of his time he tries to advance the fortunes, both material and artistic, of his friends. He defends them when they are attacked, he gets them into magazines and out of jail. He loans them money. He sells their pictures. . . . He advances them hospital expenses and dissuades them from suicide. And in the end a few of them refrain from knifing him at the first opportunity."

In many respects, Pound's entire world collapsed with the horrors of World War I; his search for the new Renaissance foundered, and the "consequent disappointment was to colour the rest of life's works," according to Clive Wilmer in a biographical portrait on the online *Modern American Poetry.* The poems immediately following that war demonstrate his new view. *Hugh Selwyn Mauberley* refers to a fictional rather than an historical poet, as does his later *Homage to Sextus Propertius.* Yet these poems also suffered at the hands of readers who misunderstood the author's intent. In a July, 1922 letter to his former professor Felix Schelling, Pound described *Propertius* and *Mauberley* as "portraits," his rendering of sensibilities. Propertius represents the character of a Roman writer responding to his age; Mauberley, the character of a contemporary British critic-poet. Both poems were, Pound told Schelling, his attempt "to condense a James novel" and both were extended dramatic lyrics. Considered by some critics to be Pound's masterpiece, "*Mauberley* is a learned, allusive, and difficult poem, extra-ordinarily concentrated and complex," Michael Alexander observed in *The Poetic Achievement of Ezra Pound;* a central difficulty the poetic sequence presents is point of view. Most importantly, however, *Mauber-*

ley served as Pound's "farewell to London" and showed, according to Alexander, "how profoundly Pound wished to reclaim for poetry areas which the lyric tradition lost to the novel in the nineteenth century—areas of social, public, and cultural life." The poem thus points toward the work that was to occupy Pound for the remainder of his life: the *Cantos.*

To Paris: The *Cantos*

By the time Pound left London for Paris in December, 1920, he had already accomplished enough to assure himself a place of first importance in twentieth-century literature. Yet his most ambitious work, the *Cantos,* was scarcely begun. And for a time, it seemed that his long poem was stalled. He had written to Joyce in 1917, "I have begun an endless poem, of no known category . . . all about everything." His original first *Three Cantos* had been published in *Poetry* (1917) and his *Fourth Canto* in 1919. Cantos V, VI, and VII appeared in the *Dial* (1921) and *"The Eighth Canto"* appeared in 1922, but except for limited editions, no new poems appeared in book form for the next decade. *A Draft of XVI Cantos* in an edition of only ninety copies came out in Paris in 1925, and *A Draft of XXX Cantos* in 1930; but commercial editions of the first thirty *Cantos* were not published in London and New York until 1933.

The significance of Pound's undertaking was recognized early. In a 1931 review for *Hound and Horn,* reprinted in *The Critical Heritage,* Dudley Fitts called the *Cantos* "without any doubt, the most ambitious poetic conception of our day." Three decades later, in *The Cantos in England,* also reprinted in *The Critical Heritage,* Donald Hall concluded, "Pound is a great poet, and the *Cantos* are his masterwork." The long poem, however, presented innumerable difficulties to its readers. When *A Draft of XVI Cantos* appeared, William Carlos Williams lamented in a 1927 issue of the *New York Evening Post Literary Review* (reprinted in *The Critical Heritage*), "Pound has sought to communicate his poetry to us and failed. It is a tragedy, since he is our best poet." Pound himself worried: "Afraid the whole damn poem is rather obscure, especially in fragments," he wrote his father in April, 1927. With fragmentary, telescoped units of information arranged in unfamiliar ways, the *Cantos* confounded critics. Fitts summarized two common complaints: "The first of these is that the poem is incomprehensible, a perverse mystification; the second that it is structurally and melodically amorphous, not a poem, but a macaronic chaos." And George Kearns in his *Guide to Ezra Pound's Selected Cantos* warned that "a basic understanding of the poem requires a major investment of time" since if "one wants to read even a single canto, one must assemble information from a great many sources." The first major critical treatment of Pound's work, Kenner's *The Poetry of Ezra Pound* paved the way for other serious scholarly attention, and intense critical activity in recent years has produced a host of explanatory texts designed to help readers understand and evaluate the *Cantos.*

Reestablishing a poetic tradition traced from Homer's *Odyssey* and Dante's *Divine Comedy,* the *Cantos* are a modern epic. In his 1934 essay "Date Line" (in *Literary Essays of Ezra Pound*), Pound defined an epic as "a poem containing history." He further declared, in *An Introduction to the Economic Nature of the United States* (1944; reprinted in *Selected Prose, 1909-1965*), "For forty years I have schooled myself, not to write an economic history of the U.S. or any other country, but to write an epic poem which begins 'In the Dark Forest,' crosses the Purgatory of human error, and ends in the light and 'fra i maestri di color che sanno' [among the masters of those who know]." Bernstein explained that Pound's concept of an epic determined many of the characteristics of the *Cantos:* "the principle emotion aroused by an epic should be admiration for some distinguished achievement," rather than "the pity and fear aroused by tragedy." Thus, the *Cantos* are peopled with figures Pound considers heroic. Historical characters such as fifteenth-century soldier and patron of the arts Sigismundo Malatesta, Elizabethan jurist Edward Coke, Elizabeth I, John Adams, and Thomas Jefferson speak through fragments of their own writings. Embodying the ideals of personal freedom, courage, and independent thinking, they represented to Pound heroic figures whose public policies led to enlightened governing. Pound searched through the historical and mythical past as well as the modern world to find those who embodied the Confucian ideals of "sincerity" and "rectitude" in contrast to those who through greed, ignorance, and malevolence worked against the common good.

An epic also encompasses the entire known world and its learning; it is "the tale of the tribe." Thus, the *Cantos* were designed to dramatize the gradual acquisition of cultural knowledge. Pound's poem follows other epic conventions, such as beginning *in medias res* (in the middle) and including supernatural beings in the form of the classical goddesses. The structure is episodic and polyphonic, but the form is redefined to be appropriate for the modern world. Christine Froula in *A Guide to Ezra Pound's Selected Poems* suggested that Pound's poem, "in its inclusion of fragments of many cultures and many languages, its multiple historical lines, its anthropological perspectives, remains a powerfully and often movingly expressive image of the modern world. It marks the end of the old idea of the tribe as a group who participate in and share a single, closed culture, and redefines it as the human community in all its complex diversity." The *Cantos* are, thus, "truly expressive of our perpetually unfolding perception and experience."

In an often quoted letter to his father in April, 1927, Pound explained that the "outline or main scheme" of the *Cantos* is "Rather like, or unlike, subject and response and counter subject in fugue: A.A. Live man goes down into world of Dead / C.B. The 'repeat in history' / B.C. The 'magic moment' or moment of metamorphosis, bust thru from quotidien [sic] into 'divine or permanent world.' Gods., etc." In the same letter, Pound also briefly outlined the themes—the visit to the world of the dead, the repetition in history, and the moment of metamorphosis—all of which have correspondences in three texts that served as his major inspiration: Dante's *Divine Comedy*, Homer's *Odyssey*, and Ovid's *Metamorphosis*. To these models, Pound added the teachings of Confucius, historical material, and information from his immediate experience. In *The Spirit of Romance*, Pound had earlier interpreted the *Divine Comedy* both as a literal description of Dante's imagining a journey "through the realms inhabited by the spirits of the men after death" and as the journey of "Dante's intelligence through the states of mind wherein dwell all sorts and conditions of men before death." The *Cantos* also dramatize such a journey. "By no means an orderly Dantescan rising / but as the winds veer" (Canto LXXIV), the *Cantos* record a pilgrimage—an intellectual and spiritual voyage that parallels Dante's pursuit of enlightenment and Ulysses's search for his proper home. Alexander noted, "If the *Cantos* are not cast consistently in the form of a voyage of discovery, they are conducted in the spirit of such a venture, and continents or islands of knowledge, like Enlightenment America or Siena, or corners of Renaissance Italy, or China as seen via Confucianism, are explored and reported on." The journey in the *Cantos* occurs on two levels: one, a spiritual quest for transcendence, for the revelation of divine forces that lead to individual enlightenment; the other, an intellectual search for worldly wisdom, a vision of the Just City that leads to civic order and harmony. These goals, personal and public, are present throughout the poem; they also sustained the poet throughout his life.

Canto I introduces these controlling themes, presenting Odysseus's visit to the underworld, where he is to receive information from the spirits of the dead that will enable him to return home. The scene also serves as an analogy to the poet's exploration of the literature from the past in hopes of retrieving information that may be significant in his own time.

Later Cantos present historical figures such as Sigismundo Malatesta and explore the relationship between creativity in the political and literary realms. By the 1930s, Pound was writing about banking and economic systems, and incorporating into the *Cantos* his own ideas about usury, which he identified as an exploitative economic system. Froula noted that the *Cantos* was "a verbal war against economic corruption, against literal wars, against materialism, against habits of mind that permit the perpetuation of political domination. It advocates economic reform as the basis of social and cultural reform, and it could not have held aloof from political reality."

Ties to Mussolini and Fascism

Pound himself was also not aloof from political reality. In 1924, he moved to Italy with his wife, Dorothy Shakespear, and was followed closely upon by Olga Rudge, a violinist with whom he had a life-long relationship and also a daughter. In Italy, his dislike of materialism manifested itself in an admiration for Mussolini, the fascist leader of Italy. Increasingly cut off from former friends, Pound retreated, unchallenged, into his own world and beliefs, finding villains in the Jews for materialism, criticizing those in the West who he felt were warmongers. When World War II broke out, Pound stayed in Italy, though he did try to return to the U.S.A. in 1941. With the bombing of Pearl Harbor, however, he was stuck in Europe and lived in Italy during the hostilities, retaining his U.S. citizenship. From 1941 to 1943, he broadcast pro-fascist propaganda in English on Rome Radio, in rambling, sometimes incoherent commentaries that often attacked Roosevelt and the Jewish bankers whom Pound held responsible for the war. "As his paranoia increased," wrote Flory, "what had been denunciations of bankers became anti-Semitic allegations about a Jewish plot to undermine gentile culture."

By 1943 the U.S. government deemed the broadcasts to be treasonous; at war's end the poet was arrested by the U.S. Army and kept imprisoned in a small, outdoor wire cage at a compound near Pisa, Italy. For several weeks during that hot summer, Pound was confined to the cage. At night floodlights lit his prison. Eventually judged to be mentally incompetent to stand trial, Pound was incarcerated in St. Elizabeth's Hospital in Washington, D.C. Ironically, while imprisoned by the army in Italy, Pound completed *The Pisan Cantos*, a group of poems that have been called among the masterpieces of this century. The poems won him the Bollingen Prize in 1949. The Library of Congress panel, which awarded the prize, felt that to allow other considerations than artistic merit to change the opinion of the committee would go counter to the spirit of the prize; up to that point *The Pisan Cantos* had earned mostly positive reviews with no critic hinting at anti-Semitic innuendoes in the verses. However, the conferring of this award also rekindled the old arguments and enmity about Pound's wartime collusion with the Italians. Critics on both sides argued the merits of *The Pisan Cantos*, some finding genius in them, others condemning the verses as a sham and anti-Semitic. The *Saturday Review* "mounted an anti-Pound and anti-T.S. Eliot campaign," according to Flory, "which soon turned into a broad-based and acrimonious controversy. Robert Hilyer's *Saturday Review* articles drew strong protest, and [the poet] John Berryman circulated a petition protesting them. Eighty-four critics and writers signed this petition, and after the *Saturday Review* refused to publish it, it appeared in the *Nation.*"

While the controversy raged outside, Pound adjusted to his hospital imprisonment, complying with all the routines. He was moved to a ward where the inmates were not the criminally insane, and allowed to have visitors. He spent over a decade incarcerated; meanwhile friends and supporters including Archibald MacLeish, T. S. Eliot, Ernest Hemingway, and Robert Frost, were working to secure his release from St. Elizabeth's, which finally came in 1958. Writing over forty years later in *World Literature Today* in a review of Pound's *Letters in Captivity, 1945-1946*, William Pratt noted that the "controversy still goes on over Pound's exact mental condition during his thirteen years of imprisonment in an insane asylum, and especially over the award of the Bollingen Prize for Poetry to him . . . while he was there. But it is clear from the notes in *Letters in Captivity* that he received the appropriate punishment for his rash abuse of American freedom of speech. Archibald MacLeish . . . wrote Ernest Hemingway as early as 1943: 'Poor old Ezra! Treason is a little too serious and too dignified a crime for a man who has made such an incredible ass of himself, and accomplished so little in the process.'" Pratt further pointed out that it is clear in Pound's letters of the time that he did not, as his lawyer and psychiatrists maintained, understand the charges brought against him.

After his release, Pound returned to Italy, where he lived quietly for the rest of his life. In 1969 *Drafts and Fragments of Cantos CX-CXVII* appeared, including the despairing lines: "My errors and wrecks lie about me / . . . I cannot make it cohere." Speaking to Donald Hall, Pound described his *Cantos* as a "botch. . . . I picked out this and that thing that interested me, and then jumbled them into a bag. But

that's not the way to make a *work of art*." Poet Allen Ginsberg reported in *Allen Verbatim: Lectures on Poetry, Politics, Consciousness* that Pound had "felt that the Cantos were 'stupidity and ignorance all the way through,' and were a failure and a 'mess.'" Ginsberg responded that the *Cantos* "were an accurate representation of his mind and so couldn't be thought of in terms of success or failure, but only in terms of the actuality of their representation, and that since for the first time a human being had taken the whole spiritual world of thought through fifty years and followed the thoughts out to the end—so that he built a model of his consciousness over a fifty-year time span—that they were a great human achievement."

Pound's Legacy

Pound's health began to fail soon after returning to Italy, living with Rudge in a house in Venice. His last decade was spent in silence, rarely speaking with anyone. Pound died in November of 1972; he was buried in his beloved Italy, on the island of San Giorgio Maggiore. In the years since his death, scholarly examination of his works have continued unabated. Several works of primary scholarship have been released, including several letter collections that trace both Pound's career and the evolution of his poetic achievements. *A Walking Tour in Southern France: Ezra Pound among the Troubadors* provides Pound scholars with the poet's notes regarding his 1912 walking trip through Provence, a landscape and cultural arena that would influence his later *Cantos.* Edited letter collections include correspondence with poets William Carlos Williams and E. E. Cummings, political ruminations with U.S. Senator Bronson Cutting, and *The Letters of Ezra Pound to Alice Corbin Henderson*, which details the working relationship between Pound and *Poetry* editor over a thirty-seven-year period.

In August of 1933 Pound, living in Italy and at work on his *Cantos*, had received a letter from a young Harvard student. The student, James Laughlin, came to visit the poet in Rapallo, sparking a correspondence that would span the remainder of the poet's life and Laughlin's own rise to founder of New Directions Press, Pound's U.S. publisher. Partially collected in 1994 as *Ezra Pound and James Laughlin: Selected Letters*, the written correspondence between these two friends was vast, numbering more than twenty-seven hundred items. Some were written from Rapallo, where the poet battled with his muse, while others were written during Pound's tenure in St. Elizabeth's, as his battle grew more inward; forbidden most correspondence as one of the terms of his punishment, Pound's letters to Laugh-

If you enjoy the works of Ezra Pound, you might want to check out the following:

The poetry of T. S. Eliot, particularly *The Wasteland* and "The Love Song of J. Alfred Prufrock."

The short stories of Irish author James Joyce, such as those found in *Dubliners.*

The works of Imagist poets Richard Aldington, H. D. (Hilda Dolittle), F. S. Flint, and William Carlos Williams.

lin were smuggled out in his wife's handbag on the days of her visits. Through the letters, noted Rockwell Gray in the *Chicago Tribune,* "Pound reminds us how much language shares with music. . . . Under the showy surface, however, the extra-poetic Pound reveals an all too human concern with vanity wounded by questions of publication, remuneration and reputation. Through it all runs a sense of alienation from a native land he needed to whip, presumably for its own good. Such themes—along with Pound's tiresome crusade against usury and modern capitalism—bedeviled his gifted mind." Pound's energetic, imagistic letters can be seen as yet unrefined cantos in themselves: "In fact," noted Donald E. Herdeck in *Bloomsbury Review,* "the Cantos are Ezra L. Pound's letters to all of us—the rant, the stubbornness, the pith and humor of the Cantos are here, as first drafts, or widening ripples of the life that became the *Cantos.*" Through his vast outpouring of creative work: poetry, translation, editorships, prose, letters, Pound fulfilled the requirement for a poet that he had set for himself in his *Selected Prose, 1909-1965:* "The essential thing about a poet is that he build us his world."

■ Biographical and Critical Sources

BOOKS

Albright, Daniel, *Quantum Poetics: Yeats, Pound, Eliot, and the Science of Modernism,* Cambridge University Press (New York, NY), 1997.

Alexander, Michael, *The Poetic Achievement of Ezra Pound,* University of California Press (Berkeley, CA), 1979.

Bernstein, Michael, *The Tale of the Tribe: Ezra Pound and the Modern Verse Epic,* Princeton University Press (Princeton, NJ), 1980.

Carson, Luke, *Consumption and Depression in Gertrude Stein, Louis Zukofsky, and Ezra Pound,* St. Martin's Press (New York, NY), 1998.

Cheadle, Mary Paterson, *Ezra Pound's Confucian Translations,* University of Michigan Press (Ann Arbor, MI), 1997.

Comens, Bruce, *Apocalypse and After: Modern Strategy and Postmodern Tactics in Pound, Williams, and Zukofsky,* University of Alabama Press (Tuscaloosa, AL), 1995.

Concise Dictionary of American Literary Biography: The Twenties, 1917-1929, Gale (Detroit, MI), 1989.

Conover, Anne, *Olga Rudge and Ezra Pound: "That Thou Lovest Well. . . .",* Yale University Press (New Haven, CT), 2002.

Contemporary Literary Criticism, Gale (Detroit, MI), Volume 1, 1973, Volume 2, 1974, Volume 3, 1975, Volume 4, 1976, Volume 5, 1976, Volume 7, 1977, Volume 10, 1979, Volume 13, 1980, Volume 18, 1981, Volume 34, 1985, Volume 48, 1988, Volume 50, 1988.

Coyle, Michael, *Ezra Pound: Popular Genres, and the Discourse of Culture,* Pennsylvania State University Press (University Park, PA), 1995.

Dennis, Helen May, *A New Approach to the Poetry of Ezra Pound,* Mellen, 1996.

Dictionary of Literary Biography, Gale (Detroit, MI), Volume 4: *American Writers in Paris, 1920-1939,* 1980, Volume 45: *American Poets, 1880-1945, First Series,* 1986, pp. 305-343, Volume 63: *Modern American Critics, 1920-1955,* 1988.

Eliot, T. S., *Ezra Pound: His Metric and Poetry,* Knopf (New York, NY), 1917.

Emig, Rainer, *Modernism in Poetry: Motivation, Structures, and Limits,* Longman (London, England), 1996.

Findley, Timothy, *The Trials of Ezra Pound,* Blizzard, 1994.

Froula, Christine, *A Guide to Ezra Pound's Selected Poems,* New Directions (New York, NY), 1982.

Gibson, Mary Ellis, *Epic Reinvented: Ezra Pound and the Victorians,* Cornell University Press (Ithaca, NY), 1995.

Ginsberg, Allen, *Allen Verbatim: Lectures on Poetry, Politics, Consciousness,* McGraw (New York, NY), 1975.

Grieve, Thomas F., *Ezra Pound's Early Poetry and Poetics,* University of Missouri Press (Columbia, MO), 1997.

Hall, Donald, *Remembering Poets,* Harper (New York, NY), 1978.

Homberger, Eric, editor, *Ezra Pound: The Critical Heritage,* Routledge & Kegan Paul, 1972.

Howe, Elisabeth A., *The Dramatic Monologue,* Twayne Publishers (Boston, MA), 1996.

Hsieh, Ming, *Ezra Pound and the Appropriation of Chinese Poetry: Cathay, Translation, and Imagism*, Garland (New York, NY), 1998.

Joseph, Terri Brint, *Ezra Pound's Epic Variations: The Cantos and Major Long Poems*, University of Maine (Orono, ME), 1995.

Kearns, George, *Guide to Ezra Pound's Selected Cantos*, Rutgers University Press (Piscataway, NJ), 1980.

Kenner, Hugh, *The Poetry of Ezra Pound*, New Directions (New York, NY), 1950.

Kenner, Hugh, *The Pound Era*, University of California Press (Berkeley, CA), 1971.

Knapp, James F., *Ezra Pound*, Twayne (New York, NY), 1979.

Kyburz, Mark, *Voi Altri Pochi: Ezra Pound and His Audience*, Birkhauser Verlag, 1996.

Morrison, Paul, *The Poetics of Fascism: Ezra Pound, T. S. Eliot, Paul de Man*, Oxford University Press (New York, NY), 1996.

Perelman, Bob, *The Trouble with Genius: Reading Pound, Joyce, Stein, and Zukofsky*, University of California Press (Berkeley, CA), 1994.

Perkins, David, *A History of Modern Poetry: From the 1890's to the High Modernist Mode*, Harvard University Press (Cambridge, MA), 1976.

Perloff, Marjorie, *The Dance of the Intellect: Studies in the Poetry of the Pound Tradition*, Northwestern University Press (Evanston, IL), 1996.

Poetry Criticism, Volume 4, Gale (Detroit, MI), 1992.

Pound, Ezra, *Drafts and Fragments: Cantos CX-CXVII*, New Directions (New York, NY), 1968.

Pound, Ezra, *Literary Essays of Ezra Pound*, edited and with an introduction by T. S. Eliot, New Directions (New York, NY), 1954.

Pound, Ezra, *Pound/Joyce: The Letters of Ezra Pound to James Joyce*, edited by Forrest Read, New Directions (New York, NY), 1967.

Pound, Ezra, *Selected Poems*, edited and with an introduction by T. S. Eliot, Faber & Gwyer (London, England), 1928, Laughlin, 1957.

Pound, Ezra, *Selected Prose, 1909-1965*, edited by William Cookson, New Directions (New York, NY), 1973.

Pound, Ezra, *The Spirit of Romance*, Dent (London, England), 1910, New Directions (New York, NY), 1952, revised edition, P. Owen (London, England), 1953.

Qian, Zhaoming, *Orientalism and Modernism: The Legacy of China in Pound and Williams*, Duke University Press (Durham, NC), 1995.

Rae, Patricia, *The Practical Muse: Pragmatist Poetics in Hulme, Pound, and Stevens*, Bucknell University Press (Lewisburg, PA), 1997.

Shioji, Ursula, *Ezra Pound's Pisan Cantos and the Noh*, P. Lang (New York, NY), 1998.

Sieburth, Richard, *Instigations: Ezra Pound and Remy de Gourmont*, Harvard University Press (Cambridge, MA), 1978.

Singh, G., *Ezra Pound as Critic*, St. Martin's Press (New York, NY), 1994.

Stock, Noel, *The Life of Ezra Pound*, Pantheon (New York, NY), 1970.

Stoicheff, Peter, *The Hall of Mirrors : Drafts & Fragments and the End of Ezra Pound's Cantos*, University of Michigan Press (Ann Arbor, MI), 1995.

Sutton, Walter, editor, *Pound, Thayer, Watson, and the Dial: A Story in Letters*, University Press of Florida (Gainesville, FL), 1994.

Tiffany, Daniel, *Radio Corpse: Imagism and the Cryptaesthetic of Ezra Pound*, Harvard University Press (Cambridge, MA), 1995.

Whittier-Feruson, John, *Framing Pieces: Designs of the Gloss in Joyce, Woolf, and Pound*, Oxford University Press (New York, NY), 1996.

Wilhelm, James J., *Ezra Pound: The Tragic Years, 1925-1972*, Pennsylvania State University Press (University Park, PA), 1994.

Wilson, Peter, *A Preface to Ezra Pound*, Longman (London, England), 1996.

World Literature Criticism, Gale (Detroit, MI), 1992.

Yip, Wai-lim, *Ezra Pound's Cathay*, Princeton University Press (Princeton, NJ), 1969.

PERIODICALS

American Journal of Psychotherapy, winter, 2000, Frederic Wertham, "The Road to Rapallo: A Psychiatric Study," pp. 102-115.

Atlantic Monthly, January, 1993, p. 127.

Bloomsbury Review, May, 1995, Donald E. Herdeck, review of *Ezra Pound and James Laughlin: Selected Letters*, p. 29.

Journal of Modern Literature, summer, 2000, pp. 535-545.

London Review of Books, January 26, 1995, p. 20.

Los Angeles Times Book Review, March 31, 1996, p. 2.

Newsweek, November 13, 1972.

New Yorker, August 15, 1994, p. 79.

New York Times, July 9, 1972; November 2, 1972; November 4, 1972; November 5, 1972.

New York Times Book Review, March 20, 1994, p. 18.

Parnassus, Volume 20, 1995, p. 55.

Publishers Weekly, November 13, 1972; January 31, 1994, p. 72; April 25, 1994, p. 62; January 15, 1996, p. 451.

Smithsonian, December, 1995, p. 112.

Time, November 13, 1972.

Times Literary Supplement, February 7, 1992, p. 7; June 26, 1992, p. 23.

Tribune Books (Chicago, IL), August 14, 1994, Rockwell Gray, review of *Ezra Pound and James Laughlin: Selected Letters*, p. 5.

World Literature Today, autumn, 2000, William Pratt, review of *Letters in Captivity, 1945-1946*, p. 828.

Writer's Digest, February, 1996, p. 12.

OTHER

Academy of American Poets, http://www.poets.org/ (April 10, 2002), "Ezra Pound."

Ezra Pound, http://www.lit.kobe-u.ac.jp/ (April 10, 2002).

Modern American Poetry: Ezra Pound, http://www.english.uiuc.edu/ (April 10, 2002), Clive Wilmer, "Pound's Life and Career."*

Pam Muñoz Ryan

■ Personal

Born in Bakersfield, CA; daughter of Don Bell and Esperanza Muñoz; married; children: four.

■ Addresses

Home—Leucadia, CA. *Agent*—c/o Author Mail, Scholastic, Inc., 555 Broadway, New York, NY 10012.

■ Career

Children's book author. Formerly worked as a teacher and administrator.

■ Awards, Honors

Early Childhood News Director's Choice Award, and National Council for the Social Studies (NCSS)/ Children's Book Council (CBC) Notable Children's Trade Book, both 1997, both for *The Flag We Love;* Children's Choice, International Reading Association (IRA)/CBC, 1997, for *The Crayon Counting Book;* Pick of the List, *American Bookseller*, Bank Street Best Books of 1998, and IRA/CBC Children's Choice, all for *A Pinky Is a Baby Mouse;* Reading Magic Award, *Parenting*, Most Outstanding Books, 1998, Teachers Choice Award, National Willa Cather Award for Best Young Adult Novel, and Southern California Center for Literature for Young People Award of Merit, all 1999, and California Young Reader Medal, and Arizona Young Reader's Award, both 2000, all for *Riding Freedom;* Pick of the List, *American Bookseller*, Best Children's Book list, New York Public Library, Reading Magic Award, *Parenting Magazine*, ALA Notable Book, and IRA Teacher's Choice Award, all 1999, and Oppenheim Platinum Award, Best Book of the Year list, *Los Angeles Times*, and Notable Social Studies Trade Book for Young People, all 2000, all for *Amelia and Eleanor Go for a Ride;* Best Book list, *Los Angeles Times*, Best Books, *Smithsonian*, and Best Children's Books, *Publishers Weekly*, all 2000, and Jane Addams Children's Book Award, Women's International League for Peace and Freedom, Excellence in a Work of Fiction Award, Children's Literature Council of Southern California, Top Ten Best Books for Young Adults, ALA, Judy Goddard/Libraries Limited Arizona Young Adult Author Award, and Pura Belpre Award, all 2001, all for *Esperanza Rising*.

■ Writings

FOR YOUNG READERS

One Hundred Is a Family, illustrated by Benrei Huang, Hyperion Books (New York, NY), 1994.

(With Jerry Pallotta) *The Crayon Counting Board Book*, illustrated by Frank Mazzola, Jr., Charlesbridge (Watertown, MA), 1996.

The Flag We Love, illustrated by Frank Masiello, Charlesbridge (Watertown, MA), 1996.

Armadillos Sleep in Dugouts: And Other Places Animals Live, illustrated by Diane de Groat, Hyperion Books (New York, NY), 1997.

Pinky Is a Baby Mouse: And Other Baby Animal Names, illustrated by Diane de Grout, Hyperion Books (New York, NY), 1997.

California, Here We Come!, illustrated by Kay Salem, Charlesbridge (Watertown, MA), 1997.

Riding Freedom (novel), illustrated by Brian Selznick, Scholastic Press (New York, NY), 1998.

Amelia and Eleanor Go for a Ride, illustrated by Brian Selznick, Scholastic Press (New York, NY), 1999.

Esperanza Rising (novel), Scholastic Press (New York, NY), 2000.

Hello, Ocean, illustrated by Mark Astrella, Charlesbridge (Watertown, MA), 2001.

Mice and Beans, illustrated by Joe Cepeda, Scholastic Press (New York, NY), 2001.

Mud Is Cake, illustrated by David McPhail, Hyperion Books (New York, NY), 2002.

How Do You Raise a Raisin?, illustrated by Craig Brown, Charlesbridge (Watertown, MA), 2002.

When Marian Sang: The True Recital of Marian Anderson, illustrated by Brian Selznick, Scholastic Press (New York, NY), 2002.

"DOUG" SERIES; BASED ON JIM JENKINS'S CARTOON CHARACTER

Doug Counts Down, illustrated by Matthew C. Peters, Disney Press (New York, NY), 1998.

Doug's Treasure Hunt, illustrated by Jumbo Pictures, Disney Press (New York, NY), 1998.

Funnie Family Vacation, illustrated by William Presing and Tony Curanaj, Disney Press (New York, NY), 1999.

OTHER

Several of Ryan's books have been translated into Spanish.

■ **Sidelights**

An award-winning author of picture books, Pam Muñoz Ryan blends colorful rhyme as well as concise texts in her books that deal with concepts, such as *One Hundred Is a Family* and *The Crayon Counting Book*, with natural history in *A Pinky Is a Baby Mouse*, *Armadillos Sleep in Dugouts*, and *Hello, Ocean*, with culture and history in *California, Here We Come!*, *The Flag We Love*, and *Amelia and Eleanor Go for a Ride*, and with family matters in *Mice and Beans* and *Mud Is a Cake*. Ryan has also penned two juvenile novels, *Riding Freedom* and *Esperanza Rising*, which feature strong female protagonists confronting life on their own terms. "I have written books for adults, picture books for children, and recently I completed my first novel for older students," Ryan noted on the *Scholastic Authors Online* Web site. "Maybe it's the teacher in me, but I want to make sure children everywhere are excited about reading, so I visit schools and go to conferences to speak about reading and literacy. I want kids to be hooked on reading and books, like I was."

"I was born and raised in California's San Joaquin Valley," Ryan noted in an autobiographical sketch for the *Scholastic* Web site. "I grew up with aunts, uncles and grandparents nearby and consider myself truly American because my heritage is part Spanish, Mexican, Basque, Italian, and Oklahoman. My grandparents on my mother's side came to the U.S. from Mexico in the 1930s." Ryan grew up in a large extended family, as she also remarked in her sketch. "I am the oldest of three sisters and the oldest of twenty-three cousins on my mother's side, so many of my childhood memories revolve around big, noisy family gatherings."

A strong influence on the young Ryan was her maternal grandmother, Esperanza Ortega. "I can still see my grandmother crocheting blankets in zigzag rows," Ryan wrote in the author's note to her year 2000 novel, *Esperanza Rising*. "She made one for each of her seven children, many for her twenty-three grandchildren . . . and for the great-grandchildren she lived to see." Ryan's grandmother would tell her stories of what it was like to come as a young girl to the United States in 1930s from Mexico, leaving her old life of wealth and grandeur for the harsh realities of life in a labor camp. It was in that same labor camp where Ryan's own mother was born.

Equally, Ryan's childhood memories revolve around books and reading. "Growing up, I spent many long, hot valley summers riding my bike to the library. The library became my favorite hangout because my family didn't have a swimming pool and the library was air-conditioned. That's how I got hooked on reading and books." In an interview with Scholastic's *Authors Online*, Ryan further commented, "I always loved books. I didn't know when I was a young child that I could be an author, because when I went to school we didn't do the great writing activities kids do in school today. I never had an author visit my school, so I didn't know it was something I could be when I grew up."

Ryan did the next best thing to writing after she graduated from college: she went into teaching to share her joy of reading. After teaching for some time and having four children and then returning to the university for a master's degree and working for some time in school administration, Ryan finally hit on her real career. "A friend encouraged me to write a book myself, and that's when I discovered what I really wanted to do with my life. Today, I am a full-time writer and I still spend a lot of time at the library. When I start a new book, if it is non-fiction or historical fiction, the first thing I do is go to the library for research."

A Beginning with Picture Books

Not surprisingly, when Ryan turned her hand to creating children's books she used families as an inspiration. *One Hundred Is a Family* is a concept book that introduces the numbers from one to ten by groups making up many different families. Ryan then extends this concept to count by tens to one hundred, still employing the family grouping in a celebration of its ever-widening circles of community, relationship, and friendship. Reviewing this debut title in *Publishers Weekly,* a contributor noted that the "politically correct concept" at the heart of the book was that family was not just about parents and children, but that "every one on earth" can be a family "caring for the fragile universe." The same critic felt that *One Hundred Is a Family* "rates high

Amelia was Amelia Earhart, the celebrated aviator who had been the first female pilot to fly solo across the Atlantic Ocean. And when two of the most famous and adventurous women in the world got together, something exciting was bound to happen.

In *Amelia and Eleanor Go for a Ride,* Pam Muñoz Ryan recounts the night in 1933 when ace pilot Amelia Earhart flew First Lady Eleanor Roosevelt over the U.S. capitol and the two toured Washington, D.C., in Roosevelt's new car.

on jolliness if low on subtlety." Annie Ayres, writing in *Booklist,* however found the book "comforting," because it "presents and embraces a world in which every form of family is welcome," both traditional and nontraditional." Ryan has noted that this first picture book is still her favorite. As she commented in her interview for *Authors Online,* "it talks about diverse families, not just Mom, Dad, and two and a half kids and a dog families."

A different sort of inspiration fueled her next picture book, *The Flag We Love.* One Memorial Day weekend she saw a flag being used to cover some cases of beer in a local grocery store. This misuse offended her and a letter to the storeowner was not enough. She discovered that there were no picture books dealing with the flag to share with her own young children, so she decided to write one herself. "Sometimes for a writer," Ryan noted on *Authors Online,* "the best inspiration of all is to realize that you might have an idea for a story that no one has done before." In the resulting book, Ryan blended patriotic verse with the artwork of Ralph Masiello to present a lyrical journey through the history of the Stars and Stripes. Ryan chose both momentous and everyday moments to commemorate this symbol of our nation, from the flying of the flag at Lincoln's funeral to the initial moon landing. "There's no hint of controversy here," wrote *Booklist*'s Carolyn Phelan, "just a bit of flag waving to celebrate the history of the Stars and Stripes." A reviewer for *Publishers Weekly* felt that the book should "delight Yankee Doodle dandies everywhere, and could help spark discussion on the basic elements of democracy."

More counting is served up in *The Crayon Counting Book,* "a high-tech approach to a low-tech subject," according to a contributor for *Publishers Weekly,* in which computer-generated crayons are featured in a "surprisingly animated" counting book. Ryan presents a rhyming text that counts by twos, first with even numbers and then with odd numbers. Ryan noted on her author Web site that she "used as many synonyms for the word 'two' as I could squeeze into the text." She also employed a hodge-podge of funny names for the crayons themselves, from iris to fiddlehead to jezabel. The *Publishers Weekly* contributor called this picture book "slight" but "colorful."

More picture books followed, including *A Pinky Is a Baby Mouse* and *Armadillos Sleep in Dugouts,* both with illustrations by Diane de Groat, and *California, Here We Come!,* with artwork by Kay Salem. *A Pinky* is a book that introduces children to the correct though little-known names of over a hundred new-

born animals, and was inspired by the world famous San Diego Zoo, close to where Ryan lives. A member of the San Diego Zoological Society, the author once read in their monthly bulletin that a baby spiny anteater is actually called a puggle. "When I saw that one word a light bulb went off in my brain," wrote Ryan on her Web site. "It occurred to me that there must be other cute, legitimate baby animal names." Researching the topic, she came up with a list, not only from the San Diego Zoo, but also from the Bug Zoo in Los Angeles, Scripps Institute of Oceanography, and even the Adelaide Zoo in Australia. *California, Here We Come!,* on the other hand, was commissioned by her publishers. "I agreed enthusiastically, because the more I traveled, the more I realized that many people have peculiar misconceptions about California," Ryan noted on her author Web site. Researching this title, she came up with a plethora of little known facts about her native state, which she integrated into a picture book for older readers. During the research for this book she hit on a topic that would inspire her first novel for younger readers.

Of Novels and Picture Books

Riding Freedom is a historical novel that features Charlotte Parkhurst, a woman who lived her life disguised as a man and ultimately became a stagecoach driver in California. Dubbed One-Eyed Charley in real life, Parkhurst found that being considered a man made life easier for her in the mid-nineteenth century West. Ryan first saw this material as a nonfiction picture book, but her editor at Scholastic thought the novel format would be better suited to the story. "Just relying on the facts alone, I couldn't have asked for a better 'bare bones' outline," Ryan noted on her Web site. "An orphan runs away and in order to survive, poses as a stable boy only to become a renowned stagecoach driver! She then is recruited to California during the Gold Rush, and even after losing the sight in one eye, continues driving stages successfully and still posed as a man, goes on to vote in a federal election fifty-two years before any woman." Ryan filled in some of the empty spaces in the life of Parkhurst, supplying how she might have become an orphan and the vile situation at the orphanage that forced her to run away at age twelve. Another fictionalized element is the friend who helped train her to drive stages. The resulting book was praised by critics and lauded by awards committees. *Booklist*'s Hazel Rochman dubbed the effort a "lively historical novel," and further noted that middle-schoolers "will love the horse adventures and the stories of [Parkhurst's] trickery," while a reviewer for *Publish-*

A wealthy young Mexican girl flees with her mother to the United States to avoid violence, only to find themselves living the lives of migrant workers in the midst of the Great Depression.

ers Weekly commented, "With a pacing that moves along at a gallop, this is a skillful execution of a fascinating historical tale."

The exploits of another daring female are recounted in the picture book *Amelia and Eleanor Go for a Ride,* a fictionalized account of the night that the aviatrix Amelia Earhart flew Eleanor Roosevelt over Washington, D.C., only to have the favor returned by the First Lady when she later drove Amelia around the city in her fast new car. Adapting freely from an actual episode in 1933, Ryan created a "sparkling picture book," according to a contributor for *Publishers Weekly.* "Ryan's inviting text adds drama and draws parallels between the two protagonists with fictional touches," the same reviewer added, concluding, "A brief but compelling slice from the lives of two determined, outspoken and passionate women." *Booklist*'s Ilene Cooper has similar praise for the book, despite the fact that in reality Roosevelt and

Earhart were accompanied by two male pilots on their flight, a fact Cooper felt that young readers might miss in Ryan's notes. However, Cooper concluded that both Ryan and her illustrator Brian Selznick "clearly did their research; and one of the book's chief attributes is its depiction, in both words and pictures, of two strong women—really pioneers."

Ryan returned to the novel for a book inspired by her grandmother's immigrant experiences. *Esperanza Flying* tells the story of young Esperanza Ortega who, at her home in Aguascaliente, Mexico, has all the luxury and pampering a rich girl could want. Servants and fancy dresses are the usual thing for her, until her father is murdered by bandits and his stepbrothers hold Esperanza's mother virtual hostage, demanding that she re-marry one of them. To let her know they are serious, they even burn down the family home. It is then that Esperanza's mother decides to flee to the United States with the cook and gardener in search of a new life. With daughter in tow, they move to California in the midst of the Great Depression only to join the hordes of others displaced during these years, working as field laborers and living in a labor camp. Esperanza, accustomed to being treated like a little princess, must adapt to these new and harsh conditions. "Set against he multiethnic, labor-organizing era of the Depression, the story of Esperanza remaking herself is satisfyingly complete," wrote Francisca Goldsmith in *School Library Journal.* Goldsmith further remarked that "this well-written novel belongs in all collections." Lynne T. Burke, reviewing the novel in *Reading Today,* had similar praise: "Written with an uncommon understanding of the plight of Mexican farm workers, this passionate novel gives a human face to an issue." A critic for *Publishers Weekly* lauded the "lyrical, fairy-tale style" of narration in this "robust novel." The same reviewer further felt that "Ryan poetically conveys Esperanza's ties to the land by crafting her story to the rhythms of the seasons." And though *Booklist*'s Gillian Engberg sometimes had difficulty with the "heavy-handed" symbolism in the book, she felt that Ryan "writes movingly in clear, poetic language that children will sink into, and the book offers excellent opportunities for discussion." Among numerous awards and honors, *Esperanza Rising* secured for Ryan the Pura Belpre award, honoring Latino authors whose work portrays, affirms, and celebrates the Latino cultural experience in a children's book.

Other picture books from Ryan include *Hello, Ocean, Mice and Beans,* and *Mud Is Cake.* In the first title, Ryan describes in rhyming couplet a young girl's journey of discovery at the seashore through each of her five senses, while in *Mice and Beans* the author tells a more earthy cumulative tale of a Rosa Maria who takes a week to prepare for her granddaughter's birthday to be held in her little house. She sets traps all around for the mice that also call her house home, not wanting them to feast on the food meant for Little Catalina and her friends. Each evening she checks her traps, and each evening finds they have disappeared. Thinking she is merely forgetful, she sets more. Then the day of the party she forgets to fill the pinata with candy, or so she thinks. The children break it open and are showered in candy. Later Rosa Maria discovers that the mice have been at work, filling the pinata for her, and decides that a house full of mice is not so bad after all. "Kindheartedness lies at the cores of this story," noted a contributor for *Kirkus Reviews*. *Booklist*'s Kelly Milner Halls also found the story "charming"; what was especially effective for Halls was "the quiet authenticity of the Hispanic characterizations." "A treat for young listeners," declared *School Library Journal*'s Mary Elam. With *Mud Is Cake*, Ryan tells the tale of a brother and sister who discover that they can turn mud into cake by using their imaginations. In fact, anything is possible on a rainy day if you can pretend. A reviewer for *Publishers Weekly* found this tale "winsome," and its "gentle tone—and dream-inspiring potential—makes it a fine choice for lazy rainy days and bedtime."

If you enjoy the works of Pam Muñoz Ryan, you might want to check out the following books:

John Steinbeck, *The Grapes of Wrath*, 1939.
Sharon Creech, *Walk Two Moons*, 1994.
Mildred D. Taylor, *The Land*, 2001.

Being a full-time writer is something that has both its advantages and disadvantages, as Ryan explained in her interview for *Authors Online*: "The part of my job that's different [from most] is that I don't go somewhere else every day and work with a bunch of other people who do the same thing I do. Teachers have a staff room, and office workers have an employee lounge, and something that I miss is not being able to talk to other people every day about my job. My job is pretty solitary most of the time. I mostly write in the mornings, and I'm usually pretty disciplined about research and writing, especially when I have a deadline! My job is like having one book report or term paper after another. But there are some fun parts of the job, too. I get to travel, and when I travel to conferences I get to meet other writers and illustrators. Sometimes I go to schools and get to speak with children in person. The best part of my job is that I get to work in my slippers."

■ Biographical and Critical Sources

BOOKS

Ryan, Pam Muñoz, *Esperanza Rising*, Scholastic Press (New York, NY), 2000.

PERIODICALS

Booklist, November 1, 1994, Annie Ayres, review of *One Hundred Is a Family*, p. 509; January 1, 1996, Carolyn Phelan, review of *The Flag We Love*, p. 841; January 1, 1998, Hazel Rochman, review of *Riding Freedom*, pp. 814-815; October 15, 1999, Ilene Cooper, review of *Amelia and Eleanor Go for a Ride*, p. 447; December 1, 2000, Gillian Engberg, review of *Esperanza Rising*, p. 708; September 15, 2001, Kelly Milner Halls, review of *Mice and Beans*, p. 233; November 1, 2001, p. 493; February 15, 2002, p. 1022.
Childhood Education, spring, 2002, pp. 173-174.
Horn Book, January-February, 2001, review of *Esperanza Rising*, p. 96; November-December, 2001, pp. 778-779.
Instructor, October, 2001, p. 318.
Journal of Adolescent and Adult Literacy, December, 2001, pp. 334-335.
Kirkus Reviews, August 1, 2001, review of *Mice and Beans*, p. 1131.
New York Times Book Review, January 1, 1995, p. 15.
Publishers Weekly, November 7, 1994, review of *One Hundred Is a Family*, p. 78; February 5, 1996, review of *The Flag We Love*, p. 88; August 26, 1996, review of *The Crayon Counting Book*, p. 96; February 2, 1998, review of *Riding Freedom*, p. 91; September 20, 1999, p. 90; September 27, 1999, review of *Amelia and Eleanor Go for a Ride*, p. 105; October 9, 2000, review of *Esperanza Rising*, p. 88; January 8, 2001, review of *Hello, Ocean*, p. 65; February 18, 2002, review of *Mud Is Cake*, p. 94.

Reading Today, October, 2000, Lynne T. Burke, review of *Esperanza Rising,* p. 32.

School Library Journal, October, 2000, Francisca Goldsmith, review of *Esperanza Rising,* p. 171; May, 2001, Sally R. Dow, review of *Hello, Ocean,* p. 133; October, 2001, Mary Elam, review of *Mice and Beans,* p. 130.

OTHER

Pam Muñoz Ryan: Children's Author, http://pammunozryan.com/ (April 10, 2002).

Scholastic Authors Online, http://teacher.scholastic.com/ (April 10, 2002), "Pam Muñoz Ryan's Interview Transcript"; (April 15, 2002), "Meet Pam Muñoz Ryan."*

—*Sketch by J. Sydney Jones*

David Sedaris

■ Personal

Surname pronounced "seh-*dar*-iss"; born 1957, in Raleigh, NC; partner of Hugh Hamrick (a painter). *Education:* School of the Art Institute of Chicago, received degree, 1987.

■ Addresses

Home—New York, NY; Paris, France; and Normandy, France. *Agent*—Steven Barclay, 321 Pleasant St., Petaluma, CA 94952.

■ Career

Diarist, radio commentator, essayist, and short story writer. Worked variously as a moving company worker, an office worker, an elf in SantaLand at Macy's department store, and an apartment cleaner. Has taught writing at School of the Art Institute of Chicago.

■ Writings

Origins of the Underclass, and Other Stories, Amethyst Press (Washington, DC), 1992.

Barrel Fever: Stories and Essays, Little, Brown (Boston, MA), 1994.

The SantaLand Diaries (play), produced off-Broadway at the Atlantic Theater, New York, NY, 1996.

Naked (autobiographical essays), Little, Brown (Boston, MA), 1997.

(With sister, Amy Sedaris) *Little Freida Mysteries* (play), produced at La Mama, New York, NY, 1997.

Holidays on Ice (short stories), Little, Brown (Boston, MA), 1997.

Me Talk Pretty One Day (autobiographical essays), Little, Brown (Boston, MA), 2000.

(With sister, Amy Sedaris) *The Book of Liz* (play), produced at Greenwich House, New York, NY, 2001.

Also author of commentaries for National Public Radio, 1992—, and of satirical plays, written with Amy Sedaris.

■ Adaptations

"Diary of a Smoker," an essay from *Barrel Fever,* was adapted by Matthew Modine into a thirteen-minute film shown at the Sundance Film Festival and on Public Broadcasting System (PBS), 1994. Audiocassette versions of *Naked* and *Holidays on Ice* 1997, and of *Me Talk Pretty One Day,* 2001, were released by Time Warner Audio Books; *Me Talk Pretty One Day* was optioned for a film, to be directed by Wayne Wang, and starring Matthew Broderick.

■ Sidelights

Humorist David Sedaris "may not be the smartest American writer, but he is arguably the funniest," wrote Sam Jemielty in a *Playboy.com* article. Sedaris had taken an IQ test to see if he could join the ranks of the "genius fraternity Mensa," according to Jemielty. And as Sedaris reported in his essay collection *Me Talk Pretty One Day,* he did not really give those heavyweights a run for their money: "There are cats that weigh more than my IQ score." But as Jemielty pointed out, it is humor and not brains that sell Sedaris's work. "His four essay collections have sold hundreds of thousands of copies. And while other popular books by 'smart' guys like Tom Wolfe or Don DeLillo often sit unread on coffee tables, Sedaris' tomes get devoured, passed from friend to friend like dirty emails, creating an underground railroad of fans."

Sedaris is the master of spin, turning the quotidian into the stuff of laugh-out-loud humor. His wry and insightful observations about daily life, tales of growing up and the alienated angst of feeling different have won radio audiences and book readers alike. He talks of his foul-mouthed younger brother, of family foibles and foils, and of his own misguided attempts to adapt to his adopted home in Paris. As Bob Hoover noted in an article in the online Pittsburgh *Post-Gazette,* Sedaris is an "elfin figure" with a "faintly nasal deadpan delivery." Hoover also noted that Sedaris is "one of life's true outsiders, a Northerner transplanted to the South, a gay man in a society of male role models, a sensitive soul in a dumb culture." Sedaris uses painful bits from his family history as well as the flotsam he finds all around him. "I'm just the friendly junk man," Sedaris told Hoover. "I take pieces of junk and make my stories out of them."

Born in New York, the second of six children in a Greek-American family, Sedaris grew up in North Carolina. Neva Chonin, writing in the *San Francisco Chronicle,* described him as an "obsessive-compulsive child [who] spent his days licking light switches and hitting himself over the head with his shoe." He dropped out of Kent State University in 1977 to travel around the country, working for a time as a field laborer in California. He moved to Chicago while in his twenties, where he attended the Art Institute, and performed readings from his diaries for audiences. After his move to New York City in 1991, Sedaris began reading excerpts from his diaries on National Public Radio (NPR), where his "nicely nerdy, quavering voice," in the words of *Newsweek* commentator Jeff Giles, delivered monologues praised for their acerbic wit and dead-pan delivery. His "SantaLand Diaries," recounting his

In his 1994 prose collection, David Sedaris examines a diverse assortment of Americans: from a department store Santa who mistreats his elves to a father who decides to save on medical expenses by performing surgery in his suburban home.

misadventures as an elf at Macy's, was an instant hit and ensured further appearances on NPR. John Marchese commented in the *New York Times:* "In the five radio pieces that he has done, Mr. Sedaris has shown remarkable skill as a mimic and the ability to mix the sweet and the bitter: to be naive and vulnerable and at the same time, jaded and wickedly funny." *Entertainment Weekly* contributor Margot Mifflin remarked: "Sedaris is a crackpot in the best sense of the word."

Sedaris's comic, and often satirical, monologues draw primarily on his experiences in the odd day-jobs he held before his work with NPR heated up his artistic career. Of his long-standing position as an apartment cleaner, Sedaris told Marchese in the

New York Times: "I can only write when it's dark, so basically, my whole day is spent waiting for it to get dark. Cleaning apartments gives me something to do when I get up. Otherwise, I'd feel like a bum." As a result of his appearances on NPR, Sedaris has received numerous job offers, both for cleaning and for writing—as well as a multi-book contract with Little, Brown which in 1994 published Barrel Fever, a collection of Sedaris's essays and short stories.

From the Air Waves to the Printed Page

Barrel Fever includes several of the pieces that brought Sedaris to national attention when he read them on the radio, including "Diary of a Smoker," in which the author declares that the efforts of non-smokers to extend his life by not allowing him to smoke in front of them only gives him more time to hate nonsmokers, and "SantaLand Diaries," a "minor classic," according to Booklist's Benjamin Segedin, in which the author chronicles his amorous and aggravating experiences playing one of Santa's elves in Macy's one Christmas. Critics remarked on the humorously exaggerated self-delusion of Sedaris's narrators in the short stories, including a man who brags on talk-shows about his affairs with such stars as rock singer Bruce Springsteen and boxer Mike Tyson, and a gay man with a persecution complex who "bemoans his suffering at the hands of society in a style so over-the-top as to be laughable," according to a critic in Kirkus Reviews.

Critical response to Barrel Fever was generally positive, with reviewers appreciating Sedaris's humorous yet accurate portrayal of such American foibles as the commercialism of Christmas and the self-righteousness of health fanatics. "Without slapping the reader in the face with a political diatribe," wrote the critic for Kirkus Reviews, "the author skewers our ridiculous fascination with other people's tedious everyday lives." A contributor to Publishers Weekly commented: "Sedaris ekes humor from the blackest of scenarios, peppering his narrative with memorable turns of phrase and repeatedly surprising with his double-edged wit." Segedin compared Sedaris's humor to Dorothy Parker, in which he demonstrates "low tolerance for human foibles." To the Booklist critic, Sedaris's humor can be "vindictive and nasty," but also "extremely, relentlessly funny." Similarly, Mifflin, writing in Entertainment Weekly called the humorist a "lacerating curmudgeon," and his "SantaLand" a "devastating taxonomy of consumer America." Allison Levin, however, reviewing the collection in Whole Earth Review, found it "uplifting, nasty, sweet, and frightening but at the heart of Sedaris's storytelling is humor born of compassion." And although Newsweek critic Giles

the new york times BESTSELLER

naked

david sedaris

author of
BARREL FEVER

More comic stories by the sharp-witted and often over-the-top Sedaris greet readers of this 1997 collection.

found some of Sedaris's commentary relatively shallow, he nonetheless concluded: "This is a writer who's cleaned our toilets and will never look at us the same way."

Sedaris's second collection of essays, Naked, appeared in 1997. These essays, according to a reviewer for Publishers Weekly, reveal that "NPR commentator Sedaris can hardly be called a humorist in the ordinary sense. . . . Sedaris is instead an essayist who happens to be very funny." In his characteristic deadpan style, Sedaris tells stories "about nutty or bizarre experiences, like volunteering at a hospital for the insane," Craig Seligman observed in the New York Times Book Review. Other essays include Sedaris on hitchhiking, working in Oregon, his personal battle with his childhood nervous disorders, and the title piece about his sojourn at a nudist colony. In still others, the essayist turns his eye on his family, especially his mother. And for Seligman, "the funniest [essays], and ultimately the saddest, have to do with the writer's family." In these autobiographical tales, wrote Mifflin in *Entertainment Weekly*, "Sedaris covers a impressive emotional range. . . . from the comically corrosive title piece . . . to 'Ashes,' his account of his mother's death from cancer—a direct, unsentimental hit to the heart." The essays that go beyond the sarcastic to touch the heart, suggested Seligman, reveal an evolution in the essayist. "He's in the process of figuring out how to go beyond the short humor piece," noted Seligman, "and the essays in 'Naked' feel transitional." As Ira Glass, the producer for Sedaris's NPR commentaries and the host of Public Radio International's *This American Life*, to which Sedaris frequently contributes, told Peter Ames Carlin in a

People Weekly profile, "People come to his work because he's funny. . . . But there's a complicated moral vision there."

Sedaris reprised some sketches from his first two collections along with some new ones for his 1997 collection, *Holidays on Ice.* According to a reviewer for *Publishers Weekly*, the three best stories of the collection come from *Barrel Fever* and *Naked:* "Dinah, the Christmas Whore," "Season's Greetings," and the ever-popular "SantaLand Diaries." The newer sketches "look very thin indeed" by comparison, thought the same critic, who concluded that "flashes of . . . customary brilliance" will keep this gift book from being disappointing.

Settles in France

Sedaris moved to Paris with his partner in the late 1990s, initially to escape the disruption of renovations on his New York apartment. However, he liked the city of light well enough to settle down there, and his attempts at navigating the treacherous shoals of French culture have provided him with more material for his self-deprecating tales of humorous misadventure. "A sequel of sorts to *Naked*, [Sedaris'] . . . 2000 book, *Me Talk Pretty One Day*, amplifies the antic family portrait he created in the earlier book, while recounting his adventures in New York and Paris," summarized Michiko Kakutani in the *New York Times Book Review*. "Although amusing, Sedaris' tales of life in France now that he's happy don't have the bite of those in the first half of the book, many of them dealing with his eccentric father, an IBM engineer who ruins miniature golf with dissertations on wind trajectory," wrote Nancy Pate in *Knight-Ridder/Tribune News Service*. As Glass observed in *Esquire:* "A lot of people think they love David for his acidic tongue—which is still there, believe me—but I think it's his empathetic side, his skill in evoking real affection and sadness in his stories, that from the beginning brought people back for more." Kakutani largely agreed, but argued that "Sedaris's bitchiness can easily wear thin . . . in the slighter pieces. . . . Indeed, the stronger chapters in this book tend to be the ones that mix satire with sentiment, brazenness with rumination. Those pieces reveal a writer who is capable not only of being funny, but touching, even tender, too." A critic for *Publishers Weekly* felt that Sedaris is "Garrison Keillor's evil twin," focusing on the "icy patches that mar life's sidewalk." The same reviewer also commented that Sedaris will exhaust readers of the new book "with helpless laughter." Lisa Schwarzbaum concluded in *Entertainment Weekly:* "These days Sedaris glitters as one

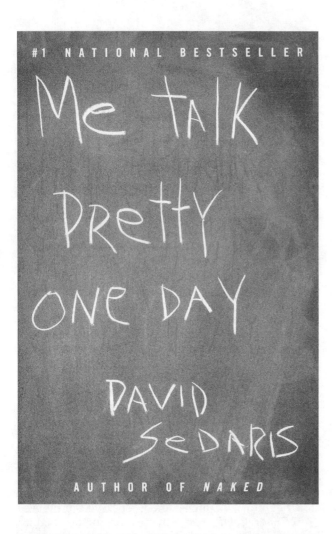

In addition to his short fiction, which includes this 2000 collection, Sedaris continues to make humorous contributions to public radio programs both in the United States and abroad.

of the wittiest writers around, an essayist and radio commentator who only appears to be telling simple then-what-happened anecdotes."

If you enjoy the works of David Sedaris, you might want to check out the following books:

Spalding Gray, *Swimming to Cambodia*, 1985.
David Eggers, *A Heartbreaking Work of Staggering Genius*, 2000.
Nick Hornby, *How to Be Good*, 2001.

Sedaris remains a master in turning personal and overheard tragedy and pathos into the material of comedy. He told *Knight Ridder/Tribune News Service* correspondent Robert K. Elder that he is not interested if he merely hears laughter in a hotel where he is staying. "I don't want to see what someone in a hotel finds funny," Sedaris commented. "But if they are screaming in pain or terror, I'm interested. I want to see what is so horrible. I want to see if I think it's horrible too." Elder commented that Sedaris is an "unapologetic voyeur of human behavior" with a talent for "finding laughter in the macabre, beauty in oddity." And writing in *Time*, Walter Kirn noted that Sedaris's target with his humor is most often himself, "vulnerable, vain, afflicted with bad habits and perpetually defending his right to self-destruct in peace." Kirn concluded that the "humor in Sedaris is transgressive, but it never feels contrived to be so. It's his legitimate, warped view of his legitimate, warped life."

■ **Biographical and Critical Sources**

BOOKS

Sedaris, David, *Me Talk Pretty One Day* (autobiographical essays), Little, Brown (Boston, MA), 2000.

PERIODICALS

Advocate, December 10, 1996, p. 54; June 20, 2000, Robert L. Pela, review of *Me Talk Pretty One Day,* p. 133.

Booklist, June 1, 1994, Benjamin Segedin, review of *Barrel Fever,* p. 1762; June 1, 2001, p. 1907.

Entertainment Weekly, July 29, 1994, Margot Mifflin, review of *Barrel Fever,* p. 55; December 13, 1996, p. S10; March 21, 1997, Margot Mifflin, review of *Naked,* p. 68; June 2, 2000, Lisa Schwarzbaum, review of *Me Talk Pretty One Day,* p. 72.

Esquire, June, 2000, review of *Me Talk Pretty One Day,* p. 38.

Fortune, June 12, 2000, review of *Me Talk Pretty One Day,* p. 358.

Kirkus Reviews, April 1, 1994, review of *Barrel Fever,* p. 430.

Knight Ridder/Tribune News Service, June 20, 2001, Nancy Pate, "Brief Reviews of New Paperbacks," p. K6846; July 18, 2001, Robert K. Elder, "Cult Writer David Sedaris Finds Mainstream Success with Acerbic Tales of the Absurd," p. K2674.

Library Journal, May 1, 1994, p. 104; April 1, 1997, p. 93; July, 1997, p. 143; October 15, 2000, Gloria Maxwell, review of *Me Talk Pretty One Day,* p. 124.

Los Angeles Times Book Review, October 16, 1994, p. 6; July 2, 1995, p. 11.

Newsweek, August 15, 1994, Jeff Giles, review of *Barrel Fever,* pp. 66-67.

New Yorker, August 1, 1994, p. 81.

New York Times, July 4, 1993, John Marchese, "He Does Radio and Windows," p. V5; February 19, 1997, p. C14.

New York Times Book Review, March 16, 1997, Craig Seligman, review of *Naked,* p. 10; June 16, 2000, Michiko Kakutani, review of *Me Talk Pretty One Day.*

Orlando Sentinel, June 28, 2000, Nancy Pate, review of *Me Talk Pretty One Day.*

People Weekly, March 24, 1997, Paula Chin, review of *Naked,* pp. 35-37; October 20, 1997, Peter Ames Carlin, "Elf-made Writer," p. 129; June 26, 2000, review of *Me Talk Pretty One Day,* p. 20.

Publishers Weekly, April 25, 1994, Review of *Barrel Fever,* p. 58; January 27, 1997, review of *Naked,* p. 88; April 7, 1997, p. 22; November 24, 1997, review of *Holidays on Ice,* p. 55; May 8, 2000, review of *Me Talk Pretty One Day,* p. 212; June 19, 2000, Kathie Bergquist, interview with Sedaris, p. 54; June 18, 2001, p. 20.

San Francisco Chronicle, March 14, 1999, Neva Chonin, "Sedaris in Paris."

Time, June 19, 2000, p. 139; September 17, 2001, Walter Kirn, "Wry Slicer," p. 86.

Tribune Books (Chicago, IL), February 2, 1996, p. 2.

Variety, November 11, 1996, p. 66.

Wall Street Journal, June 2, 2000, Robert J. Hughes, review of *Me Talk Pretty One Day,* p. W10.

Washington Post, March 22, 1997, p. B1.

Whole Earth Review, winter, 1995, Allison Levin, review of *Barrel Fever,* p. 63.

OTHER

David Sedaris Unofficial Home Page, http://home. pacifier.com/ (April 14, 2002).

January Magazine, http://www.januarymagazine. com/ (April 14, 2002), Linda Richards, "January Interview: David Sedaris."

Playboy.com, http://www.playboy.com/ (April 14, 2002), Sam Jemielty, "David Sedaris."

Post-Gazette.com, http://www.post-gazette.com/ (October 23, 2001), Bob Hoover, "Book Review: Sedaris' Wit Entertains at Byham."

Steven Barclay Agency Web site, http://www. barclayagency.com/ (April 14, 2002), "David Sedaris."

Tucson Weekly, http://www.tucsonweekly.com/ (June 15-June 21, 2000), Keith Pandolfi, "This American Icon."*

Mildred D. Taylor

■ Personal

Born September 13, 1943, in Jackson, MS; daughter of Wilbert Lee and Deletha Marie (Davis) Taylor; married Errol Zea-Daly, August, 1972 (divorced, 1975). *Education:* University of Toledo, B.Ed., 1965; University of Colorado, M.A., 1969.

■ Addresses

Home—Boulder, CO. *Agent*—c/o Author Mail, Random House, Inc., 201 East 50th St., New York, NY 10017.

■ Career

Writer. U.S. Peace Corps, English and history teacher in Tuba City, AZ, 1965, and in Yirgalem, Ethiopia, 1965-67, recruiter, 1967-68, instructor in Maine, 1968; University of Colorado, study skills coordinator, 1969-71; proofreader and editor in Los Angeles, CA, 1971-73.

■ Awards, Honors

First prize in African-American category, Council on Interracial Books for Children, 1973, and outstanding book of the year citation, *New York Times,* 1975, both for *Song of the Trees;* American Library Association Notable Book citation, 1976, National Book Award finalist, *Boston Globe-Horn Book* Honor Book citation, and Newbery Medal, all 1977, and Buxtehuder Bulle Award, 1985, all for *Roll of Thunder, Hear My Cry;* outstanding book of the year citation, *New York Times,* 1981, and Jane Addams honor, American Book Award nomination, and Coretta Scott King Award, all 1982, all for *Let the Circle Be Unbroken; New York Times* notable book citation, 1987, and Christopher Award, 1988, both for *The Gold Cadillac;* Coretta Scott King Award, 1988, for *The Friendship,* and 1990, for *The Road to Memphis;* Christopher Award, 1991, for *Mississippi Bridge;* Alan Award for Significant Contribution to Young Adult Literature, National Council of Teachers of English, 1997; Jason Award, 1997, for *The Well: David's Story;* Coretta Scott King Award, and Top Ten Black History Books for Youth, *Booklist,* both 2002, both for *The Land.*

■ Writings

Songs of the Trees, illustrated by Jerry Pinkney, Dial (New York, NY), 1975.
Roll of Thunder, Hear My Cry, Dial (New York, NY), 1976, 25th anniversary edition, Phyllis Fogelman Books (New York, NY), 2001.

Let the Circle Be Unbroken, Dial (New York, NY), 1981.

The Friendship, illustrated by Max Ginsburg, Dial (New York, NY), 1987.

The Gold Cadillac, illustrated by Michael Hays, Dial (New York, NY), 1987.

The Road to Memphis, Dial (New York, NY), 1990.

Mississippi Bridge, Dial (New York, NY), 1990.

The Well: David's Story, Dial (New York, NY), 1995.

The Land, Phyllis Fogelman Books (New York, NY), 2001.

Kevin's Story, Penguin Putnam (New York, NY), 2002.

■ Adaptations

Roll of Thunder, Hear My Cry was recorded by Newbery Awards Records in 1978, and as a three-part television miniseries of the same title by American Broadcasting Corporation (ABC-TV), 1978. *Let the Circle Be Unbroken* was made into an audio book by Recorded Books, Incorporated, 1998. *Roll of Thunder, Hear My Cry*, and *The Land* were made into audio books by Listening Library, 2001.

■ Sidelights

The author of ten novels for young readers, Mildred D. Taylor shares pride in her racial heritage and provides historical fiction about life for black Americans in her award-winning series of novels about the fictional Logan family. Such novels do not sugarcoat historical or contemporary realities; instead Taylor presents realistic accounts of growing up black in a white-controlled world. In her acceptance speech for the 1997 Alan Award for significant contributions to young adult literature, Taylor noted: "I have to be honest with myself in the telling of all my stories. I realize I must be true to the feelings of the people about whom I write and true to the stories told. My stories might not be 'politically correct,' so there will be those who will be offended, but as we all know, racism is offensive."

As a child, Taylor was regaled with stories of proud, dignified ancestors, but she received a different version of history from white, mainstream America. Believing that school history texts diminished the contributions of blacks and glossed over the injustices to which they had been subjected, Taylor vowed to write stories offering a truer vision of black families and their racial struggles. The author drew upon family narratives to produce her books, using a first-person voice that mirrored her relative's rendition of such tales, and she has been praised for the authentic ring of her characters' ordeals. Taylor invented the chronicle of the Logan family, and the series of books follows the group's activities and experiences throughout the mid-twentieth century. Taylor uses this time frame because she wishes to emphasize the importance of this generation's experience of and reaction to segregation and discrimination in helping pave the way for the reforms of the Civil Rights movement and an improvement in racial conditions in the United States. These Logan books, which feature various members of the family as well as members of the nearby community, include *Sons of the Trees, Roll of Thunder, Hear My Cry, Let the Circle Be Unbroken, The Friendship, The Road to Memphis, Mississippi Bridge, The Well: David's Story*, and *The Land*. For the second title in the loosely knit series, Taylor won the prestigious Newbery Medal; other titles have garnered honors ranging from the Coretta Scott King Award to the *Boston Globe-Horn Book* Honor citation.

Taylor sets many of her books in the rural South of the 1930s, something she learned about through family stories, research, and personal experience. Though growing up in Ohio, Taylor's family made annual pilgrimages to Mississippi, where they had come from. "I grew to know the South—to feel the South—through the yearly trips we took there and through the stories told. . . . In those days, before the civil rights movement, I remember the South and how it was. I remember the racism, the segregation," Taylor related in her 1988 *Boston Globe-Horn Book* acceptance speech. Taylor's ability to mix the events of everyday life with volatile issues and complex characters has gained the author both wide critical acclaim and popular appeal.

Growing up in Two Worlds

Taylor brings a unique vantage point to her fiction. Born in 1943, she was part of a transitional generation who witnessed both blatant discrimination against black Americans as well as legislative reform to amend historical transgressions. The author also experienced the differing racial climates of the North and South. Although born in Jackson, Mississippi, Taylor moved north with her family when she was only three months old. In an essay for *Something about the Author Autobiography Series* (*SAAS*), she recounted that her father, infuriated by repeated racial incidents, decided to leave the South in the mid-1940s because "he refused to allow my older sister, Wilma, and me to live our lives as he had to live his, in a segregated, racist society that allowed little or no opportunity to blacks." Although racism was persistent throughout the country, the North was perceived as an area offering greater freedom and job opportunities. Despite their relocation, the family did not abandon their Southern roots; they made an annual trek to visit relatives.

Reminiscing about such trips in her Newbery Award acceptance speech printed in *Horn Book*, Taylor remarked, "As a small child, I loved the South. . . . In my early years, the trip was a marvelous adventure; a twenty hour picnic that took us into another time, another world." At that time Taylor did not understand that the nature of these trips was a direct result of the racist policies of the South; the family packed food because they were not allowed in Southern restaurants and hotels, and they traveled back roads out of fear of harassment from bigoted police officers. Yet Taylor soon realized that she was expected to act—and was treated—differently in the South merely because of the color of her skin. She continued, "One summer I suddenly felt a climbing nausea as we crossed the Ohio River into Kentucky" because of the blatant discrimination in the South and the fear it inspired. Despite the uneasiness these vacations involved, Taylor's father insisted that his daughters be aware of these injustices commonly invoked in the United States. His reasoning, as she explained in her *SAAS* essay, was "that without understanding the loss of liberty in the south, we couldn't appreciate the liberty of the North."

Yet, for the author, the South also held pleasant memories as the home of her ancestors. In an article for *Horn Book* she remarked, "I also remember the other South—the South of family and community, the South filled with warmth and love—and how it opened to me a sense of history and filled me with pride." This vision of the South was passed down in an oral tradition; when Taylor's extended family gathered, relatives would re-create the family's history with stories acted out on porches and around bonfires. Her father was a noted storyteller, engaging family members with fascinating tales of colorful, proud ancestors who retained dignity even when faced with the inhumanity and degradation of slavery. Such tales had an encouraging effect on Taylor: she began to see herself as a storyteller. A shy child, she knew she would not be able to participate in the oral tradition. Instead, she turned inward, creating daydream stories that she soon began committing to paper.

When the author was ten years old, her family moved into a newly integrated Ohio town, and she was the only black child in her class. This was a scene repeated throughout her formative years, and

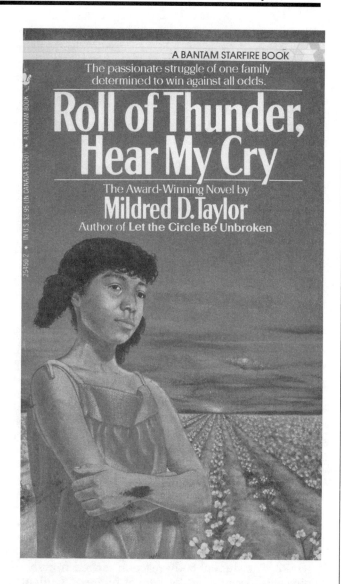

A BANTAM STARFIRE BOOK
The passionate struggle of one family determined to win against all odds.

Roll of Thunder, Hear My Cry

The Award-Winning Novel by
Mildred D. Taylor
Author of *Let the Circle Be Unbroken*

Taking place in Mississippi during the pre-civil rights era of the early twentieth century, Mildred D. Taylor's award-winning 1976 novel finds the Logan family fighting for equality while suffering threats and Mama's loss of work.

Taylor felt burdened by the realization that her actions would be judged—by whites unfamiliar with blacks—as representative of her entire race. In school, when the subject was history, Taylor was uncomfortable because her understanding of black heritage contrasted sharply with that presented in textbooks. In *Horn Book* she commented that such publications contained only a "lackluster history of Black people . . . a history of a docile, subservient people happy with their fate who did little or nothing to shatter the chains that bound them, both before and after slavery." Knowing this to be false, the young author tried to think of ways to repudiate the information in those books. In her *SAAS* essay she recalled, "I remember once trying to explain those [family] stories in class, about the way things really were. . . . Most of the students thought I was making the stories up. Some even laughed at me. I couldn't explain things to them. Even the teacher seemed not to believe me. They all believed what was in the history book."

The bias of such accounts had a motivating effect on the young Taylor. In *Horn Book* she explained, "By the time I entered high school, I had a driving compulsion to paint a truer picture of Black people. I wanted to show the endurance of the Black World, with strong fathers and concerned mothers; I wanted to show happy, loved children. . . . I wanted to show a Black family united in love and pride, of which the reader would like to be a part."

When Taylor entered high school, the civil rights movement had begun to gain momentum. A number of incidents—including the murder of a young black boy named Emmett Till, the Montgomery bus boycott, and the Supreme Court decision in *Brown v. The Board of Education of Topeka*—had raised awareness of racial discrimination to new levels. Despite the publicity surrounding these and other incidents, Taylor felt somewhat removed from the problem. "I was in Toledo after all, in the North, and though there certainly was discrimination, certainly prejudice, and certainly open violation of civil rights, I had seldom felt open hostility," she wrote in her *SAAS* essay. One incident, however, helped draw Taylor into the fray. In 1957, a black senior was chosen as homecoming queen at Taylor's high school. The student body reaction ranged from happiness (especially on the part of minority students) to anger that exploded into violence. The author recollected: "Though things returned to normal . . . those days of my freshman year hammered home to all of us that racism was not only part of the South, but of the North as well."

A visit to Toledo by then-senator John F. Kennedy further stimulated Taylor's interest in civil rights. Elected to report on the senator's visit, Taylor was impressed by both Kennedy's charisma and his interest in the civil rights movement. "I loved the promise of the future he offered, and hearing him I very much intended to be a part of it," she noted in *SAAS*. Inspired by Kennedy's speech, Taylor began making plans for her own future, plans that included faraway places and people. "Before John F. Kennedy, I had never known I could achieve this," she recorded in *SAAS*. "It was something I intended to do, but until John F. Kennedy it was only a dream."

The Making of a Writer

Part of Taylor's plans included college. When not preparing for classes, she wrote stories (some of which were later submitted to various writing contests). In many ways, Taylor found writing difficult. At first, she tried to pattern her efforts after writers that she admired, such as Charles Dickens and Jane Austen: "I was trying to emulate a literary form that left my work stiff and unconvincing. It was an unnatural style for me," she commented in *SAAS*. Taylor wrote her first novel at age nineteen; told using a first-person narrator, "Dark People, Dark World" explores the retreat of a young, blind, white man into Chicago's black ghetto. Although a publishing house expressed some interest in the work in a shorter, edited format, Taylor abandoned the project, largely because she was "very naive and full of artistic self-righteousness."

After graduating from college, the author was invited to join the Peace Corps. While Taylor was elated over the prospect of going to Ethiopia to teach, her family was unsettled by the prospect. Taylor's father was worried about the distance and potential danger; Taylor's mother, although resigned to her daughter's decision, was sad about the amount of time she would be gone. Eventually, Taylor's enthusiasm overrode her parents' concerns. During her Peace Corps service, Taylor taught English as a second language on a Navajo reservation in Arizona and later traveled to Ethiopia, where she taught at a small school.

Taylor enrolled in graduate school after her stint with the Peace Corps. Inspired by another graduate student, she became involved with the Black Student Alliance and other organizations established by the Alliance, such as the Black Education Program. "In addition to putting together plans to force the university into meeting our demands for black enrollment and black programs, we studied black culture, black history and black politics," Taylor notes in her essay. At one point, Taylor was approached by *Life* magazine about writing an article describing the Black Studies movement. Unfortunately, the magazine felt that the final product did not capture the spirit of the organization and the article was never published; Taylor's ensuing disappointment made her question the direction her life was taking. She wrote in her *SAAS* essay: "I began to question whether or not individual goals must be suppressed to the will of the group in order for the group's goals to flourish." Eventually, Taylor returned to Ethiopia to regroup.

After returning from Africa, Taylor moved to Los Angeles. There, she worked at a number of temporary jobs to help make ends meet, all the while applying for positions more in keeping with her work experience and education. At one point, Taylor was offered a job as a reporter for CBS; after much self-analysis, she turned the position down in favor of concentrating on her writing. Taylor's first success in the latter area came about when she entered a contest sponsored by the Council on Interracial Books for Children. Much to her surprise, Taylor's revision of an old manuscript won in the African-American category.

The Logan Saga

Taylor produced the manuscript for the award-winning *Song of the Trees* in only four days. Three months later she received a telegram naming her the winner in the African-American category of the Council on Interracial Books for Children contest. *Song of the Trees* introduced the Logan clan: Big Ma, Papa, Mama, Uncle Hammer, Stacey, Christopher-John, Cassie, and Little Man. This book, based on an actual incident, is told through the voice of the Logan daughter, Cassie. Jobs are scarce in 1930s Mississippi because of the Depression, and Cassie's father is away in Louisiana trying to earn enough money to pay the taxes on the family's land. In his absence, white men threaten to cut down trees on the Logan's property. However Papa returns in time to take a stand against the white men. Ruby Martin, in a *Journal of Reading* review, praised *Song of the Trees* as "so beautifully told, the prose rings poetry." Other critics agreed with such praise, emphasizing the lyrical nature of the narrative. For example, a reviewer for *Bulletin of the Center for Children's Books* called the narrative "fairly brisk, verging on the poetic," and a *Horn Book* contributor also applauded "Cassie's descriptions of the trees [which] add a poetic touch."

Taylor's next book, *Roll of Thunder, Hear My Cry*, which earned the prestigious Newbery medal in 1977, continues the story of the Logan family in "a remarkable family portrait," according to David A. Wright in *Dictionary of Literary Biography*. Using a limited time frame, the book examines the family's life and demonstrates how discrimination is an everyday occurrence. Stacey, Christopher-John, Cassie, and Little Man all attend school, suffering humiliations such as being splashed by the school bus that only picks up white children and receiving school texts in poor condition that are available only because the white school no longer had a need for them. Mama loses her teaching job because she defies school district officials by including a discussion of slavery in a history lesson even though it is not in the book. After a horrifying racial incident in which several black men are set on fire, the Logans

help orchestrate a boycott of a crooked white merchant's store, a suspected ringleader in the burnings. This act sets off a series of events, including the threat of foreclosure on the Logan's land, the near lynching of the Logan children's classmate, and a suspicious fire.

"I have to be honest with myself in the telling of all my stories. I realize I must be true to the feelings of the people about whom I write and true to the stories told. My stories might not be 'politically correct,' so there will be those who will be offended, but as we all know, racism is offensive."

—Mildred D. Taylor

Stuart Hannabuss, writing in *Junior Bookshelf*, commented that *Roll of Thunder, Hear My Cry* is "full of episodes of emotional power." Noting the effect of such scenes, David Rees, in his work *The Marble on the Water: Essays on Contemporary Writers of Fiction for Children and Young Adults*, remarked that "it's impossible not to feel anger and a sense of burning in reading this book." And *Interracial Books for Children Bulletin* contributor Emily R. Moore concluded, "*Roll of Thunder, Hear My Cry* deserves to become a classic in children's literature."

In the next addition to the Logan chronicle, *Let the Circle Be Unbroken*, "Taylor's recurrent theme of family unity has its strongest appearance," according to Wright. Cassie recounts the hardships of the Depression for both white and black sharecroppers and shows how sometimes people of the same economic status work together regardless of race. Yet, the author also presents more situations of racial struggle. The Logan children's classmate is unfairly convicted for his part in a robbery that took place in *Roll of Thunder, Hear My Cry*. Cassie helps an elderly black woman memorize the state constitution so that she can register to vote, but nonetheless the woman is refused this basic civil right. *New York Times Book Review* contributor June Jordan praised the book for its "dramatic tension and virtuoso characterization." In a review of *Let the Circle Be Unbroken* for the *Christian Science Monitor*, Christine McDonnell observed, "Though many of Cassie and Stacey's experiences happen because they are black, their growing pains and self-discovery are universal." McDonnell added, "The Logans' story will strengthen and satisfy all who read it." And Holly Eley, writing in the *Times Literary Supplement,* felt that Taylor "gives us a historical perspective on racial issues which she insists can only be successfully resolved by recognizing the fundamental equality of all human beings."

The Friendship, written in 1987, presents a racial confrontation between two men in 1930s Mississippi that is witnessed by the Logan children. Tom Bee, a black man, had saved the life of John Wallace, a white storekeeper, when the two were young men. In gratitude, John insisted that the two would always remain friends, evidenced by their using first names to address each other. However, years later, John reneges on this promise and shoots Tom for addressing him by his first name in public—an act considered insubordination because blacks were supposed to refer to white men or women as mister and misses. Frances Bradburn, writing in *Wilson Library Bulletin,* stated, "This is a story that children will experience rather than simply read. . . . The humiliation, the injustice, but above all the quiet determination, courage, and pride of Mr. Tom Bee will speak to all children." Similarly, a reviewer for *Bulletin of the Center for Children's Books* commented that the novel "elicits a naturally powerful response in depicting cruel injustice" with writing that is "concentrated to heighten that effect."

New Dimensions

With *The Gold Cadillac,* Taylor takes a break from her Logan cycle, setting her tale in the 1950s and chronicling a black family's car trip to the South to visit relatives. Much like the family vacations of Taylor's youth, the family is confronted with "whites only" signs and suffers harassment from white police officers who are both jealous and suspicious of the family's car and the prosperity it represents. Such incidents help the two young sisters appreciate the greater freedom and opportunity they enjoy in their Ohio hometown. Writing in *School Library Journal,* Helen E. Williams praised Taylor for her "clear language and logical, dramatic sequencing of story events [that] make this story bittersweet for adult readers but important for the social development of beginning readers."

Taylor returned to the Logan saga with her 1990 title, *The Road to Memphis,* in which Cassie is a high school senior dreaming of becoming a lawyer. She attends school in Jackson, Mississippi, and is for the first time without the protection of her parents and grandmother. Her brother Stacey and a friend are also in Jackson working in factories. There the trio faces more racial incidents and also must contend with the outbreak of World War II. After Stacey's friend is forced to flee the city because—even though he realized he would be punished—he defended himself against a white attack, Cassie grapples with her decision to pursue a career in the white-controlled legal system. Susan Sculler, reviewing the novel in *School Library Journal,* concluded that it "is a dramatic, painful book."

Another of Taylor's works, *Mississippi Bridge,* is loosely related to the Logan cycle, in that it is told from the point of view of Jeremy Simms, a white character who befriended the Logan family in previous books. In these works Jeremy was distinguished from the racist townsfolk in that he continually made offers of friendship to the Logan children. *Mississippi Bridge* chronicles another racist incident in which, during stormy weather, black bus passengers are forced to get off of the bus to make room for white riders. This story concludes in an incident that some critics perceived as judgment for the white's discriminatory actions: the bus goes off a bridge drowning all the passengers. A contributor for *Publishers Weekly* noted that "the ironies and injustices presented in [Taylor's] story will be strongly felt and remembered."

A critic for *St. James Guide to Young Adult Writers* also felt that *The Road to Memphis* and *Mississippi Bridge,* published in the same year, "add a new dimension to the author's work," in that "each appears designed to complement the other and makes a statement regarding all that has taken place before." For this critic, *The Road to Memphis* shows the "desolation of black life" more intensely than in Taylor's other work, while *Mississippi Bridge* is "at once a study in deific payment for wrongs and human kindness."

In 1995 Taylor published *The Well: David's Story,* further chronicling the Logan family, this time focusing on ten-year-old David Logan (father of Cassie in *Roll of Thunder, Hear My Cry*) and his family, who share their well water with both black and white neighbors in Mississippi in the early 1900s. Despite their kindness, the Logans are still treated with disrespect by the white neighbors. A reviewer writing for *Publishers Weekly* noted, "Taylor, obviously in tune with these fully developed characters, creates for them an intense and compelling situation and skillfully delivers powerful messages about racism and moral fortitude." *Booklist's* Hazel Rochman noted that though the cast is large, the Logan family "is beautifully individualized." Rochman concluded that the "well of the title is also a metaphor for the history of the place: both the bigotry that lies beneath the surface and the sweet strength of family ties." *Horn Book*'s Mary M. Burns also commented on the size of the cast of characters, noting that "Taylor has enriched her story" by introducing characters outside the main plot line. Burns concluded, "Like all of Taylor's work, this story reverberates in the heart long after the final paragraph is read."

Taylor's next book, *The Land,* is also a prequel to *Roll of Thunder, Hear My Cry* and deals with Paul-Edward Logan, Cassie's grandfather during the period right after the Civil War. Writing in *Publishers Weekly,* a reviewer said that, "Like any good historian, Taylor extracts truth from past events without sugarcoating issues." Noting that Taylor's tone "is more uplifting than bitter," the reviewer added, "Rather than dismissing hypocrisies, she digs beneath the surface of Paul-Edward's friends and foes, showing how their values have been shaped by the social norms." A reviewer for *Horn Book* noted Taylor's masterful use of the realities of racism "to frame a powerful coming-of-age story of a bewildered boy becoming a man beholden to no one." Finally, Rochman, writing for *Booklist,* pointed out, "The novel will make a great discussion book in American history classes dealing with black history; pioneer life; and the Reconstruction period, about which little has been written for this age group."

If you enjoy the works of Mildred D. Taylor, you might want to check out the following books:

Yvette Moore, *Freedom Songs,* 1991.
Christopher Paul Curtis, *The Watsons Go to Birmingham—1963,* 1995.
Harriet Gillem Robinet, *Forty Acres and Maybe a Mule,* 1998.

With each of her books, Taylor has provided a glimpse into the history of black Americans. Even though her characters face repeated racial indignities, they show courage and resourcefulness in overcoming their problems. With her Logan series Taylor has earned esteem and recognition, but she gives her own father the credit for much of her success because of the stories he told that formed the basis of her books and for the example he set in responding to discrimination. The author accepted her Newbery medal for *Roll of Thunder, Hear My Cry* on be-

half of her father and remarked that "without his teachings, without his words, my words would not have been." Taylor added in *Horn Book* that she hopes her books about the Logan family "will one day be instrumental in teaching children of all colors the tremendous influence that Cassie's generation . . . had in bringing about the great Civil Rights movement of the fifties and sixties." In her acceptance speech for the 1997 Alan Award, Taylor also pointed out, "In the writing of my books I have tried to present not only a history of my family, but the effects of racism, not only to the victims of racism but also to racists themselves." Taylor has said that she still has a final book to write about the Logans and will be returning to Cassie's voice to tell the story.

■ Biographical and Critical Sources

BOOKS

Beacham's Guide to Literature for Young Adults, Beacham Publishing (Osprey, FL), Volume 3, 1990, pp. 1135-1143, Volume 8, 1994, pp. 3890-3897.
Children's Literature Review, Volume 9, Gale (Detroit, MI), 1985.
Contemporary Black Biography, Volume 26, Gale (Detroit, MI), 2000.
Contemporary Literary Criticism, Volume 21, Gale (Detroit, MI), 1982.
Crowe, Chris, *Presenting Mildred D. Taylor,* Twayne (New York, NY), 1999.
Dictionary of Literary Biography, Volume 52: *American Writers for Children since 1960: Fiction,* Gale (Detroit, MI), 1986, pp. 365-367.
Rees, David, *The Marble in the Water: Essays on Contemporary Writers of Fiction for Children and Young Adults,* "The Color of Skin: Mildred Taylor," pp. 108-109.
Something about the Author Autobiography Series, Volume 5, Gale (Detroit, MI), 1988, pp. 267-286.
St. James Guide to Young Adult Writers, 2nd edition, St. James Press (Detroit, MI), 1999.

PERIODICALS

ALAN Review, spring, 1995, Barbara T. Bontempo, "Exploring Prejudice in Young Adult Literature through Drama and Role Play"; spring, 1998, Mildred D. Taylor, "Acceptance Speech for the 1997 Alan Award."
Booklist, December 1, 1990, p. 740; December 15, 1994, Hazel Rochman, review of *The Well,* p. 754; November 1, 1995, p. 494; May 15, 1997, Karen

Harris, review of *The Road to Memphis,* p. 1596; August, 2001, Hazel Rochman, review of *The Land,* p. 2108; February 15, 2002, Stephanie Zvirin, "Top Ten Black History Books for Youth," p. 1034.

Bulletin of Interracial Books for Children, Volume 7, 1976, Emily R. Moore, "The Bookshelf: 'Roll of Thunder, Hear My Cry,'" p. 18.

Bulletin of the Center for Children's Books, October, 1975, review of *Song of the Trees;* December, 1987, review of *The Friendship.*

Christian Science Monitor, October 14, 1981, Christine McDonnell, "Powerful Lesson of Family Love," pp. B1, B11.

Horn Book, August, 1975, review of *Song of Trees;* August, 1977, Mildred D. Taylor, Newbery Award Acceptance Speech, pp. 401-409; April, 1982, review of *Roll of Thunder, Hear My Cry,* p. 174; July-August, 1995, Mary M. Burns, review of *The Well,* pp. 461-463; September, 2001, review of *The Land,* p. 596.

Journal of Reading, February, 1977, Ruby Martin, "Books for Young People," pp. 432-435.

Junior Bookshelf, October, 1982, Stuart Hannabuss, "Beyond the Formula: Part II," p. 175.

New York Times Book Review, November 15, 1981, June Jordan, "Mississippi in the Thirties," pp. 55, 58; May 20, 1990.

Publishers Weekly, April 13, 1990, review of *The Road to Memphis,* p. 67; July 17, 1990, review of *Mississippi Bridge,* p. 234; January 2, 1995, review of *The Well: David's Story,* p. 77; August 13, 2001, review of *The Land,* p. 313; October 22, 2001, Jennifer M. Brown, "Stories behind the Book," p. 24.

School Library Journal, September, 1987, Helen E. Williams, review of *The Gold Cadillac,* pp. 171-172; June, 1990, Susan Sculler, review of *The Road to Memphis,* p. 138; February, 1995, pp. 63-64, 100; April, 1995, p. 37; August, 2001, Bruce Anne Shook, review of *The Land,* p. 190.

Times Literary Supplement, March 26, 1982, Holly Eley, "Cotton Pickin' Blues," p. 343.

Wilson Library Bulletin, March, 1988, Frances Bradburn, "Middle Readers' Right to Read," p. 42; May, 1995, p. 100.

OTHER

Edupaperback.org, http://www.edupaperback.org/ (April 16, 2002), "Mildred Taylor."

Mildred Taylor Teacher Resource File, http://falcon.jmu.edu/ (April 16, 2002).*

Chris Ware

■ Personal

Born December 28, 1967, in Omaha, NE; son of M. B. Haberman and Doris Ann Ware (a newspaper reporter); married, 1997; wife's name, Marina. *Education:* Attended Skanregan School of Painting and Sculpture, 1989; University of Texas, B.F.A. (painting), 1990.

■ Addresses

Home—Chicago, IL. *Agent*—c/o Fantagraphics Books, 7563 Lake City Way, Seattle, WA 98115.

■ Career

Author and illustrator of comic strips.

■ Awards, Honors

Harvey Award for Best New Series and Special Award for Excellence in Presentation, 1995, Harvey Award for Best Letterer, and Special Award for Ex-cellence in Presentation, 1996, Harvey Awards for Best Colorist, Best Single Issue or Story, and Special Award for Excellence in Presentation, 1997, Harvey Award for Best Colorist and Special Award for Excellence in Presentation, and Ignatz Awards for Outstanding Series and Outstanding Comic, all 1998, Harvey Award for Special Award for Excellence in Presentation, 1999, Harvey Awards for Best Letterer, Best Colorist, and Special Award for Excellence in Presentation, and Ignatz Awards for Outstanding Comic and Outstanding Story, all 2000, and Harvey Award for Best Continuing or Limited Series, 2001, all for "Acme Novelty Library"; Harvey Award for Best Graphic Album of Previously Published Work, and Special Award for Excellence in Presentation, and First Book Award, *Guardian*, all 2001, all for *Jimmy Corrigan: The Smartest Kid on Earth.*

■ Writings

Jimmy Corrigan—The Smartest Kid on Earth, Pantheon Books (New York, NY), 2000.

Author of comic strips "I Guess," in *Raw*, Volume 2, number 3; "Quimby the Mouse"; "Big Tex"; "Rocket Sam"; "Jimmy Corrigan—The Smartest Kid on Earth"; "Blab!"; and "Rusty Brown." Editor and publisher of "The Ragtime Ephemeralist," 1998—. Author of "Acme Novelty Library" comic book series, 1993—. Ware's work has appeared in the *New York Times* and *New City.*

Young, lonely Jimmy Corrigan is grilled about his school day in this award-winning strip collected in Chris Ware's *Jimmy Corrigan—The Smartest Kid on Earth,* published in 2000.

■ Work in Progress

A serialized story, set in the 1970s, about a boy named Rusty Brown who grows up to be a toy collector.

■ Sidelights

Dubbed the Emily Dickinson of comics by one fan, cartoonist Chris Ware is the creative force behind several comic strips, including "Quimby the Mouse," "Big Tex," "Rocket Sam," and "Jimmy Corrigan—The Smartest Kid on Earth," all of which have been collected from their original publication in various newspapers and subsequently published in self-designed periodicals. The Corrigan strips were also collected for the 2000 book *Jimmy Corrigan—The Smartest Kid on Earth,* the first graphic novel ever to win a major British literary award when it earned the *Guardian* First Book Award in 2001. Ware's precisely detailed, warmly colored artwork has been compared to Islamic miniatures, Maya glyphs, and Egyptian hieroglyphs. "The pictures are ideograms," Ware told Beth Nissen writing for *CNN.com,* "drawn words, if that makes any sense. The pictures tell the story—I'm a terrible writer." A meticulous draftsman, Ware has commented that creating just two pages of story takes about twenty hours to write and draw, another ten hours to ink, and then a further four to color. But these pages take only about twelve seconds to read.

Gary Groth of *Comics Journal* divided Ware's work into three "untidy and overlapping" categories: "the doggedly visual gamesmanship,. . . ; the bigfoot humor, laced with irony, black humor and *pastiche* . . . ; the tragi-comic world of 'Jimmy Corrigan.' It's the last that seems to me the most substantial and it's here that Ware's investigation into how formal visual properties impart meaning comes into play most successfully." Other critics have concurred with that assessment. Jonathan Goldstein, for example, writing in the *New York Times,* called *Jimmy Corrigan* a "great work of art, deep and moving, pretty much unlike anything that's come before it." "Ware's book is arguably the greatest achievement of the form [of the graphic novel], ever," declared author Dave Eggers, writing in the *New York Times Book Review.* And *Time*'s Andrew Arnold called *Jimmy Corrigan* a "haunting and unshakable book [that] will change the way you look at your world." High praise for a self-confessed loner who started cartooning to win friends. "Drawing was the only way I had of distinguishing myself," Ware told Nissen, "of trying to impress people—impress people with my one pathetic ability. There's nothing less impressive than a scrawny kid with poofy hair, drawing superheroes."

The "Albino"

Ware was raised in Omaha, Nebraska, by his mother, a newspaper reporter, and his maternal grandparents, and did not know his father, who abandoned the family when Ware was a baby. His grandmother was an important person in Ware's life. "She and I spent whole days together every week, as I preferred being indoors to being out," Ware told Groth. "I liked going on errands with her, and drawing at the desk that she had set up in the basement of their house. She had it divided right down the middle so I would have half of it to work at and she had the other half." Ware's grandfather and mother were both journalists, and thus he was introduced to the world of printing at an early age. Comics were also an early passion for young Ware, who got his first taste for the medium through a stack of back copies kept in his grandmother's basement. For a few years Ware took art lessons at the Joslyn Art Museum in Omaha, and he also

learned rudimentary drawing techniques from watching a PBS television program. Soon he was trying to copy the pictures he admired in the comics. "I would just find panels I liked and try to figure out how they were making all those thick and thin lines," Ware recalled to Groth. "I'd try to do it with a pencil, because I had no idea they were using a brush or a pen."

Like many teenagers of his generation, Ware enjoyed popular music and television shows. He developed an interest in ragtime piano music, and he took up the piano, though he eventually decided against pursuing a career in music. When he moved from a private high school to a public one, he began to hang out with kids who were reading so-called

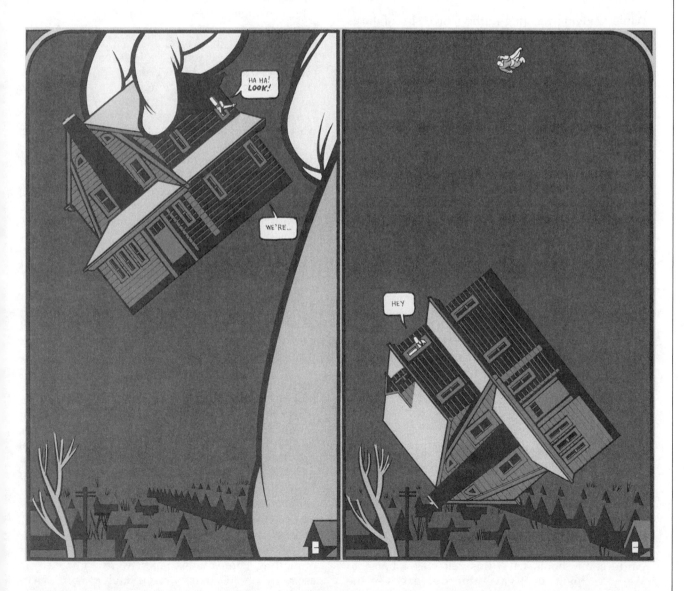

In drawing his "Jimmy Corrigan" strip, Ware employs such careful draftsmanship and attention to detail that an average of 16 hours are devoted to each full page of colored graphics and text.

"underground" comics. When a friend started drawing his own "alternative" comics for fun, Ware did the same.

Largely, however, Ware "grew up bullied," as he told Nissen. "As a kid, I was, shall we say, not the favored one. Kids were threatening me all the time. I ate lunch by myself. I had some friends I talked to on the weekends—but they wouldn't talk to me at school. And I wasn't good at games—I was about as physical as an inert gas." Ware's nickname at the time was "Albino" because of his pasty complexion. Drawing became a refuge for him. "Ware came through it all," Nissen commented, "with an enduring empathy for the ridiculed, the awkward, the maladept."

While studying painting at the University of Texas at Austin, Ware drew comic strips for the student newspaper, the *Daily Texan.* A friend on the paper introduced Ware to older comic strips, and soon the fledgling cartoonist was immersing himself in the history of the medium. "Comics haven't really developed much since about 1920," Ware told Chip Kidd in an interview for *Print* magazine, reprinted on the Random House Web site. "If one wants to tell stories that have the richness of life, their vocabulary is extremely limited. It's like trying to use limericks to make literature." Ware took note of the early masters, including Winsor McCay and his "Little Nemo," Frank King and the "Gasoline Alley" strips, George Herriman's "Krazy Kat," and, of course, "Superman." The omnivorous Ware also took inspiration from the mundane: the Sears catalogue, advertising from the first half of the twentieth century, and old newspaper comic strips. Each of these sources and traditions later came to play in Ware's own artwork. McCay had "Impeccable craftsmanship," Ware told Kidd, adding that the early twentieth-century cartoonist was "Firmly rooted in the principles of realism and Renaissance perspective, invariably to stunning effect." From King he saw the power of a "real-time chronicle of American domesticity," and Herriman's "Krazy Kat" simply awed him. "A masterpiece. A world unto itself, eluding strict explanation." Such a world unto itself would present itself to Ware, as well.

Making It in the Underground

In 1987, when he was a sophomore, Ware received a call from Art Spiegelman, publisher of the avant garde comic book *RAW*; this call was a boost to Ware, as Spiegelman gave him four pages in the next issue of *RAW*, and then another assignment after that. One early strip in *RAW* became emblematic

of the Ware style: "I Guess" draws on his childhood memories growing up with his journalist mom and his grandparents. In the story, the protagonist is a somewhat odd-looking superhero who had to deal with the slings and arrows of domestic life rather than super-villains. With his alternate takes on growing up in America, Ware was soon on his way to a certain degree of underground notoriety.

He was not gaining any points with his art teachers, though. The cartoonist has spoken at times of "art school damage" he and others like him have suffered, and he explained this concept to Travis Fristoe and Chris Waldronn in an interview for *Indy Magazine*. By this Ware means "the sort of mental 'self-policing' that was encouraged in college when I attended, from 1985-1993. The sort of 'thinking' which included notions that 'talent' interferes with 'expression,' and that reading about art was better than looking at the world, and that anything which made sense wasn't really art. I encountered a number of 'instructors' who considered my cartooning a 'gig,' some kind of 'side thing' I was doing to make cash. (Needless to say, this was from people who were having to teach to pay the bills.) Of course I wasn't making any money at it, but the simple fact that I was doing artwork for reproduction was more than some could swallow. . . . They reduced artmaking to the level of the essay. . . . If you weren't trying to 'expose' racism, or sexism, or tainted beef packing then you weren't an artist." Ware happily went his own way, despite such advice from instructors.

However, as Neil Strauss noted in the *New York Times*, Ware "might never have hit his stride in illustrating but for an event that took place a couple of years later. He was working on what he describes as a pretentious, conceptual comic when his girlfriend dumped him." Depressed by the event, Ware trashed everything he was working on and started improvising with some stories he had in his sketchbooks. These "mostly wordless and action-free tales of a potato-shaped character" bear a "remarkable resemblance to Mr. Ware," Strauss commented. In these stories and sketches "one can see the beginnings of an immense vocabulary of loneliness, economical use of space and dark humor," according to Strauss. Jimmy Corrigan was born.

Ware continued to improvise, however, playing with other artwork, experimenting with cartoons that are virtual flow charts, deeply intricate visual displays of plotting. Some of his comics "were crammed with as many as 300 panels on a single page," wrote Strauss, "an attempt . . . to create a comic that could be read like musical notes on a score." Other early

Ware compellingly illustrates that loneliness will not be eradicated by technological advancements in this strip, *The Tales of Tomorrow* from the "Acme Novelty Library."

cartoons from Ware include "Quimby the Mouse," "Big Tex," and "Rocket Sam."

In 1993 Ware moved from Austin to Chicago, and felt more isolated than ever. At this time he began to focus on the semi-autobiographical comic strip "Jimmy Corrigan—The Smartest Kid on Earth,"

which he published in a local alternative weekly *New City*. Corrigan appears to be the quintessential loser, although Ware told Groth, "It's not my goal to present a deliberately dark view of life." Instead, according to Ware, he is simply presenting life in a "realistic" manner, even if the result seems ironic or cruelly humorous. Ware, who thinks popular cul-

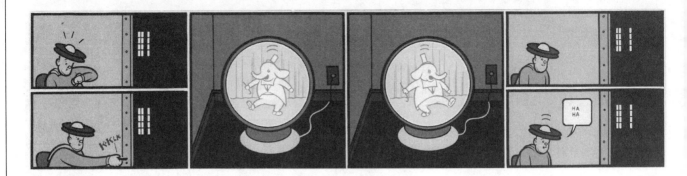

Ware's vision of the future offers little cause for celebration for his aging protagonist, shown living a life of "quiet desperation" in *The Tales of Tomorrow.*

ture falsely misleads people into believing they should be happy all of the time, draws from events in his own life and the lives of others for material. Jimmy Corrigan, like his creator, grew up without a father. The storyline follows Jimmy as he learns of the existence of this absent father, as he tries to become independent of his domineering mother, as he establishes a relationship with an African-American stepsister he never knew he had. One of the centerpieces of the strip is the story within a story of his grandfather, also named Jimmy Corrigan, who himself was abandoned at the 1893 World's Columbian Exhibition in Chicago. Thirty-six now, Jimmy works long hours in a silent cubicle, calls his mother daily, and is terrified by women.

When Ware set out to draw his weekly comic strip, he did not plan the work in detail ahead of time. Instead he used a semi-improvisational method. He explained to Groth: "I'll have a vague idea and start working on the strip, and before I know it, by the time I'm to the bottom of the page, it's gone somewhere completely different from where I'd thought it might." As for technique, Ware has explored a number of different styles in his comics. "I could point to elements in my stuff that I've picked and chosen from hundreds of cartoonists," Ware told Groth. As an artist, he is constantly trying to push the boundaries of comic-strip language; through page layout, the rhythms of the panels, the framing of characters and their faces, and the amount and position of text Ware tries to find new ways of visually communicating emotions and sensations not traditionally associated with this American art form.

From Underground to Mainstream

The "Jimmy Corrigan" strip became so popular that Ware soon had two full pages weekly, and he also launched the "Acme Novelty Library" to publish

the collected volumes of this venture. Fantagraphics in Seattle, Washington, picked up on these, and published the first number in 1993. Over the course of the series, Ware developed stories within stories for his hapless hero. "The compact imagery, the compacted plot and subplots, make 'Jimmy Corrigan' more akin to a novel by [William] Faulkner or [Charles] Dickens than to 'The Adventures of Spiderman,'" wrote Nissen. Ware spent hours not only drawing each strip, but also researching. For the story of the grandfather abandoned in 1893, Ware researched art and architecture books of the period during his long convalescence when he broke both his legs in 1995. "I guess my graphic style draws from the past," Ware told Nissen. "Turn-of-the-[twentieth]-century—I prefer things from that era. The style then seemed to have more respect for the viewer. What was presented was something hand-made, something crafted with care and skill."

A central part of the comic is a call Jimmy gets from his father and their poignant meeting during which they have little to say. Ware himself received such a call from his own father, halfway through the writing of "Jimmy Corrigan," and the resulting meeting was equally as poignant as the imagined one. Neither had much to say. "I was probably a little hostile," Ware told Nissen. "There were so many regrets." His father died a short time after that meeting.

After seven years of weekly strips and more than a dozen volumes in the "Acme Novelty Library" series, Ware—who initially thought he might have enough material for a few months of the strip—published the entire collection as the graphic novel *Jimmy Corrigan—The Smartest Kind on Earth.* The book jacket itself attests to the care with which the project was mounted. The jacket folds out to a poster-size diagram of the multiple storylines of Jimmy Corrigan, and is a piece of artwork in itself.

With an initial printing of 25,000, the book went back for subsequent printings as word-of-mouth and rave reviews boosted sales.

A reviewer for *Publishers Weekly* called the book "graphically inventive" and "wonderfully realized." It is a graphic novel that "follows the sad fortunes of four generations of phlegmatic, defeated men while touching on themes of abandonment, social isolation and despair within the sweeping depiction of Chicago's urban transformation over the course of a century," according to this same reviewer. It is hardly the usual comic book fare. Arnold, writing in *Time,* also applauded the depth in Ware's book, calling it a "graphic version of the anomie found in a Raymond Carver short story, with a social-historical sweep and unexpected, if fleeting, grace notes. And that may be this melancholy book's uplifting message: even in the most emotionally barren settings, there is still something not to deaden us but to makes us stronger."

Other reviewers added to the praise. "Clearly," wrote Stephen Weiner in *Library Journal,* "Ware is one of today's premier cartoonists." *Booklist*'s Gordon Flagg noted Ware's antecedents in McCay and in turn-of-the-twentieth-century advertising images, and how the cartoonist transforms these into "something new, evocative, and affecting." Flagg further commented that Ware's "daunting skill transforms a simple tale into a pocket epic and makes Jimmy's melancholy story the stuff of cartoon tragedy." Laura J. Kloberg, writing in *National Forum,* concluded that Ware's "use of color, the rhythm of the panels, attention to details and details within details, and the repetition of themes—keep the reader interested in a story that on the surface is mundane. The many layers of history and images keep the mind engaged. It is ultimately a very complex tale, one that bears rereading. I loved the interconnectedness of it all." And Phil Daoust, reviewing the book in the *Guardian,* called *Jimmy Corrigan* "a rare and uplifting example of an artistic vision pushed to the limits."

The unpretentious, unaffected Ware is not only a maker of books, but also is a collector of ragtime ephemera, having played piano since he was a teenager. He publishes *The Ragtime Ephemeralist,* "a fascinating, dryly amusing periodical . . . devoted to ragtime," according to David Wondrich writing in the *New York Times.* Ware told Wondrich that with his publication he "aims to provide a dense sense of the whole era, not simply a dissected examination of the music apart from it." In his periodical, he publishes newly rediscovered sheet music and articles on ragtime composers, both known and obscure. He also includes pictures of performers,

minstrels, banjo players, and pianists from the time. "You cannot read *The Ephemeralist* without beginning to understand just how intimately ragtime is bound up with the perennial issue in American music, race," wrote Wondrich.

Ware has also continued his comic book odyssey in other avenues since putting the final "The End" to Jimmy Corrigan's adventures. In 2001 he brought out the fifteenth number in his "Acme Novelty Library," titling it "The Big Book of Jokes," and its publication ensured, according to Arnold, writing in *Time.com,* that Ware's reputation will "remain intact." Arnold described the issue as large enough to reach the "proportions of menus at Italian 'family-style' restaurants," at ten inches wide and eighteen inches tall. Ware reprises some characters, such as Quimby the mouse, but also deals with new ones, such as Rusty Brown "a nasty collector of pop-cultural detritus," according to Arnold, who "lives in filth but owns the complete Summer '87 Happy Meal toy series." Arnold concluded, "Those who have never picked up a copy of Chris Ware's 'Acme Novelty Library' owe it to themselves to do so. His dedication to the holistic experience of a single comic book issue has vastly increased the prestige of the medium."

If you enjoy the works of Chris Ware, you might want to check out the following books:

Art Spiegelman, *Maus: A Survivor's Tale I: My Father Bleeds History,* 1986, and *Maus: A Survivor's Tale II: And Here My Troubles Began,* 1991.
Ben Katchor, *Julius Knipl, Real Estate Photographer: Stories,* 1996.
Daniel Clowes, *Ghost World,* 1998.

This final sentiment is echoed by Strauss, writing in the *New York Times:* "Thanks in part to Mr. Ware's Acme Novelty Library, alternative comics have been slowly but steadily moving out of their underground niche over the last decade." Yet despite all the critical fuss, fan response, and even interest from Hollywood, Ware remains "profoundly unimpressed with himself," explained a contributor to the *Guardian.* "Beside the towering reputations of his comic-strip heroes—Art Spiegelman, Frank King, George Herriman—Ware says he feels 'like a real hayseed.'"

■ Biographical and Critical Sources

PERIODICALS

Book, January, 2001, James Sullivan, review of *Jimmy Corrigan—The Smartest Kid on Earth,* p. 66.

Booklist, February 15, 1998; November 15, 2000, Gordon Flagg, review of *Jimmy Corrigan,* p. 598.

Bookseller, December 7, 2001, review of *Jimmy Corrigan,* p. 7.

Chicago, February, 1998, pp. 68-72.

Comics Journal, December, 1997, pp. 15-16, 119-171.

Creative Review, July, 2001, review of *Jimmy Corrigan,* p. 66.

Entertainment Weekly, February 23, 2001, p. 156.

Graphis, May-June, 2000, review of *Jimmy Corrigan,* p. 13.

Guardian (London, England), December 7, 2001; "I Still Have Overwhelming Doubt about My Ability," pp. G4-G5; July 21, 2001, Phil Daoust, "Daddy, I Hardly Knew You."

Library Journal, November 15, 2000, Stephen Weiner, review of *Jimmy Corrigan,* p. 64.

National Forum, summer, 2001, Laura J. Kloberg, review of *Jimmy Corrigan,* p. 44.

New York Times, January 21, 2001, David Wondrich, "Ragtime: No Longer a Novelty in Sepia," p. 2; April 4, 2001, Neil Strauss, "Graphic Tales Mine His Own Life and Heart," p. E1; February 8, 2002, Jonathan Goldstein, "Notes from Chicago."

New York Times Book Review, November 26, 2000, Dave Eggers, "After Wham! Pow! Shazam!," p. 7.

Publishers Weekly, September 4, 2000, review of *Jimmy Corrigan,* p. 87.

Time, September 11, 2000, Andrew Arnold, "Right Way, Corrigan," p. 116.

Wall Street Journal, October 20, 2000, Andrew Horton, "Beyond Archie and Spidey," p. W10.

OTHER

CNN.com, http://europe.cnn.com/ (October 3, 2000), Beth Nissen, "A Not-so-Comic Comic Book."

Fantagraphics Books Web site, http://www.fantagraphics.com/ (April 17, 2002), "Chris Ware."

Indy Magazine, http://www.indymagazine.com/ (April 17, 2002), Travis Fristoe and Chris Waldronn, "Chris Ware Interview."

Lambiek.net, http://www.lambiek.net/ (April 17, 2002).

Metro Active Books, http://www.metroactive.com/ (November 9-15, 2000), "Chris Ware."

Print, http://www.randomhouse.com/ (April 17, 2002), Chip Kidd, "Please Don't Hate Him."

This American Life, http://www.thislife.org/ (April 17, 2002), "Chris Ware."

Time.com, http://www.time.com/ (November 27, 2001), Andrew Arnold, "The Depressing Joy of Chris Ware."*

Author/Artist Index

The following index gives the number of the volume in
which an author/artist's biographical sketch appears: